United Nations In
Economic Development -
Need For A New Strategy

by

SUDHIR SEN

1969

OCEANA PUBLICATIONS, INC.
DOBBS FERRY, NEW YORK

Library of Congress Catalog Card Number 70-83745

SBN 379-00385-6

PRINTED IN THE UNITED STATES OF AMERICA

TO THE MEMORY

OF

ADLAI E. STEVENSON

"Nourish your minds on trust in good and
have the courage to be ever its proclaimers and promoters."

Pope Paul's Easter Message on 27 March 1967

"Blessing all my thorns the rose will blossom."

TAGORE

"This must be the context of our thinking—the context of human interdependence in the face of the vast new dimensions of our science and our discovery. Just as Europe could never again be the old closed-in community after the voyages of Columbus, we can never again be a squabbling band of nations before the awful majesty of outer space.

"We travel together, passengers on a little space ship, dependent on its vulnerable reserves of air and soil; all committed for our safety to its security and peace; preserved from annihilation only by the care, the work and I will say the love we give our fragile craft. We cannot maintain it half fortunate, half miserable, half confident, half despairing, half slave—to the ancient enemies of man—half free in a liberation of resources undreamed of until this day. No craft, no crew can travel safely with such vast contradictions. On their resolution depends the survival of us all."

ADLAI E. STEVENSON

CONTENTS

List of Abbreviations

ACC	Administrative Committee on Coordination
ACABQ	Advisory Committee on Administrative and Budgetary Questions
AOS	Administrative and Operational Services (cost)
ECOSOC	Economic and Social Council
EPTA	Expanded Programme of Technical Assistance
FAO	Food and Agriculture Organization
GA	General Assembly
GATT	General Agreement on Tariffs and Trade
IAEA	International Atomic Energy Agency
IBRD	International Bank for Reconstruction and Development (World Bank)
ICAO	International Civil Aviation Organization
IDA	International Development Association
IFC	International Finance Corporation
ILO	International Labour Organization
IMCO	International Maritime Consultative Organization
IMF	International Monetary Fund
ITU	International Telecommunications Union
OECD	Organization for Economic Cooperation and Development
OPEX	(Programme for) Operational and Executive Personnel
SUNFED	Special United Nations Fund for Economic Development
TAB	Technical Assistance Board
TAC	Technical Assistance Committee
UN	United Nations
UNCDF	United National Capital Development Fund

UNCTAD	United Nations Conference for Trade and Development
UNDP	United Nations Development Programme
UNDP/SF	Special Fund Component of UNDP
UNDP/TA	Technical Assistance Component of UNDP (formerly EPTA)
UNESCO	United Nations Educational, Scientific and Cultural Organization
UNIC	United Nations Information Centre
UNICEF	United Nations Children's Fund (formerly United National International Children's Emergency Fund)
UNIDO	United Nations Industrial Development Organization
UPU	Universal Postal Union
WHO	World Health Organization
WMO	World Meteorological Organization

Note: The phrase "specialized agencies" has all along been used in its broad functional, and not strictly juridical, sense. IAEA is technically not a specialized agency, but in practice functions as one; and the same is largely true of UNCTAD and UNIDO, though they are classified as "subsidiary organs" of the General Assembly.

Acknowledgements

My deepest gratitude is due to those who must remain unnamed: old friends and colleagues at the United Nations headquarters, in the specialized agencies, and in the field offices, who have, through numerous discussions, helped clarify many issues and have from time to time encouraged, and urged, me to undertake this critical study; also some eminent authorities in the field of international development, both inside and outside the UN family, whose positive reactions to the basic ideas have given me the needed inspiration to pursue the subject and complete this write-up.

To the authorities of Brown University I am under a special debt for having provided me with a visiting professorship, initially under the auspices of the National Science Foundation of Washington, D.C., and later supplemented from the University's own resources.

In the Department of Sociology and Anthropology of Brown University I found a most congenial and stimulating milieu for my work, for which I want to record my deep personal appreciation. My special thanks are due to Professor Sidney Goldstein and Professor Basil Zimmer for the generous facilities they have provided within the Department; also to Professor James Sakoda who has been ever ready to help with secretarial and other assistance.

I am particularly thankful to Mrs. Joyce Coleman and to Miss Rheta Martin for the help they have readily given in handling the typing work.

On the professional side, I am under a debt of gratitude to Professor Whitney Perkins who has read the entire manuscript and has made valuable comments, also to Professor Goldstein who made a special effort on the eve of his sabbatical to look into parts of the manuscript and offered some useful suggestions. Needless to say that for the contents of the book and the views and opinions expressed in it, the writer takes the sole responsibility.

Author's Preface

This work springs from a twofold conviction that has grown, and deepened, over a period of ten years of service in the United Nations: that the UN family has not been making anything like the contribution it can and it must make towards the development of the world's poorer nations; and that it has been unable to do so mainly because of its defective machinery and its desultory approach.

It is not a book intended to praise or please, nor to criticize and deprecate. Neither is it a narrative study. Such literature on the United Nations and its affiliates is already more than sufficient.

The need for a critical analysis of the development activities of the United Nations became unmistakably clear to me several years ago. The decision to embark on it was far from easy. Could a single-handed study of admittedly complex problems and far-flung organizations and programmes serve much useful purpose? Would it not look like an audacious, even pretentious, undertaking? Long reflection helped subdue the initial qualms. Even more decisive were the views of others, the encouragement and the urgings received from several quarters, until it looked to me almost mandatory to go ahead with the task.

Although this study has been prepared on a university campus, its purpose transcends purely academic interests. Its focus is primarily on practical problems, arising out of deficiencies in organization, methods, programmes and procedures, which have been visibly impeding the performance of the UN family. Its main object is to clarify the issues and to indicate the directions in which one must look for their solutions in order to secure better management of the UN programmes.

I have relied mostly on my personal experience as Director of the Programme Division of the Technical Assistance Board at New York headquarters (1956-61), Resident Representative in Accra, Ghana (1961-62), Deputy Administrator of the United Nations Temporary Executive Authority (UNTEA) in West New Guinea/West Irian (1962-63), and Resident Representative in Belgrade, Yugo-

ix

slavia (1963-66). Previously, I had first-hand experience in dealing with the practical problems of development in India in different fields for fifteen years, particularly as the chief executive officer of the Damodar Valley Corporation (1948-54), a multi-purpose river valley project that used to be referred to as "India's TVA."

In short, what is presented in this study is a kind of crystallization of this experience mainly in the form of reflections, observations, and practical recommendations. It has not been deemed necessary to burden the presentation with full-scale historical reviews of the growth and ramification of the UN programmes, or with detailed descriptive accounts of their substantive contents. Nor have I resorted to the fashionable device of case studies. These could be largely dispensed with because this analysis is concerned, above all, with the fundamentals of management, which have their own logic and whose violations can be detected and analyzed quite meaningfully without exhaustive description and illustration. References and quotations have been used sparingly and selectively. A short bibliography, mostly of documents of the UN family, has been appended for the benefit of those who might seek more information about the financial, operational and substantive aspects of the programmes.

Almost two years have passed since I began this task. Events during that period have, if anything, further reassured me about the need for it and its timeliness. The UN family is now groping for a new strategy in its anxiety to avoid, in the 1970's, a repetition of the widespread disappointments experienced in the first development decade. Yet it is still unable to grasp the simple truth that no future strategy will ever succeed unless it is first able to retool, restyle, and re-orient its own programmes and its own machinery.

The need for such a study was highlighted by some forthright remarks recently made by Secretary-General U Thant. Opening the forty-fifth session of the Economic and Social Council in Geneva on 8 July 1968, he referred, inter alia, to the "preoccupations" which governments were expressing "more and more frequently and more and more insistently." He treated them as an indication that "new efforts should be made to streamline our machinery, our procedures and perhaps some of our activities." Mr. Thant then proceeded to make the following significant statement: "The fact is that many questions continue to be asked, many doubts nurtured—not to speak of the more open hostilities—in regard to our young international bureaucracy. Soul-searching examination of possible improvements is therefore very much the order of the day."

That all is not well with the UN effort in the field of economic development should be clear. Obviously, reforms are needed. But general dissatisfaction with the present state of things will lead us nowhere. Nor will good intentions cure mismanagement due to organizational and other shortcomings. It is equally clear that the remedy will not come of itself, and it will not come on the UN family's own initiative.

Self-reform, in any large institution, is always a difficult matter if only because of the need to counter vested interests and the forces of inertia. In the case of the United Nations, this difficulty is magnified many times. For one thing, one has to deal here with a whole system of organizations—the United Nations and all its specialized agencies.

There is yet another, even more formidable, impediment in the case of the UN. More or less the same governments are represented in the UN General Assembly and in the legislative bodies of the specialized agencies. Yet their representatives are used to speak in different voices in different forums without being troubled about their overall coherence, sometimes even about their compatibility. In other words, the representatives of the various ministries or departments of a member-government, in their dealings with international affairs, are themselves apt to behave very much like the specialized agencies, and not as representatives of a national government acting on the basis of a firm set of predetermined national policies.

Clearly, reform within the UN family can come only in one way—only if its most important members will carry out a careful diagnosis, decide on the specific measures needed, and take the initiative to secure necessary support from other member-governments, leading to their approval by the Economic and Social Council, and ultimately by the General Assembly.

To all this one has to add another essential pre-condition: As a starting-point there should be wide and intelligent discussion on the fundamental issues involved. True, not all discussions lead to the desired reforms. But what is even more true is that there will be no reform if there is no discussion, and if the issues continue to be missed, shelved or ignored.

The primary object of this book is to help this first step—to start a discussion and to guide it to the heart of the real problems. It has therefore been considered essential to identify the main weaknesses of the UN system—structural, procedural, functional and managerial—and then to set forth, in clear and concrete terms, what specific measures are needed as remedy in each case.

This is an intensely practical task. One of its major objectives is to help the member-governments represented on the various policy-making bodies of the United Nations and its specialized agencies to see the problems of development in the right perspective and to arrive at the right decisions. Given this action-oriented approach, I have deemed it best to try and present the facts and ideas, as far as possible, in a simple and direct style. For the same reason it has been assumed that candour will do no harm. The search for euphemisms has, accordingly, been minimized.

The winds of change have long been blowing through the underdeveloped countries, and have been increasingly assuming stormy proportions. It is time for the winds of change also to blow through the cosy international establishments if the United Nations is to fulfil its historic mandate in this tumultuous age. The analysis given here will, it is hoped, make some contribution towards clarifying the kind of changes the UN family urgently needs today.

On the Dedication

The dedication of the book calls for a brief comment. This, I confess, is a sentimental act.

On 29 April 1953, Governor Stevenson, then on a round-the-world trip after his first defeat as the Democratic Presidential nominee, came on a visit to the Damodar Valley Corporation, a multipurpose river valley project which, as mentioned earlier, was known as India's TVA.

It was a typically bright April morning in Calcutta. We received the Governor at the airport and flew over with him to Asansol (135 miles), where the DVC Chief Engineer Mr. Andrew M. Komora (an ex-TVA engineer) joined us. We visited two of the DVC dams—Konar and Maithon—which were then nearing completion.

As we left for Konar by road, the conversation immediately turned to the domestic political scene of America.

"We have the privilege of meeting you for the first time, Mr. Governor. Yet we have a feeling as if we have known you for a long time", I said.

The remark took the Governor by surprise. He looked intently at me, waiting for an explanation.

"Your campaign speeches, even though reported in the Indian press in a summary form, have already made you so familiar to us." Then, after a brief pause, I added on a more personal note: "As I read those reports I could not help feeling as if American politics had been suddenly raised to a new level, in line with its best traditions, and I was constantly reminded of Jefferson, Lincoln, Wilson and Roosevelt."

The Governor was visibly moved. "It's gracious of you to say so. Those have always been my heroes." This was his gracious reply.

I could have said then, as I can say now, that Adlai Stevenson was my hero then, as he has remained so all these years. It could not be otherwise because of the teachings of Tagore and Gandhi I had deeply imbibed in my early life.

Truth, Tagore emphasized all along, has no geography. A good idea—no matter where it is born, scientific knowledge—no matter where it is discovered, is the common property of all, the heritage of mankind. Every nation has the right to draw upon it for its own growth and well-being.

And throughout his life he preached the gospel of what may be called transcendental patriotism: It is the values that matter—the values we preach, practise and uphold. And it is the allegiance to the right values, irrespective of their origin, that is the essence of true patriotism, not a blind allegiance to the land of one's birth.

This was the keynote also of Gandhi's philosophy. He built his eclectic model of ethics with ingredients collected from such diverse sources as Tolstoy, Ruskin, Thoreau, the Bible, and the Bhagavat Geeta. And he upheld his spiritual values uncompromisingly, rebelliously—and non-violently, for what he believed was the common good of India as well as of mankind.

Adlai Stevenson's system of values was derived from different sources, but in its essentials it was strikingly similar. Two historic charters largely charted out the path for him in the treacherous world of politics: the American constitution and the United Nations charter. To the ringing words of the Declaration of Independence about the self-evident truths—that all men are created equal, that they are endowed with certain inalienable Rights, that among these are Life, Liberty and the pursuit of Happiness—he sought to impart fuller meaning in actual life with his ringing oratory. To the principles of the United Nations charter, which is based on identical values and assumptions, which, as a co-architect, he had helped to shape and mould, he devoted a good deal of his eloquence along with the last six years of his life.

An even more significant fact about Adlai Stevenson is that he saw the unbreakable link between the two charters, how the realization of the one depended directly and inexorably on the

xiii

realization of the other. If the United Nations is the "last best hope" for mankind, the USA, in his unerring vision, remained the last best hope for the UN.

From this clear perception flowed much of his inspired oratory. Could the world's greatest leader—with all its wealth and power, and with its liberal and humanitarian tradition—shirk the moral leadership in a desperately ailing world? Could it do so in good conscience, without being untrue to its highest ideals, without sacrificing its own long-range interests? His answer to these questions was a clear, resounding No—an answer which for years echoed around the world, which is echoing even today in the hearts of countless men and women, though somewhat muffled by the confused din of Vietnam.

But we must not lose sight of the perspective. What we are experiencing today—in Vietnam and in the extravagant spiraling of expenditures on destructive armaments—must be treated as a tragic diversion, away from the challenging agenda facing mankind today. It must be assumed that this is no more than a passing cloud that will soon blow over, that the liberal spirit of America, though partially eclipsed today, will shine once again in its full glory on a world needlessly over-burdened with misery and unhappiness.

"We shall conquer, no doubt, the dark face of the moon", said Adlai Stevenson in his last address. "But I would hope we can with equal confidence conquer the dark face of poverty and give men and women new life, new hope, new space on this planet."

This must be our hope, too. To despair about the future of mankind, to quote Tagore once again, is the ultimate sin. "For we are saved by hope."

This book is dedicated as a token of allegiance to what Adlai Stevenson stood for, worked for, fought for, and died for, and as a testament of a shared faith in the victory of those ideals and in mankind's march, through ups and downs, towards a better United Nations.

Sudhir Sen

Brown University
Providence, R.I., USA
November 1968

xiv

PART I

INTRODUCTION

CHAPTER 1

U. N. Role in an Explosive Age

*"With these promises and these prospects of
the Great Revolution the United Nations must
identify itself."*

WALTER LIPPMANN

We live in what is now commonly regarded as the most explosive
age in man's history, characterized by multiple revolutions that impinge
on it from many directions. The facts, though well-known, may be
briefly recalled.

Since the United Nations was established the world has changed.
First, the tide of decolonization has swept virtually over the whole
world. In the few residual pockets now stubbornly holding out, colonialism is in its last breath. Meanwhile the number of the United
Nations members has gone up by leaps and bounds. Fifty-one states
signed and ratified the charter in 1945, as original members; the total
now stands at 125; and this includes a large number of very small states.

Second, a demographic revolution of unprecedented magnitude has
burst upon the world. And the most explosive growth of population is
taking place just where one can least afford it—in the undeveloped,
poverty-stricken countries of Asia, Africa and Latin America. Population in these countries is mounting at an average rate of close to 3 per
cent per year. Even according to the medium estimates of the United
Nations, it will double itself between now and the end of the century
—from, say, 2.3 billion to about 4.7 billion.

Third, there has been another explosion the explosion of knowledge. The world of science and technology is crowded with discoveries
and breakthroughs, and they continue to pile up at an amazing rate.

It is now possible to prevent epidemics, to curb deaths, and prolong life; also to forestall unwanted births and plan families; to produce cheap power out of the atom; to turn sea-water into fresh water with this power and to make the desert bloom; to harvest the oceans; to boost the output from land—food, fibre, and other crops—to astonishingly high levels; and to use this imposing range of scientific tools to produce enough for all.

Freedom from want need no longer remain a remote ideal. Modern science has brought it within man's reach. Mass poverty, for ages regarded as inevitable by mankind, has lost its traditional justification in this scientific age. Even religion has shifted its emphasis from finding solace for the impoverished to an improvement of their conditions. This was no doubt the essence of Pope Paul's encyclical "Populorum Progressio"[1] issued in March 1967, with its anguished call to lift the poorer nations out of their misery and suffering.

And finally, the knowledge about the new knowledge is spreading fast all over the globe, with the message of hope implicit in it for the developing countries; and this in turn has created a new restlessness verging on revolt against their present conditions which are no longer acceptable because they are no longer looked upon as immutable.

Modern science has already affected their lives at least in two vital respects. International communications have been revolutionized; and as contacts between peoples multiply in a shrunken world, the gulf between the developed and the underdeveloped, between the conditions as they are and as they can be and should be, looks increasingly more glaring and less tolerable.[2] Besides, the fruits of modern medicine —for disease control, for public health and environmental sanitation— have been carried to the remotest corners of the earth, bringing about a steep decline in mortality and an explosive growth of population, which has tremendously aggravated the already desperate problems of development.

2

What should be the role of the United Nations in such a fast-changing, revolutionary epoch?

This question was perhaps most neatly answered by Mr. Walter Lippmann in an address he delivered at the United Nations a few

---

[1] Encyclical Letter "On the Development of the Peoples," 26 March 1967.

[2] President Johnson's remark: "The wall between rich and poor is a wall of glass through which all can see" (speech at Associated Press luncheon, New York City, 20 April 1964) is now largely true of the world as a whole.

years ago in a series to celebrate the "International Cooperation Year 1965."[3] The ultimate goal before the United Nations is "to organize a universal society," and the immediate tasks before it, he emphasized, were threefold. Put in a succinct form, they are: *make peace*—there are still too many jobs of peace settlement to be completed—in Central Europe, in Eastern Asia, in Africa; *keep peace*—there are still too many sporadic fires, "little wars" which threaten to get out of control, and which must be isolated and contained; and *build peace*—on the foundation of what he called the Great Revolution, a product of man's advancing knowledge that has made, for the first time in human history, the conquest of poverty "a rational object of policy for all states."

The United Nations "will not live by peace alone," said Mr. Lippmann. "That is too gray an horizon. The horizon should be vivid with splendour and hope." To the masses of mankind—from the poorest to the richest—it is this Great Revolution that brings the promise and the prospect of the fulfilment of their hopes. "With these promises and these prospects of the Great Revolution", Mr. Lippmann concluded, "the United Nations must identify itself."

The underlying idea is of course not new, though the emphasis is here much sharper. Development, it has long been recognized, can make the quest for peace more meaningful, also help build it on a more solid foundation. Peace-building and economy-building are interlinked and interdependent. They can, and inevitably will, either strengthen or weaken each other.

This conclusion is reinforced by several factors. Whatever may have been the shortcomings of colonialism—they were many, and often grave—it did involve direct responsibility on the part of the colonial powers for their colonies, and this in turn led at least to some measure of development for their welfare. With decolonization this responsibility has disappeared, giving place to new relations, diplomatic and commercial, supplemented at times by a modest quantum of aid. Thus decolonization for which the United Nations had served as an active forum, has created a vacuum that logically can be filled only by the United Nations itself.

In the face of an all-embracing world revolution, the ideological gulf is narrowing down, and the cold war is fast becoming a costly irrelevance.[4] Indeed, in the last third of this century there can be

---

[3] Delivered on 1 March 1965 under the caption "The Great Revolution."

[4] Vietnam, no doubt, has clouded the prospects of a détente. But as the New York Times remarked in a leader on 4 May 1968, "relations between Washington and Moscow can improve rapidly once the irritant of the Vietnam conflict is removed."

only one legitimate war of liberation—the war to liberate the human kind as a whole from the age-old bondage of poverty and want. There is hope that some day the world's biggest and richest powers will close their ranks and join their forces in a common effort to build a better world community.

But the process has only just begun; and even on a most optimistic view it will be years before one could expect to see its consummation. Until then, the United Nations is likely to enjoy greater acceptability than the members of either ideological bloc. Thus, by a curious turn of history, responsibility for development in the newly-independent and in other developing countries has come to be placed largely on the world organization.

3

The United Nations, Mr. Lippmann urged, must "identify" itself with the Great Revolution. Has it not already done so? The voluminous literature of the UN family would give a loud affirmative answer. After all, the Expanded Programme of Technical Assistance had been in existence since 1948, the Special Fund since 1959, and the two were brought under one roof in January 1966 to form the United Nations Development Programme (UNDP). Besides, the 1960's were proclaimed as the United Nations Decade of Development; and though the march of this decade has brought little glory to the United Nations family and little comfort to the developing countries, the intention was clear: to speed up their development.

The snag, no doubt, lies in the word "identify." Clearly, passive identification will not be enough. The United Nations family must play an active role; it must inspire and promote development; indeed, as far as practicable, it must help initiate, guide, and manage development along sound lines.

There is no escape from such an active UN role. The problems of development are highly complex; the governments of the developing countries are seldom equipped to tackle them; all too often they are dazzled and puzzled by the plethora of choice displayed before them by modern science and technology. To pick and choose wisely would call for a high degree of sophistication which they frankly lack. No wonder that their action is often prompted less by reason than by impulse, and is based less on a logical analysis of given conditions than on hit-or-miss methods.

This difficulty, inherent in the developing countries, has been compounded by outside pressures to which they have been continually exposed: from the protagonists of rival ideologies vying with each other to extend aid often with the thinly veiled object of winning their political allegiance rather than promoting their economic development; from the representatives of numerous agencies and organizations anxious to put over their own pet projects on a piecemeal basis, without caring to ask if these are the projects that would do the maximum good to them; from the stream of commercial salesmen who would talk the governments into hasty deals to earn quick profits. Such pressures could hardly promote clarity of thought. They could only make the initial confusion worse confounded.

There is yet another complication of a different nature but no less formidable. The leaders who led the national movements for independence are still in the saddle in most countries. And here is the paradox: the great leaders of political movements seldom make great leaders for economic development—usually they make poor ones. Yet, hero-worshipped and idolized by the masses, they wield great authority, and they exercise it to take crucial decisions in the economic field. Thus the great leaders, often with the best of intentions, can make, and have made, great blunders.

In the post-decolonization world, the developing countries urgently need light and guidance from outside. In today's world this light and guidance can come primarily from one source, the United Nations.

4

The UN family has, in one form or another, been actively involved in economic development almost from its earliest days. The start was modest and had little more than symbolic value, but the imperatives of our times have pushed it deeper and deeper into this venture. Its resources have appreciably increased, especially since 1960, and its activities have broadened in scope. Today it has become a significant factor in the field of international development. All this represents an encouraging trend.

What is not so encouraging, however, is the fact that while the apparatus of the UN family has been mobilized to promote development, it has not been able to make any real impact. The progress made in the last two decades under UN auspices has been fitful and painfully slow.

It is customary to blame these disappointing results on two things. First, it has been argued that the financial resources available to the UN programmes have been far from adequate. This is unquestionably true; the UN family could, here and now, effectively utilize twice the amount it has been currently handling for technical assistance and pre-investment work; and if it were equipped with a substantial capital development fund as well, this amount would easily be several times bigger. Similarly, the developing countries could, here and now, productively absorb a vastly larger sum of money as development capital. A few years ago the World Bank estimated that they needed something like $4 billion *more* a year to finance carefully screened projects. Such an amount would undoubtedly accelerate the rate of their progress. Yet the fact is that while their needs and their absorptive capacity have been rising rapidly, the total flow of "aid," net of amortization, has been stagnating around the level of $6 billion reached in 1961.

The second reason frequently cited is no less obvious: the problems of development are immensely complicated. What is involved here is modernization of traditional economies and societies on a global scale. The time-dimension appropriate to this task should not be overlooked; it is bound to take not years, but decades even with the best of efforts.

The crucial words are, however, the ones just mentioned. Can it be said with enough reason that the UN family has really been making the best of efforts, that its contribution to development has already reached the highest *attainable* level after full allowance has been made for the twofold limitations mentioned above? Or, is it possible that the UN family, too, has been at fault, that because of its own deficiencies it has been unable to stimulate progress to anything like the full extent of its latent capabilities?

These questions point to a third reason which is no less relevant in this context, although it is seldom mentioned and has never been subjected to a sufficiently objective analysis, namely, the effectiveness of the UN system itself as an instrument for development.

In a sense, this last factor is even more decisive than the other two. For, the UN family, functioning as it does between the aid-givers and the aid-receivers, is clearly called upon to discharge a threefold task: to decide imaginatively how the available resources can be put to the most productive use in the receiving countries; to try and induce their governments, to the utmost possible extent, to utilize *all* their resources —national as well as international—so as to achieve the best possible results; and to persuade the donor countries to show more foresight and greater generosity in making their contributions.

These tasks are by no means unrelated. The better the judgement and the greater the wisdom, along with understanding and sympathy, that the UN family is able to bring to bear on the problems of development, the easier will be its task of persuading the governments with friendly advice and guidance, and the speedier will be their rate of progress. Better utilization of funds, coupled with speedier and more tangible progress, will in turn immeasurably strengthen its own hands in attracting more liberal contributions from the major donors.

5

How well is the United Nations performing these functions today? It is a curious fact that this question is almost never raised or discussed, at least in public. As a result, the UN family has come to enjoy a kind of immunity from any critical examination of its activities. Several rather peculiar factors seem to account for this omission.

There is, first of all, a general tendency to look upon the UN programmes as something above criticism; the cause, it seems, is so sacred that criticism would be almost anathema. Such an attitude is as unhelpful as it is superficial. For no cause, however sacred or noble, can afford to dispense with objective self-analysis and periodic reform without in the end undermining the cause itself. It is hardly necessary to recall this fact at a time when the Catholic Church is struggling to adjust its centuries-old tenets and dogmas to the needs of a new age, and, as a result, is going through a revolutionary process of self-questioning and self-reform.

The dictum of Justice Oliver Wendell Holmes that general propositions do not decide concrete cases is no less valid here. The cause of development can be effectively served not simply by focussing attention on its overriding significance, but only when the right kind of machinery is carefully forged and when, in addition, appropriate policies and methods are adopted to tackle the specific problems that have to be faced and resolved.

This particular point is all the more important because economic development of the poor nations, however idealistic or humanitarian its objective, is an intensely practical matter, and constantly calls for the essentials of sound management, along with what may be called a kind of new and benevolent diplomacy. In a sense this is not unlike the attitude of the pilgrim fathers and many of their immediate descendants who often uniquely combined the pursuit of high ideals with efficient management of mundane affairs to augment material wealth.

Secondly, there is an institutional reason. The UN system is so vast and complex, also so fragmented and scattered, and so heterogeneous in its composition, that it is not easy to focus public attention on its doings and performances. In spite of its essentially democratic structure, it can and does escape the discipline of public assessment and criticism to an extent that would be unthinkable in a national democracy.

It is also an undeniable fact that in the United Nations politics invariably steals the limelight and runs away with most of the statesmanship. With a plentiful supply of crises in the contemporary world, the best minds and brains are mostly preoccupied with the immediate challenges affecting the vital issue of war or peace. Trouble-shooting absorbs most of the energies; and so, at the top levels, not enough is left for trouble prevention, for building peace through long-range development.

Thirdly, the UN family has its own quota of apologists who, at times from high levels, preach the philosophy of muddling through. Experience has repeatedly shown that those who begin with such laxity are apt to muddle right through until the objective itself is seriously compromised. Yet as in most large undertakings, they can easily command a sizable following who specialize mainly in finding suitable arguments to rationalize the existing order of things in spite of its palpable deficiencies.

Finally, there is what may be called the success-story argument. The technique is simple and, at least prima facie, plausible enough. One can string together projects where success has been, or is being, achieved in varying degrees under the UN programmes and treat the accounts as concrete evidence of their effectiveness. Yet this is clearly a non sequitur. It sheds no light on the negative side, i.e., what could have been, but has not been, achieved. Besides, the underdeveloped countries cover two-thirds of the world; they are rich in natural resources; and they have unlimited possibilities for development. One can barely scratch the surface and yet show results. For the same reason these results cannot be construed as a measure of the effectiveness of the operations. They are, above all, an index to the vast potentialities that lie untapped in these countries.

The fact is that the UN family has hitherto been able to realize no more than a fraction of its great opportunities for sponsoring economic development. The performance of its programmes, it would be no exaggeration to say, resembles that of primitive agriculture: unimproved seeds are sown on ill-prepared ground to raise indifferent crops. Even a poor crop is, of course, better than no crop. But it would make poor sense, in both instances, if goals were set no higher.

CHAPTER 2

Some Paradoxes

"By the year 2000, we can be living in a world that has overcome poverty—a world without want."

PAUL G. HOFFMAN

To say that there is room for improvement in the UN operations would be the understatement of this development decade. The truth is that the UN family launched its development programmes without an overall policy or a sound strategy; it has been groping for one ever since. Ill-organized for the tasks, it is still stumbling and fumbling along an uncharted path.

The programmes have proliferated from resolution to resolution, while the agencies for handling them have grown steadily in number. The establishments of the UN, the agencies, and latterly the UNDP have undergone rapid expansion. Ad hoc decisions of all kinds, impinging on development directly or indirectly, have been juxtaposed or pyramided over the years. The complex structure of the UN family has grown steadily in complexity, and with it the procedures and regulations. No wonder that the principles of management should have disappeared in a flood of improvisation. Lip service to priorities and coordination are paid routinely year after year. But one scans in vain the UN horizon for the signs of what could be legitimately called a strategy for development.

Today the UN programmes are studded with paradoxes and contradictions. The Expanded Programme, the oldest one of any size, was established to give technical assistance to the underdeveloped countries. Yet riddled with compromises and strangled with procedures, the Programme itself has been badly in need of technical assistance.

9

Even after two decades it is still debating what procedures it should follow for preparing country programmes!

The UN family has asked the governments to strengthen the machinery for coordinating their development activities, but it has not been able to resolve its own problems of inter-agency—in several instances also intra-agency—coordination. It wants the governments to choose only those projects which are worthy of high priority; yet it displays no clear-sighted view of the priorities, and it has been unable to lay down guidelines for the benefit of the governments.

For many years the UN family has been giving assistance in the field of public administration. But it has long been clear to many insiders that the UN—and most of the specialized agencies—would themselves greatly benefit from a substantial dose of assistance in this field. Similarly, the UN family gives assistance in business management, but forgets to apply the principles of management to its own business.

Development is, above all, a function of creative imagination and needs an atmosphere of open and free discussion. Yet creativity is being squeezed out through increasing bureaucratization which is concerned primarily with dull routine and conformity to rules.

Developing countries are blamed for subordinating development to politics. But the UN family has not been able to lift its programmes above its own brand of politics, well-concealed behind the scenes but no less damaging in its effects.

Development is held up as a sacred cause. Yet how many are inclined to ride the cause rather than to serve it!

And finally, there is the super-paradox—the growing fashion to send out ad hoc missions to the field to evaluate past results. The missions consist of safe men; they enjoy the short-term assignments, and in return gratefully bless the status quo with judicious expressions of pious wishes and familiar recommendations.

2

There is yet another paradox which must not be overlooked. It may be best called phenomenon Hoffman.

Of the manifold achievements of Dag Hammarskjöld as the UN Secretary-General, one that will always stand out was his success in inducing Mr. Paul G. Hoffman to join the UN family and to serve as the Managing Director of the newly-established Special Fund. It guaranteed the success of the new programme. It also marked the beginning of a new era for the UN in the field of development.

From the start Mr. Hoffman's dynamic leadership transcended the narrow limits of his immediate assignment. He set out to strengthen the UN family as a whole, to draw its members closer together, to lay down more meaningful guidelines for development, to raise funds for the programmes and to knock more sense into the entire UN operations. He has no doubt made a good deal of progress, but he has also been knocking his head against a dead wall.

A direct beneficiary of Mr. Hoffman's fund-raising campaign has been the Expanded Programme. Having stagnated around $25 - 30 million level a year in the late fifties, it gave a sudden spurt, rose from year to year, and reached $75 million in 1968. But despite the so-called merger with the Special Fund, it still remains a separate entity. This artificial dichotomy, which has continued at the very heart of the UN development effort, has badly hurt its effectiveness.[5]

In other respects, too, history has been less than kind to Mr. Hoffman. He had to deal with a large family of specialized agencies with a strong tradition of centrifugal tendencies and with field representatives who faithfully reflected the disjointed pattern of the UN family with divided responsibilities. Besides, the Special Fund was concerned only with pre-investment activity, without any guarantee that investment capital would be available for the completed projects.[6]

What a contrast all this presented to his experience as Marshall Plan administrator in post-war Europe! There he could start with a clean slate and a free hand. He could draw upon a vast reservoir of talents waiting to be mobilized. And thanks to the far-sighted generosity of the USA, he was assured of a large flow of funds—$13 billion in about four years.

Reconstruction, it has been pointed out, is not development, and there can be no valid comparison between the Marshall Plan and the UN development programmes. Nevertheless, it is intriguing to speculate how much more Mr. Hoffman could have achieved in the UN had his hands been relatively free, and had he not been compelled to grapple incessantly with the inner contradictions of the UN family.

"Do the best you can where you are and with what you have"—this old maxim perhaps best sums up his approach. In the teeth of manifold obstacles he has been striving to achieve whatever results are humanly possible.

---

[5] See in particular Chapter 17.
[6] Discussed in Chapter 18.

A UN aide once remarked: "Mr. Hoffman stays in the engine room of the ship; others do the steering." The analogy could be misleading. It would be more correct to say that Mr. Hoffman has been struggling to build a UN fleet out of a dozen ships, now based at half a dozen scattered ports, all flying the UN flag, all plying the seas according to their own charts, often criss-crossing each other's routes; and that with this unified fleet he would embark upon an exciting journey to reach—by the shortest route, at the fastest speed, and before the deadline of 2000 A.D.—the shores of the promised land, a world without want.

It has been an exhilarating experience to see this grand old man at work in the UN—patting and prodding, achieving and failing, but never flagging or despairing, sparing none and, least of all, himself.

He has been moving from gathering to gathering to put across his threefold theme: Poverty in this age is an anachronism which can and should be eliminated within the next few decades. Raising the entire human kind above the poverty line is not simply a fascinating ideal; it is also good business, for both the rich and the poor, because it will guarantee indefinitely expanding world markets. It is good business for another reason too: prosperity is the only effective antidote to war and threats of war, and it can be achieved at a fraction of the vast expenditures now incurred for armaments.

With this recurring theme he has coupled a threefold plea: the governments, especially those of the developed countries, must give more generously; the developing countries must use the limited funds carefully to achieve the best possible results; and the UN organizations must work together more closely and more efficiently.

In unfolding his theme, Mr. Hoffman rolls out key statistics, including what are very rough approximations or intelligent guesswork, thus using figures at times as a kind of figures of speech to make an argument more telling or to drive home some essential points. In all his utterances he brings to bear a rare combination of experience and authority, that of businessman, administrator, and statesman. And to all this he has added something else: a missionary zeal. No wonder that his speeches readily acquire the overtones of sermons. His gospel on economic development tends to turn every gathering he addresses into a congregation on behalf of the poor nations. No one with a spark of idealism can listen to this humanitarian businessman and not feel inspired. But how easily, alas, is this spark extinguished in a large, modern establishment!

Besides, familiarity is apt to breed insensitivity. As time goes on and as Hoffman sermons multiply, they seem to spark fewer and fewer minds. Meanwhile quite a few, it would seem, are less interested in the ideas he preaches than in their aftereffects, and wistfully watch the fruits of his fundraising drive.

The drive continues as before, for more funds, for their better utilization and for improved management. But the point of diminishing returns has already been reached. The contributions are flattening out; the $200 million target set for 1966 is yet to be realized.[6a] On the other fronts, too, progress has been far from commensurate with efforts. There is a limit beyond which even Mr. Hoffman cannot inspire a vast international conglomerate.

The diminishing response hardly affects Mr. Hoffman's own attitude. As time goes on, his idealism, if anything, looks even more invincible. Striving tends to become an end in itself. With prodigious effort he pushes back a few yards the mountain of inertia and derives immense satisfaction from the outcome. The satisfaction, one suspects, is derived not from the outcome, but from the effort.

For the developing countries the advent of Mr. Hoffman on the UN scene was a matter of singular good fortune. Over the years they have given eloquent proof of their trust in him and of their gratitude for his services. But it is also their misfortune that they could not benefit remotely as much from these services as they were entitled to; that the tremendous input of idealism gave such low output because of the defective organizational media he had inherited and through which he had to work.

The conclusion is clear. Future progress will hinge directly on the ability of the UN family to come to grips with its own paradoxes which have been indicated above.

3

That all is not up to the mark with the UN programmes has long been known to many serving within the UN family. This has also been sensed or suspected by interested observers from outside. Glowing tributes, both sincere and conventional, continue to be paid by many people for its achievements. But the tributes are interspersed with gnawing doubts expressed by others from time to time.

For example, speaking at the twentieth anniversary of FAO on 23 November 1965, Mrs. Barbara Castle, the then Minister of Overseas

---

6a. To judge from the last pledges, the target should be reached in 1969 for which the voluntary contributions are expected to total slightly over $200 million.

Development in the U.K. Government, made a hard-hitting appeal to make the international organizations more effective in terms of results. If the multilateral agencies were to have their responsibilities increased, "they must be ready to overhaul their organizations, integrate their work, eliminate waste and overlapping, close some of the gaps that still remain; in short, fashion a streamlined and coordinated instrument which has a visible impact in the field." FAO faced an especially crucial period, she stressed, because of the urgent need to develop the world's capability to feed itself.

In his address to the Board of Governors at the annual meeting held on 27 September 1965, Mr. George Woods, President of the World Bank, forcefully stated some home truths. In many underdeveloped countries, "economic performance can be greatly improved." After recounting the various fields where these countries must make a bigger effort and take more effective measures, Mr. Woods referred to "the frustration and disillusionment that the industrial countries feel about development finance," and underscored the dilemma it posed: "Governments which provide development finance are subjected to searching questions by their legislatures and peoples about it. The most careful use of aid by each of the recipient countries is constantly necessary if they are to expect continued assistance, and on a large scale. Performance will have to stand up to close scrutiny."

There is an inescapable corollary to these remarks. The performance in a developing country can be "greatly improved" if, above all, the UN family, as an aid-administering body, greatly improves its own performance. This is the only conceivable way out of the dilemma highlighted by Mr. Woods.

A similar note was struck by Sir Arthur Lewis, and with the same forthrightness. In an address he delivered in June 1966 at a global meeting of the UN field representatives, he observed that: "We are now in a phase where aid to underdeveloped countries is under sharp criticism. The major donors are disenchanted with the results, with the consequence that ... the volume of aid has been nearly stationary for the last five years. The volume of American aid is actually falling ... Part of the disenchantment is due to the wasteful manner in which much of technical assistance has been administered, both bilaterally and multilaterally ... There is just about as big a waste of technical assistance personnel, bilateral and multilateral, in these countries, as there is of capital."

To take a more recent example, speaking at FAO's annual conference held in Rome in November 1967, the Canadian delegate, Minister of Agriculture John H. Greene, urged the FAO to strive for "greater internal efficiency" and "to examine its own house." Mr. Greene wondered whether increases in FAO's operating budget (currently $70 million a year) and in personnel (a field force of some 1,700 experts) had been passed on in terms of greater assistance to the developing countries, and whether FAO was not "suffering from over-centralization and bureaucracy."

In fairness to FAO it should be pointed out that while this agency provided the forum for Mr. Greene's remarks, their validity is by no means confined to it. They hold good, in varying degrees, for the entire UN family.

4

Quotations like those given in the preceding section could be easily multiplied. In the last few years critical voices have been increasingly heard in the various UN bodies, reflecting misgivings about the present operations of the UN programmes.

One significant offshoot of such misgivings has been the growing emphasis on evaluation. In resolutions 908 (XXXIV) and 991 (XXXVI) the Economic and Social Council stressed the need for undertaking "systematic and objective evaluations of the impact and effectiveness of the programmes." Since then several other resolutions have been passed on the subject, stressing the need for "pilot evaluations" to be carried out in a limited number of countries. They have also steadily widened the scope of such evaluations to include an assessment of "the overall impact and effectiveness of the combined programmes of the United Nations system of organizations in terms of performance and results achieved;" "possible deficiencies and short-comings," as well as the successes of the technical co-operation programmes and activities; and "co-ordination and co-operation among the organizations concerned at the country level." So far pilot evaluations have been carried out in Thailand, Chile and Tunisia; and other evaluation missions are contemplated for the future.

The growing emphasis laid on evaluation reflects an increasingly widespread feeling that the current operations of the programmes leave much to be desired, that their quality can and should be improved and that this should be done as a matter of urgency. It also reflects an inability on the part of the policymaking bodies to identify the specific weaknesses the programmes now suffer from and the specific remedies they call for. And so it is hoped that a series of evaluation exercises will furnish the right answers, in terms of both diagnosis and cure.

This hope may well be belied. The operations of the UN programmes are too complex, too heterogeneous and too wide-ranging to lend themselves readily to such an evaluative treatment. The missions are too short-term, and they have too much of an ad hoc character to carry out evaluations in depth. To crown it all, their findings have to run the whole gamut of clearances; and since these would include clearances from those on whose performances they are supposed to sit in judgement, their final reports are likely to contain no more than watered-down versions of their findings.

The truth is that for a proper diagnosis of the existing deficiences it is not necesary to go far afield. Indeed, the evaluation missions, as now contemplated, are more likely to sidetrack the central issues than to reveal the shortcomings. Lao Tzu's remark, "The further one travels, the less one knows," is almost literally true in this case.

The search for remedies will begin in earnest only when the United Nations family decides to turn the searchlight on itself—at the headquarters of each organization—and begins to do some genuine soul-searching. The concept of evaluation, already overworked, will take on real meaning only when the UN family decides to launch resolutely on a process of honest self-evaluation.

If that happens, it will be easy to recognize another simple truth: that the real need is not to carry out elaborate post-mortems of results, but to create those conditions which are the sine qua non for sound programming and effective execution. Once these essential prerequisites are clearly recognized and built into the UN system, there will be far less reason to worry about the results which will automatically register a vast improvement.

5

What, then, are these essential prerequisites? They cover a wide range and will be examined at length in the rest of this book, but briefly:

They call for a real, and not superficial, consolidation of the UN programmes; an immediate termination of the absurd procedures hitherto followed for formulating technical assistance programmes; and a reappraisal of the proper role of technical assistance, which is at present both misconceived and grossly exaggerated.

They call for deliberate, stepped-up effort in such eye-catching high-priority fields as agriculture, with emphasis on food production and agro-industries, and population control.

They call for structural changes within the UNDP, the UN, and the specialized agencies to make it possible to treat development, above all, as a serious business and not as a primarily bureaucratic affair, and to pursue it according to the established canons of business management.

They call for complete unification of responsibilities in the hands of a single field representative in each country or group of countries, ending once and for all the long equivocation in this vital matter.

They call for radical rethinking and readjustment in the headquarters-field relationship, so as to provide for a far more substantial delegation of responsibilities to the field representatives to enable them to supply to the governments, on a continuous basis, the advice and guidance which they sorely need.

They call for a frank adoption, to the utmost possible extent, of an imaginative and nonpolitical approach to personnel management; for this, more than anything else, will determine the degree of ultimate success or failure of the other measures of reform.

And finally, they call for what is easily the Number One prerequisite: the will to reform. Given the will, we shall, even without evaluation missions, inevitably arrive at the broad diagnosis outlined above. Without it, we can only continue, as before, on a merry-go-round of dizzy excitements, lost motions, low performance, and worst of all, self-delusion.

PART II

EXPANDED PROGRAMME OF
TECHNICAL ASSISTANCE

CHAPTER 3

Guiding Principles and Forgotten Guidelines

*"Within the wide range of activities envisaged,
the participating organizations should practise,
especially in the initial stages of their programmes, concentration of effort and economy."*

ECOSOC RESOLUTION 222A (IX)

An analysis of the development programmes of the UN family now
at work can best begin with the United Nations Expanded Programme
of Technical Assistance. Though EPTA had some modest precursors,
it was the first programme of significant size which specifically aimed
at the economic and social development of the underdeveloped world,
and it brought together the entire UN family—the United Nations
and its specialized agencies—as participants in a global undertaking.
As the oldest programme, it also set the tone and pattern which have
exercised a decisive influence ever since on the development activities
of the United Nations as a whole.

Almost from its birth the Expanded Programme was caught in a
procedural tangle from which it has never been able to extricate
itself. Its history has been characterized by a series of ad hoc decisions,
with compromises strewn all along the way. Expediency, rather than
any clear-cut principles, has inspired and determined the nature of
these compromises. Or, to put it more correctly, the only principle it
has consistently recognized and applied in practice has been expediency.

The result has been a jungle of procedures. A senior official of
one of the specialized agencies remarked some time ago: "In their intricacies the EPTA procedures could now vie with the diver's code of
a leading maritime nation." The remark reflected, though in a more
vivid form, the view widely held by professional people working in

21

the UN organizations. The worst feature of this code is that it frequently runs counter to the principles of sound programming and good management.

The fact is that, in EPTA's concept, programming has all along been more or less synonymous with money-sharing. All its elaborate rituals in the end subserve this primary objective. A number of formulae were laid down for this purpose with the agreement of all concerned; they were periodically discussed at great length, and then were varied from time to time, mostly within very narrow limits. How to pick one's way skilfully through the procedural maze became a specialized job in itself, and the major concern of a great many people. Meanwhile the quality of the projects, that is to say, what the funds were actually spent upon, was tacitly relegated to the background. Clearly, no rational programme of development could emerge in such circumstances.

The EPTA's balance sheet contains other debit entries no less serious. The problems of development are inherently complex, and almost always they are further complicated by domestic politics. They would be hard to resolve even if seasoned minds with a scientific approach were brought to bear on them. In such a situation the Expanded Programme has been instrumental in introducing not light, but a fresh dose of confusion, aided by interagency competition at the country level. And this in turn has further dimmed the prospects of an objective search for the right priorities or proper formulation of projects in a recipient country.

Nor is this all. The Expanded Programme, thanks to its unique procedural code, has led to the creation of an expanding corps of senior officers, both at the headquarters of the participating organizations and in the field offices; these have been imbued with its peculiar spirit and tradition. As a result, they have been dedicated to routine, and accustomed to treat meticulous adherence to its money-sharing formulae as the essence of the programming function.

Finally, the Expanded Programme has developed, as was perhaps inevitable, a strong personality of its own. Despite a change in its name and its encasement in UNDP with effect from 1 January 1966, it has managed to survive with most of its dubious characteristics more or less intact. This amazing performance has been due to a combination of factors, and an attempt will be made later to shed some light on them.[7] What cannot be overstressed at this stage is the fact that

---

[7] See in particular Chapters 8-9 and 13-15.

the former EPTA, even after its rechristening as the "Technical Assistance Component of the United Nations Development Programme"
or UNDP/TA, remains by far the most important single source of
weakness, the Achilles heel of the UN programmes. A victim of false
premises and nebulous concepts, it has, by deflecting attention away
from the essentials, often tended to impede rather than promote development.

What, then, are the specific weaknesses of the EPTA procedures?
And how did the Programme get into such a tangle of procedures?
Why have they continued so long, and survived even its "merger" with
the Special Fund? Can the Programme be rescued from its procedural
stranglehold, and if so, how? These are not just academic questions,
but have far-reaching practical implications for the future. For, no
attempt to enhance the effectiveness of the UN programmes will ever
succeed unless they are squarely faced and adequately dealt with.

2

The Expanded Programme of Technical Assistance was created in
1949 by Resolution 222 (IX) of the Economic and Social Council and
Resolution 304 (IV) of the General Assembly, which also laid down
that the Programme would be financed by voluntary contributions
pledged by member states on an annual basis.

The concept of technical assistance was not entirely new. In fact,
some organizations were already giving such assistance, though on a
small scale, as is clearly reflected in the qualifying word "Expanded"
which was added to the title of the new programme.[8] Nevertheless,
there is no doubt that EPTA represented the first concerted effort
made on a significant scale by the UN family on behalf of the underdeveloped countries.

The objectives and the guiding principles of the Programme have
not changed over the years. They are still the same as were laid down
in Resolution 222 (IX) and its annex, although certain parts, especially
those relating to programme planning, have been amended almost with
bewildering frequency. One of the most important tasks before the
EPTA administration was to evolve programme-planning procedures

---

[8] For example, the International Telegraph Union and the Universal Postal
Union gave advice to member governments even before 1900. The International
Labor Organization had extended technical assistance to requesting governments
on labor and social problems since its creation in 1919. The United Nations was
asked to provide technical assistance on a modest scale by General Assembly
resolutions passed in 1946-48. The fields initially covered were economic development, social services, and public administration.

that would best serve the declared objectives of the Programme within the framework of the basic resolution. Procedural changes came thick and fast; but, as we shall see later, the problem still remains largely unresolved.

For a proper understanding of the questions relating to EPTA it is essential to have some idea about the main provisions of Resolution 222 and its subsequent amendments. The legislative picture is far from simple, especially because of the voluminous changes in the programming procedures. It is however not necessary to burden this analysis with anything like a complete historical account of all the changes that have taken place in EPTA's procedures, rules and regulations since its establishment. Instead, attention will be focussed, in this and the next two chapters, on those specific aspects of legislation and of administrative practices which have a direct bearing on the quality of the programme and its overall performance.

The "guiding principles" as laid down in Resolution 222 for the Programme, are of an abiding interest. A summarized version of these principles is therefore given below:

1. The primary objective is to help the underdeveloped countries to strengthen their national economies through the development of their industries and agriculture with a view to promoting their economic and political independence and to ensure the attainment of higher levels of economic and social welfare for their entire populations.

2. Technical assistance shall be provided only in agreement with the governments concerned and on the basis of requests received from them, or through them.

3. The kinds of services to be rendered shall be decided by the government; shall be provided as far as possible in the form which it desires; and shall be designed to meet the needs of the country concerned.

4. Countries desiring assistance should perform, in advance, as much of the work as possible in order to define the nature and scope of the problem involved.

5. Technical assistance shall not be a means of foreign economic and political interference in the internal affairs of the country and shall not be accompanied by any considerations of a political nature.

6. It shall avoid all distinctions arising from the political structure of the country requesting assistance, and from the race or religion of its population.

7. The highest professional competence should be maintained in all services undertaken by the participating organizations. Experts should be chosen not only for their technical competence, but also for their sympathetic understanding of the cultural backgrounds and specific needs of the countries to be assisted. They should be adequately prepared for their tasks before starting their assignments. And the scope of their duties should be strictly defined in each case by agreement with the country concerned.

8. The requesting governments will have the following obligations:

   a. to help the participating organizations in obtaining necessary information about the problems on which they have been asked to help;

   b. to give full and prompt consideration to the technical ad-advice they receive;

   c. to maintain or set up, as soon as practicable, governmental coordination machinery to ensure that their own technical, natural and financial resources are utilized in the interest of economic development;

   d. to assume, normally, responsibility for a substantial part of the costs of technical services, at least that part which can be paid in their own currencies;

   e. to undertake sustained efforts required for economic development; therefore to provide continuing support for projects initiated at their request;

   f. to make available information on the results of technical assistance so that it may be of value to other countries and to the international organizations;

   g. to supply information to the participating organizations, whenever technical assistance is requested, about all assistance which they are already receiving or requesting from other sources in the same field of development; and

   h. to give publicity to the Programme within their countries.

9. Participating organizations will deal with projects falling within their respective fields of competence. They should coordinate the work among themselves, due regard being paid to their constitutions and the relations established between them.

10. Their work under the Expanded Programme should be such as is suitable for integration with their normal work.

11. Requests for assistance falling within the sphere of two or more organizations should be handled jointly by them, with co-ordination made among them at the planning level. Programmes of training should be the subject of cooperative effort.

12. Activities which at present are not a special responsibility of any specialized agency, such as certain aspects of industrial development,[9] manufacturing, mining, power, land and water transport should be undertaken by the Secretary-General of the United Nations.

3

There were two other guiding principles which deserve special attention. "Within the wide range of activities," the Resolution stipulated, "participating organizations should practise, especially in the initial stages of their programmes, *concentration of effort and economy.*"[10]

The other principle laid down, in broad terms, the criteria for the selection of projects. After reiterating that, in furnishing technical assistance, the organizations should be guided by the Charter of the United Nations, the principles of the technical assistance programme, and the appropriate resolutions of the General Assembly and the Economic and Social Council, the Resolution set forth some definite guidelines:[11]

a. "The services envisaged should aim at *increased productivity* of material and human resources and a wide and equitable distribution of the benefits of such increased productivity" to raise the living standards of the *entire populations.*

b. Due attention and respect should be paid to national sovereignty, national legislation and to the social conditions having a direct bearing on economic development.

c. Technical assistance projects should aim at economic development for the welfare of the population as a whole including the *promotion of full employment.* They may also deal with specific

---

9 Industrial development activities have meanwhile been transferred to the United Nations Industrial Development Organization (UNIDO) which was established as a specialized agency on 1 January 1967.

10 and 11. Italics supplied.

social improvements necessary to permit effective economic development and to mitigate the social problems—particularly dislocation
of family and community life—that may arise as a concomitant of
economic change.

d.   Special attention should be given, *in timing and emphasis,* to
activities tending to bring about *an early increase in national productivity* of material and human resources. This point was specially
stressed because the capacity of a government to finance welfare
activities would depend on national production and income.

e.   Before undertaking work of an extensive character involving
substantial cost, organizations should assure themselves that the
governments concerned are giving *full consideration to major capital
investment* or large continued governmental expenditure which
may be needed as a result of the technical assistance.

f.   Equipment and supplies may be provided in so far as they form
an integral part of a technical assistance project.

4

The guiding principles relating to concentration of effort and economy and to the selection of individual projects had an overriding
significance. It was obvious that the ultimate success of the Expanded
Programme was going to depend on how effectively and imaginatively
they were applied in practice. On these points the letter and the spirit
of the Resolution were unmistakably clear.

No less clear were the tasks that devolved on the EPTA administration, namely: to work out the full implications of these programming
guidelines; to spell out, on their basis, more detailed and objective
criteria for its own guidance; to enforce them all along the line in all
its operations; and to do so in a way that would be compatible with
the other provisions of the basic legislation. The administration chose
to act differently. It ignored these vital principles, and quietly consigned them to oblivion.[12]

A 15-year anniversary review of the Expanded Programme, published by the Technical Assistance Board in 1965, bestows high praise
on the guiding principles of Resolution 222 A (IX). But it made no
more than a cursory reference to the directive that the services envisaged

---

[12] In my ten years with the UN programmes I never came across a single
reference to these guidelines. No one had the time, or the inclination, to worry
about them.

under the Programme should aim at increased productivity. And it made no mention at all of the need for concentration of effort and economy.[13]

The worst deficiencies of the Expanded Programme sprang primarily from this single source: from its inability, or unwillingness, to recognize the crucial importance of these guidelines. And this in turn foredoomed it to its present status: a pretentious mini-programme indiscriminately littering the underdeveloped world with countless mini-projects.[14]

---

[13] "15 Years and 150,000 Skills," United Nations, New York, 1965. Pages 9-10 and 49-51.

[14] See Chapter 7 on "A Many-Splintered Thing," also EPTA statistics in Appendix 1A. The annual and biennial programme documents of EPTA clearly reflect the bewildering number of tiny and disjointed "projects."

CHAPTER 4

Management by Consensus

> *"...Special attention should be given in timing and emphasis to activities tending to bring an early increase in national productivity of material and human resources."*
>
> Resolution 222 A (IX), Annex I.

Like the great majority of decisions in the UN family, Resolution 222 was a product of multiple compromise. This was inevitable since, as usual, conflicting viewpoints had to be harmonized. What is surprising is not that there were some weak spots in it, but that they were so few. Its guiding principles reflected wisdom and foresight. With a few exceptions which related above all to certain aspects of programming procedures, the Resolution did provide a general framework that was essentially sound.

As with all good pieces of legislation, what mattered most at this stage was not what the Resolution provided for, but how its provisions were actually worked. A great deal therefore depended on the Technical Assistance Board which was charged with the administration of the Programme. A wise Board, acting with foresight and statesmanship, could have helped improve upon the governing legislation. The Board, however, chose to follow the line of least resistance, relied heavily on compromises, and worked mainly on the basis of consensus that could seldom yield inspiring decisions. As a result, the initial weaknesses of the legislation were not remedied, but reinforced.

The programming procedures and their implications will be examined later in some detail, so also the actual functioning of the EPTA administration. To start with, however, it would be useful to note, even if briefly, the other major provisions of Resolution 222, in par-

ticular those relating to the financing of the Programme and the obligations of the governments receiving assistance.

2

A noteworthy feature of the Expanded Programme is that it is
financed by voluntary contributions made by all governments, rich or
poor, who are members of the United Nations or its specialized agencies. A Technical Assistance Conference, also called Pledging Conference, is convened annually during the General Assembly session when
the members pledge their contributions to the Programme to cover the
operations of the following calendar year. All contributions are credited
to a Special Account for technical assistance for economic development,
which was established by General Assembly resolution 304 (IV).

The governing legislation, as amended from time to time, made
several stipulations which are worth noting. Contributions should be
made "without limitation as to use by a specific agency or in a specific
country, or for a specific project." They should be, "to the fullest extent possible, in a form readily utilizable for programmes purposes."
A currency was to be considered not readily usable "if an amount
greater than the equivalent of $500,000 and greater than the total of
the previous year's pledges in any currency remains uncommitted for the
approved programme at the time of the Pledging Conference." Governments were urged to make "that part of their contributions exceeding
the equivalent of $500,000 in the form of, or convertible into, readily
usable currencies."

The legislation further enjoined that the multilateral character of
the Programme should be strictly respected and that, to ensure this, no
contributing country should receive special privileges or treatment with
respect to the contribution. Information regarding the availability of
not-readily usable currencies might be supplied to the receiving countries by TAB (see below) and its participating organizations. But direct
negotiations for the use of currencies between contributing and receiving countries were disallowed as an infringement of the multilateral
character of the Programme.

The contributions were received in a large number of currencies
—some sixty or more.[15] Utilization of these resources was always a

---

15 In addition, there were two special contributions though the amounts involved were relatively small: the "Brazilian Catalogue of Services," which amounted
to $162,162 in 1960-61 when they were merged with other contributions; and the
"Danish restricted contribution"—fixed at 50% of Denmark's annual pledge for
EPTA, it rose in value from $325,000 in 1960 to $2.3 million in 1969, but from
1970 they will be assimilated with other contributions.

major administrative headache. This was, however, unavoidable in a global programme financed with voluntary contributions made by a great many states, rich and poor, each according to its own volition and in a form it can best afford.

What is avoidable, and, consequently, what makes so little sense, administratively or otherwise, is to go through the same chores more than once because separate programmes are maintained side by side with the same currency management problems.

3

To ensure that expenditures would not exceed the available resources, the Resolution made several specific provisions. Each organization must at all times keep its obligations within the limit of funds earmarked by the Board. For each financial period, earmarkings should be based initially on the most conservative estimates of contributions likely to be available, to avoid possible cancellation of authorized programmes for shortage of funds; supplementary earmarkings were allowed as and when justified by the receipt of contributions.

And finally, the funds earmarked to the participating organizations were available to them for "assuming obligations or commitments during the programming period." Actual expenditures, too, had to be made within the same period except that obligations for fellowships could be liquidated over the full period of the fellowships, provided that "placement arrangements had been completed prior to the obligation of funds." As for equipment, delivery could take place with considerable time lag, provided funds were committed on the basis of firm orders within the programming period.

Until 1960 the "programming period" consisted of one calendar year, which has always been, and still is, the fiscal year in the United Nations. Thereafter the programme was placed on a cycle of two calendar years, and, in keeping with this, actual expenditures too were allowed to extend over the two corresponding fiscal years, while the rules regarding obligations for fellowships continued as before.

The concern of the legislators to prevent authorizations in excess of the available resources was easy to understand. From a purely financial angle, the system devised for earmarkings and obligations could hardly be improved upon. It fully secured the immediate objective, namely, that the coat would be cut without fail according to the cloth. What was overlooked, however, was the fact that projects, too, suffered arbitrary cuts in the process, and that it encouraged piecemeal programming for very short durations.

Annual appropriations was in itself a serious limitation. Writing in mid-fifties about the U.S. bilateral programme, Mr. Harlan Cleveland lamented the mistaken insistence on "tackling twenty-year problems with five-year plans using two-year personnel with one-year appropriations."

In the case of EPTA things were even worse because of the earmarking rules which meant instalment appropriations within the same financial year. A determined effort to evolve sensible programming procedures might have helped, if not to rid the Programme of these shortcomings, at least to mitigate their effects. But what happened was just the opposite. The weaknesses resulting from the financial regulations were aggravated by the programming procedures that were actually followed.[16]

The governing legislation provided for the establishment of a so-called Contingency Fund with 5 per cent of the estimated resources, which was placed at the disposal of the Executive Chairman of TAB.[17] Its main purpose was to finance contingencies which might arise during the implementation of the annual programme. It was later renamed the Working Capital and Reserve Fund (WCRF) and was also given some additional functions, such as to make advances against firm pledges of contributions to finance the TAC—approved programme;[18] to improve and facilitate currency management; and to make advances to participating organizations to provide working balances in their bank accounts.

It was stipulated that advances made from the Fund to finance projects authorized by the Executive Chairman under his contingency authority must constitute a priority charge against the resources of the following year.

The size of the WCR Fund was determined by TAC from time to time. The amount that could be drawn by the Executive Chairman to meet "contingencies" was raised in stages. After the introduction of the two-year programme the ceiling was fixed at 10 per cent of the estimated total resources for the year. We shall have occasion to comment on the use of these funds while examining the EPTA operations in detail.[19]

---

16 See Chapters 5, 7, and 9.
17 See Section 5 below for functions of TAB and its Executive Chairman.
18 See Section 5 below for functions of TAC.
19 See Chapter 7.

4

In addition to the voluntary contributions made to the Special Account of the Programme every year, a recipient government is required to bear part of the living costs of technical assistance experts serving in its country. Arrangements for the payment of these costs were made in considerable detail. For several years the local cost payments were made on the basis of meticulous calculation of the actual costs incurred for the services of each individual expert; and this involved an enormous amount of book-keeping, at headquarters and in the field offices, for what were, after all, very small sums of money.

The method of assessment and payment was changed but only in 1960, by resolution 787 (XXX) which provided that the local cost contribution to be made by a government "shall be computed on the basis of a percentage of the total cost of expert services provided to that government." The percentage was fixed at 12.5, and it has remained at that level since then. The shift to a fixed percentage method of assessment was a much-needed simplification which, if anything, was long overdue.

Even now the local cost issue involves a large amount of routine work. Before the beginning of each year a preliminary assessment is made by applying the 12.5 per cent rate to the *estimated* cost of the approved programme; the governments are required to pay the amounts in advance as assessed; the accounts are finally adjusted at the end of the year on the basis of the actual costs.

There are further complications about regional projects. It is not easy to identify the shares of each recipient government under such a project, the more so since, even after all the talks of all these years, regional projects are still mostly conceived and initiated by the agencies, while the government attitudes toward them range generally from indifference to lukewarm support. A compromise was therefore necessary on this point, and it was decided that the new mode of assessment would be applied to regional projects only where the shares of each government could be clearly identified and where an appropriate agreement to that effect had been reached with the government concerned.

Local cost payments could be waived "in cases of extreme hardship." Authority was given to the Executive Chairman to grant, in consultation with the Board, general waivers to a recipient country for limited periods covering its entire programme. In exceptional cases waivers could be extended to certain specific projects.

In an international programme that has been established for the sole purpose of extending assistance to the underdeveloped countries to promote their economic and social development, an issue like local cost contributions may appear too insignificant to be given so much attention. There are, however, good reasons why this attention is justified.

First of all, the issue has in practice loomed large in TAB and TAC discussions. It has claimed much of their time and attention, generated a large amount of routine work, consumed a great many staff man-hours at headquarters and in the field offices, and continues to do so even now. In these respects it provides a good example of how, in EPTA operations, minor issues were blown out of all proportion and how they tended to overshadow the essentials.

Secondly, it illustrates how much could be gained, in terms of administrative efficiency, rationalization of work, and economy in over-head costs, if the different programmes of the UN family were merged into one, instead of each programme going its own way with local cost assessment and collection, as is the case at present.

And thirdly, these payments show that technical assistance from UN sources carries a higher price tag than one might imagine; that the recipient governments have to pay the local costs and incur other obligations.

In fact, when all these obligations are put together, the total burden falling on the governments would appear to be quite consider-able. Apart from the 12.5 per cent contribution towards the local costs of experts, they have to provide a number of facilities, in cash or in kind, such as: local personnel services, technical and administrative, including necessary secretarial help and interpreter-translators; office space and other premises; equipment and supplies produced within the country; transportation of personnel, supplies and equipment for official purposes within the country; local transport; postage and tele-communications for official purposes; and such medical services and facilities for technical assistance personnel as may be available to the civil servants of the country.

Clearly, UN technical assistance is not cheap; it has to be matched by a recipient government, and the matching costs, when all the items are expressed in terms of money, are quite substantial. In the poorer countries, especially of Africa, much of their meagre resources can be tied up in the process.[20]

---

[20] To alleviate the hardship in specific cases, certain measures were taken by the Special Fund, such as extending financial assistance towards construction of office buildings.

5

The administration of the Expanded Programme was entrusted, under Resolution 222, mainly to three bodies. The overall responsibility, particularly at the policy-making level, devolved naturally on the Economic and Social Council (ECOSOC)[21] of the General Assembly. In actual practice, however, it was a standing committee of the Council, called the Technical Assistance Committee or TAC, that discharged the functions on its behalf, subject to what was mostly a purely formal review and endorsement by it. The execution of the Programme, within the framework of ECOSOC-TAC policy decisions, was left to an inter-agency body called the Technical Assistance Board, or TAB.

The TAC, as originally established, consisted of eighteen members, i.e. the same members as the ECOSOC. Its membership was raised to twenty-four when, by Council resolution 647 (XXIII) of 1 May, 1957, six members elected from among the member-governments, were added to it. This latter figure was doubled, by Council resolution 863 (XXXII) of 22 December, 1964, so that thereafter the Committee consisted of thirty members. As is customary in the case of such UN bodies, the governing legislation also laid down that, in electing the TAC members, due regard should be paid to geographical distribution and to the representation of both the contributing and the receiving countries.

The Committee, which used to meet twice a year, had the responsibility, among other things, to review and approve the overall programme submitted to it by the Board, to authorize the allocation of funds to the participating organizations; to receive reports from the Board, and review the progress under the Programme; to interpret resolutions, to recommend new legislation, and to take decisions on questions submitted to it by the Board.

The Committee reported to the Council which in turn reported to the General Assembly of the United Nations.

The coordination of EPTA was the function of the Technical Assistance Board (TAB) which consisted of the Executive Heads, or their representatives, of the organizations participating in the Pro-

---

21 The Economic and Social Council, it may be recalled, is one of the four main organs created under the UN Charter to help the work of the General Assembly, the other three being the Security Council, the Trusteeship Council and the International Court. The ECOSOC, as its name implies, was made competent for all economic and social matters. It was established with eighteen members, but in 1965 the number was raised to twenty-seven to reflect the big rise in the membership of the United Nations itself. The relevant Article 61 of the UN Charter was amended by General Assembly resolution 1991 B (XVIII) of 17 December 1963, which however went into force only on 31 August 1965.

gramme and a full-time Executive Chairman. The representatives of the International Bank (IBRD) and the International Monetary Fund (IMF) might attend TAB meetings, but not vote; and after the establishment of the UN Special Fund in 1959, the same right was extended to its Managing Director. Other programmes, such as UNICEF, could send observers where appropriate.

The Board met three times a year. The executive heads of the larger organizations never attended the meetings, nor were they, as a rule, represented at a very high level. The IBRD and IMF never showed much interest in the Board's proceedings, and they seldom, if ever, sent representatives to its meetings.

Extensive responsibilities were vested in the Executive Chairman of the Board, who was appointed, on a full-time basis, by the Secretary-General *"after consultation with the executive heads of the participating organizations."* Continuity in the Expanded Programme operations has been maintained through continuation of the same Executive Chairman since the Programme was established twenty years ago.

He has the responsibility, among other things: to examine programme proposals submitted by requesting governments, and to make appropriate recommendations about them to the Board; to earmark and to allocate funds after TAC has approved the overall programme and authorized such allocation; to exercise continuous supervision of the Programme, and to appraise the effectiveness of its activities and of the results achieved; to review coordination of the activities with those financed from the regular budgets of the agencies as well as with other programmes, bilateral and multilateral, and make recommendations to the Board; to convene and preside over Board meetings and, in the intervals between meetings, to act on its behalf; to execute basic and comprehensive country agreements with governments under conditions agreed to by the Board; to establish, after consultation with the Board, administrative rules and procedures; to report, on its behalf, on the Programme; and to supervise the work of the Board's secretariat.

Finally, the Executive Chairman was given another function of great practical significance: *"In agreement with the Board, to appoint* resident technical assistance representatives and to determine their terms of reference; to *supervise* the activities of such representatives and to establish an effective system of *reporting between himself and such representatives."*[22]

---

22 Italics supplied.

6

How were decisions to be taken by a Board that consisted of so many organizations? Here, again, Resolution 222 furnished the guideline: "Decisions relating to recommendations or proposals made by the Executive Chairman or by members of the Board will normally be taken by general agreement between the Executive Chairman and all members of the Board."

The governing legislation also provided that in the absence of a general agreement, decisions would be taken by a majority of the members of the Board present and voting and the Executive Chairman, provided there was agreement among them; otherwise the matter could be referred to TAC either by a majority of the members or by the Executive Chairman.

Such occasions of disagreement never arose. The Board always managed to evolve agreed decisions. This was a remarkable achievement, especially in view of its heterogeneous composition. The secret of such exemplary teamwork was no less remarkable. Agreement was treated as by far the most important objective, if not an end in itself; issues were carefully screened in advance, and whatever might give rise to disagreement or to controversies was kept out of the Board's agenda. By far the most important items on the agenda were financial—estimated resources, allocation of funds, earmarking, contingency funds, and the primary concern of each member was its own share of the total resources. And as long as the member organizations were reasonably satisfied with their respective shares, harmonious teamwork was practically assured.

To maximize the prospects of agreement, the Board eschewed such issues as priorities among the fields of activities, quality of projects including their size and duration, efficiency in their execution, and follow-up action by the governments, and status, functions and responsibilities of the field representative. Such issues are no doubt fundamental to a programme, both according to common-sense view and to all accepted business standards. But they were, in general, treated as extraneous matters. For, in the Board's concept there was something even more fundamental though it was never mentioned in so many words, namely, to be in agreement.

A no less important factor has been the long experience of the Executive Chairman who has served the Expanded Programme since it was establisched twenty years ago. He has provided continuity in its operations; supplied leadership and guidance; and has been the chief architect of consensus at the Board level.

CHAPTER 5

A Procedural Roadblock

"What obvious truths the wisest heads may miss.!"

WILLIAM COWPER

The first question which an administration in charge of a development programme has to face and answer is: *"What* kind of programme should one prepare"? The Expanded Programme has the unique distinction of being an exception to this logical approach. It has expended a vast amount of energy on a different question: *"How* should one prepare a programme"? The *how* has overshadowed the *what* from the start, and has elbowed it into the background. In short, the primary preoccupation of EPTA has been not with the substance of the Programme, but with its procedures.

And incredible as it may sound, even after almost two decades, this procedural question remains unresolved. It is still being debated with renewed ardour, though the issues involved long ago took on a hoary look.

For an elementary issue like this to remain alive all these years is an unusual phenomenon. How it happened makes a fascinating story; and an attempt will be made later to shed some light on it, particularly in Chapter 15 on "Why Anomalies Die Hard." For the present let us take a look at the salient features of the procedures, how they have been shaped and reshaped from time to time, and how, on each occasion, they were improvised without regard to their effects on the quality of the programme.

2

In the evolution of the EPTA programming procedures four main phases can be distinguished:

38

a. The *agency allocation system* which prevailed in the first five years of the Programme through 1954;

b. Country-programming procedures with country targets, *annual programming*, "agency planning shares" and "agency sub-totals," which was introduced with effect from 1955 and lasted six years through 1960;

c. Modified country-programming procedures with country targets and *two-year programming*, but without "agency planning shares" and "agency sub-totals"; and with a new distinction between "short-term" and "long-term" projects. The two-year cycle was first introduced, on an experimental basis, for the biennium 1961-62. Since then it has been renewed every two years, and each time on the same experimental basis.

d. The final phase began in summer 1967 with a new proposal which is expected to come into force in January 1969, that is to say, after the expiration of the current biennium. The new system will be based on "project programming" and "project budgeting"; two-year cycles will be abolished; and authorization will take place, project by project, *on a continuous basis* throughout the year.

It is evident from this that the Expanded Programme did not lack a dynamic quality. It has shown a rare genius to expand—in a procedural sense. Nor is the end of this dynamism yet in sight. For it is safe to predict that even the fourth phase is not going to be the last. It may help rectify some errors, but it retains others and will, in addition, create some fresh complications. And in any case it does not come firmly to grips with the essentials of sound programming, nor with the problems of inter-programme relationship, not to speak of simplification and rationalization for which there has long been a crying need. The new procedural gambit may, like its predecessors, dazzle the onlookers for a while, but it is unlikely that its deficiencies will escape notice very long.[23]

3

The Expanded Programme began to function in 1950. The Technical Assistance Board held its first meeting in February of that year when it attended to the preliminary administrative arrangements. A

---

[23] See Chapter 9: "Plus ça change . . . ." The new procedures duly came into effect on 1 January 1969, and they are already being subjected to a growing criticism, both inside and outside the secretariats of the UN and the agencies.

skeleton programme soon emerged with a pooling of isolated projects recommended by the participating organizations. The Technical Assistance Committee, meeting for the first time, in midsummer 1950, reviewed the Board's activities and its recommendations. Then followed the first "pledging conference" which had been unexpectedly delayed by six months. At this conference 54 countries promised to contribute the equivalent of just over $20 million for the 18-month period ending 31 December 1951. With funds available, the Programme now became operative.

In the Committee's view, EPTA "had got off to a good start." And so indeed it did, but only in the narrow financial and administrative sense. From a programming angle, the start, as we shall soon see, proved ill-starred. The course was well set—but in the wrong direction.

In the early years of the Programme the available resources were allocated among the participating organizations according to a fixed formula agreed among themselves, after setting aside a small amount to meet the costs of the central secretariat. Each organization was virtually left free to develop its own programme, in consultation with the governments as and when it deemed necessary.

This practice had serious limitations which were by no means unforeseen. Fixing the shares of the organizations was in itself a sensitive task. Nor could it be disposed of as a one-time affair; it continued to crop up as a perennial issue. The 15-year anniversary review[24] of the Expanded Programme contains enough hints of this, though in well-guarded, euphemistic terms. Each agency with a special technical competence in its own field evinced "a special zeal in exercising it" (p. 12). The principle that each organization, with some margin of flexibility, should "automatically receive a fixed proportion of the resources" tended "to freeze the main components" of the Programme in terms of agriculture, health, education, and so forth; and the resultant pattern might not necessarily correspond to the needs of the receiving countries. Within the TAB itself "this had proved a divisive issue" (p. 15).

Moreover, under such an approach the quality of projects could not be of a high standard. The requests emanating from the governments were often no more than expressions of intentions or of impulses, and did not provide a sound enough basis for formulating projects. Nor were the headquarters-inspired proposals which bulged conspicuously in the Programme in its early years, necessarily superior, especially since they were not based on a deep enough knowledge of local conditions and local needs.

---

[24] Ibid., footnote 13 *ante.*

There were also some financial paradoxes. In the initial stages of the Programme the flow of funds did not sufficiently match the pledges. The time-lag between the two was often considerable. Yet the organizations were unable to develop projects fast enough to utilize the available funds.

The programme had to be prepared on a calendar-year basis; and funds unobligated by an agency from its own share by 31 December lapsed and automatically reverted to the Special Account. Yet the capacity of the agencies to develop programmes had no visible relationship to their planning shares; some might receive more than they could spend, while others might not have enough funds to finance the projects on hand. Obviously, the situation was untenable and could not last long.

However, in those early years tangible progress was made in certain other directions. Field offices were gradually established; a TAB Resident Representative was appointed in Pakistan in 1950, and this was followed by similar appointments in several other countries. Administrative rules and regulations were formulated; and fairly uniform terms and conditions were established for the services of all EPTA project personnel even when appointed and serving under different agencies. And finally, there was a growing realization that the right place to prepare projects was not at the headquarters of the agencies, but within the countries served by the Programme.

In 1952 the United Nations as a participating organization indicated its clear preference for a system under which all funds should be allocated *on a project basis*. It further argued that this could be best brought about as part of the process of greater centralization of executive authority which was then under way. The preference of WHO had always been in favour of "project programming" and "project budgeting." It is to the credit of WHO that, right from the start, it adopted and adhered to this approach in giving technical assistance under its own regular programme; and, with remarkable consistency, it has pleaded all along that there is no valid or rational alternative to it, whether for EPTA or any other development programme.

It is the misfortune of the Expanded Programme and of its well-wishers that this wise counsel did not prevail, that the dictates of commonsense were brushed aside. As a result, the stage was set to proceed from one initial blunder to another, this time to a more profound and longer-lasting one because it was no longer readily visible to the naked eye, and because it rested on premises which, though intrinsically fallacious, had a deceptively plausible look and could therefore easily escape outside probing.

4

It took about four years for the Programme to realize fully the awkward contradiction it had stumbled into. Its declared objective was to meet the needs of the receiving countries to promote their development. Yet it had adopted a system of automatic allocation of funds to the agencies which, in turn, distributed them among the countries as they deemed best. There was no guarantee that the subtotals of the agencies in a given country would, under such conditions, correspond to its real needs. The two could not coincide, except by a miracle.

In short, trying to serve the countries through preprogramming allocation of funds to the agencies was self-contradictory. And so it was decided that the recipient governments should themselves draw up their requests to meet their own needs. The verdict against the agency allocation system was unquestionably right. But the conclusion drawn from it was only half valid, even to start with. And it became a full-fledged non sequitur when it was used to justify the switch from a system of agency laissez faire to a system of government laissez faire.

The new principles were embodied in resolutions which were adopted by the Economic and Social Council and the General Assembly in 1954.[25] Thus came into existence the so-called *country-programming procedures* which, with some modifications, have remained in force up to this day.

In all, six annual programmes were prepared on the basis of the new procedures, for the years ending 1960 when the cycle was changed to two years. It is worth looking at the salient features of the system of annual programming as it was adopted in 1955.

The first step, as before, was to prepare a realistic estimate of the resources likely to be available for the Programme, based on the results of the pledging conference and the anticipated carryover from the current programme. The timetable for the pledging conference had already been adjusted so as to precede, and not follow, the commencement of the programme year, when late in 1953 it was held for the 1954 resources. This practice, which has continued since then, has made it possible to prepare better financial forecasts.

The next step was a five-way division of the resources. First, an amount was set aside to reimburse the Working Capital and Reserve

---

[25] Council resolution 542 B II (XVIII) and Assembly resolution S3 (IX).

Fund for the sums previously drawn from it to finance "contingency projects" and for other authorized purposes. As noted before, such replenishment of the Fund constituted the first charge against the available resources. In the early years, before the creation of the WCRF, a slightly different procedure was followed—five per cent of the estimated resources were earmarked to meet contingencies that might arise in the course of executing the approved programme.

The second and third deductions were made to meet respectively (a) the administrative costs of the TAB secretariat and its field offices, and (b) the "operational services costs" of the participating organizations—that is, the expenses incurred by them in carrying out their respective parts of the approved programme.

The balance of the estimated resources, which were considered available for the field programme, or for "project costs," was then divided into two parts for "regional projects" and for "country programmes."

The amount earmarked for regional projects—initially fixed at ten per cent of the total resources but raised in successive stages[26] was directly allocated to the agencies according to a previously agreed formula. The initiative for the preparation of projects remained with them, and it was also left to them to decide when and to what extent the governments concerned were to be consulted. In the earlier years such consultation was rare, and though its frequency has increased somewhat, it has mostly been a matter of formality. Regional projects have been, and still are, virtually made by the participating organizations. So far as this part of the Programme is concerned, the agency allocation system has survived all legislative changes.

The real innovation was in the preparation of the "country programmes," to which the rest of the funds was devoted. Here, again, the system had several facets. The first and the most complicated task in TAB was to set up a whole series of "targets" for each individual country and territory receiving assistance from EPTA.

Target-fixing was an arduous and delicate exercise. Theoretically, the criteria applied embraced almost every conceivable factor. Due weight was supposed to be given to the size of the population of a recipient country or territory, its stage of economic development; its current and future needs, the assistance it had already received from various sources, the current volume of assistance received from other sources, especially the U.S. bilateral programme. But obviously, the

---

[26] It will amount to 17 per cent in the technical assistance programme for 1969.

targets would have to cover, above all, the "continuing commitments" on account of the existing projects; and these alone, as a rule, accounted for 80 to 85 per cent of the annual programmes. The weights that could be given to the other factors had to be light indeed!

In fact, they were even lighter than one might at first imagine. Only the participating organizations could supply complete data about the continuing commitments; in doing so, they tended to give an elastic interpretation to this phrase and thereby stretch it as far as possible; and in any case the yearend rush into obligations always had the effect of inflating the commitments for the following programme year. While communicating these data, the organizations also recommended provisions for new projects, country by country, usually on the basis of discussions or correspondence already carried out by them. The result was a mass of subtargets or "sub-totals" given by each organization for every country or territory.

Then began the real agony. For invariably the total of all the suggested subtargets far exceeded the estimated resources available for country programmes. Sometimes the total of continuing commitments alone, as defined by the agencies, were in substantial excess of these resources! So the task now was to examine the subtotals country by country; to cut them down, often drastically, in animated discussions with the agencies; and to bring them in line with the assumed resources. This is how targets were fixed in actual practice.

Another refinement was introduced after the initial experience with country programming. While fixing the country targets, a sum, usually varying between $1 and $2 million, was kept aside as the "planning reserve" of the Executive Chairman; it was used later to make marginal adjustments in the final programme requests of the governments. The need for such adjustments arose for reasons such as oversights in providing for continuing commitments in isolated instances, marginal excesses due to re-costing of projects, need for supplementary allocations made ex gratia in special cases.

The mechanics of programming had another notable feature. For each country not one, but two targets were fixed. The first one was for what, in TAB parlance, was called "Category I programme"—projects that were given the first priority. This was the operative programme that determined the actual volume of assistance in each case, apart of course from whatever extras a country might get as contingencies and through its participation in regional projects.

In addition, each country had a second target, for the so-called "Category II programme," the level of which was fixed almost mechanically at 50 per cent of Category I. Its professed purpose was to keep a reserve list of projects readily available in advance for each country, so that they could be implemented as and when more funds became available, either from savings on Category I projects or from additional earmarkings. In practice, Category II consisted overwhelmingly of projects that could not be accommodated within the modest Category I targets.

What about costing the three components of technical assistance? For equipment, provisions had to be made on the basis of estimated actual costs. But for experts and fellowships costing was in general based on standard figures, which have been revised upwards from time to time in keeping with the rising trend of prices and costs. The practice however showed some variations among the participating organizations. For example, the UN standards for fellowships made some allowance for regional variations of costs. The most striking exception has been WHO which has consistently followed the practice of costing its expert posts and fellowships not by any global standards, but on the basis of meticulous calculations of estimated cost in each case. This is in keeping with the agency's practice of preparing its projects in depth, from start to fiinish, with realistic costing in each case even though the EPTA procedures forced it to fit them artificially into its one-year, and later two-year, cycles.

Once this preliminary exercise was over, the two targets were communicated to the governments through a letter issued from headquarters. This letter spelled out at great length the details regarding the procedures to be followed, the standard costs to be applied to expert posts and fellowships, the timetable for submitting the programme requests, the implications of the two categories, the need to pay some heed to the problem of difficult currencies. It also entered a caveat that the targets did not mean allocation of funds and that the delivery of the programme would be contingent upon the adequacy of the available resources.

The letter communicating the targets also gave the subtotals, agency by agency, as they had emerged out of the target-fixing exercise, mentioning at the same time that the governments need not consider themselves bound by them. This practice was continued until the suppression of the agency planning shares and subtotals in 1960.

The letter itself was recomposed and reissued every year in its entirety, although the variable points were only a few, such as the size of the targets, standard costs, and the timetable. A standard manual on programming procedures could have eliminated a great deal of labour. But the fact is that such a manual could not be prepared because the procedures were, or at least appeared to be, always in a state of flux.

There was another feature which distinctly harked back to the days of automatic allocation. The participating organizations wanted protection against the risk of a sudden sharp reduction of their programmes. This they obtained through the so-called "85 per cent rule" which was written into the Council resolution 542. This rule provided that the global share of a participating organization in the overall programme should not shrink by more than 15 per cent from one year to another. It thus set a floor to the downward slide of their shares. However, the protection was only psychological, and it has never been necessary to evoke this rule. The reason was what one might suspect. The freedom given to the governments to deviate from the agency subtotals was sldom used by them. The subtotals proved extremely sticky. They seemed to carry a *de facto* sanction and were adhered to in practice more or less consistently.

In fact, even after their formal suppression, the spirit of the subtotals continued to dominate the individual country programmes. And as we shall soon see, given the nature of the country-programming procedures, this was more or less inevitable.

5

With the communication of the targets to the governments, the centre of gravity would shift to the field, and there would begin in each country the so-called programming exercise, starting usually around January and lasting four to five months.

In preparing their "programme-requests" the governments had to satisfy three main conditions. As the first charge against the target, they had to make adequate provisions to cover all continuing commitments; they had to do the costing of the projects correctly, according to the standard costs; and it was, of course, imperative for them to stay within their respective targets. Subject to these conditions, the governments were given a free hand to prepare their requests.

In actual practice their hands were far from free. The continuing commitments for projects already under way usually claimed a big chunk; in countries where the programme had been in operation for a few years, this might be as high as 80 to 85 per cent of the country target.

Meanwhile, the agencies were ready with their lists of "recommended projects" or, more correctly, their "shopping lists." These were discussed with the ministries concerned—mostly on a bilateral basis through their own representatives, sometimes through correspondence, and occasionally through the Resident Representatives. (The United Nations has been an exception and has always relied on the latter for all discussions and negotiations with the governments, and so also the smaller agencies). The ostensible purpose of the agencies' discussions with the ministries was, and still is, to give them technical advice. It is an open secret that this technical function has seldom been unrelated to the nontechnical objective of securing a slice of the cake. And in determining the slice to be aimed at, neither the agencies nor the ministries could be expected to err on the side of modesty.

Add to the agency-stimulated proposals those that would in any case originate within the country, reflecting the needs and demands of ministers, officials, politicians and the public, and it would be easy to visualise the impossible task that would confront the coordinating unit, assuming that such a unit did exist and was reasonably well organized. Even the most developed coordinating unit in the least underdeveloped country would be helpless in the face of such pressures. It could survive only by making a whole series of political compromises all along the line.

It should not have been too hard for the veteran administrators of the UN family to grasp this elementary fact. All that they needed to do was to cast their eyes around to see the behaviour of governmental organizations even in the most developed countries; or, easier still, to turn their eyes on themselves to see their own behavior.

The period of the programming exercise has traditionally been a period of considerable excitement. This is not surprising. Not only are there numerous deadlines to be met; strenuous efforts have to be made to stay within the target. The sum total of requests coming from different sources almost invariably exceeds this target by a wide margin. For example, it happened to be 100 per cent higher for the 1963-64 programme in Ghana, and 500 per cent higher for the 1965-66 programme in Yugoslavia. Given this swollen volume of requests, the government is faced with the agonizing task of drastically cutting them down, pushing many of them into Category II, dropping some altogether, and chopping off man-months from others.

This is the true nature of the programming exercise. One could see some Resident Representatives and senior government officials emerge from it, like battle-scarred heroes, to announce proudly that they had finished the job, without betraying the least concern, even awareness, about the real implications of their performance—how they had axed and mutilated the projects. The so-called programming exercise thus boils down to a predominantly political exercise, a kind of financial gymnastics, that makes a mockery of the programme in a substantive sense.

6

The field exercise undoubtedly marks the high point in the programming cycle. Even thereafter the pressure continues, but its locus shifts back to headquarters, and its character also changes; a mountain of routine mechanical work has to be completed to meet further deadlines set for consolidation, review and approval of the programme.

The programme requests from one hundred odd countries and territories must flow in by a fixed date, usually in May or June. The defaulter must therefore be reminded, sometimes prodded. Copies of the requests went from the field simultaneously to the participating organizations who would review the parts relating to their respective competence and submit their comments to TAB headquarters.

The TAB secretariat had a heavy load to carry in consolidating the draft programme. It had to scrutinize each programme request, item by item; detect errors, if any; make sure that costing was based on the prescribed standards and, above all, that the targets had not been overrun. Serious errors would have to be corrected through correspondence with the governments concerned. Minor adjustments were made in some of the programmes by adding to them small sums from the reserves set aside at the planning stage.

Some projects, usually a small number, might apparently involve conflicts of jurisdiction between agencies. An attempt was made to have them straightened, as far as possible, through bilateral discussions between the agencies concerned. In exceptional cases, the good offices of the secretariat were used, generally as the last resort.

What deserves special mention is the fact that the TAB headquarters did not concern itself with the substance of the programmes. This was the established practice and it was scrupulously followed, barring the few cases where the requests had a glaringly dubious quality. For example, the government of one country was persuaded to withdraw the request for an expert to advise on methods to detect drunken driving. Another government was talked out of a request for a short-term expert to advise on the construction of air-raid shelters. Such cases were very few indeed. Of some 1200 so-called projects figuring in the annual programme, perhaps not even one per cent was subjected to a substantive query.

As for regional programmes, they were prepared by the participating organizations and submitted to the TAB secretariat around the same time. As a rule, they were given no more than a cursory scrutiny, just to be sure that they were kept within their respective financial quota.

7

Then began a massive operation in paper-processing. The draft of the global programme had to be consolidated in three parts: the country programme in Categories I and II, and the regional programme. Even the mechanical work involved in the reproduction and circulation of these bulky documents was far from negligible.

The *draft* programme emerging out of these operations was reviewed by the Board at its full session, usually held in October, and recommended to TAC for approval.

The *recommended* programme was then reproduced and submitted to TAC, along with an analysis of its main features, such as the size of the global programme and its year-to-year variation, shares of the participating organizations, geographical distribution by regions, and distribution by fields of activities.

The review of the programme by TAC took place at its November-December session, and by early December it would receive formal approval together with allocation of funds to the participating organizations and other essential authorizations, such as for administrative costs for TAB and its field offices and for drawal of funds from the Working Capital and Reserve Fund to finance contingency projects.

The TAC allocations would receive the endorsement of the General Assembly, usually on the eve of the dissolution of its annual session. The Assembly action marked the completion of the cycle. At last there was an *approved* programme to be put into operation.

One further step was still to be taken—the communication of the approved programme to each government. This was done by an official letter from the Executive Chairman, which, by a happy coincidence, was issued around Christmas time.

The programming cycle, it will be noticed, consisted of almost exactly fifteen months—from October of one year when the first estimate of the probable programme resources was prepared, to the end of December of the following year when the approved programme was communicated to the governments.

Until 1960 this gigantic globe-girdling exercise was carried out once in every twelve months. And so, in the last quarter of the year, TAB was busy working simultaneously on three annual programmes— an approved programme already in operation, a draft programme proceeding through the assembly line towards TAC approval, and a new programme for which the financial exercise had just begun. For a programme of $30 million—this was the approximate size of EPTA in the late fifties—the work-creating capacity it developed was extraordinarily high. It easily outdid normal operations of the Parkinsonian law.

The switchover to two-year programming with effect from 1960 somewhat reduced the work-load, but not significantly. By and large, this incredibly cumbersome machinery continued unchanged through the programme for 1967-68, while the newly adopted measures, as will be seen later, have changed some of its features but not reduced its overall complexities.

8

This chapter has admittedly been loaded with dreary procedural details. But no apology need be offered for this. Procedures and substance are sometimes interlinked as cause and effect. With the Expanded Programme it has been unquestionably so.

The label "country programming" has, without doubt, strong attractions. What could be more appropriate than to insist that programmes should be made, not at the TAB or at agency headquarters, but in the countries, by the countries and, of course, for the countries? To put the question was as good as to answer it, or so it seemed to most people who were content to assume the excellence of country programming, and raised no further question about it. They accepted in good faith the package as it was served to them, and did not bother to remove the label and look into its contents. Nor was this surprising when its virtues were being so well advertised by an authoritative international body.

Yet why should the *principle* of country programming be wrapped up in such absurd *procedures?* The policy-makers had debated the issue "agency allocation or country programming," and they had rightly voted for the latter. But there was a cognate question no less vital: how to ensure *good* country programmes since, obviously, their quality could show wide variations. The second question was never discussed. Apparently it had not even been posed, beyond assuming that the governments would establish coordination units which would, by some magic, produce the right programmes.

Thus the blessing given to the principle was automatically carried over to the procedures; and this, in turn, had two far-reaching consequences. It perpetuated the anomalies, and, as will be seen later,[27] it became instrumental in impeding sorely needed consolidation and rationalization of the two major programmes.

Meanwhile, the country programming procedures, as practised hitherto, have revealed their excellence far more in terms of their political convenience, than of their relevance to economic development. They have the undeniable merit of keeping a large number of people happy with very limited resources. But so far as rational and systematic development is concerned, they have become a formidable stumbling block.

The fifteen-month programming cycle consumes an enormous number of manhours of a great many people. Under a well-planned system, these could be cut down to a fraction and the rest diverted to far more productive use. Besides, the result of this global fanfare is a programme of poor quality produced at high cost. In fact, quality and cost in this case are, it would seem, inversely correlated. The excitement of the programming exercise is matched by the confusion of thought; the confusion is matched by the waste of effort and money; and this direct waste results in what is the saddest feature of this whole operation— a misdirection of a country's efforts and its limited domestic resources.

There should be no illusion about the true character of the country-programming procedures, so frequently extolled and so zealously safeguarded by some. It is a political pandora's box presented to the struggling countries of the underdeveloped world, that let loose forces which have been hard to control, and which have merrily made a mess of the principles of management.

---

[27] See Part III, Chapters 13-15.

CHAPTER 6

Serving Through Abdication

> *"But, alas, you are ... grasping at majesty in the least things, while you abdicate it in the greatest."*
>
> RUSKIN

The programme in 1956, the first to be prepared and approved according to the country-programming procedures, has been called, in the 15-year anniversary report, "a landmark in the history of EPTA."

The new programme, the report further claims, "was without doubt the most carefully prepared in the life of EPTA thus far, owing much to the work of hundreds of officials in Government departments and ministries, in the headquarters of the TAB and Participating Organizations and in their regional and country offices."[28]

A landmark it certainly was; for there can be no doubt that it landed the Programme in a deep political morass. Vested interests have since then shown all their ingenuity to frustrate every rescue effort.

The following observations on the new system, also extracted from the same authoritative source, are characteristic of a studied superficiality about an all-important subject:

> "An effective country programming exercise would have seen, over a period of many months, representatives of the international agencies (or the TAB Resident Representatives acting as such) discussing with technical ministries their urgent needs and suggesting how some of them might be met under EPTA; the ministries forwarding their requests to a central Government authority, which might be a branch of the planning commission,

---

[28] Ibid., p. 20.

and inter-ministerial committee, or a single ministry charged with the function of co-ordination; the Resident Representative, assisted by technical advice from agency specialists, continuing frequent consultation in person and by mail and cable with the agencies and with the Government's co-ordinating unit, and also with bilateral and other sources of assistance in order to avoid duplication of effort; and the programme gradually taking shape as a series of projects, continuing or new, which not only corresponded in cost to the country target figure but also, and more importantly, reflected some of the country's most urgent and well-defined needs for expert assistance, education and training in its endeavours to achieve its own properly planned development objectives.

"This was still rather the ideal than the typical picture of country programming. There remained countries where planning techniques were not sufficiently advanced to determine true priorities; there remained cases of projects of questionable value being maintained and new ones being pressed upon insufficiently experienced ministries; and there remained countries where, within the administrations or among the Participating Organizations and the Resident Representatives or both, the concept of co-ordination was not fully appreciated. But the net result was a global EPTA Programme more soundly planned and better balanced than before, and the Technical Assistance Committee gave it unanimous approval."[29]

Here is a masterpiece of question-begging assumptions with a sprinkling of self-criticism that serves to give an overtone of objectivity. The remarks were made about the first country programme prepared for 1956. They are no less applicable to the last one prepared for 1967-68.

Even the ideal which the first paragraph of the above quotation seeks to glorify, suffers from some grave defects; while the deficiencies, gently touched in the second paragraph, flow logically from them. And these deficiencies, far from being the exception as implied here, have always been the rule, for reasons sufficiently indicated in the previous chapter. Nevertheless, the official panegyrics sung from time to time with the dull monotony of a lullaby, and at a slightly more raised voice on the fifteenth anniversary of the Programme for the benefit of a

---

[29] Ibid., p. 20.

wider audience, cannot be passed over without some additional comments.

2

It is assumed that programming spread over many months and involving a great many people would, ipso facto, produce a high-grade programme embodying the wisdom of all. The reality is quite different, as any administrator should know. The involvement of a multiplicity of minds does not necessarily make for excellence in a programme; indeed, it is more likely to ensure its mediocrity, and it will do so the more easily when programming is treated, as in the case of EPTA, as almost everybody's business.

The fact is that the participants are far from disinterested parties. The country target becomes a bone of contention among them as soon as it is communicated to a government. They insist on having their say in formulating the programme. And along with this say, they want something more tangible—a share.

The ideal postulates a strong coordinating unit at country level. This is an odd assumption coming from a Board whose own record in coordinating interagency activities was not exactly brilliant. Even more incongruous is the remark that in some countries "the concept of coordination was not appreciated." The Board's own concept in this matter was not marked by shining clarity; nor can it be said that the kind of coordination it actually practised was the most commendable. In effect, it was coordination through surrender to special interests.

And how could a Board that was so keenly aware of the pressures of agency politics, that was not always able to resist them even when it was genuinely willing to do so, overlook the fact that the coordinating unit in a country would also be exposed to political pressures and would be forced to make all kinds of compromises, even to the detriment of the programme? Matters were made worse through the very programming procedures which left the governments at the mercy of divergent influences coming from international organizations. Strange as it may sound, the Board, by implication, was counting on a far more enlightened behaviour from the government of an underdeveloped country than its own.

The programme, according to the official view, was "better balanced" than before. This claim can be readily conceded, not only for the first programme but for all the others that followed. The claim is, however, valid mainly in the *political* sense: the new procedures did help keep conflicting interests in better balance. For the same reason the programmes made far less *economic* sense. There was better balance, and greater interagency and interdepartmental harmony. But both were bought at the cost of the Programme.

The "unanimous approval" given by TAC calls for a comment. All the country programmes—from the first to the last—were approved by the Committee unanimously, and more or less automatically. It could not be otherwise. The Committee itself was a political body; its representatives were subject to frequent turnover; it was never strong on development economics; the so-called programmes, being catalogues of expert posts, fellowships and equipment, did not lend themselves to intelligent scrutiny from outside; and, of course, there was the unanimous recommendation of TAB comprising the United Nations and its specialized agencies, which could not but exercise a strong influence.

The unanimous approval given by the Committee year after year to the country programmes was a measure of its faith in the Board and of its own helplessness, not of a conviction about the excellenec of their quality. Indeed, from time to time voices were raised and questions were asked that pointed in the opposite direction.

3

The general tenor of discussions at TAC sessions left no doubt that many of the members were far from reassured by the kind of information they received about the actual results achieved under the Programme. Some were haunted by a feeling that there was considerable room for improving the quality of performance; and this feeling found recurrent expression in the growing emphasis laid on priority-fixing, coordination, and evaluation.

For example, at its 1961 summer session, the Committee raised the question of "guidelines for fixing priorities within the framework of the Expanded Programme." It received the assurance that the matter would be considered by the Board and that the outcome of its deliberations would be reported to it in due course. The Economic and Social Council, too, stressed the same point in resolution 854 (XXXII) and decided that TAC, at its 1962 summer session, should prepare the most appropriate principles for the guidance of governments wishing to establish priorities for assistance under the Expanded Programme.

The Board's deliberations were significant primarily because of their evasive character. The recipient countries had a free choice in the selection of projects within the EPTA's scope of assistance, so the Board argued. Any attempt to lay down criteria for priorities would place the Board and its members in a difficult position since they would then be regarded as "supranational bodies" granting assistance only on predetermined conditions. Freedom of choice for governments, the Board concluded, was not compatible with direct policy guidance on priorities for the selection of projects within EPTA's framework.

The Board had a second argument to support its negative stance, which ran as follows: Conditions vary from country to country regarding the stage of development and the available human and material resources. Therefore, no pattern of priorities could be laid down that would hold good for all recipient countries. Besides, EPTA was only one, and not the major, source of technical assistance received by them; priorities could be usefully set only for individual countries or perhaps for groups of countries having essentially similar economic and social background. Accordingly, assistance could be given only on the basis of requests received from the individual countries.

To soften this negative conclusion the Board made some suggestions which more or less bypassed the central issue. The Committee, it suggested, might wish to discuss a set of considerations to be taken into account by the recipient countries in fixing priorities, such as: the government's own development plan or programme where it existed; and in the absence of such a programme, whether the project was "meaningfully related" to the country's needs, i.e., whether it would have an "important impact" on the economic and social development of a country; special attention could be given to projects which might later be financed from multilateral sources.

The governments might be advised also to take into account their commitments, both for current and follow-up action, on technical assistance projects, and therefore their own ability to provide counterpart personnel and necessary administrative support and facilities; and to weigh the benefits and costs of a project in the light of possible alternatives including prolongation of long-continuing projects.

As for priorities between expert posts and fellowships, it would be for each government to decide the relative emphasis to be placed on each, bearing in mind its own development needs and the assistance it received from other sources.

On the question of setting priorities among fields of activity, the Board was unable to make any recommendations. All that it could do was to draw the Committee's attention to the comprehensive list of fields of assistance contained in the "Explanatory Booklet on the Expanded Programme."[30] and to the various reports and proposals[31] which were then due to be submitted to the Council in response to the General Assembly resolution 1710 (XVI) declaring the nineteen-sixties as the Decade of Development.

4

The Board's views as summarized above show how, in its collective wisdom, it chose to evade an issue of overriding importance, also the arguments it used to bolster a strange thesis. Since these arguments are still very much in vogue in the UN family and still exercise a direct influence on critical policy-making decisions, it is worth examining them a little more carefully.

First, here was a relatively small technical assistance programme—its total resources were then of the order of $30 million a year. It tried to extend assistance to a great many countries and territories—their total number in the 1960's has been around 130. It encompassed an extremely wide range of functions as listed in the "Green Book" or the "Explanatory Booklet"—the list is so comprehensive that almost anything with any relation, howsoever remote, to economic and social development, would qualify for assistance. Inevitably, the limited resources of the Programme were spread far too thinly over far too many projects which numbered between 1300 and 1500. The need for concentrating the resources on a much smaller number of truly significant projects was quite obvious. This is what had been worrying the Committee and had prompted it to raise the question of fixing priorities. What did the Board do? As we have seen, it chose to refer the Committee to the Explanatory Booklet, and the proposals for the Development Decade! Thus the Board, in effect, passed the buck back to the governing body, and left the Programme where it was, encumbered by the countless items it was being called upon to finance.[32]

---

[30] The reference here was to document TAB/1/Rev. 3. In its early years TAB published the so-called Green Book which contained the governing resolution with amendments and other basic information relating to the Expanded Programme, including its principles and objectives, organization, methods and procedures of operation. This was later replaced by a more comprehensive version called the "Explanatory Booklet on the Expanded Programme", which was revised from time to time to keep it up to date. For the scope of the Programme or its "fields of assistance," see Appendix I of the Explanatory Booklet (pages 28-42), TAB/1/Rev. 4.

[31] These were later incorporated in "The United Nations Development Decade —Proposals for Action." E/3613, United Nations, New York 1962.

[32] See Chapter 3 on "Guiding Principles and Forgotten Guidelines."

Second, the Board clearly implied that fixing priorities was none of its business; that it was very much a matter for the recipient governments to decide. It overlooked the simple fact that many governments were just not able to work out a proper pattern of priorities if only because, being in the very early stages of development, they lacked the requisite experience. Indeed, proper guidance in fixing the right priorities is by far the most important service that the UN family could render to the underdeveloped countries. The Board failed to realize this, and implicitly extolled the virtues of a laissez faire approach to justify what was equivalent to a grave default.

Third, on this as on so many other occasions the Board took its stand on certain provisions of Resolution 222, especially the following: Technical assistance shall be rendered "only in agreement with the Governments concerned and on the basis of requests received from them"; and "due attention and respect should be paid to the national sovereignty and national legislation of the underdeveloped countries and to the social conditions which directly affect their development."

Such provisions are axiomatic for all programmes that aim at promoting economic and social development of the low income countries. But to uphold them in isolation from, and to the neglect of, the provisions relating to the concentration of efforts and the criteria for the selection of projects with emphasis on their productivity and maturity periods can make no sense at all. Surely, the task of the Board was to respect the sovereignty of the governments *and* to serve them effectively, where necessary by providing top-level guidance and advice. It is not a question of "either or"; it must be both. For a Board in charge of a UN programme to miss such an elementary point seems incredible. Yet this is the thesis it virtually pleaded for and acted upon.

Implicit in the Board's attitude was the assumption that the provision of guidance and advice regarding the selection of priority projects was not compatible with, if not an infringement of, the sovereignty of the recipient governments. This was indeed a strange assumption, as was evident from the operation of the Special Fund just next door. The Fund clearly demarcated the fields of activity in which its support would be available; laid down unequivocal guidelines for preparation of projects; and even after they were formally requested, frequently readjusted or remoulded them in consultation with the governments concerned.[33] There never has been any suggestion from any quarter that this involved an infringement of their sovereign rights. And as is well known, the World Bank has, from the outset, given a successful

---

[33] For Special Fund procedures see Chapter 11.

demonstration of how to combine effective service to sovereign governments with friendly counsel and guidance.

Thus, the Expanded Programme posed as more royal than the king, anxious to respect sovereignty rather than to serve sovereign governments. This, however, is not the whole story—far from it. If it was curious that the Board should have developed such a one-sided thesis, even more so was the fact that the thesis should have been honoured more in breach than in observance. The specialized agencies, through their representatives, have all along been vigorously active at the country level—ostensibly to provide "technical advice" to the governments through the ministries concerned, but frequently "to sell" to them their own, often headquarters-inspired, projects and to ensure, as far as possible, that these would be formally requested by the governments, no doubt in exercise of their sovereign rights. While the Board maintained a façade of noninterference to the point of declining to offer legitimate and much-needed guidance, the governments were in practice left vulnerable to the pressures emanating from the powerful specialized agencies. Their lobbying was equated to technical advice, and was thus easily legitimized.

This is the background of the famous TAB lore: The government must choose and request; the Board can only respond; and it can respond positively only when it has the funds.

Such a lore had an all-round soothing effect. It kept peace at the Board level, since the contents of the programme and the shares of individual agencies were the outcome of decisions taken by the recipient governments. It kept peace at the TAC session, and even pleased the masters who could not but be impressed by such an exemplary demonstration of obedience by the international family to their own sovereignty.

Finally, it kept peace at the country level. For, though the agencies enjoyed the freedom to promote projects and to stimulate official requests, the governments could not complain since they were free to accept or reject such advice. And if the weak governments of underdeveloped countries bowed, as they often did, to the pressures exercised by awe-inspiring international organizations, this was treated as a bow only to their own sovereignty, and not to any extraneous parties.

True, some discordant voices were heard, with the jarring note that such a lore, however well-suited to peace-keeping, was fatal to programme-making. But such voices were few and far between; they were frowned upon, and drowned in the clamour of the programming exercise.

CHAPTER 7

A Many-Splintered Thing

"He would rather make three bites of a cherry."

FRANÇOIS RABELAIS

All these years the Expanded Programme has been held up as a many-splendoured thing, an impressive mosaic of delicate, painstaking work. On a close-up view the splendour begins to wear away, its inherent clumsiness becomes more and more vivid until it appears as what it has always been in reality—a many-splintered thing.

The programming procedures are ideally suited to promote endless fragmentation of projects. The headquarters parcels out funds to the agencies and the countries, and then for all practical purposes it abdicates. A recipient government is supposed to formulate its programme freely in its own wisdom within a given target. The government, in its turn, subjected as it is to all kinds of pressures and counter-pressures, tries to make the best possible compromises and usually to placate as many parties as possible. Such pressures originate not only within the country, but almost always also from outside—from the specialized agencies which sponsor their own projects, mostly through the particular ministries concerned with their respective activities. Even within an agency or organization, the various departments often compete among themselves in an attempt to promote their favourite projects and to build up their own business. This is particularly true of the larger agencies. It has long been customary in the UN family to speak of their "internal TAB" under which the available funds are informally subdivided among the various departments within an agency.

The regional programmes were no less fragmented, though for somewhat different reasons. To start with, ten per cent of the programme funds were set aside for these programmes. But the share was raised in stages—for the 1967-68 programme it amounted to 16 per cent. Some members of TAC were unhappy about this trend. They wanted to keep the percentage at ten and, if possible, to push it down even lower, on the ground that it meant diversion of funds away from the country programmes. The participating organizations, on the other hand, were interested in keeping it as high as possible since the amount involved was directly distributed among them without being put through the country-programming procedures.

Whatever the percentage, the amount involved was relatively small —it ranged from $2.5 million in 1955 to about $8 million a year under the 1967-68 programme. This sum was divided among the participating organizations, and each of them used its share to cover a large number of countries and territories. As a result, the bulk of the programme has always consisted of very short-term "projects," especially seminars, conferences, symposia, ad hoc training centres lasting a few months each, individual consultants giving advice to groups of countries. Significant projects designed to make real impact were few. The size of the regional programmes and the approach to them were hardly conducive to the formulation of such projects.

Another curious feature of the programme is that even after it has been formally approved, it can be amended with surprising ease. The gimmick prescribed for the purpose is worth noting. The approved programme of a government, as has been noted earlier, consists of two parts: Category I which comprises the "first priority" projects, becomes the operative programme after its approval by the governing body; and Category II which contains a reserve list of projects, usually those which could not be accommodated within the country's target at the time of preparing the programme.

In the operational phase, a Category II project can be promoted to Category I for immediate implementation provided there is enough "savings" to finance it. Such savings may arise when some approved project or projects are actually costing less than was anticipated, or when they are curtailed in scope, or are altogether dropped. Incidentally, additions to Category II are freely allowed so that entirely new projects may be added to it and immediately promoted to Category I, if necessary savings are available.

Such promotion is almost automatically given. At present the Resident Representative is competent to give the approval, provided no interagency transfer of funds is involved. In the latter case approval can be given only by UNDP headquarters which would normally do so, but only after consulting the organizations concerned. Transfer of funds from one agency to another is much easier today than used to be the case a few years ago, mainly because, thanks to the growth of the Special Fund and the Expanded Programme, the agencies now have much more business to do so that they can afford to be somewhat more generous.

Thus a country programme which is produced with so much labour and which goes through so many complicated motions before its approval by the governing body, can be amended radically, often substituting completely new projects for the existing ones, provided funds can be found from within the programme itself, and provided some procedural rituals are duly complied with. Well might the wit say: "In EPTA's concept a programme is something to get money with!" The substance matters much less to it than the bookkeeping aspects.

3

The funds for financing contingencies have shared the same fate as those for the country and the regional programmes, if anything in a more marked fashion. Piecemeal allocations were made during the programme year until the available funds were more or less committed. The number of allocations made for "contingency projects" would be 250 to 300 in a typical year.

In 1955, when the country-programming procedures first went into force, the ceiling for contingencies was set at five per cent of the available resources. With the transition to two-year programming it was raised first to seven and one half per cent, and later to ten per cent a year.

The rationale for the contingency authority may be briefly noted. Critical situations might arise as a result of natural disasters or other causes, such as earthquakes in Chile, Turkey or Yugoslavia; an outbreak of the foot-and-mouth disease in the Middle East and elsewhere; food poisoning in Morocco; an outbreak of fire destroying the public library in Kabul. The mechanism made it possible to respond promptly to government requests for assistance in such emergency situations.

Or, a country might suddenly become independent and urgently need assistance from the UN programmes. Such cases could not, as a rule, be fitted into the long programming cycle, and had to be dealt with on an ad hoc basis.

Besides, individual projects in the approved programmes, no matter how carefully costed, needed adjustments from time to time. Contingency funds could be used to give marginal support to going projects.

And finally, during the implementation phase of the approved programme, governments might come up with entirely new projects which were worthy of high priority, but which could not be absorbed in the current programme as funds were already committed. In such cases contingency finance provided the only practicable means of initiating the projects without waiting until the formulation and approval of the next programme, annual or biennial, which would involve considerable delays.

Clearly, this type of contingencies would be more likely to arise under a two-year programming cycle than under annual programming. This was the reason why the ceiling for contingencies was raised sharply after 1960. It may be noted in passing that some important members of TAC were never too happy over contingency finance in general, and they were particularly unhappy over its subsequent increase.

The argument commonly adduced in support of the contingency authority is that it imparts a much-needed flexibility to the programme. So indeed it does. Yet despite its plausible ring, it begs the main issue. Why should the programme be cast into a strait-jacket in the first place to discover later that it cannot function without exaggerated doses of contingency finance and an avalanche of ammendments? It would make just as much sense to have first a custom-made garment that is too tight and then to switch to the loose comfort of the pyjamas in order to breathe more freely!

The fact is that contrary to the notion prevalent in the UN family, flexibility is not a virtue in itself; one can have not only too little, but also too much of it. The EPTA programmes are both over-rigid and over-flexible. The two traits do not, and cannot, cancel each other, any more than two defects, when juxtaposed, can add up to a virtue. The result of these twin defects is what one might easily imagine: good programming became needlessly more difficult.

The philosophy behind contingency finance is that it made it possible to give flexible response to government requests in emergency situations. The participating organizations had, predictably enough, a different philosophy—they looked upon it and treated it, sometimes quite cynically, as just another source of funds. Their primary concern has been to secure as reasonable a share as possible which also dictated their strategy—to stimulate contingency requests in good time, to stake their claims early, and therefore to have them submitted in the opening months of the programme year, before the funds are substantially committed. As a result, there has always been a heavy concentration of contingency projects in the first few months of the year.

The contingency authority has undoubtedly been used over the years to meet many genuine contingencies arising out of national calamities and other sudden and unforeseen causes. But the proportion of pseudo-contingencies has been far from negligible. The bulk of the projects financed from this source were indistinguishable from those included in the approved programme. They could be classified as contingencies mainly because of the rigidity of the programming procedures with fixed cycles, and sometimes it was hard to find even this justification.

The allocations were made from time to time on a case-by-case basis. They were too many in number, mostly too small in size, too disparate and disjointed to make much sense from the programming angle; and they were hardly immune from political influences or considerations. A top-level administrator of the UN family, in an informal personal talk, did not hesitate to apply a different label to the so-called contingency fund: "It is essentially a pork-barrel"—this is how he chose to characterize it.

4

The basic statistics relating to the growth of EPTA for the period ended in 1965 are given in Appendix IA.

In its first fifteen years the Programme did show considerable expansion. The number of participating organizations grew from six to eleven, and of the contributing countries from 54 to 109. The Programme began with contributions totalling $20 million for the 18-month period ended on 31 December, 1951; the contributions pledged for 1964 exceeded, for the first time, the $50 million level; there have been further increases since then—for 1968 they reached a record level of $74 million.

During its first fifteen years the Expanded Programme received and spent $457 million, apart from $26 million contributed by recipient governments as local costs and the substantial amounts received from them in kind as supporting services and other facilities.

In all, 180 countries and territories received assistance from this source. Of the total amount of $457 million, 60 per cent or $276 million was spent on expert assistance; 14 per cent or $64 million on fellowships; eight per cent or $36 million on equipment; and 18 per cent or $81 million on administrative and operational costs.

Country projects accounted for $323 million, or 85.8 per cent of total project costs; while the share of regional and inter-regional projects amounted to $53 million or 14.2 per cent. These figures include projects financed from contingencies.

Altogether, 13,500 experts—men and women—drawn from 90 different nationalities served under the Programme; on an average, they served about two and one half years each, or a total of 32,000 expert-years. The number of fellowships awarded was 32,000; the trainees came from 168 countries and territories, and were placed in 128 host countries.

As the data will show, the growth of the Programme has been visibly accelerated since 1960. In the last eight years it has more than doubled, for reasons which were indicated in Chapter 2. The data, particularly the number of experts and fellowships, would testify to the fragmented character of the Programme. Or, one may take the global programme of technical assistance as approved for the 1967-68 biennium. It consisted of over 3000 projects at a total cost of $140.2 million; of this $110.7 was earmarked for field projects, $26.0 million to meet the administrative costs of the United Nations and eleven participating organizations, and $2.5 million for a special programme for Indonesia after it rejoined the UN family. The programme provided for over 6000 experts on field service, whether as single specialists for a few weeks or in teams over longer duration, and more than 8000 fellowships to be awarded to men and women for training abroad.

Over 3000 projects for some $110 million! This once again highlights the need for "family planning" in the technical assistance programming. In fact, the word "project" as used in this connection is a misnomer. Man-months of experts and fellowships, sometimes with a modest quantum of equipment, are strewn around without any visible pattern or any noticeable concern for securing optimum results. In general, their relationship to real projects is not unlike that of a few bricks or some pieces of steeel or lumber to a building; to call them projects would be like equating the latter to the building itself.

Proliferation of projects has another serious consequence. The need for experts is mounting just at a time when there is a growing shortage of qualified experts. Recruitment often suffers long delays; experts, it is increasingly found, are not up to the standard; misgivings have been expressed from time to time in responsible quarters about their quality. Their job descriptions are not infrequently vague and elastic, and consequently their duties are ill-defined. The duration of their assignments has often proved much too flexible in practice; and not surprisingly, individual experts at times try to stimulate requests for extensions of their services through the ministries concerned.[34]

Finally, there is no guarantee what action will be taken on the experts' recommendations after they leave on completing their assignments. Their reports have a restricted circulation, and they seldom, if ever, reach the public. On too many occasions they have been consigned to oblivion with surprising speed.

Thus the result of proliferation is not only waste of money, but also waste of valuable expert man-months. Not that the Programme has not achieved results. It certainly has; it would have been impossible to spend half-a-billion dollars and 32,000 expert man-years in underdeveloped countries with unlimited opportunities, and not to show results. The official literature is therefore able to compile enough success stories to impress the uncritical reader.

An alert mind will, however, be provoked to put some counterquestions. Has the Programme been doing enough? Could it not, and should it not, have done a great deal more? If the demonstrably arbitrary and superficial programming has been able to produce these results, how much more could have been achieved if projects were selected with the requisite care and judgement, if they were deliberately slanted towards productivity and prepared in the right dimensions to achieve the best possible results in the conditions prevailing in a country, and if steps were taken in advance to ensure that everyone of them would be carried through systematically—from preliminary planning to execution? This was the sole purpose of the Programme. Its founding resolution had left little room for doubt about it.

There is no means of measuring the gap between what could have been and what has been, the implications of the vast opportunities that did exist but were not availed of, the so-called opportunity cost. Those who understand the process of development and are familiar with the problems and possibilities in the underdeveloped world can have no doubt on this score. The opportunity cost, though invisible, must have been staggering. The net result of this for the underdeveloped countries has been truly tragic. What could have been a powerful force in guiding and accelerating their economic growth has been wantonly dissipated.

---

[34] An extreme example was cited by a colleague from a country where an expert serving as an economic adviser had married the daughter of the minister of planning. "From now on, this expert will have to be included in every technical assistance programme," remarked the colleague, adding wittily, "unless there is a divorce."

CHAPTER 8

Making Status Quo Safe

"Where there is a will there is a way."

In the early years of country programming, deviations from the ground rules were numerous, sometimes embarrassing. Continuing commitments on account of going projects were not always covered. "Savings" were transferred by the agencies from one country to another, without the knowledge of the governments and of the Resident Representatives concerned. And as mentioned in the previous chapter, the agencies showed a strong tendency to milk the contingency fund. Considerable efforts were needed to plug these loopholes.

Grappling with the irregularities became a major preoccupation and, in the eyes of many, an end in itself. The progress made with rule enforcement was noted and reported with some enthusiasm. The deviations no doubt needed correction; but they were mere peccadillos compared with the far more fundamental defects from which the whole system suffered.

After the first couple of annual programmes, these defects stood out with a clarity that could no longer escape an objective eye. Nor could the well-standardized praise of the new system indefinitely deflect attention from the need to do something about them. The first timid soundings made in 1957-58 revealed that a number of people in key positions within the participating organizations were veering round to the idea of reform.

And so there emerged the first reform proposal, which was kept deliberately simple to facilitate agreement among the agencies, and yet would have effected a major improvement. Briefly, it was a three-part

67

plea: to keep a "project" and the allocation made for it neatly tied together, and not to allow the fiscal-year deadline of 31 December to disrupt this as happened, for example, when delays occurred in recruiting experts; to prepare each project for its full duration—from start to completion; and to confine the annual programming exercise to an annual review of these projects, to make such marginal adjustments in their contents and costs as might appear necessary, and to add new projects to the extent they could be absorbed within a given country target.

The main idea was to prepare projects as entities, even when they consisted of single expert posts, and to keep them and treat them as such right up to the end. The advantages of such an approach—the so-called project programming and project budgeting—were obvious: it would avoid the year-end rush to commit funds, remove worries about provisions for continuing commitments on going projects, greatly simplify programming which would cover only new projects, enable all to see the programme more clearly and better judge its performance and results, and, of course, reduce the voluminous routine work to a fraction of its historical dimensions.

2

Early in 1959 the time looked ripe for a constructive move on these lines. The response of the agencies was surprisingly positive and surpassed earlier expectations. The World Health Organization, perhaps the most efficient and methodical of all the specialized agencies, lent its unstinted support to the proposal; as a long-time practitioner of the project-programming approach it had consistently supported it, and had refused to accept that there could be any rational alternative. Most of the other organizations saw the underlying logic and recognized its merits. The remaining few, particularly the smaller agencies, had no strong feeling either way and were willing to follow the majority lead. All that was needed to clinch the matter was just a little leadership.

The attitude of the agencies threw a new light on the situation. It clearly showed that the blame put on them had been grossly exaggerated; that they had been unduly maligned in some quarters. True, they had their own special interests, and often they took a narrow view to defend their own positions; but this was only natural and no different from what would have happened anywhere in the world, given a similar organizational pattern. What came as a surprise was not how narrow they were in their outlook, but how ready they were to rise above this narrowness in response to right leadership.

That leadership never came. Instead, something extraordinary happened. All of a sudden, out of the blue, came the suggestion to replace annual programming by a two-year cycle. The representative of one agency enthusiastically championed it, using logic that sounded almost boastfully cynical: "If we must go through all these motions for our programmes, let us agree to do so once in two years, and not every year. That will greatly reduce our headaches." A brief discussion followed; others agreed; the proposal was accepted.

This episode illuminated a fact that is seldom suspected even within the UN family. While agencies are blamed for dissensions, there are other powerful, well-disguised vested interests to which the chaotic status quo is far from unwelcome.

3

What justification was there for this abrupt switch to a two-year cycle? From the angle of the Programme itself—none; from the angle of entrenched interests—a great deal. It was a shrewd move. At one stroke it made the status quo safe for a number of years—three years or more for one cycle, and at least another three years for a future change of course since this would have to go through the slow-moving legislative processes of the UN family.

And there could be little doubt that, by 1959, the safety of the status quo had become a major policy objective before the EPTA administration, overriding other considerations.

For, by then, the decision had been taken to establish the Special Fund of the United Nations as a separate programme. Politics—in the delegations to the UN and within the UN Secretariat—had done its best, or worst, to pave the road to a major blunder: to set up two separate programmes to operate side by side to achieve the same objective, i.e., the development of the underdeveloped countries. The price for that initial blunder has been, and continues to be, heavy.[35]

The Expanded Programme felt itself eclipsed and threatened; and driven by the instinct of self-preservation, it began to fight back, subtly but resolutely. The similarities between the two Programmes and the identity of their goals were deliberately played down; the differences between them were played up out of all proportion; where they were non-existent, every effort was made to trump them up skilfully, and to make them more vivid through differences in procedures. This strategy had already proved its effectiveness and had prevented the Expanded

---

[35] See in particular Part III, also Chapter 17.

Programme from being gobbled up by the Special Fund. But one round of initial victory was not enough since the threat was a continuing one. The future of the Programme had to be made secure, and this could be best achieved by erecting a solid procedural bulwark around it.

Project programming? It sounded like an invitation to suicide! For, this is exactly what the Special Fund was adopting from the first day of its existence. The retention of the country-programming procedures had become a matter of life and death—to highlight how different EPTA was from the Special Fund, and why it must continue to move independently on its own orbit. This was not the time to jettison the old procedures, the most potent means of self-defence. It was the time to make a firmer commitment to them on a longer term basis.

4

Yet the project-programming concept could not be entirely bypassed. It had been discussed so long and had been given so much support that at least a modest, even if superficial, bow to it was indicated. So it was decided to incorporate, within the two-year programme, not only short-term projects with duration up to 24 months, but also long-term projects with duration not exceeding four years or two programming cycles. These were to be "produced in depth"—by now the phrase had come to be used with a cliché-like frequency that robbed it of all depth of meaning—and was to be carried over automatically from the first to the second cycle, unless a project was so radically modified as to require fresh authorization. Thus, the advocates of project programming were not left quite empty-handed, while the virtue of compromise was demonstrated once again to the outside world.

To those who were unacquainted with the intricate happenings in the submerged nine-tenths of a large international establishment, the modified country-programming system appeared reasonable enough. It even created an illusion of progress. Development problems are intractable and do not admit of instant solutions; one must inevitably learn from experience, and it is the readiness to learn that matters most. It was to the credit of EPTA that it was ever ready to do so, as evidenced by its latest proposal to move from annual to biennial programming. Rationalization on such lines was easy, and it proved effective in securing the blessings of the governing body.

And it was made even more attractive by labelling it as an *experiment*. This magic world had a dual appeal. No firm commitment was made, and so further changes could be freely made at a later date. It also showed how enlightened was the administration that kept an open mind, was ready to embark upon new experiments, learn from their results, and introduce new improvements, all as parts of a forward movement toward perfection.

How easily minds were trapped by this kind of reasoning! The problems of actual development in the field were confounded with what was no more than artificial wrestling with procedural problems at headquarters. The end was overlooked in an endless preoccupation with the means.

And why should experiments of this type be at all necessary in the twelfth year of the Programme? There was, for example, the Special Fund of the United Nations which found no difficulty in laying down rational procedures almost immediately after it was established, and these have stood well the test of time. Why should one embark on a trial-and-error process to learn from the costly school of experience what calls for only some elementary commonsense? No one stopped to ask such questions. There were no probing minds to do so; no sharp eyes to penetrate through the smoke-screen; and, alas, no wit to recall Oscar Wilde's irreverent but not irrelevant dictum: "Experience is the name that everyone gives to his mistakes."

5

At the TAC session the main concern expressed by some members was about the proportion of short-term and long-term projects, and the potential risk that too large a part of the programme might be frozen for too long a time, leaving very little margin for shorter term projects. The Board was therefore asked to take appropriate steps to forestall such risks.

Two-year programming, as mentioned before, was approved for 1961-62 on an experimental basis. Neither the Board nor the Committee was in a hurry to enquire about the results of this experiment after the first two years were over. It was extended without questioning through the second, third and fourth biennia, aided no doubt by the potent force of inertia. And so it proved once again the old truth: nothing tends to be more permanent in life than the temporary. Meanwhile, the experiment has been an undeniable success so far as its undeclared objective was concerned. It protected the independence of the Expanded Programme and averted the threat of its absorption by what was fast bcoming a senior partner, the Special Fund.

As for its other results, there was little noticeable change, except that the agony of the programming exercise was experienced at somewhat longer intervals. Otherwise the Programme continued as before —an amalgam of anomalies.

CHAPTER 9

Plus Ça Change....

"Warum einfach, wenn es auch kompliziert geht?"[36]

In January 1966 the inevitable happened. The two programmes—EPTA and the Special Fund—were merged, and the United Nations Development Programme, or UNDP, came into existence. But something else, perhaps no less inevitable in the UN family, happened at the same time. The so-called merger resolution[37] specifically provided that the two programmes should retain their "special characteristics." The Expanded Programme once again demonstrated its uncanny capacity for survival.

This meant survival also of its shortcomings. Once they had managed to receive omnibus blessing under a politically inspired resolution, there was only one course of action open to the UNDP administration —to find ways and means to whittle them down, step by step, in practice; in short, to achieve administratively on a *de facto* basis what it had not been possible to achieve legislatively on a *de jure* basis.

Almost immediately after the establishment of the UNDP attention turned inexorably to the vexed problems of EPTA, now rechristened as UNDP/TA. Fresh proposals were formulated for project programming; they were discussed at a global meeting of the Resident Representatives held in Turin, Italy in June 1966; they were then reviewed and discussed by the specialized agencies and the newly-created Inter-Agency Advisory Board; and in June 1967 they were formally approved by the Governing Council of the UNDP. Accordingly, project pro-

---

36 "Why simple, if it can also be done complicatedly?"

37 Resolution 2029 of the General Assembly, see Appendix III. For the merger debate and related developments, see Part III, especially Chapters 13-14.

72

gramming will come into force after the expiry of the current biennium
—on 1 January 1969.

The weaknesses of the two-year programming system were now
recognized with a refreshing candour, all the more remarkable for a
Programme that had not distinguished itself by its capacity for self-
introspection, not to speak of self-reform.

A one-time programming operation in two years, it was admitted,
built up a sudden peak; and the primary concern of the governments
became formulation of requests in haste up to the full level of the
targets, irrespective of their quality. The so-called long-term projects
were prepared in a perfunctory fashion, as was evidenced by the project
data maintained at headquarters; with allocation of funds limited to
two years at a time there was no incentive to look beyond and to
prepare them even with minimum thoroughness.

Too many changes were found necessary in the governments' requests, even in the intervening months between their submission and
their formal approval; for the 1967-68 programme such pre-approval
changes were about 250 within a seven-month period. Though prepared
for only two years, a great many projects continued longer for various
reasons, such as ill-defined scope and duration, practical difficulties in
execution, including delays in the recruitment of experts.

These facts, long known and long pushed under the carpet, were
now brought out into the open to argue the case for reform.

2

How far will the new system remedy these and other defects discussed earlier, and help sound programming in future? Let us first
take a look at its main features.

Resources estimated on an annual basis will be allocated virtually
on the same lines as before. The system of country targets will be
retained, but it will be put back from a two-year to an annual basis.

The allocation to regional projects will be raised from 16 to 17 per
cent, and, as before, one per cent will be specifically earmarked for
the smaller agencies; six per cent will be set aside initially as a planning reserve; for contingencies the initial provision has been fixed at
$4.5 million; the agency overheads will be calculated by applying 14
per cent to one half of their respective shares in the programme for
the 1967-68 biennium plus contingency projects; the UNDP overheads
for technical assistance will be calculated as before, and will amount
to about three per cent. The balance of the resources would be used for
country targets.

These targets will be fixed on the same basis as before. In fact, "notional targets" for 1969, as approved by the Governing Council at its 1968 January session, have already been communicated to the governments. They will be firmed up after the pledging conference in October 1968; and definitive targets will be established in similar fashion every year while looking several years ahead. The first set of notional targets should hold good for 1969-72.

There will, however, be no one-time programming exercise. Instead, projects will be prepared and submitted, on a continuous basis, throughout the year; each project will be considered as a whole, from beginning to end; and, when approved, allocation will be made for its entire duration. Each project will therefore have its own schedule, and the programme will be freed from the tyranny of an overall timetable determined by the calendar. Though long delayed, this is a real improvement as far as it goes.

Unfortunately, the system does not go far enough. It retains most of the old and undesirable features of the Expanded Programme. Its main accent is still primarily on the money-sharing aspects, on the so-called financial equity, and not on the quality of the programme. In these respects it is more of the same and, on balance, is unlikely to leave the Programme in a significantly better shape. Meanwhile, the new system clearly betrays an ominous trend towards overcentralization of programming responsibilities at headquarters.

Why should there be country targets at all? The official answer given is that, in some mysterious ways, it improves the management of the programme; that it ensures equitable geographical distribution of its activities. But an assertion, however emphatically made, is certainly not a proof. There are other programmes, as for example the Special Fund, which do not communicate any targets, national or otherwise, to the governments. It would be inequitable to imply that they are impervious to considerations of equity.

Once a target is communicated to a government, it virtually becomes an allocation. In fact, the new system has specifically laid down that it would constitute "an undertaking" to deliver assistance to the approximate level of the target, subject only to one condition: the adequacy of the funds available to the technical assistance component as a whole. The unprogrammed or uncommitted balance, if any, at the end of the year will be carried forward and added to the next year's target. Such carryover is, however, limited to 50 per cent of the original target; any excess over this will revert to the UNDP/TA account.

Experience has abundantly shown the fatal weaknesses of the country target device. The pressure of various interest groups will, as before, make it impossible to draw up any sensible programme at the country level. The new system seeks to provide an apparent safeguard in the sense that all projects will be subject to head-quarters review and approval. While the headquarters may well derive added satisfaction from this direct financial control it will henceforth exercise over individual projects, its capacity to improve their quality through such a central review can be easily over-estimated. It is likely to prove no more than wishful thinking. For, it is hard to see how and on what grounds headquarters could turn down requests prepared by governments within their respective targets and submitted with the full technical backing of the specialized agencies. To judge from past experience, it will, barring exceptional cases, almost certainly give more or less automatic approval to the requests subject to purely financial checks.

Headquarters review and approval of projects could be more meaningful if projects were to be far fewer in number and much larger in dimension, similar to those of the Special Fund. But such prospects, however devoutly to be wished, have been explicitly dashed to the ground. The UNDP, it is stipulated, must provide "the full gamut of field services" requested by the governments without any "artificial or arbitrary distinctions in the administration of this continuous range of assistance." This, it is averred, is *inter alia* the meaning of the injunctions of Resolution 2029 calling for retention of the "special characteristics" of the two components of the UNDP.[38]

No interpretation of the special characteristics of the technical assistance component could be more arbitrary, less relevant to the cause of development, also less worthy of the UNDP. It ignores the fact that the gamut of services, as they have been developed, is far too wide and embraces almost every conceivable subject, while the resources are still pitifully small. It ignores the elementary fact that all expenditures or investments cannot yield the same benefit; that to maximize the benefit they must be rationally concentrated. It connives at the inescapable fact of life that a country target inevitably becomes a playball of internal and external politics, and that the end-result is overwhelmingly political, not development, programming. And, finally, it continues to flout the injunctions of Resolution 222 of 1949 regarding the concentra-

---

[38] First operative para. of General Assembly resolution 2029 (XX). For text see Appendix III.

tion of effort and selection of projects.[39] Legally, those injunctions are still in force; they have never been repealed; what was repealed long ago, and has remained so ever since, is the honesty of purpose in the former EPTA administration to give effect to them with good sense and good judgment.

As for the regional programmes, they will, as hitherto, consist mostly of mini-projects without any guarantee that they will represent activities truly worthy of high priority. This is inevitable when 17 per cent of the available resources are allocated, according to an agreed formula, among twelve participating organizations, each of which will try to cover a wide range of projects embracing a large number of countries.

As in the past, the regional projects will be prepared and submitted by the agencies; each of them will be outlined on the same data sheet as a country project; and in addition, each submission will have to indicate that at least three governments have expressed direct interest in the particular project. If past experience is any guide to the future, the agencies should experience no insuperable difficulty in procuring such certificates of legitimacy.

3

Other salient features of the new system may be briefly noted. Requests for technical assistance will be submitted through the Resident Representatives to the UNDP, with copies to the Participating and Executing Agency concerned, in a prescribed form giving all the required information including cost estimates. And the agencies concerned will communicate the results of their "technical appraisal" of the requests to the UNDP headquarters.

The procedures for approval are worth noting. Recommended projects, catalogued by country and agency, are to be bunched together and submitted to the Governing Council for review and approval at each session, which means twice a year. The submission to the Council shows for each country—there are over 100 in all—the approved country target figures, year by year, for 1969-72; the allocations approved to date, again by country and year; the allocations by year in accordance with the latest recommendations; and the balance avaialble for future programming.

Once a project is approved, financial authorization will be conveyed to the agency concerned as an "allocation." Project allocations are to

---

[39] See in particular Chapter 3 on "Guiding Principles and Forgotten Guidelines."

be made to agencies on a cumulative basis broken down by year starting with 1969.

The Council delegates to the Administrator of the UNDP the interim authority to approve, without waiting for a future session, urgent requests within the limits established by the country target and to allocate the necessary funds. Projects so approved are to be reported to the ensuing session of the Council.

There are other gimmicks on the financial side which may be noted in passing. Agencies will open project accounts, crediting allocations and debiting obligations and/or commitments, project by project and year by year. They will report promptly every quarter to the UNDP headquarters, with copy to the Resident Representative, on the status of the countries concerned, showing expert and fellowship man-months and equipment costs planned and delivered, and resultant savings with regard to each project. Savings reported by agencies will be surrendered and restored to the unprogrammed balance of the country target, for reprogramming in the manner described earlier; and allocations to the agencies will be revised accordingly.

Finally, agency overhead allocations are to be calculated as a percentage of the programme approved for execution by the agency, subject to a minimum guarantee.

What happens if a project costs more than the actual allocation? Presumably all excesses would require prior headquarters approval and would normally have to be accommodated within the country target concerned.

As for contingency authorizations, an amount of $4.5 million has been kept provisionally in what is now called the "UNDP revolving fund" for financing country and regional contingency projects under the Technical Assistance component. It is likely to be increased later. The procedure for processing these projects will remain practically unchanged. Costs of continuing such projects beyond the end of the financial year will, however, be debited against the respective country targets. Expenditures incurred for contingency projects in a given year will be reimbursed as a first charge on the global programme resources for the following year. All projects financed as contingencies are to be reported to the Council for information.

What about amendments of approved projects? As in the past, governments will be free to request changes as and when the need arises. Such requests will be channelled through the Resident Representatives to the UNDP, with copies to the agencies; they will be reviewed in the UNDP, based on the comments of the Resident Repre-

sentatives and the Agencies; approved changes will be reported to the
Governing Council for information. Minor changes of an administrative nature will be approved by the Resident Representative in consultation with the agency concerned, and reported post facto to the UNDP
and to the Council.

These, then, are the main provisions of the new system or, more
accurately, of the old system clothed in a slightly re-tailored guise with
some new frills. Once again the Technical Assistance programme has
demonstrated its genius to ensure that a tremendous ado will produce
a minimum of change, and to impart a new look to what is old and
outworn.

4

Obviously the latest changes contain no hint of work-simplification;
if anything, the hint is the other way—towards work-multiplication.
A small technical assistance programme—and so it is despite the increased contributions of recent years—will continue to operate with
incredibly complicated procedures; and, as in the past, compliance with
these will tend to become the be-all and end-all of programming.

Under the modified system, the financial control will be considerably tightened, with the reins more firmly held at the UNDP headquarters. Every project will be meticulously accounted for; project
savings will have to be surrendered by the agencies periodically—they
will no longer have the leeway to use them at their own discretion.
The governments will be sure of receiving programmes up to the full
amount of their respective annual targets; they will no longer be
deprived even fractionally of their shares through intercountry transfer
of savings, although such transfers have progressively diminished to a
point where they no longer pose a serious problem.

One thing is certain. The over-elaborate accounting and book-
keeping for each country, target by target, year by year, and project by
project, and for each agency substantially on the same lines, particularly
for regional projects, will consume a vast number of man-hours of
high-salaried professional people. Is the game worth the candle? Is it
beyond the wit of man to devise far simpler, more rational and more
efficient methods to administer a development programme of this size?

With the tightened financial control, every dollar-and-cent may be
better accounted for; and with all loopholes carefully plugged, the
principle of no expenditure without prior headquarters approval may
be made more fool-proof. But will the dollars available to the programme be invested wisely and intelligently on projects that really

matter most in the underdeveloped countries? The answer to this crucial question remains as problematical as before.

Efficient budgeting and accounting, highly desirable as they are, cannot by themselves guarantee high quality programming. This sounds like a platitude, but it is far from irrelevant in the present context when old-style treasury control threatens to monopolize attention.

Programming responsibilities are generously delegated, as before. Requests for technical assistance, it is reiterated, will be prepared at the country level, based on consultations between the technical ministries, the participating and executing agencies, the coordinating organ of the government, and the Resident Representative. All of them are mentioned in one breath. It is assumed that whatever emerges out of such quadrilateral discussions will automatically represent the best possible programmes one could expect in a given country. No assumption could be more unrealistic.

High quality programmes can be produced only when high-grade judgment and experience of competent people are directly brought to bear on them. How to ensure this is by far the most important single task to which an administration like the UNDP should address itself. Of this there is as yet little or no suggestion. Instead, its entire thrust is in the direction of a finance-conscious, quality-callous approach.

The truth is that collective consultations of the type postulated above all too often degenerate into collective bargaining, with the result that the programme, under the weight of multiple compromises, sinks to a mediocre level. This is what one would expect even on a priori reasoning based on the facts of life—about national governments, international organizations, and human nature. And this is what has been repeatedly confirmed all these years by actual experience.

True, with project programming it will henceforward be possible to see projects as entities—for their full length from the beginning to the end. But what kind of entities are they going to be? Thin, anaemic, stunted, dismembered and disjointed, unable to excite and to inspire, to make impacts, to produce visible, tangible results; entities which in their ensemble will make a programme procedurally foredoomed to needless, senseless mediocrity, to remain as in the past a many-splintered thing; eluding any intelligent judgment and evaluation from outside; indeed, making it impossible even for those dealing with it on a day-to-day basis to figure out whether, in a given country, first things are really being put first, and whether the options among a great many potential projects are being wisely exercised.

To sum up, the emphasis of the programme is still overwhelmingly on how projects should be financed, not on how they should be selected, formulated, piloted and executed. This cart-before-the-horse approach has, not surprisingly, produced an odd result—the UNDP/TA is going to have project programming, but without projects in a valid sense of the term.

5

As a footnote to this chapter reference may be made to an episode that occurred at the global meeting of Resident Representatives held in Turin, Italy during 27-30 June 1966.

The general idea of project programming which culminated in the procedures outlined above was broached at this meeting to obtain first-hand reactions of the field representatives; and it immediately met with warm, spontaneous support. This should have been no surprise. Most of the representatives had long been tired of the dreary routine and bookkeeping aspects of the EPTA activities, barring of course a few who were too securely wedded to the cosy status quo to care for a change. It was quite obvious that most of them had been quietly waiting for a lead of exactly this kind.

Some could hardly restrain their enthusiasm, and greeted the proposal as "a revolution," "a renaissance"! Little did they know how strikingly precise they were in their exclamations, how they had stumbled on *le mot juste*. The ceremony of resurrection was not marred by any unceremonious reference to a similar proposal which had been made about eight years previously and had been given a decent burial with a speed that was none too decent.[40]

This is how the stage was set for future revolutions. How long will they continue, one wonders.

---

[40] After the meeting two old-time colleagues came to me and said in a voice that betrayed some agitation: "What nonsense is this? It is all a rehash of the old proposals that had been thought through more thoroughly and presented more systematically. Yet it is now served as something new!" I had attended the solemn function as a bemused observer. The remark came as a surprise. It was unusual, to say the least, to have such long memories for the dead past.

CHAPTER 10

Country Programming -- Right and Wrong

> *"And beware of seeming truths that grow on the roots of error."*
>
> M. TUPPER

The adoption of project programming has been hailed as a resounding victory of commonsense; and rightly so. The only uncommon thing about it was that it took such a long time in coming.

"I do not want to see the distant scene; one step's enough for me"—this may be an ennobling thought in certain situations. But it is not germane to development projects, where it can only encourage a superficial approach, or planlessness.

Put in simple language, project programming only means that even baby projects must be conceived, produced, nursed and raised as full entities. This is how projects and programmes should in any case be prepared in any responsible administration that professes to father the cause of international development. The Expanded Programme had to grope for twenty years before it was able to grasp this axiom. In fact, it was grasped, on behalf of this Programme, by Mr. Paul Hoffman, and it is mainly because of his strong and unflinching support that we are at last able to celebrate the victory of an axiom.

This phenomenon is worth pondering. The UN family is engaged in its historic mission to work for the economic salvation of the underdeveloped countries. Yet it had to struggle in vain all these years to salvage its oldest programme from primitive contradictions in which it had been entangled. It was unable to match its noble intentions with enough practical wisdom. For this the blame should be placed squarely where it belongs—not on the tasks of development, difficult as they are, but on the failure to work out and adopt a sensible strategy.

81

Meanwhile, one victory is not enough. There are several other axioms which have to be recognized, accepted, and built into the UN administration to make its programmes really effective.

2

In the late fifties whenever the suggestion was made that the EPTA programming left a good deal to be desired, it met with the stock reply, at times mingled with some impatience: "Are we in a position to do the programming from headquarters for a hundred odd countries with all their diversities? The programmes must be prepared within the countries."

More recently, an able young colleague while discussing the current trends in the UNDP, expressed his own view in these words: "I am all in favour of country programming. My reason is a simple one. To put it bluntly, the countries should be saved from our own tyranny at the headquarters."

Both remarks contain an important truth. Both also suffer from a serious flaw.

The programming must be a decentralized operation and carried out within the countries. The headquarters cannot and should not dictate the contents of the programme. But it does not follow that the only alternative is to adhere to the country-programming procedures followed by the Expanded Programme since 1955. Thinking went off the track because it was preoccupied with what was a right question, but wrongly formulated, and so yielded a wrong answer.

The EPTA practice, as should be abundantly clear from the preceding chapters, suffered from three major drawbacks. First, the headquarters practically divested itself of all responsibility for the substance of the programme. Surely, the alternative to centralization should not be abdication. Second, its over-generous delegation of powers did not go in the right direction. Responsibilities for programming were vested in the governments and the agencies, and only nominally in its own field representatives who should really play the central role. And third, it decentralized the wrong way inasmuch as it gave the recipient government, to all intents and purposes, a *carte blanche* for preparing the programme, subject only to a given financial ceiling.

In short, it delegated too much, to too many parties, and too soon; in so doing it did not just decentralize, but actually dispersed the responsibility. It is futile to expect that any sensible programme could emerge under these conditions.

The root cause of the trouble lies in a basic misconception, a failure to differentiate between two things: the country-*level* programming as a general principle and the particular brand of country-programming *procedures* as they have been evolved over the years, whether by accident or by design.

3

An example will best illustrate the results of this confusion in thinking.

Yugoslavia was one of the first countries to take advantage of the Expanded Programme. In the fifteen years ended in 1964 it received from this source technical assistance totalling $9,475,267.[41] From the beginning the Yugoslav programme consisted predominantly of very short-term fellowships and worker-trainees. No less than 4,665 fellowships were awarded to Yugoslavia during the 15-year period, out of a global total of 31,792; its share worked out to almost 15 per cent. For expert services, on the other hand, the proportion was strikingly low. The global total of expert assignments during the same period was 31,542; the share of Yugoslavia was only 631, or two per cent. The actual number of experts was very much smaller—perhaps one-third to one-half—since the same expert often served on more than one assignment, usually for a couple of months or even less.

Within a few years it became the standard practice at headquarters to take a rosy view of this programme. Nor was it hard to find the necessary rationalization to bolster it. Yugoslavia was a relatively developed country, so ran the long-distance logic; its educated nationals needed experience abroad, which could be well acquired through short-term fellowships; in this way, by giving foreign training to several hundred nationals every year, it was clearly making the best conceivable use of the slender resources made available to it from the Expanded Programme. In any case, a country knows its interests best; therefore what Yugoslavia was doing must be to its best interest.

This view was reflected, year after year, in EPTA's annual reports. And it was duly supported by isolated examples carefully picked out to show how Yugoslavs trained with EPTA fellowships had effectively utilized their newly-acquired knowledge for the benefit of national development.

---

[41] Its own voluntary contributions to the Programme during the same period totalled $1,499,900,

The feeble logic was reinforced by yet another fallacy, which is also somewhat more subtle though no less treacherous, as happens all too often in the field of development. Most people, at headquarters and in the agencies, were unconsciously inclined to compare Yugoslavia's performance with that of other recipient countries, often overlooking, curiously enough, what they themselves had been at pains to stress all along—that Yugoslavia cannot be regarded as a typical underdeveloped country.

Clearly, there could be only one valid comparison in a case like this—between the Yugoslav programme as it was and what the same programme could and should be, between its actual and its potential performance. The gap between the two could be the only correct measure of the effectiveness, or otherwise, of the programme.

On a critical, on-the-spot view of things, that gap, contrary to previous expectations, appeared surprisingly wide.[42] It contradicted the facile assumptions that had prevailed so long; the rationale underlying the fellowship programme looked far less attractive; it turned out to be the weakest, and not the strongest, feature of the Yugoslav programme.

In theory, under the present system of country programming, the government is supposed to identify high-priority projects, carefully assess the requirements in each case in terms of experts, fellowships and equipment, formulate its programme request on this basis within a given target, and thereby ensure the best possible utilization of the funds.

In practice, things have been quite different. As soon as the target was communicated to the Federal Government, a great many interests staked their claims. The first task was to accommodate the six Republics, each of which received a slice of the cake in varying thickness. Within each Republic there were numerous communes, institutes and enterprises, all enjoying a high degree of independence under the Yugoslav constitution with its system of decentralization and workers' councils, and all of them having their claims against the target. So the Republican portion had to be cut skilfully into razor-thin slices in order to give something to each claimant, and to make all concerned feel that the principle of distributive justice was fully respected.

Given the modest country target and the large number of parties, the share of each had to be extremely small, only a few thousand dollars. And given the tiny size of the amount, it could be used most

---

[42] The writer was "Resident Representative" in Yugoslavia from September 1963 through December 1966.

easily for short-term fellowships, and only exceptionally for very short-term experts with or without a sprinkling of equipment. Whatever may be the philosophy of programming, its politics was clear. And it is the politics that determined the programme with its highly fragmented contents.

The Resident Representatives have been frequently pressed to submit periodic reports evaluating the results achieved under the Expanded Programme. But how on earth should one carry out such an evaluation? Even the thinly spread resources to finance short-term fellowships and expert posts are of course not entirely wasted; here and there they will show some useful results. But even in such cases the correlation between the results achieved on a particular project and the few thousand dollars spent by the Programme on an expert or a fellow intended to serve on it would be well-nigh impossible to establish. Besides, such an account of results could at best only give some indication of what had been achieved in spite of haphazard programming; but it would shed no light on the all-important question of how much more could have been achieved with the same resources had every single project been screened to meet the first-priority needs and formulated in more rational dimensions.

And finally, no honest evaluation could blink at what was by far the most conspicuous weakness of the technical assistance programme in Yugoslavia (and, by and large, in all receiving countries) viz., its senselessly splintered character; nor could it ignore the fact that this indiscriminately sliced-up programme was a direct outcome of the system which had been instituted by the headquarters in its own wisdom. What was needed was not evaluation of results, but rectification of bad programming.

4

Could the programme be rescued from this planned fragmentation? The need was no longer in doubt, but the task was far from easy.

For one thing, programming under EPTA was considered to be a prerogative of the Government, and the Yugoslav authorities were fully conscious of this. The Resident Representative was not supposed to have any say about the substantive aspects of the programme.

Worse still, the technical assistance programme was not making any worthwhile contribution because of the way it was conceived and prepared. Yet wrong programming had led a lot of people to a wrong conclusion. The view often heard from headquarters was that Yugoslavia had already reached a point of development where it could dispense with technical assistance. Such a view had, at least for some people, the flattering implication that in this particular case the Expanded Programme had more or less fulfilled its mission!

Yugoslavs, too, were by no means enthusiastic about the programme, which was continued partly because of the past tradition, but mainly as a handy source of foreign exchange, amounting to about one half million dollars a year. Some were, however, frankly inclined to forego this amount, and also the support for two projects Yugoslavia was at that time receiving from the Special Fund. It could then abandon the status of a recipient country and belong to the elite club of donors of aid. The prestige, it was felt, would be well worth the sacrifice.

A close study of the conditions in Yugoslavia revealed not only the poor performance of the technical assistance programme, but also excellent opportunities where both the Expanded Programme and the Special Fund could make an impressive contribution. In fact, at this juncture of Yugoslavia's development, there are a number of vital areas where a joint international-Yugoslav effort holds out the promise of far better and more effective results. To ignore these opportunities would be tantamount to a default, all the more so when valuable services could be rendered at a small net cost to the Programme. To do so on the ground that the Programme had outlived its necessity in the country would be even less warranted.

The first task was to provide a convincing demonstration, for the benefit of the sceptics, of what the UNDP could achieve through tailor-made projects designed to meet some of the most urgent needs of the country and with a judicious combination of national and international experts.

For this the reconstruction of Skopje, the capital of Macedonia, after the devastating earthquake of 26 July 1963 provided an ideal testing ground. About 50 per cent of the buildings in the city, with a population of 180,000, had collapsed; another 25 per cent had been severely damaged; the total loss was estimated around $750 million. Emergency aid was rushed to the city from all parts of the world in a remarkable demonstration of international fellow-feeling. And it included modest, but nonetheless valuable, assistance from the various United Nations programmes.

Once the first phase of immediate relief measures was over, it was necessary to plan for the future. The authorities, at both the Federal and the Republic level, had taken the decision to reconstruct the city on the same spot, and this was supported by well-known international experts. The decision, which involved capital investment ultimately totalling one billion dollars, was underwritten by the Federal Government.

Clearly, it was to the interest of all concerned to integrate into the project the latest findings of seismology and earthquake engineering, and to plan for building a better and safer city. Intensive discussions spreading over several months were needed before the practical advantages of a joint UN-Yugoslav approach were fully grasped. But thereafter it was not only accepted wholeheartedly; it became the corner-stone of official policy for reconstruction of Skopje.

After some preliminary assistance financed with contingency allocations of $250,000 from EPTA, three major Special Fund projects were developed. The most important of them was the Skopje Urban Planning project (UNSF allocation: $1,457,400; Executing Agency: United Nations) for preparing a new Master Plan for the city of Skopje. The project was all along aided by a high-level International Board of Consultants drawn from Japan, USSR, Poland, Czechoslavakia, Hungary, France, Netherlands, UK, USA and, of course, Yugoslavia. The Master Plan was submitted to the Yugoslav authorities in October 1966 and was formally accepted by them.

The second project called "Training Centre for Building Construction Personnel" (UNSF allocation: $485,000; Executing Agency: the ILO), aimed at upgrading the skills of local workers and initiating them in modern techniques of antiseismic construction. It was conceived as an essential part of the overall programme since it was the local workers who would ultimately have to rebuild the city on the basis of the new Master Plan. The UNDP part of the project was practically completed in summer 1967.

The third project related to the regulation and control of the Vardar river (UNSF allocation: $1,479,300; Executing Agency: United Nations). The city of Skopje has long been subjected to periodic floods from the Vardar which flows through the heart of the city. This, it has been held, aggravates the seismicity of the area; in any case, there is no doubt that the flood of December 1962 had undermined the foundations of many buildings and had thereby directly contributed to the heavy damages caused by the earthquake. Obviously, a city rebuilt at enormous cost and protected against earthquakes with modern engineering techniques, could not be left exposed to floods. And so the Vardar regulation project, which is still under way, was added to the list.

Mention should be made of yet another project which, on a long view, must form an integral part of the strategy for reconstruction and future development of this area. An Institute of Seismology, Earthquake Engineering and Town Planning was established in 1965 to deal with the long-range problems of high seismicity not only in Skopje and Macedonia, but in the whole of Yugoslavia and some day perhaps of the Balkan region. The Institute, modestly supported from EPTA, has been making slow progress. Meanwhile, the importance of its functions can hardly be exaggerated. Development in this area is proceeding at a fast rate. It is therefore all the more essential to insist that every single structure to be erected on this unstable terrain will be built according to the latest techniques of earthquake engineering.

The Skopje package of projects with their ancillaries served as an eye-opener. They revealed the true potential of the UNDP, also the multiplier effect of intimate collaboration between the Yugoslav and carefully chosen international experts. And as a by-product, they generated a new confidence in the UN programme—in its capacity to help steer development towards new and attractive goals; and this, in turn, created a favourable background of understanding and good-will for tackling the delicate question of EPTA reprogramming.

5

Around mid-1964 the time seemed ripe for the first gentle sounding. This was done in the course of a talk with a senior official who was then in charge of administering all technical assistance (officially called "technical cooperation") programmes, both bilateral and multilateral. A hint was thrown out that the current EPTA programme might not be the best conceivable for Yugoslavia, as it appeared unrelated to her most important problems and consisted mainly of very short-term and rather isolated fellowships. Could it be remodelled so as to serve her more immediate needs? This way Yugoslavia could also set an example to others.

The reaction of the administrator was unforgettable. He laughed, signified his unqualified agreement and then, with a disarming frank-ness frequently evinced by Yugoslavs at high levels, added: "The pro-gramme is certainly not doing us much good. We have a joke among ourselves. We call it the Yugoslav programme for tourism on United Nations account!"

This last phrase had evidently been in circulation for quite a while. For it was independently repeated by others in similar dis-cussions.

A somewhat different comment heard around the same time was equally illuminating. On expressing some misgivings about the usefulness of certain fellowships in one of the Republics, the local Director in charge of technical cooperation activities quoted a proverb in Serbo-Croat,[43] which turned out to be the equivalent of: "Don't look a gift horse in the mouth!" And then he explained that if their own money were involved, they would never think of spending it on such fellowships; but since this was a gift from the UN, they did not mind too much.

A major psychological hurdle was overcome. The need for programme reorientation was recognized in responsible quarters. And it was further underlined by the far-reaching economic reforms introduced in July 1965, which aimed at higher industrial efficiency, freer trade and gradual integration of the domestic economy into international division of labour. The currency reforms with a sharp devaluation of the dinar from 750 to 1250 to the dollar, were accompanied by the abolition of a host of subsidies, decentralization of managerial responsibility, and greater emphasis on some sectors of the economy, particularly agriculture, flood control and river valley development, and the tourist industry.

The EPTA programme for 1965-66 to some extent reflected this new trend. It provided for 265 fellowships totalling, 1,100 man-months at a cost of $488,300, or 60.4 per cent, out of a programme for $807,900. The fellowship component in the 1963-64 programme had been much higher —there were no less than 485 fellowships, totalling 2,299 man-months, at an estimated cost of $816,000, or 81.2 per cent out of a total programme for $1,015,900. The provision for expert services, on the other hand, rose appreciably between the two programmes—from 19 posts or 49.5 man-months, costing $79,900 or 7.9 per cent of the total in 1963-64, to 42 posts or 138 man-months costing $221,700 or 27.5 per cent of the total in 1965-66. The equipment component, as a percentage of the total, remained practically unchanged in the two programmes.

The "element of tourism," as measured by the number of fellowships, was significantly reduced in the 1965-66 programme. It was a move in the right direction, but it was still a modest one. To be really effective the programme needed to undergo many more adjustments. Meanwhile, experience showed how difficult it was to make even minor adjustments in the programme, once it had taken final shape; in particular, attempts to squeeze out funds by suppressing nonessential projects encountered

---

43 "Poklonjenom konju ne gledaju se zubi."

formidable resistance even when the intention was to finance some new projects of high national priority.

For example, a short-term UN-FAO mission of two consultants to carry out a preliminary study for multipurpose development of the Sava river basin could not be financed within the current programme. It needed a contingency allocation of about $12,000 early in 1965.

Again, a seven-member mission on tourism, assigned also in 1965 under United Nations auspices, made comprehensive recommendations on the future development of the tourist industry, which, because of its foreign exchange earning potential, was now placed in the forefront of Yugoslavia's planning. The mission could not be accommodated within the normal programme, and so it had to be financed with a special allocation of about $22,000 from the regular budget of the United Nations.

In 1966, two other short-term missions were requested by the Government, in pursuit of the policy of programme reorientation which was now clearly under way. The first one consisting of five consultants —four from the USA and one from Switzerland—was to assist in preparing a master plan to deal with the rising tide of transit tourism in Yugoslavia. It fell within the United Nations field of activity and was estimated to cost about $16,000. The second mission related to the rehabilitation and economic utilization of the forestry resources in the Republic of Bosnia-Herzegovina. It was agreed that a mission consisting of four members drawn respectively from Austria, Italy, the UK, and the USA, would be organized and assigned by FAO. The cost was estimated around $15,000.

In both cases the primary object was to bring together competent international and Yugoslav experts who would jointly go over the whole range of problems, prepare action-oriented programmes and submit them to the authorities concerned to facilitate policy-making at the top level, which was expected to be followed in due course by sizable investments of domestic and foreign capital. In both cases, financing the missions became a major hurdle. Further contingency allocations could not be justified; the only practical alternative was to make room for them within the current programme by eliminating some fellowships; but no one was willing to make the sacrifice—the enterprises—tightly guarded their shares of the programme as if these represented some inalienable rights. In the end the programme was amended, and funds were released, but only after a great deal of effort which involved, inter alia, several interventions at the ministerial level.

6

The experience in Yugoslavia only provided fresh evidence for a curious fact already been well established: To do the right things for the programme is incredibly difficult; to do the wrong things for it is ridiculously easy. This, in a nutshell, is the result of the peculiar constraints the programme had created for itself.

Its focus, as of all development programmes, should be on the quality of projects; yet its concern for this has always been remote. And if, in isolated cases, individual servants of the programme, gripped by a nonconformist zeal and favoured by luck, succeeded in identifying high-grade projects and in mobilizing high-level support in the government, it proved exceedingly difficult to channel the programme funds towards them.

The strategy for the future now emerged with unmistakable clarity. The programme for the 1967-68 biennium offered the first real opportunity to try to secure a greater concentration of funds, and to help promote and finance projects worthy of high priority, particularly in the context of Yugoslavia's post-reform economic development. This was obvious; but no less obvious was the fact that this could be achieved only if the programme were prepared on a firm basis well in advance, and in any case *before* the country target for Yugoslavia was officially communicated to the Government. Otherwise commitments would be made for the distribution of the funds according to the traditional pattern, and it would be too late to influence the substance of the programme.

The target communication was expected to arrive in December 1965. This was the fateful deadline that had to be beaten. In short, the programme had to be prepared, and fully firmed up, before the "programming exercise" was scheduled to begin. This is the strategy that was followed, and it worked.

The Federal authorities supported the approach. A long process of persuasion began; intensive discussions were held in each Republic explaining the case for a reorientation of the programme, the needs that had acquired special urgency after the reforms, and how and where UNDP/TA could help meet them, if the authorities so wished. Out of all these discussions emerged a draft programme which, after necessary review, was submitted to the Federal authorities. In November 1965 it received the blessings of the Federal cabinet; and this, to all intents and purposes, marked the completion of the programming exercise.

It is not necessary to go into the details of the programme. Suffice it to say that the amount—only $700,000—was deliberately concentrated on projects which, above all, satisfied three main criteria: that the projects chosen really deserved high priority in Yugoslavia's economy; that they represented fields where a joint approach by Yugoslav and international experts would yield far more effective results; and that they would, where necessary, either provide essential supplementary support to important projects already under way, for example, under the Special Fund or they would pave the way to the formulation and initiation of new pre-investment and investment projects. Application of nuclear energy to agriculture and the Institute for seismology and earthquake engineering may be cited as examples of projects which eminently satisfied these criteria.

The programme was saved from its own procedures. A clean break was made with the past practice. What cannot be overstressed is the fact that at no stage of this arduous and delicate reprogramming operation was there the slightest suggestion from the Yugoslav authorities of any encroachment on their time-honoured prerogative. On the contrary, they went out of their way to record, in an unusual gesture, their appreciation for all the initiatives that had been taken on behalf of the UNDP to develop a programme that would best serve their own national interests.

These reactions underlined another fact never doubted by knowledgeable people but too often ignored in practice: The recipient governments not only do not resent, they welcome initiatives from the United Nations family, if taken in the right spirit and in the right way.

When initiatives are prompted solely by a genuine desire to serve, when the proposals made are concrete, well-informed, and are based on a full understanding of local conditions and a sympathy or, better still, a concern for the people, when proposals are made only in the form of suggestions, but are supported fully by facts and logic, and when the final decision in each and every case is left explicitly to the government, it is safe to say that no government will ever take exception to such an approach; that all governments will appreciate the motives and will treat this as a valuable service to themselves; and that most governments, in the vast majority of cases, will end up by giving full support to the proposals. It is precisely here that the UN family has its unique opportunity; and it is precisely this opportunity that makes it so eminently qualified to be the vanguard of international development.

7

The example of Yugoslavia, and no doubt of other receiving countries, has other lessons to teach which, though negative, are no less pertinent.

The Yugoslav case shows that country-programming, as now followed in practice, is a misnomer; it is essentially a sharing of funds, or of *devisen,* among numerous interested parties within the country. It is an example of pseudo-programming.

It shows that getting away from programming by the calendar, whether at twelve or twenty-four month intervals, as now proposed, will be an improvement. But it also shows why the retention of programming based on country targets with advance commitments to them will be a major error. The system of "allocation first, programme next" —and this is what it essentially boils down to—has damaged the programme in the past. It now seems that the future too will bring no respite from it.

Finally, the Yugoslav example, which holds good also for other countries, shows the vital role the field representative must play in all programming operations, and therefore the inescapable need to decentralize responsibilities on a substantial scale from headquarters and to centralize them in the hands of one single representative at the country level. Of this there is as yet little indication. Indeed, the trend under the new system is in the reverse direction—towards centralization of responsibility at headquarters, using old-fashioned treasury control as its primary instrument. This is trying to cure an ill with a wrong remedy. No wonder that the young colleague should have been so much at unease regarding the growing trend towards what he called "our tyranny from headquarters."

A final comment is in order. One of the cardinal principles of administration in any programme involving expenditure of public funds is to devise effective safeguards to forestall the risks of patronage. It cannot be said that the Expanded Programme, or UNDP/TA, has betrayed keen awareness of this problem. Indeed, the worst feature of the system of country-programming it has stumbled into, no doubt with the best of motives in most of the people, lies in the fact that it lends itself to patronage with dismal ease. This is inevitable where money matters more than the programme. After all, this is the quintessence of any well-conceived system of patronage.

Too many people have in the past been trapped by the propaganda about country-programming; too few have been able to detect its fatal flaws. Is it not time to recognize the simple fact that good intentions cannot by themselves produce good management, to go beyond the theory to see the realities of the system as it has developed in actual practice, to understand how badly it has been hurting the entire UN operations in a vital field?

One thing is clear. The UN family will never be able to play its historic role in the underdeveloped world until it decides to remove this self-erected roadblock from its path.

PART III

SPECIAL FUND AND
THE MERGER MOVEMENT

CHAPTER 11

Special Fund: A New Dimension

"There is nothing so well done but may be mended,"

The establishment of the United Nations Special Fund, almost exactly ten years ago, was an event of great significance for the developing countries. A no less significant event was the appointment of Mr. Hoffman as head of the new programme. Under his creative and energetic leadership the Fund has rapidly grown in size as well as in the volume and range of its activities. This new dynamism spilled over into other programmes and other sectors of the UN life.

Without doubt the Special Fund has added a new dimension to the United Nations. Its impact is now being felt over the entire underdeveloped world. By June 1968, the Governing Council had authorized 929 projects, and by that time actual operation had started on 700 of them. When completed, the 929 projects will have cost $2,324 million. The UNDP allocations will, by then, amount to $911.9 million, or 40 per cent. The balance will be the contributions directly made by the governments themselves.[44]

In reciting these impressive figures one must beware of a pitfall: they represent activities *relating to* development, *not actual* development. For, the Special Fund is explicitly confined to pre-investment work—surveys, research, training; as such, it is a preparation for the future, for a harvest yet to come. That harvest, in the great majority of cases, is nowhere in sight. In fact, all the present indications are that

---

[44] By January 1969, the UNDP had approved a total of 1,025 Special Fund projects; their average duration was four and a half years; and their total cost, on completion, was estimated at $2,441 million, of which the UNDP will provide $1,003 million and the recipient governments $1,438 million.

the end-results, when measured in terms of economic growth, will fall short of the hopes that have been aroused in the developing countries.

2

Two main currents of thought converged and led to the creation of the Special Fund. The first was the proposal to set up a Special United Nations Fund for Economic Development. The SUNFED proposal, which was first broached in 1952, became a contentious issue between the "have" and the "have-not" countries. The USA explicitly made it contingent upon the question of disarmament on the ground that given progress in disarmament, funds would be released, which could then be partly directed toward development. There was no disarmament, and therefore no SUNFED. But the proposal, like a hardy annual, continued to crop up at various meetings and conferences of the UN bodies. The drawn battle was repeatedly fought with unabated enthusiasm, enlivened with a plentiful exchange of verbal shafts.

The second current had its source in the Expanded Programme. By the mid-fifties, the Technical Assistance Board was ready with a proposal for widening its own activities. In a report[45] submitted to TAC and ECOSOC in May 1956, it reviewed the first six years of its activities and sought to take what it called "a forward look." Its main conclusions were: The Programme was rendering services which proved "increasingly useful." A beginning had been made; valuable experience had been gained, some useful results had been achieved, also the main lines of future development had been laid down. "But the surface of the great task has barely been scratched, and its long-term implications scarcely recognized."

This pointed to the need for additional financial resources to enable the Programme to make a larger contribution to the tasks of development.

Since future requirements, even when conservatively defined, would far outstrip the resources of the Programme, the report suggested for consideration two possible levels of expansion. The first would involve a modest increase in resources to finance activities on a somewhat larger scale, but within the then existing scope of the Programme. The specific suggestion made was to aim at an annual target of $50 million, or double the then available resources, and to reach the target in stages "over the next few years." The second alternative was to go in for a more substantial expansion, both in the scope of the Programme and

---

[45] "The Expanded Programme of Technical Assistance—A Forward Look." E/2885, 11 May 1956.

in the provision of support in the form of equipment, supplies and expert services.

The parallel deliberations on the SUNFED and EPTA's forward-look proposal blended in 1958 to produce an unforeseen compromise. The majortiy of the governments ruled out the first alternative proposed by EPTA and clearly favoured a bolder move. The advocates of SUNFED went a step further; they opposed the idea of merely enlarging the Expanded Programme and argued, rightly or wrongly, that it would mean the demise of their long-cherished objective. So they made another desperate attempt to sway the policy-makers to establish a capital development fund for the United Nations, but with no more success than on previous occasions. The only concessions they managed to extract was that, instead of an enlargement of the Expanded Programme, there should be a separate fund which, in its initial stages, would be confined exclusively to pre-investment activities; and that the idea of a UN capital development fund could be considered again at some unspecified future date.

So was established a new programme. As the supposed forerunner of the SUNFED or UNCDF it was, rather symbolically, called the United Nations Special Fund. Its fields of activity, though not very different from what had been envisaged for EPTA under its second alternative mentioned above, carried the generic label "pre-investment work." This, too, had its psychological value as it created an aura that the UN family had now moved closer to the establishment of a fund for supplying investment capital.

Meanwhile, the forward-look school had sensed the futility of pressing for a forward move on behalf of the Expanded Programme; by 1958, it was convinced that a new and more substantial programme was going to be established. So its concern thenceforward was twofold: to defend the existence of EPTA as a separate programme, and to build up its own financial resources, taking full advantage of the fundraising drive launched by Mr. Hoffman. In both respects it achieved, as we have seen, a disconcerting measure of success.

3

The governing legislation of the Special Fund,[46] benefiting from a decade of experience with technical assistance, carefully avoided the pitfalls which had inpeded the operations of the Expanded Programme.

---

[46] General Assembly Resolution 1240 (XIII) of 14 October 1955. For the text see Appendix II.

Its main provisions, particularly where they differ from the founding resolution 222 A (IX) for EPTA, are well worth noting.

One, resolution 1240 explicitly provided, in Seciton 2(a), that the Special Fund should concentrate, as far as practicable, on "relatively large projects and avoid allocation of its resources over a great number of small projects." This is a significant provision. Implied in it is a stricture on the EPTA practice. The authors of the resolution were well aware of the danger that the Special Fund might, like its predecessor, dissolve itself into a mass of tiny projects and thereby largely dissipate its effort. They were anxious to forestall the risk.

Two, Section 2(c) laid down that only such projects would be undertaken as would "lead to *early results*" and would have "the *widest possible impact* in advancing the economic, social or technical development of the country or countries concerned, *in particular by facilitating new capital investment.*"[47]

The governing resolution of EPTA contained a similar provision which, however, was quietly set aside from the start. The Special Fund has been far more vigilant in this respect. It has successfuly avoided fragmentation of projects; it has also exercised much greater care in selecting them, although there has all along been, and still is, considerable room for improvement. It is in attracting or facilitating new capital investment that the Special Fund has been less than a stunning success (see Chapter 18, especially sections 6-7).

Three, projects might be approved for the period of time needed for their execution, even if more than one year (Section 4). This was reinforced by Section 51 which clearly stated that "programmes shall be developed on a project basis." For the same reason, the section further provided, there should be "no *a priori* allocation of funds on a country basis or among basic fields of assistance."

Thus, the Special Fund was based, as any rational programme of development must be, on project programming and project budgeting, unlike EPTA which, having debated and resisted the obvious all these years, has at last reluctantly agreed to surrender part of its irrational modus operandi.

The idea of country targets, it should be noted, was clearly ruled out; yet it was laid down, in Section 2(d), that "due consideration should be given to wide geographical distribution in allocations over a period of years." The Special Fund did not consider it necessary to subscribe to the thesis to which EPTA has stubbornly adhered to this

---

[47] Italics supplied.

day, namely, that without country targets there can be no equitable geographical distribution of the programme.

The resolution, it will be noticed, also ruled out the idea of any agency targets or *a priori* allocation of funds to the agencies, whether for country or for regional programmes.

Four, the basic fields of assistance, as laid down in Section 5, covered a fairly wide area: resources, including assessment and development of manpower, industry including handicrafts and cottage industries, agriculture, transport and communications, building and housing, health, education, statistics and public administration.

However, since the resources "prospectively available at this time," were not likely to exceed $100 million annually (Section 1(c)), the projects to be assisted by the Fund were required to be in one or a combination of the following forms: surveys, research and training; demonstration, including pilot projects. And they were to be implemented by the provision of staff, experts, equipment, supplies and services, and fellowships in such proportions as might be judged necessary by the Managing Director (Section 6).

These provisions, which further underscored the preinvestment character of the Special Fund, also sought to secure concentration of its resources on a rather small number of carefully selected projects.

Five, the resolution left it to the Managing Director to decide the precise form in which the governments should present their requests for assistance. Nonetheless, it laid down the broad framework for the preparation and submission of requests, each of which was required to provide all possible information on the intended use of the Special Fund assistance and the benefits expected from it, evidence to establish the technical soundness of projects, data bearing on their economic appraisal, and statements on counterpart costs to be borne by the recipient governments (Section 32).

The Managing Director had the responsibility for evaluating the project-requests. For this he was expected to rely normally on the facilities available within the UN family, but was authorized to contract the services of outside agencies, private firms or individuals, should the UN family's service be unavailable or considered inadequate (Section 34).

The Managing Director was specifically required to see that each project, when submitted to the Governing Council, was accompanied by: an evaluation of the expected benefits, a summary of its technical evaluation, a proposed budget showing the full financial implications of the project for its entire duration, also a statement on the cost to be borne by the recipient government or governments, a draft agreement with the latter and, where appropriate, a draft agreement with the agent or agents responsible for executing the project (Section 37).

These clear-cut provisions present a refreshing contrast to the practice followed by the Expanded Programme. And undoubtedly they have made for far greater efficiency in the Special Fund operations.

Six, of overriding significance is Section 21 which provided that the Special Fund "shall be administered by the Managing Director under the policy guidance of the Governing Council," and that he "shall have *the over-all responsibility* for the operations of the Fund, with *sole authority* to recommend to the Governing Council projects recommended by the Governments."[48]

The resolution provided for a small Consultative Board consisting of the UN Secretary-General, the Executive Chairman of TAB, and the President of IBRD, or their designated representatives. As its name implied, the function of the Board was solely to assist the Managing Director *with advice* in examining and appraising requested projects and proposed programmes (Section 26). It was left to the Managing Director to invite, "as appropriate," agency representatives to attend the Consultative Board meetings when projects falling mainly within their fields of activity were being considered (Section 27).

All this represented a clean break with the tradition of the Expanded Programme which was operated collectively by a Board consisting of the UN and the specialized agencies, all enjoying equal status and all representing their special interests, and an Executive Chairman whose main function, as it developed in practice, was to maintain harmony among these interests by working out suitable formulas for mutual accommodation.

Seven, the Managing Director was expected to appoint "a small group of officials" to assist him in his work, and to rely on the existing facilities of the UN family for other services, although he was authorized to engage expert consultants as required (Sections 28-29). Similarly, for work at the country level he was to rely on the resident representatives, and to facilitate field coordination, he was required to enter into an agreement with the Executive Chairman of TAB (Section 30).

Eight, the immediate intergovernmental control of policies and operations was vested in an 18-member elected body called Governing Council with equal representation for the developed and the less-developed countries respectively (Section 11-14).

---

48 Italics supplied.

The Economic and Social Council had the responsibility for formulating general rules and principles which would govern the administration and operation of the Fund; also for reviewing the Fund's operations based on annual reports to be submitted by the Governing Council (Section 9).

The ECOSOC was required to transmit the Governing Council report, along with its own comments, to the General Assembly which would then review the Fund's progress and operations as a separate subject on its agenda and make appropriate recommendations (Section 10).

These arrangements paralleled those of the Expanded Programme with one notable difference in practice. The members of the Governing Council were invariably represented at a significantly higher level than was the case with the Technical Assistance Committee, the governing body of EPTA.

Nine, recipient governments were expected to bear part of the project costs, at least that part payable in local currency, although this general rule could be waived in the case of needy countries unable to make even a local currency payment (Section 52).

This provision is similar to that of EPTA in the sense that the recipient governments have to make contributions in local currency towards the local costs of EPTA experts and provide other counterpart support. However, the total burden of costs borne by the recipient governments for Special Fund projects is much heavier—on an average, it amounts to 50 to 60 per cent of the total project costs.

As for finance, both programmes follow an identical pattern, that is to say, both are financed by voluntary contributions made in some 60 different currencies to two different accounts, so that each programme has to keep its own books, do its own accounting, and independently wrestle with its currency management problems.

The main differences between the two programmes should be clear from what has been said above. They can be summed up in a few words. Management, in EPTA, is equated with consensus-building, and consensuses are built with compromises that seek primarily to accommodate the special interests of agencies and pay scant heed to the principles of management or to the imperatives of development. Resolution 1240, on the other hand, provided a legislative framework which not only made it possible for the Special Fund to adopt and apply the canons of sound management, but also made it as difficult as possible to stray too far from them.

4

The difference between the EPTA and the Special Fund approach can be best illustrated with a couple of examples.[49]

An EPTA expert, of New Zealand nationality, was assigned to Ghana in 1957 for range management and pasture improvement in an area 30-40 miles from Accra. There was no question about his high professional competence, nor about his devotion to the work allotted to him. For almost five years he worked single-handed against all kinds of odds, both physical and administrative, and did the best he could under the circumstances.

But even the best he could do was not good enough, through no fault of his. For, grassland management is only one aspect of the complex problem of animal husbandry which had been a neglected subject in West African countries. To make a real impact on livestock development it should have been necessary to launch a simultaneous attack on four broad categories of problems: dry weather water supply; feed and fodder supply, especially in the dry period when there was an acute shortage; disease control based on adequate research and experiment; and upgrading of the local stock including introduction of new breeds. It was distressing to see this able and genial New Zealand expert gallantly struggling on year after year, but without making a dent in the problem. The result was a frittering of resources, waste of expert man-months, job frustration, and little or no real development.

Examples of this type could be easily multiplied in Ghana, and indeed in all receiving countries. This built-in waste, as mentioned before, has characterized the Expanded Programme from the outset, and it continues to do so even now despite the so-called merger.

The extent of this waste was vividly brought home in the course of the so-called evaluation exercises carried out annually during the five years ended in 1961.[50] There was of course evidence of progress in a good many instances, also some examples of conspicuously successful projects. Yet it was equally clear that with $30 to $40 million a year and with some 2000 international experts recruited from different countries, EPTA was not making anything like the impact it could have made with better priorities, better preparation of projects, and a

---

[49] Based on the writer's experience during 1961-62 when he was stationed in Ghana as Resident Representative.

[50] The writer, then serving as Director of TAB Programme Division in New York, was largely responsible for these exercises.

more rational allocation of resources. The overwhelming impression was one of lost or untapped opportunities and of wasted effort. It was customary to justify the splintered projects on the plea that resources were limited and one had to cut the coat according to the cloth. This was an idle analogy. What was being done constantly was to cut the cloth according to—whim!

Now, contrast all this with another example, also from Ghana. Not far from where the EPTA expert was at work on grassland experiments, there was a Special Fund project called "Lower Volta Flood Plains Survey." The project, covering an area of about 30,000 acres, aimed at introducing irrigation and cultivation of irrigated crops. Accordingly, provision had been made in it for contour survey and preparation of contour maps, soils survey with complete soil maps, preparation of blue-prints showing the alignment of canals, cultivation of new crops, especially sugar-cane and rice, on experimental plots brought under pump irrigation. All these pre-investment activities were completed in about three years, by 1962. The experiments with sugar cane yielded such excellent results that the Government decided, even without waiting for the full results on ratoon yields, to set up a sugar factory in the area with a capacity of 24,000 tons of sugar a year.[51]

This Special Fund project well illustrated how projects ought to be conceived and executed. It aimed at utilizing idle resources—land and water—for producing food crops—rice, sugar-cane, maize—that were urgently needed, on a scale that would add substantially to agricultural production and support a sizable sugar mill, thereby promoting the much-needed diversification of agriculture; and the project was carried out by a team of experts, supplemented by a firm of consultants, up to a point where follow-up action by the government was fully assured. A project of this nature could not help but make a real impact on the economy.

The two examples from Ghana also illustrate the important point that was stressed earlier. Even where *physical* priorities have been sorted out reasonably well, *financial* priorities may still go awry unless projects are developed on the *right scale* to make sense from an economic angle. Historically, the EPTA resources have been spread far too thinly over too large an area, large not only in a geographical, but also in a functional sense.

---

[51] The follow-up investment made a less exciting story. President Nkrumah signed a contract with a Czech firm for a turn-key job financed from supplier's credit. The firm was well-known for its experience, but only in beet-sugar production.

And this policy has been usually defended with the standard argument that development depends on the national effort of a recipient country, while all that UN assistance can do is to supplement it modestly at points decided by the government. What has not been asked, however, is how much more could the same Programme with the same resources achieve by way of helping the governments.

5

The Special Fund procedures, as elaborated in practice on the basis of Resolution 1240, have many commendable features. Each project aims at attaining some clear-cut objectives, and is therefore prepared on a meaningful scale, for which a floor has been set at $250,000. To achieve the given objectives, each project seeks to combine, in some rational proportion, the three ingredients—services of international experts, essential equipment and supplies that have to be imported, and fellowships to provide advanced training in developed countries to national experts who would later serve on the project.

Besides, each project is provided with a "Project Manager" as head of an international team of experts; each is launched for a specific period of time not exceeding four years; and each is based on a plan of operation which sets forth in detail the mutual obligations, including the government's counterpart support in terms of professional and other personnel as well as physical facilities. The government is required to designate a national expert to serve as co-manager who could later head the project on its termination. Major alterations in the plan of operation are renegotiated with the government as and when found necessary.

The Governing Council approval of a project carries with it an allocation of funds to cover the costs for its entire duration. After approval the project is entrusted for execution to one of a dozen organizations—the United Nations and eleven specialized agencies, including the World Bank. The Executing Agency has well-defined responsibilities and submits periodic progress reports according to the terms of the plan of operation.

Even the Special Fund operations, despite its admirable features, are capable of improvement, especially in three important directions —in the initial selection of projects; in the speed and efficiency with which selected projects are authorized, initiated, and executed; and in ensuring that a project, on completion, will be actually followed by the requisite capital investment.

These questions will be examined critically at a later stage (in Chapter 18). Suffice it to say here that the Lower Volta project referred to above should not be treated as the rule; it is, in fact, very much of an exception. The proportion of such high-grade projects designed to make a decisive impact on the economy is unfortunately not high in the lengthening inventory of Special Fund undertakings, especially when the question of actual capital investment is taken into account.

CHAPTER 12

Special Fund: A New Problem

"Wise it is to comprehend the whole."

EDWARD YOUNG

The compromise that gave birth to the Special Fund has left a dubious legacy, the full implications of which are yet to be grasped by the UN family and the outside public, by the donors as well as the receivers of aid.

There is, first of all, the basic question: What is the Special Fund? Is it a percursor of the SUNFED or at any rate of some kind of a UNCDF, or is it merely an extension of technical assistance, that is, of the Expanded Programme? From the start the answer has been different in different minds. That duality of concept has continued to this day.

Yet facts should have spoken louder than words or labels. All that the Special Fund has been engaged in all these years is technical assistance par excellence—in carrying out surveys, in conducting research and training, in providing demonstration, including some pilot projects. The only real difference as compared with EPTA is that the Special Fund is giving this assistance more selectively, in heavier doses and in a more concentrated form, and therefore more rationally and more effectively. Should this be an argument for two separate programmes, or for one, more comprehensive in character, with EPTA cast into the more sensible Special Fund mould? There can be no doubt about the answer—if logic, not politics, is the guide.

The Special Fund, according to Resolution 1240 (XIII), was "envisaged as a constructive advance in United Nations assistance to the less developed countries." The advance, in its substantive aspects, largely comprised the area that EPTA had demarcated for itself in its "Forward Look" proposal. Its fifteenth anniversary review pointed out, with some legitimate pride, how "significant" this proposal had proved in "shaping the thinking" for the Special Fund.[52]

The fact that the Special Fund was designated as a "pre-investment" programme, has helped to keep alive the hope for a capital development fund, but the result so far has been far from salutary. What was ignored in the process was the fact that, under Resolution 222 A (IX), the Expanded Programme, too, had been given the task to promote economic and social development to the utmost possible extent; that, to be really effective, this Programme, too, had to be concerned primarily with pre-investment work since only then it could expect to make the maximum possible impact on production. The fortuitous distinction that arose between the two programmes has clouded thinking on basic problems of development; it has also powerfully aided the separatist tendencies of the Expanded Programme, and has thus hampered attempts to rationalize its procedures and operations.

Not only that; two programmes operating in the same field to perform the same functions and to serve the same objectives gave rise to interminable discussions on such questions as: How different they were. Were they really so different after all? Why should there be any difference between them at all? Since their essential similarity could not be indefinitely suppressed or ignored, the discussions mostly ended with anguished queries if the two programmes were being coordinated effectively enough in practice. What was never asked nor discussed was what losses, if any, would have ensued if there were only one programme working with right procedures, and how much could have been gained in terms of better programming and more efficient management.

Nor was this all. The emergence of two programmes—one for technical assistance with no investment, the other for pre-investment work also with no investment and only a vague hope for it—reflected what was feasible in the UN forum, given the alignment of political and bureaucratic forces. It did not in any way correspond to the real needs of development in the recipient countries. Here is a vitally important fact that has been virtually ignored in practice. As a result, the intrinsic worth of technical assistance and pre-investment activity *per se* has been exaggerated out of all proportion.

---

[52] "15 Years and 150,000 Skills." Ibid., page 31.

Thus, the very success of the Special Fund threatens to produce lop-sided results. It has been pushing one dimension—that is, pre-invest-ment—too far and too rapidly, while the most critical dimension—ac-tual capital investment— is not moving fast enough, nor has it been receiving the amount of attention it deserves.

2

The Special Fund was formally established on 1 January 1959. By 1962, Mr. Hoffman reportedly set his sights on 1,000 pre-investment projects for the developing countries to be reached as quickly as pos-sible. With this target in mind, and as a major plank in the platform for the first development decade, he launched his relentless drive which has continued to this day with undiminished vigour.

The year-by-year growth of the Special Fund activities is summed up in the statistical tables given in Appendix 1 B. No doubt there has been some delay in reaching the coveted target of a thousand projects. However, it is now almost within grasp; next year, no doubt, the Fund will be able to celebrate its fulfilment.[53]

By mid-1968, the 700th Special Fund project actually went into operation. The number of completed projects stood at 178 in December 1967 and should be close to 200 by the end of this year. The word "completion" in this context has, however, strictly limited connota-tions. It means no more than the completion of the preparatory phase of development in the particular segments covered by the projects. As such, they are, as a rule, neither able nor expected to make any im-mediate, visible impact on the developing economies.

This is too obvious a fact to need any specific mention. Yet how often it tends to be forgotten in practice! Take, for example, the follow-ing observation made by Secretary-General U Thant: "There are few, if any, tasks more urgent than that of speeding economic and social progress in the low-income countries. And there are few, if any, pro-grammes of international assistance helping more effectively in this task than the United Nations Special Fund."[54] Few will question the first part of the statement today. But few with firsthand knowledge of the Special Fund operations will be ready to subscribe to its second part.

The statement, evidently, was not intended to apply to the World Bank which has set up a record of unparalleled achievements in inter-national development if only because it has been equipped with, or has

---

[53] The one-thousand mark was crossed in January 1969 when the number of authorized projects reached a total of 1,025. See footnote 44.

[54] Quoted in a UN Fact Sheet on the Special Fund, July 1965.

managed to equip itself with, substantial long-term development capital which it has been investing in carefully screened high-priority projects. The Special Fund is admittedly bigger and more important than the other United Nations programmes, such as former EPTA, the World Food Programme, UNICEF, regular programmes of the UN and of the specialized agencies. But this, in itself, could hardly be a matter for gratification. The fact is that the Special Fund, despite its strong points, has not been 'speeding economic and social progress in the low-income countries" to any noticeable extent.

That this should be so is a reflection mainly on the inherent deficiencies from which the Special Fund has suffered as a programme for economic development. It has been given a great cause—raising the living standards of the people of Asia, Africa and Latin America; but only half a goal, that is, to deal with pre-investment studies and investigations; limited means—$100 million or thereabouts a year; a disjointed apparatus of specialized agencies with ingrained sectional attitudes; and no unified control and guidance at country level. The greatest contribution made by Mr. Hoffman has been in selling the cause of development to the world at large and to the developed countries of the West in particular. Some headway has also been made in combatting the other shortcomings. But progress here has been painfully slow, uneven, and far from decisive.

As the Special Fund projects multiplied, means and ends began to be easily confused; the intrinsic limitations of pre-investment projects were overlooked; the part began to be treated increasingly as the whole, and the starting point almost as the destination.

The agencies—and within an agency, its various departments—tried hard to enlarge their respective portfolios of Special Fund projects. The governments too, often aided and guided by the agencies, soon began to submit requests in increasing numbers. Given their unlimited needs for development, present and future, they had no difficulty in doing so. As a result, the demand for assistance from the Fund rose rapidly. The overall number of projects which the Fund could authorize at any given time was, of course, determined by the available resources, that is, by the voluntary contributions of the member governments. However, their distribution among the organizations, and also among the various departments within the same organization, was largely a matter of personality—and luck.

What guarantee is there that the projects selected in such circumstances would correspond to the most pressing needs of the recipient countries, and to no other? There is, of course, no such guarantee.

Not only have projects been promoted more or less at random, without any assurance that they represented, really and truly, what were the most desirable ones at a given time in a particular country. Something else has happened which is even more disturbing—a massive diversion of effort away from investment to pre-investment, from actual development here and now to only a preparation for development in some unknown future.

Because it was confined exclusively to pre-investment work, the Special Fund has ignored the manifold opportunities that are ripe for capital investment right now; and it has also ignored a great many others that could be opened up easily, perhaps only with a few months' preliminary work and at a very small cost, where capital investment in small and medium doses could yield solid results in terms of increased production. What the developing countries need most urgently is quick pre-investment work leading to actual capital investment. What the Special Fund has been offering them instead is a large number of extended pre-investment projects with no assurance that investment will follow.

There is, admittedly, genuine need for pre-investment studies in certain cases, such as for mineral development that requires survey and prospecting, for land utilization that involves crop experiments, for major industrial projects that require careful feasibility studies, for large dam projects for which the blue-prints can be prepared only after a considerable amount of studies and investigations. But a truly development-oriented programme must take great care not to overload itself with such projects. Yet this is precisely the bias the Special Fund has zealously cultivated. As a result, it has made virtually all its development effort contingent upon time-consuming pre-investment projects, each running into several years.

The Special Fund has erred no less seriously on another major hypothesis. It has assumed that only when its pre-investment studies are completed, would it be possible to attract, on the strength of their results, capital for long-term investment, usually from abroad. It has therefore ignored what the Fund and the UN family can do by way of directing into productive channels the investment resources, domestic as well as foreign, that are already available.

Thus, the denouement of Special Fund operations, so impressive at first sight, should also be a cause for profound misgivings. It has heavily mortgaged the present to the future, and has thus been instrumental not for speeding, but for retarding, economic growth. And this is happening at a time when the UN is pursuing the goals of the first development decade; when the underdeveloped world is tumultuously clamouring for a better economic life; when, in the words of Eric Hoffer, hope has become desire, and the future is now.

3

The Special Fund, it has been suggested, was born as a cripple. It was denied a capital development fund without which it could hardly achieve any real economic development. This again harks back to the old question of a SUNFED. What are the chances that the UN will be provided with such a fund? And what can and should it do without one?

The SUNFED hope springs eternal in the UN breast. No enlightened person in any part of the world today will question the urgent need of the developing countries for far larger development capital. The question is not the need for more funds, which is transparent, but how to attract the funds which no nation today is overly anxious to part with, even on reasonable commercial terms. The policy hitherto pursued in the forums of the UN family has not helped matters. It has ignored some obvious facts, invited frustrations for itself and for the developing countries, and has generated much ill-feeling into the bargain.

The SUNFED proposal has a long and chequered story behind it. In its first version, it was called the United Nations Fund for Economic Development, which gave the rather unappealing abbreviation of UNFED. This led to the prompt addition of the word "Special" in front of the already lengthy designation.

The proposal, as mentioned in the last chapter, came to a head with particular force in 1957-58, but it ended with the creation of a United Nations Special Fund coupled with a vague expectation that it would some day be converted into a capital development fund.

Hardly was the ink dry on General Assembly resolution 1240 (XIII) establishing the Special Fund when the prospects for such an eventuality receded into deeper uncertainty. For, around the same time, the decision was finally taken to create the International Development Association as a soft-loan subsidiary of the World Bank. Given this decision, the main concern of the major donors was to keep IDA equipped with enough funds. And it was quite clear that they would be even less inclined than before to bless the idea of setting up a separate fund under United Nations control.

Nevertheless, at its fifteenth session, the General Assembly decided,[55] in principle, that a United Nations Capital Development Fund should

---

[55] In resolution 1521 (XV) of 15 December 1960.

be established and resolved that a committee of twenty-five member-states should consider concrete preparatory measures for it. The Committee on a Capital Development Fund submitted its first proposals in 1962. The attitudes of the governments whose views mattered most continued to be negative or noncommittal. The outcome was another compromise resolution passed by the General Assembly at its eighteenth session. All that it did was to ask the Secretary-General "to prepare, in consultation with the appropriate organs of the United Nations and such other institutions as may be necessary, a study of the practical steps to transform the Special Fund into a capital development fund in such a way as to include both pre-investment and investment activities."

Three more years passed without any decision. At last, in December 1966, at its twenty-first session and after a rather prolonged deadlock, the General Assembly passed a resolution[56] authorizing the creation of a Capital Development Fund for an "experimental period." Most of the potential donor governments, including the USA, explicitly dissociated themselves from the resolution, and, after it was passed, made it clear that they would not be able to participate in the Fund. Contributions made to the UNCDF by 1 May 1968 amounted to $1,296,542. Meanwhile, the UNDP Administrator, to whom the management of the Fund has been entrusted under the general supervision of the Governing Council,[57] has decided that the best course would be to allocate this small sum of money to the Asian Development Bank and other Regional Banks. At last the United Nations has a capital development fund. But so far it has remained—unfed!

Thus, the last move, like its predecessors, has been an exercise in futility. That it was bound to be so, could—and should—have been foreseen, particularly at a time when the whole climate for foreign aid had so visibly worsened, when IDA was finding it extremely difficult to obtain a fresh supply of funds. It was, to say the least, unrealistic to assume that the major donors could be *compelled* by resolutions to increase their *voluntary* contributions.

What, then, can the Special Fund or, more correctly, the UN family do in such a situation? There is a tremendous lot it can do. The procedures so carefully developed by the Special Fund could be applied almost in toto to investment projects. In that sense it has been a faithful forerunner of a SUNFED or a UNCDF. Yet it would be wise for the

---

[56] Resolution 2186 (XXI) of 13 December 1966 on Establishment of the United Nations Capital Development Fund (UNCDF).

[57] In accordance with General Assembly resolution 2321 (XXII) of 15 December 1967.

UN not to count on any significant capital development fund of its own, nor even on its ability to attract follow-up investment capital on a substantial scale.

The wisest course for the UN would be to gear its efforts boldly to a far broader and more urgent objective—to help direct the best possible utilization of all the resources that are already available for development in the low-income countries—domestic and foreign, multilateral and bilateral, public and private. Together, they add up to some $30 billion a year—about $6 billion of net external capital and $24 billion generated domestically. This is the greatest—and almost a revolutionary—contribution that the UN family could make in the context of economic development.

For another reason, too, there is no rational alternative to such an approach. What happens to these resources will determine the pace of progress in the developing countries, far more than any additional funds that might be raised abroad today. And this pace of progress—the demonstrable results achieved here and now with the resources ready to hand—will, in its turn, determine their capacity to raise national incomes, to enlarge the volume of domestic savings, to absorb investment capital in productive undertakings, and to attract fresh resources, public and private, from abroad.

Can the UN family undertake such a comprehensive job? It certainly can, provided, however, it knows how to make effective use of the rare assets it possesses, and is able to free itself from the grave liabilities it has created for itself; to be more specific, provided it can make one single programme out of the present congeries of programmes; clear the jungle of procedures that now strangle development; overhaul the administrative machinery in the interest of better management; use the impressive skills of the agencies, but with skill and sense instead of giving free rein to them; appoint top-grade men, with unified responsibility and authority, to serve as country-level representatives; and use the revamped UN machinery and the available UN resources to achieve the primary objective mentioned above.

These questions will be discussed in PART IV in all their ramifications, including a critical examination of the various mental roadblocks and semantic traps that are frequently encountered and that will have to be negotiated. Before doing so, however, it would be worth reviewing, even if in its broad outline, the so-called merger movement in order to understand how the first attempt to merge the UN programmes and to improve their performance foundered on invisible rocks within the UN family.

CHAPTER 13

The Merger Debate: Ad Hoc Decisions Of Ad Hoc Committee

"Reason stands small show against the entrenched power of habit."

ELBERT HUBBARD

The nineteen-sixties began with high expectations for world development under UN auspices. There were many hopeful signs on the horizon. Within a few years, however, they disappeared almost completely. Several factors contributed to that unhappy end. Not the least potent of them was the senseless defence of the old order by veteran old-timers.

The curtain-raiser on the decade was the inaugural address of President Kennedy on 20 January 1961 which brought to vision the grandeur of a new vista of possibilities. To the United Nations which he called "our last best hope," he renewed the pledge of support—"to enlarge the area in which its writ may run." To the people of half the globe struggling to escape from mass misery, he pledged the best efforts to help them help themselves, "for whatever period is required," not to compete with others, not to seek their votes, but "because it is right." And he climaxed this trend of thought with a remark that will not soon lose its relevance to the future of mankind: "If a free society cannot help the many who are poor, it cannot save the few who are rich."

Nine months later—on 25 September 1961—President Kennedy reverted to this theme, when, addressing the United Nations General Assembly, he observed: "Political sovereignty is but a mockery, without the means of meeting poverty, illiteracy and disease. Self-determination is but a slogan if the future holds no hope." That is why he proposed, on hehalf of the USA, that the 1960's be officially designated as the United Nations Decade of Development.

By then, the Special Fund was already an established fact, and its operations had begun to pick up momentum. The voluntary contributions to the UN programmes, too, were rising much faster than before.

At the same time there was a new awareness of the key role of the Resident Representatives. At Secretary-General Dag Hammarskjöld's personal initiative, the Resident Representative's post in Nigeria was elevated to the level of an Under-Secretary, and a former ambassador of Canada was appointed to it. He also combined the post of Resident Representative in India with that of the Director of the United Nations Information Centre (UNIC) as an experimental step with the evident intention of extending it later to other countries. It may be mentioned in passing that both experiments proved short-lived. From the start, they were cordially disliked by old-liners who waited to celebrate their failure, and seized the earliest opportunity to revert to the status quo ante.

Meanwhile, decolonized Africa began to turn increasingly to the UN for assistance. This, Mr. Hammarskjöld emphasized, was easy to understand in view of the fact that the United Nations, since it came into existence, "has had special responsibilities" toward all non-self-governing territories—and of course the trust territories in particular. Besides, "it is understandable," he said, "that assistance, whether financial or technical, may be easier for them to accept when extended through, or in association with, an international body of which they are full and equal members."[58]

This thesis was readily accepted by most people not only in UN circles, but also outside. Simultaneously, there was strong support for channelling US bilateral aid increasingly through the UN system. And this clearly conformed to the trend of thinking of many within the Kennedy administration.[59]

There still remained the practical question, namely, the capacity of the UN family to administer aid effectively and on a substantially increased scale. In knowledgeable circles there was no illusion in this matter. They were well aware of the latent weaknesses of the UN system.

---

[58] Address before the Economic Club of New York on 8 March 1960.

[59] There were, of course, other trends as well. Some, for example, favoured concentration of US aid in countries where it would show the best results.

What, then, could be done to improve the system itself? This immediately became an important question.

2

A major attempt to overhaul the UN machinery was initiated in the early days of the Kennedy administration. On 27 June 1961, at the 32nd session of the Technical Assistance Committee of the ECOSOC, Mr. Harlan Cleveland, then Assistant Secretary of State for International Organization Affairs, made a statement which was equivalent to a keynote address on "Strengthening Technical Cooperation through the United Nations." Among the points he made were the following:

—The moment had come to draw hard on a dozen years of intensive experience, to prepare to take on the greatly expanded job that was waiting to be done, to qualify the UN family of agencies for a larger and more central role.

—The need for better country programming, based on a rational sense of priorities, was perfectly obvious. This was the fundamental prerequisite for rapid yet sound development.

—The UN system of organizations had, for economic and social development, special opportunities and hence a special responsibility.

—There was the great contribution the UN Resident Representatives could and must be expected to make to sound programming in the countries to which they were assigned.

—The specialized agencies—charged as they were "with only a piece of the overall task of development"—were "diffident" about getting into questions of priorities. And the Resident Representatives were not yet concentrating on planning advice as a central concern.

—What was needed was a more tightly coordinated group of all the country representatives of the UN system, headed by the Resident Representative in each country. Such a group needed to reproduce within itself "in microcosm," as it were, the very process of development with all major functions represented in it, and the country's own interest in terms of development as its "primary focus of concern."

—The questions that called for answers related, inter alia, to the best relationship between EPTA and the Special Fund. "Should they be more closely integrated—or even merged?"

—There was also the problem of coordinating the many aid programmes available to a country. The leaders of each developing country were faced with fifteen or twenty and sometimes as many as twenty-five or thirty agencies, international and bilateral, purveying varying forms of technical assistance and investment aid. The problem of coordinating the aid programmes could be solved only at the country level. And a more unified group of the UN system's representatives at country level could assist in relating this remarkable variety of outside aid to the most desirable kind of development within a country.

—Here again, the UN family was in an excellent position to provide "important, nay crucial services" to the development process—if, but only if, the UN family "is organized aggressively for the tasks ahead."

These questions had been "talked" for almost twelve years. "Let us resolve to put enough effort into answering them, in the next twelve months," pleaded Mr. Cleveland. The questions have not yet been answered. Intead, they have been kept "aggressively" alive to this day.

The points raised in this statement, along with the comments made by TAC members, resulted in a draft resolution which was introduced by Brazil, El Salvador, Ethiopia and the USA. The draft, with considerable modification in the light of the subsequent debate, was adopted by TAC and recommended to the Economic and Social Council for adoption. This culminated in ECOSOC resolution 851 (XXXII), which established the Ad Hoc Committee of Eight.

The resolution provided that the Committee should consist of representatives of eight member-states appointed by the ECOSOC President on as wide a geographical basis as possible. Its main task was to undertake a study of the further steps which might be needed:

—To organize the technical cooperation activities of the UN family so as to provide greater aid to the member-states, "on their request, in the preparation of country development programmes," it being understood that the preparation of such national programmes, their implementation and coordination were the prerogative of the governments concerned.

—To bring about a closer coordination, wherever possible, of the technical cooperation and pre-investment activities of the UN family in order to advance the achievement of country development objectives.

—To assist member states by providing technical cooperation services which would be most conducive to their national development.

To explore ways and means to bring about in developing countries "a closer relationship" within the UN system of agencies, giving special attention to the potential role of the resident representatives, so as to provide more concerted advice to countries that request it.

The United Nations, the specialized agencies and IAEA, and the Special Fund were invited to transmit to the Committee any comments they might deem appropriate. The countries designated by the President of the Council as members of the Committee were: Brazil, Ethiopia, France, Japan, USSR, UAR, UK and USA.

So began an arduous and ill-fated experiment in self-reform. The tenor of discussions in TAC, the divergences of views they revealed, the voices of no-changers that were already audible, the objections raised against the text of the resolution, and the caveats that were carefully built into its final version—all these were portents that did not bode well for the future.

3

Whatever prospect there still was of a competent analysis of the problems leading to constructive conclusions was soon dashed by two factors: the preponderantly political composition of the Committee and the patently political approach it adopted in dealing with questions relating to economic development.

The Committee held its first series of meetings in January, 1962. After a preliminary exchange of views, it drew up a consolidated list of some fifty questions reflecting the various points made by its members. This list was addressed to the United Nations, UNICEF, the agencies, the Executive Chairman of TAB, and the Managing Director of the Special Fund, asking for their replies by a specified date. The Committee reassembled after a few months, held ten sessions—during April-May 1962—to discuss the issues mainly on the basis of the replies received to its questionnaire, submitted an interim progress report[60] to the ECOSOC, and decided to resume its work later in the year.

The interim report makes a fascinating study in many respects. It showed once again how widely the views differed; how profound was the lack of understanding of the processes of development; also how little concern there was to understand them; how views were assembled faithfully and mechanically, but without any attempt to sift or evaluate them; how, as a result, all its major conclusions remained glaringly inconclusive.

A point-by-point analysis of such a soulless document would be a meaningless exercise. A sampling of the views, which is representative but not exhaustive, should be in order.

The time had come, some members urged, for a review of technical assistance and pre-investment activities and procedures. In the preceding ten years new programmes, new agencies and new patterns of operation had come into existence; as a result, rigid habits, narrow interests, and "understandable loyalties to well-worn procedures" could have developed. It was imperative that programmes and procedures were well adapted to the tasks of development.

The urgency of improving the Expanded Programme procedures was stressed by a member who submitted concrete proposals to that effect. He wanted the Committee to consider the possibility of "aligning" EPTA procedures with those of the Special Fund, also the desirability of merging the two programmes.

The debate that followed was notable for the diversity of views. There was no common ground, not even a common concern to improve matters. For example, some members saw no need for any basic modification of structure; in their view, the machinery for coordinating the two programmes was, by and large, working satisfactorily.

Another held that the distribution of the resources—of both EPTA and the Special Fund—among the governments was inequitable; and that its rectification should be a matter of high priority.

There should be no "pre-allocation" of funds through such devices as country target figures, urged some members. Others quibbled that fixing country targets under EPTA was not a pre-allocation; that this was only a device to indicate to the countries what volume of assistance they could expect.

The real problem, in the opinion of others, was the inadequacy of resources. The Committee, it was therefore suggested, should endorse

---

[60] Programmes of Technical Cooperation—Report of the Ad Hoc Committee of Eight. E/3639, 21 May 1962.

the Executive Chairman's view that "the most desirable element in the orderly development of EPTA activities and efficient use of resources" was an assurance that the Programme would expand at a steady rate of $5 to $10 million a year. Other members pointed out that the target of $150 million set by the General Assembly for the two programmes had not yet been realized; that the immediate task before governments was to reach this target rather than to consider further expansion. Some questioned whether the Ad Hoc Committee had any competence to recommend financial targets.

Meanwhile, one member took a line that was as striking as it was original. There were large unutilized resources, he stated in obvious reference to the "difficult currencies"; if fully used, they would lead to an expansion of the activities of the programmes. As for a sizable increase in their volume, he emphasized the responsibility of the "colonial powers" in this respect; and also urged the United Nations to respect the principle of "genuine international universality" and therefore to accept contributions from all sources, irrespective of the countries by which they were offered.

The discussion on priorities and concentration of efforts revealed no greater accord. The UN family, suggested a member, should fix priorities for their own programmes, since their limited resources could obviously not meet all requests for assistance; while, within this framework, the governments should be left free to fix their own priorities, with the help of the UN organizations if and when they so desired.

Against this were pressed the familiar views: Any guidance about priorities would "impinge upon the freedom and responsibility of the governments;" the present system with diverse objectives and procedures, though complex, was well adapted to the varied situations and requirements of the developing countries; what was needed was "appropriate coordination without too limitative concentration of activities."

Also on programme review and approval, the established TAB position was well represented in the Committee: The programme authorities were normally in no position to appraise the relevance of individual projects to the development objectives of a recipient government; nor should it be permissible to encroach upon its sovereignty; the country programming procedures of EPTA provided for project review at both the country and the agency level, a system well adapted to a programme with a large number of projects; longer-term projects could, under the latest procedural changes, be prepared on "project programming" basis, while sufficient flexibility was retained for the rest of the Programme; additional flexibility was provided by the Executive Chairman's contingency authority; it could and should be further enhanced by raising the limit for contingency authorizations from 7.5 to ten per cent of the overall EPTA resources.

This testimony, above all, testified to one fact—how well some of the Committee members had been briefed on the traditional TAB approach.

The debate on questions relating to EPTA could produce only a general agreement on some principles, so general that they were almost pointless, viz: it was essential to get the best possible value out of the programme resources; priority in the use of those resources must reflect the genuine needs of the governments; technical assistance requests should be examined carefully and not automatically approved.

As for the Special Fund, the only question raised was about the increased participation of the agencies and of the regional economic commissions of the UN in the examination of projects. In this case, interestingly enough, no one felt concerned that there was any risk of encroaching upon the sovereignty of the recipient governments! There was no discussion of the relative merits and demerits of the radically different procedures followed by the two programmes. Nor was anyone perturbed over the continued coexistence of such vivid incongruities.

As for coordination in the field, members emphasized that this was a responsibility of the recipient governments. The UN family, it was suggested, should help them, when requested, in setting up effective governmental coordination machinery, and organize seminars on technical assistance coordination to familiarize the appropriate officials of the recipient governments with the UN machinery, programmes, procedures and activities.

As regards the Resident Representatives and their relations with the agencies' mission chiefs or representatives, the Committee, with one exception, endorsed the guidelines laid down by the ACC in October 1961,[61] including informal meetings of the agency representatives to be convened periodically under the chairmanship of the resident representatives; and suggested that a report should be compiled, at some suitable time in 1963, on the extent to which the ACC-inspired agreement was being put into effect.

Several other questions were discussed by the Committee, mostly in the same inconclusive fashion, such as the location of TAB and Special Fund headquarters—whether it should be New York or Geneva, OPEX-

---

[61] See Chapter 19, Section 2.

type appointments,[62] recruitment of international experts, regional economic commissions and the question of decentralization and their relations with the Resident Representatives, recruitment of international experts, and the administrative and operational services (AOS) costs of the programmes and of the agencies. As for this last item, the Committee felt that the Secretary-General, with the assistance of the Advisory Committee,[63] should study the question of financial procedures and overhead costs.

4

Finally, and overshadowing all other items, there was the question of a merger of the Expanded Programme and the Special Fund. One delegation, which could only be the USA, proposed that the Secretary-General, with the assistance of the Advisory Committee and such consultants as he might wish to select, should study the possible advantages and disadvantages of a merger of the two programmes in due course.

The comments of the members revealed once again the deep differences of opinion. The present system, according to one member, was unduly complicated and confusing for the developing countries; it was not conducive to effective coordination, to concentration of efforts, or to establishment of priorities. A study therefore should be made of the means to improve the situation so that the question of merger could be considered on its merits.

Another member felt that there would be considerable advantages in merging not only EPTA and the Special Fund, but also the regular programmes, and argued that this would require some major organizational changes involving the governing bodies of the agencies, so that it could be brought about only in stages. He saw no advantages, however, in merging just EPTA and the regular programmes.

On the other hand, some members held that the merger was not technically desirable at this time at least, that it would upset the delicate balance of the present system and would, in effect, impede the efficiency it was supposed to promote. They did not elaborate the arguments further. One member went so far as to state categorically that the statutes, the scope, objectives and activities of the two programmes were different, that his government was opposed to a merger and considered a study of this question quite unnecessary.

---

[62] See Chapter 17, Section 6.

[63] I.e., Advisory Committee on Administrative and Budgetary Questions (ACABQ) of the United Nations.

Some urged that the proposed study should embrace also the regular programmes of the UN and the agencies. They took special care to stress that the study should in no way prejudge the main issues—that is, whether or not a merger was desirable, and whether or not the Special Fund procedures were the best, on the ground that there might well be other and better alternatives.

A few members made it clear that, in their view, the study was not urgently needed, but that they would not oppose it provided that it did not prejudice the establishment of a United Nations Capital Development Fund!

One member entered a different caveat, but no less striking in its implications. In requesting the study, care should be taken, he insisted, not to affect the specific objectives of the various programmes and the flexibility they provided.

Disagreement could hardly be more profound. All that the Committee could agree upon was to recommend to the Council to consider requesting the Secretary-General—with the assistance of the Advisory Committee on Administrative and Budgetary Questions and such consultants as the Secretary-General might consider necessary—*to study*, in consultation, as appropriate, with the specialized agencies, the Executive Chairman of TAB, and the Managing Director of the Special Fund, the possible advantages and disadvantages of a partial or complete merger in due course, *without running counter to the basic objectives of each programme*, of some or all of the technical assistance programmes of the United Nations, i.e., the Regular Programmes, the Expanded Programme and the Special Fund.

The decision, it will be noticed, was both weak and vague. For one thing, the Secretary-General was only to study the issues and assess the pros and cons of a merger, partial or complete. He was to consult, as appropriate, the other members of the UN family. Clearly, no Secretary-General could appropriately deal with such issues without fully consulting them, and consultation could serve only one purpose, namely, reveal all the differences that were known to exist, including strong, at times determined, opposition of the smaller programmes against any merger proposal. Besides, the Committee explicitly stated that the study was not to run "counter to the basic objectives of each programme." The anti-merger ring in the phrase was loud and clear.

Finally, the UN itself was far from a disinterested party. It had its own regular programme, and it was no more willing to give up control over it than the agencies were ready to surrender control over theirs.

The Committee could not have been unaware of these facts. Evidently, as the reform proposal bogged down in endless dissensions, its prime supporter brought up the proposal for further study by the Secretary-General as a last-minute formula in a desparate attempt to avert a complete failure and to keep alive a ray of hope, however faint, for the future.

5

The report of the Committee was submitted to the thirty-fourth session of the Economic and Social Council, in summer 1962. The Council, in its stylized fashion, commended the work of the Committee, considered the proposals for further study and, with due solemnity, rubber-stamped its approval.

The Council Resolution 900 A (XXXIV), as adopted in this session, requested the Ad Hoc Committee to continue its work, and to submit a progress report to its thirty-sixth session (in summer 1963) and a final report to its thirty-eighth session (in summer 1964). It also provided for the appointment of two more members to the Committee which, with this addition—the new members were Indonesia and Jordan—became a Committee of Ten. The Secretary-General was requested to undertake the study as proposed in the Committee's interim report.

Thus, what was conceived as a short-term exercise to carry out overdue reforms now grew, at the least, into a three-year project, not an insignificant victory for those who had been opposed to any change.

The Committee convened for its second session in March 1963, held fourteen meetings, and went over the same dreary round of debate over the same divisive views, occasionally with fresh refinements and new ramifications, but all leading, step by step, further away from the original purpose for which it had been set up. By then, the merger issue was well merged in hopeless disagreements.

As required by Resolution 900 A (XXXIV), the Committee submitted a progress report[64] to the thirty-sixth session of the Council, in which it, once again, faithfully recorded all the conflicting views and was therefore unable to report any progress. A fiasco seemed imminent, but for the second time the Committee shied away from it.

The device adopted on this occasion to put off the inevitable was slightly different. The Council, under the promptings of the Committee, adopted Resolution 954 (XXXVI) in which it requested the Secretary-General: (a) to transmit the interim report of the Ad Hoc

---

[64] In document E/3639.

Committee, as well as the records of the debate in TAC and the ECOSOC, to all member-states of the United Nations or of the specialized agencies and "to invite their comments and observations on the issues raised in this report;" and (b) to prepare an analysis of the views received in time for consideration by the Ad Hoc Committee early in 1964 to assist the ECOSOC and the General Assembly in their consideration of the Ad Hoc Committee's final report.

This *ad hoc* decision was taken by the second highest legislative organ of the UN family, even though its futility could be clearly foreseen. How were the governments to comment on the bulky documents that were mainly records of irreconcilable differences voiced in the Ad Hoc Committee and in TAC? And why should they respond at all to such a request when they knew only too well that they stood, not by choice but by chance, at the receiving end of an unedifying buck-passing ceremony?

The decision had some ironical implications as well, although they went almost universally unnoticed. The UN family was supposed to help the developing countries, with advice and guidance in their development, under the UN programmes. Yet its members were unable to agree among themselves as to how best to handle this business; and so they decided to seek from those very countries guidance on methods and procedures! Thus, the relations between the givers and the receivers of technical assistance were, by some strange twists of events, turned-topsy-turvy.

Assuming that the Secretary-General did receive comments and observations from the governments, how was he to analyze them meaningfully? All he could do was to bunch them together or at best prepare a fresh catalogue of discordant views and opinions. It was hard to see how such an operation could ever help the Council and the General Assembly in considering the Ad Hoc Committee's final report.

One again the effect of the Council's resolution was only to prolong indecision, and to keep the whole question of merger in a state of suspended animation.

CHAPTER 14

UNDP or Half-A-Merger

"Just think of all the efforts we put in only to achieve this puny merger!"

AN OLD-TIMER.

The Ad Hoc Committee was set up in the hope that it would draw up a blueprint for reform. What it produced, in two voluminous instalments, was a babel of views. The Council resolutions were, predictably enough, leading nowhere. All the actions taken so far seemed only to consolidate a deadlock with no sign of a break anywhere in sight.

At this point, the major donor, according to reliable reports, decided to intervene, informally but decisively. One of its senior aides made a démarche to the appropriate quarters in the UN secretariat and let it clearly be understood that his government was far from happy over the way things were going in the Ad Hoc Committee, nor did it have any doubt about the real source of the difficulty—some had been playing the bureaucratic game of defending the status quo rather too well; that the Expanded Programme had hitherto done the best it could, but that the time had definitely come to look ahead and to take some decisive steps, to revamp the UN programmes and machinery in the interest of speedier development; that, as an essential step in that direction, the two programmes—EPTA and the Special Fund—would have to be merged.

This presentation, according to the same report, was supplemented by a clear indication of the consequences that would otherwise ensue. If the merger continued to be resisted, then there would be no other alternative than to advise his government to withold contributions to the Programme pending settlement of the issue.

Apparently, the démarche had its effect. Things began to move; from then on it was no longer a question of whether or not there was to be a merger, but only of what kind of merger it was going to be.

2

What followed next can be best summed up with an old Sanskrit saying: "When danger threatens the whole, the wise part with one-half." Given the inevitability of a merger, the anti-merger school changed its tactics. It moved from a stalemated situation to an attempt to salvage as much of the status quo as possible; in short, to accept a merger in form but to surrender only a minimum of substance. In this it achieved a large measure of success, aided by two notable factors—a favourable climate of deep differences within the UN system and a none-too-deep understanding of the processes of development.

Late in 1963, on the personal initiative of the Secretary-General, some merger proposals were evolved, which were first discussed with the executive heads of the specialized agencies and of the two major programmes, and then submitted, in a two-part report,[65] to the Ad Hoc Committee and the Council for consideration in January 1964. In this report the Secretary-General made two main recommendations: First, the Expanded Programme and the Special Fund should be merged, at the intergovernmental, inter-agency and management levels, to create a United Nations Development Programme (UNDP). And second, there should be no merger of the regular programmes of the United Nations and the agencies, which could be left as before.

The report was prepared in response to Resolution 900 A (XXXIV) based on the recommendation of the Ad Hoc Committee made in its first interim report. The Committee had suggested that outside consultant or consultants "who are expert in administrative and organization matters," might assist in the study, as determined by the Secretary-General. No such experts were employed. The Committee had requested a study of the possible advantages and disadvantages of a partial or complete merger. The Secretary-General preferred not to deal with them in his report and to state, instead, the conclusions to which he had been led by his study.

No wonder that the report should have been surprisingly thin in substance. It left many questions unanswered, while at least some of

---

[65] Co-ordination of Technical Assistance Programmes—Report of the Secretary-General under Resolution 900 A (XXXIV). Part I—EPTA and Special Fund, E/3850, 9 January 1964; and Part II—Regular Programmes of UN and the Agencies, E/3851, 31 January 1964.

its statements sounded more like downright assertions than like well-argued propositions. In fact, the proposals emerged not out of any objective, scientific analysis undertaken in the interest of development, but out of intensive soundings of the various interests—the executive heads of the agencies and of the programmes, and some key delegations. As such, they represented what was politically feasible, not economically desirable.

The main conclusions arrived at by the Secretary-General, as stated in the introductory part of his report, are worth noting. He was "not unmindful" of the reasons that had led to the creation of the Special Fund as separate from, in spite of its being complementary to, the Expanded Programme of Technical Assistance. But he believed that those very reasons now pointed to their unification within a broader structure. The report did not elaborate further.

The Secretary-General believed that "certain organizational rearrangements would offer obvious advantages and be entirely feasible." He was recommending them irrespective of the outcome of the discussions that were then in process on the question of establishing a United Nations Capital Development Fund. But he believed that the proposals would provide "a more solid basis" for the future growth of the UN programmes "in this direction or in others." This was evidently intended to disarm those who held out for some kind of a SUNFED and opposed a merger on that ground.

His consultations with the executive heads of the agencies and the two programmes—EPTA and the Special Fund—had revealed general agreement on the advantages of a merger at the intergovernmental, inter-agency and management levels. But they had also revealed that no attempt at closer integration would be fruitful, that "the most valuable elements in the machinery and methods of work of both the TAB and the Special Fund" had to be preserved. This was a masterpiece of petitio principii. Nobody in his senses would have suggested that the most valuable elements should be jettisoned, just as every intelligent person would have liked to know what precisely these elements were and why they were considered valuable. This was a thumping omission, and it left an alert mind wondering about the cogency of the proposals.

Moreover, the merger, to be fruitful, had to respect "the constitutional relationships" among the participating organizations and "the responsibility of each of them" within its respective fields. Again, the most important questions were those that were not asked: What were the real needs for development? Was there any conflict between them and the so-called constitutional rights of the agencies or their special responsibilities? If so, how best could it be resolved? For, the task before a conscientious programme of development is how to maximize development, and not to compromise it at the first sight of some obstacles.

In making his proposals the Secretary-General, according to the report, aimed at securing "the most efficient implementation of the present programmes of EPTA and the Special Fund," also at enabling the UN family to undertake additional activities of an international character (but without prejudice "to the autonomous expansion of the existing organizations under their respective constitutions"). It was more or less assumed that, given the proposed merger, the industrialized countries as a whole would be inclined to channel more development assistance through the UN system.

These were laudable aims, eagerly sought after by all well-wishers of the UN programmes and of the developing countries. What was not recognized, however, was that they could not be realized in the absence of radical reforms in programming procedures and methods, at headquarters and even more at the country level, about which the report said practically nothing.

3

After these preambular observations, the specific proposals made in the report appeared very much like an anticlimax. First, the countries contributing to and benefiting from the UN programmes would, it was averred, be best served "by bringing EPTA and the Special Fund together in a new *United Nations Development Programme.*" The circumlocution was perhaps not accidental. It seemed to imply that there was to be no merging, but only a "bringing together" of the two programmes, though subsequently the operation came to be hailed by others as a merger.

Second, there would be a single intergovernmental body, tentatively called the *Inter-Governmental Committee,* to provide general policy guidance and direction for, and necessary supervision over, the Programe as a whole. This new Committee was intended to replace the then existing governing bodies, that is, TAC of the Expanded Programme and the Governing Council of the Special Fund.

Third, an *Inter-Agency Board* was to be established with the participation of the Head of the combined Programme or UNDP, the Secretary-General of the UN, the executive heads of the specialized agencies (including the President of the IBRD), or their representatives.

This new Board, which was to participate in and facilitate the process of decision-making and policy formulation, was conceived as a substitute for the Technical Assistance Board of EPTA and of the Consultative Board of the Special Fund.

And finally, the Programme would be managed by a "Head" and a "Co-Head"—the exact titles were to be determined later—who would exercise their responsibility for the combined Programme under the policy guidance and direction of the Inter-governmental Committee and in full consultation with the Inter-Agency Board.

The proposals, as sketched in the report, left open one big question: how was the new Inter-Agency Board going to function? Or, more specifically, was it going to be a prototype of the Technical Assistance Board of EPTA where authority was shared equally by its members and decisions were taken collectively by them? Or, was it to be a magnified replica of the Consultative Board functioning, as its name implied, only in an advisory capacity? In short, should the so-called merger be the TAB way or the Special Fund way?

This was an issue of seminal importance. And it was on this issue that views differed most strongly and the negotiations proved most difficult. The Secretary-General's proposals, even in their final formulation, were rather indecisive on this point, although the nomenclature used was more akin to the TAB tradition: an Intergovernmental Committee—not Governing Council, an Inter-Agency Board—not Consultative Board, Head and Co-Head—not Managing Director and Co-Director. Also significant was the remark that the Head of the Programme would consult with the Board and "would express a consensus of its views to the fullest extent practicable and consistent with his responsibilities to the Programme as a whole." This remark, and particularly the word "consensus" as used here, seemed to imply that the Board was intended to be something more than just consultative.

The TAB protagonists would, no doubt, have plumped for a merger if they could have it their own way. This had been their dream all along, and it would have made belated amends for the disappointment they had suffered in 1957 when the Special Fund was established as a separate programme. However, they soon realized that it was too late to turn the clock back, that there was no chance of a merger being consummated the TAB way; that the only alternative they had was to defend the TAB position to the utmost possible extent, as had been done in 1957 when EPTA had successfully resisted a real risk of being swallowed up by the Special Fund.

The long tussle ended with a three-way compromise. It was agreed that the Consultative Board of the Special Fund would be enlarged —from four to sixteen members—in order to accommodate all the specialized agencies. But the Board must function only in a consultative capacity, and not as a collective decision-making body. On this point the Special Fund school was adamant from the start. The result was an agreement in favour of creating what was finally called an Inter-Agency Consultative Board that would resemble TAB in its composition, but the Special Fund's Consultative Board in its function.

The third compromise was far more fundamental and in many ways decisive, at least for the immediate future. It was agreed that the merger should be confined only to the three points mentioned above and would not be extended to the programmes; that each programme would there- fore continue to be administered as before with its own funds, its own methods and procedures, its own philosophy whatever it might be, and in any case with no change in the character of country pro- gramming or in the responsibiilty and authority of the Resident Rep- resentatives.

The report concluded with observations which could not be easily reconciled with facts. A consolidation along the lines proposed was con- sidered desirable as it sought to maintain "all that has proved most valuable to governments in the existing arrangements." In actual fact, the proposed consolidation was best suited to maintain what had proved "valuable" to some programme-managers and to the specialized agen- cies, often at the cost of actual development.

Again, retention of "the best practices" of the Expanded Programme and the Special Fund, the report stated, would help meet the fun- damental desire of all, namely, to enable assistance channelled through the UN system "to produce maximum constructive effects." It would have been much more to the point to say that by indiscriminately retaining the practices of both programmes, including the worst fea- tures of EPTA, the new move only prejudiced the prospects of im- proving the effectiveness of the UN programmes.

And finally, it was held that the proposed action would make a notable contribution toward other objectives such as simplification of administration, strengthening inter-agency cooperation, more adequate assessment of the priority needs in the developing countries, and more fruitful utilization of resources. Here, evidently, wish was father to the thought. In any case, all these objectives could unquestionably have been far better served if the two Programmes were not simply "brought together" or "consolidated" as provided in the Secretary-General's scheme, but completely merged and administrated with business-like methods and procedures.[66]

4

The second part of the Secretary-General's report was devoted to the question of a possible merger of "regular" and other programmes.[67] It reviewed in detail the purpose, growth, nature of operations and the size of each regular programme, that is, of the United Nations, the ILO, FAO, UNESCO, WHO and IAEA respectively; the other agencies, i.e., WMO, ITU and ICAO had no regular programmes. It then briefly considered the desirability and the feasibility of a merger. The conclusion it arrived at was that a merger would solve no problems and would bring new ones in its wake, even if it were constitutionally feasible; that the best course would therefore be to leave the regular programmes as they were. The arguments used in support of this conclusion looked, prima facie, cogent and persuasive. Yet as a closer examination would show, they rested largely on shaky premises.

First, the regular programme, for example, of the United Nations was able to respond more quickly to the needs of the recipient governments since, unlike EPTA or UNDP/TA, it had neither established country targets nor a fixed two-year programming cycle. This, however, was clearly an argument for eliminating the rigid procedures of UNDP/TA, and not for maintaining separate regular programmes. To justify first the continuation of these procedures lock, stock and barrel, as was done in the first part of the report, and then to use them as an argument for continuing the separate existence of the regular programmes was not very convincing logic.

Second, the regular programmes "act as a spearhead" for the initiation of new types of assistance, and therefore they formed "a natural complement" to EPTA or UNDP/TA. It was not explained how several spearheads pointing at the underdeveloped countries were going to help development; why new types of activities would in themselves be a desirable thing. And assuming that some very desirable areas of development actually fell outside the ambit of EPTA, should it not have been an argument for widening the latter rather than for continuing separate programmes? To regard EPTA as something immutable in

---

66 This is discussed fully in Chapter 17. For the Secretary-General's most recent criticism of the present operations of the UN system, see extracts quoted in the Author's Preface.

67 Co-ordination of Technical Assistance Programmes. Ibid., Part II on Regular Programmes. E/3851, 31 January 1964.

scope and in methods was unwarranted, and therefore also the conclusion drawn from such a premise.

Third, the regular programmes were handled by the same staff within each organization as the activities financed by EPTA or the Special Fund. Their merger would therefore produce no significant saving in administrative costs. Indeed, its result, according to some, might even be not simplification, but greater complexity leading to increased rather than reduced administrative expenditure. Those with inside knowledge of the organizations will find it hard to subscribe to this thesis. The merger should reduce the total workload—for programming, operation, reporting, and routine administration, and should therefore make it possible to reduce significantly the staff and the overhead costs.

Besides, workload and administrative costs are largely a function of methods and procedures. And it is always possible to compress an excessive amount of both even into a small programme, as EPTA or UNDP/TA has so clearly demonstrated. This, however, need not be the case.

Fourth, there was the question of the "additional resources" that would be needed to finance "all the activities" of the regular programmes, assuming these were merged with the UNDP. This, according to the report, was a question that could be answered only by governments.

The point was no doubt valid, but it was far from helpful. All matters requiring legislation could, after all, be decided only by governments acting through the appropriate UN organs. In raising the very question of a merger, they were, by implication, indictaing a desire to review and, if necessary, to amend the various legislation they had passed from time to time. And in referring the issue to the Secretary-General with an explicit request to study and report on the pros and cons of a possible merger, they were, in effect, seeking from him guidance and recommendations for future action. Of these they received very little.

And finally, the report stressed, and quite rightly, that the merger issue was linked to the "fundamental questions" regarding the structure of the United Nations system. Yet it was clear that the UN family, with all its structural problems, had already embarked upon the field of economic development on a significant scale, and was constantly pleading, despite these fundamental issues, for an expansion of its activities. Was it not also a responsibility of the UN family to face up to the question as to how best it could adapt its own structure to deal adequately with the multiplying problems of development, visibly aggravated by its own organizational weaknesses? Of this there was no hint or suggestion in the report.

The arguments led up to a patently negative conclusion. A merger of the regular programmes, whether with EPTA or with the proposed UNDP, "would raise more problems than it would resolve," and its "disadvantages would outweigh any possible advantage." What was needed was "a central" United Nations Development Programme "complemented" by the regular programmes of the various agencies with "their distant characteristics and procedures." This, according to the report, was the most effective means for the United Nations system as a whole to fulfil "its diverse responsibilities" towards its member-states.

This last phrase contains the key to the whole problem. Are the responsibilities so diverse, after all, so far as the programmes in question are concerned? Do they not—and should they not—aim at an identical objective—the development of the economically backward countries? The question that was not answered, not even considered, was the one that should have been overriding in this context, namely: what kind of programme and approach were needed to enable the UN family to serve this primary objective with maximum effectiveness.

5

The Secretary-General's proposals were considered by the Ad Hoc Committee of Ten in its final session—in February-March 1964 when it held fifteen meetings. The Committee also had before it the replies received from governments. Only twenty of them had sent some kind of comments, and only eleven of them had done so by the prescribed deadline. Some members were less than happy over the number of replies received, the absence of any secretariat analysis of those replies, also over the fact that the Secretary-General's report had set forth only his conclusions, and not a study of the possible advantages and disadvantages of a partial or complete merger, as had been requested in the Council resolution.

The debate that ensued once again revealed a wide divergence of views. However, a majority of the Committee favoured the creation of one intergovernmental body and of some inter-agency advisory body for both EPTA and the Special Fund. Even within this majority, however, there was considerable disagreement on questions relating to a merger at the management level. Some favoured one centralized management with one single fund for both programmes. This, however, had to be ruled out to avoid a split within the pro-merger majority.

The final decision was to maintain two funds, as well as most EPTA procedures, especially country targets and country programming.

The majority decisions were embodied in a draft resolution which was introduced, at the thirty-ninth meeting of the Committee, by the representative of the United States. The draft, with some amendments, was adopted by 6 votes to 3 with 1 abstention.[68]

The opponents of the resolution used several arguments. The issues involved, they held, had not been studied with sufficient thoroughness. Besides, the merger, in their view, would prejudice the prospects of converting the Special Fund into a Capital Development Fund, which was then under consideration. The assurance given by the Secretary-General on this point cut no ice with them.

They also felt that the benefits expected from the proposal had been overstated. For example, a merger, it had been claimed by its supporters, would result in a larger flow of funds to the Programmes. The Managing Director of the Special Fund had stated his conviction that, given the merger, further increases would be forthcoming; "otherwise, we are going to have difficulty in holding our own." This, presumably, reflected what was going on behind the scenes at that time. But several members did not see the relevance between the merger and the volume of contributions; nor did they agree that the reorganization was necessary to provide a more solid basis for the future growth of the UN programmes, as was stated in the resolution.

Finally, it was held that the merger would mean the absorption of EPTA by the Special Fund, and that this would reduce the effectiveness of the programmes. This was the view expressed all along by the USSR representative.

What is particularly worth noting is that even the United Kingdom and France had serious reservations. They were not convinced that the merger would have all the advantages that had been claimed for it. They supported the resolution for two reasons: first, because the separateness of the two programmes was going to be preserved; and second, because the majority considered it desirable to create a combined governing body and a single inter-agency consultative body. In fact, but for this half-hearted support given by the UK and France, there would have been no majority even for the halfhearted merger proposal.

---

[68] For the text of the resolution, including the first draft and the amendments, see the Final Report of the Ad Hoc Committee, E/3862, 10 March 1964. The roll-call vote showed: in favour—Jordan, UK, USA, Indonesia, France, Japan; against —USSR, UAR, Brazil; abstaining—Ethiopia.

As for the regular programmes, some members wanted them to be merged with the EPTA on the basis of EPTA principles. This, they held, would advance the cause of country development objectives. Another suggestion made was only to merge, with certain given conditions, the United Nations regular programmes with EPTA. This evoked the prompt reply that it would be "illogical" to leave the programmes of the specialized agencies untouched and yet "to deprive" the United Nations of its own regular programme.

The UK representative submitted a 4-point formula designed to maintain the regular programmes as they were and to help work out a kind of modus vivendi between them and EPTA. Activities that could be carried out equally well under EPTA, it was suggested, should be left to that Programme; the regular programmes should concentrate on types of assistance not suitable for EPTA procedures, such as research programmes at headquarters, advisory assignments of a regional or inter-regional character. It was also suggested that there should be "maximum flexibility" in drawing up the programmes, whatever this overworked phrase might mean. Finally, there was the commonplace or revolutionary proposal, depending on one's viewpoint, namely that the specialized agencies should, like the United Nations, make use of the Resident Representatives for negotiating their regular programme activities.

Much of the discussion centred round these proposals. Of particular interest was the stand taken by WHO. From the very start of the merger debate, in 1962, the agency made its position clear. First, the United Nations Charter, in Article 17, paragraph 3, provides that the General Assembly "shall examine" the administrative budgets of the specialized agencies with a veiw to "making recommendations" to the agencies concerned. The Executive Board of the agency held that funds appropriated by the World Health Organization must continue to be governed solely by WHO; that, therefore, a merger of its regular programme would run counter to the provision of the UN Charter.

Second, the WHO constitution provides that assistance should be given to member-governments in direct consultation with them. The agency could not deviate from this constitutional provision and was therefore unable to depend on the Resident Representatives for programe negotiation, nor use them as the channel of communication with governments.

Third, WHO had always considered that Expanded Programme was "to supplement, not supplant," its regular programme of technical assistance. Any other approach would, in effect, be repugnant to its constitution.

And finally, the agency, unlike other members of the UN system, made no distinction between developed and underdeveloped countries in giving its assistance. The problems of disease and promotion of health transcended this primarily economic distinction. As an example it cited the case of smallpox which had suddenly appeared in Europe in 1962-63. It had been transported from another part of the world where smallpox was a chronic and serious problem. The developed countries were keenly interested in eradicating smallpox at its source, and in this respect they had a common concern with the developing countries.

The strong WHO stand had been largely anticipated. In fact, interested parties had confidentaly counted on it in their strategy for forestalling change. It reinforced the negative conclusion of the Secretary-General's report. In spite of some disagreement in the Committee, the majority of its members had no difficulty in agreeing on his no-merger recommendation.[69]

6

The final report of the Ad Hoc Committee of Ten was next reviewed by the ACC. Out of this emerged a draft Assembly resolution which incorporated the recommendations of the Ad Hoc Committee and was patterned closely on the resolution adopted by it. The Economic and Social Council, in its Resolution 1020 (XXXVII) of 11 August 1964, recommended the draft to the General Assembly for approval.

This approval had to suffer an unexpected delay as the nineteenth session of the Assembly foundered on the question of finances for the peace-keeping force. It was finally adopted, on 25 November 1965, as General Assembly resolution 2029 (XX).[70] And as provided in paragraph 8, it went into force on 1 January 1966 when the United Nations Development Programme came into existence.

The structure of the UNDP followed closely what had been envisaged by the Secretary-General and the Ad Hoc Committee. The inter-governmental committee was called the Governing Council, as in the case of the Special Fund. It was to consist of 37 members to be elected by the ECOSOC—19 seats were allocated to the developing countries, 17 to the economically developed countries, one seat was earmarked for Yugoslavia.

---

[69] The questions relating to a merger of the regular programmes are examined in Chapter 17, Sections 8-9.

[70] For the text of the resolution, see Appendix III.

The heads of the UNDP were now called Administrator and Co-Administrator, and the first incumbents of these posts were the Managing Director of the Special Fund and the Executive Chairman of TAB respectively.

So ended the marathon debate that had begun on a distant summer day in 1961, at the TAC session in Geneva. The goals which the sponsors of reforms had in view are still almost as remote as ever. The finale came as a veritable anticlimax. Well might an old-timer call it "a puny merger."

This represented the inner feeling of many officials within the UN family, and they included most Resident Representatives. "They speak of a merger, but where is it," wondered a senior UN aide after watching the first year of UNDP operations. "Things are going on as before." The fact is that the programmes have not been merged; only their problems, particularly those of EPTA, have been submerged.

How well this has been done is borne out by another fact. The General Assembly resolution creating the UNDP was heralded as a historic event of great moment. It served as a signal for more vigorous effort to publicize the achievements of the UN programmes. The problems that had dogged them for years faded before these glowing accounts, or were lost in the stepped-up din of the fundraising campaign. The Assembly resolution carried the enticing title: "Mobilizing for Progress." It could, more correctly, be called: "Mobilizing for Publicity."

Several factors conspired to bring about this odd consummation. The sponsors who had initiated the reform movement, soon realized the uphill nature of their task. As the prospects of a complete failure stared them in the face, they were anxious to salvage at least something out of it. There followed, as indicated before, more determined moves behind the scenes to bring about a merger of the two main programmes. They ended in what was, in effect, a shotgun wedding.

This enforced union, it has been suggested, was a face-saving device on the part of its sponsor. It was certainly more than that. In the sponsor's view, half-a-merger was evidently better than no merger. No doubt they had also entertained a strong hope that, despite all its imperfections, it would provide the new UNDP administration with enough leverage to bring about essential reforms and, through suitable administrative measures, to attain gradually the cherished goals which had eluded the legislative arm of the UN system.

This hope, however natural, was misplaced. For one thing, it took inadequate account of the fact that those very powerful forces which had successfully reduced the reform movement to a stalemate, would continue to work and with no nobler motivation than before. It also made insufficient allowance for another fact: that the mood and behaviour of partners in a shotgun wedding might develop in unpredictable ways; that, in short, the newly-formed UNDP might undergo changes, evolve erratically, even lose sight of the goals in question.

It was amusing to see how gratified some were now that the two programmes were put together and added up to a larger sum of money. What was not so amusing, however, was to watch how many old critics of the TAB operations developed, almost overnight, a new tolerance for its weird procedures they used to run down in caustic terms; how deeply committed some were to the acquisition of power rather than to the cause and the quality of management; how fast the swollen UNDP establishment began to contract the grand disease of our times—over-centralization with rule-ridden exercise of authority, regulated thinking, and no elbow-room for creative deviation; and how many felt surprisingly at ease with it.

The long and sad story of the merger movement and its aftermath can be summed up in two simple sentences: The entrenched no-changers, through adroit manoeuvres and capitalizing on the multiple rifts in the UN system, won an outstanding victory. The cause of development of the world's impoverished nations suffered a resounding defeat.

CHAPTER 15

Why Anomalies Die Hard

"The bee's life in its channel of habit has no opening,—it revolves within a narrow circle of perfection."

TAGORE

The UN family has been loud in proclaiming its special responsibilities and special opportunities in guiding the development of the world's poorer nations. Yet it has been surprisingly slow, nay unwilling, to organize itself sensibly for its great tasks. This contradiction set the stage for one of the worst defaults of our times.

Much of the preceding discussions has been concerned with machinery and methods, with the modus operandi of the programmes instead of their actual substance. This may appear unusual, but the explanation is quite simple. It is the defective organization and methods of the programmes and machinery of the UN family that have hurt it most, that have been a prolific source of its woes, that continue even today to undermine its practical value as a tool of economic progress.

This, as mentioned previously, was perfectly clear to the Kennedy administration. For example, in concluding his statement at the TAC session on 27 June 1961 (see Chapter 13) Mr. Cleveland made the following observation: "Organizational and administrative techniques are not as dramatic as the genuine substance of technical assistance, and general economic and social aid. Yet in their prosaic context they can spell the difference between success and failure—between effective and wasteful use of resources." This is precisely what has happened to the UN development effort. And it explains, far more than any other factor, the tragically wide gap between what the UN family could have achieved in this troubled world with a more orderly approach, and the actual record of achievements it has to its credit so far.

Why, then, have anomalies proved so obdurate and have endured so long within the UN system? And what, if any, are the likly remedies? The answers to these questions have, at least to some extent, been implicit in what has been said in the foregoing pages. It should, however, be useful at this stage to bring them to a better focus and to shed a little more light on them.

2

The Ad Hoc Committee worked for three full years. During this period it did not seek advice from any professional consultants or experts. It did not visit any recipient countries; and it did not interview any Resident Representatives for their views and suggestions as derived from their actual experience. Instead, it heard or received statements made on behalf of the UN, the agencies, the Expanded Programme and the Special Fund. And for the rest, it confined itself to discussions among its own members.

Such an approach was doomed to fail as could, and should, have been foreseen. Each party reiterated its own viewpoint, and defended its special interests with a shield that the Committee could hardly penetrate. All that it was served was a rehash of old ideas and policies. The approach it followed was ideally suited not to formulate and push through reform proposals, but to keep things on an even keel—as before.

True, the Committee did issue a comprehensive questionnaire which contained 51 questions, but they touched the real problems no more than tangentially. They almost conveyed the impression that the Committee was engaged in a kind of information-gathering enterprise rather than in a thorough diagnostic investigation.

Moreover, the circulation of the questionnaire was confined to the same parties mentioned above, i.e., the UN organizations and the heads of the programmes. The Technical Assistance Board did consult the field representatives in preparing its own replies. The whole questionnaire was sent to half-a-dozen selected Resident Representatives, while most of the others were asked to comment on five questions directly relating to the field offices. The replies received from them were supposed to have been taken into account by the TAB administration in preparing its own replies for the Committee. How much bearing they actually had on the latter was not visible. What was visible was that the TAB replies hewed undeviatingly to the traditional line. Several field representatives were unhappy over this indirect mode of consultation. In their eyes, its real value was mainly ritualistic.

3

That a programme or an agency should tend to grow and expand— build its own "hive," so to say—and to defend itself with all conceivable means is a common phenomenon. It springs no doubt from deeper human impulses and is therefore manifest both in national and in international life.

However, public undertakings or institutions, especially in the developed countries, are subject to a number of checks and balances, such as an independent and vigilant legislature, higher audit of policies and performance on a regular basis, periodic investigations of major segments by ad hoc bodies of experts, a watchful public that wants to see results, an alert press, and, of course, periodic changes of regimes with reshuffles of key personnel. They serve as brakes and help counteract undesirable trends.

These safeguards are weak or nonexistent in the case of UN programmes and agencies; as a result, even though headquartered in the developed countries, they are not disciplined in a similar fashion. For one thing, there is no world public opinion, except perhaps on major issues like war and peace. And whatever opinion exists mostly suffers from a two-way or three-way split, which is reflected in the composition of the legislative organs of the UN system and in many of their decisions.

The existence of a whole series of specialized agencies, each with its own constitution and its governing body, has accentuated the sectional or compartmental approach far beyond what is encountered in a national government, and has thereby introduced enormous complications into the decision-making processes.[71]

The great majority of the members of the legislative or governing bodies are not distinguished by their capacity to comprehend the practical problems of development, not to speak of their ability to bring mature judgment to bear on their solution. Only too often their outlook is coloured by purely political considerations. On top of this, there are constant changes in the composition of the legislative bodies because of their rotating membership and the practice, widespread among the member-governments, to change the personnel of their delegations from year to year, sometimes even from session to session.

The result has been an almost complete dependence of the legislative bodies of the UN family on its executive branch, that is, on the secretariats of the UN, the agencies and the different programmes. And

---

[71] See Chapter 18, sections 1-2.

this provided an ideal climate in which secretariat politics could flourish more or less unchecked. Each establishment was engrossed in what it considered to be its own interest, and began to revolve within a "narrow circle of perfection."

Meanwhile, the ideological cleavage that has characterized the contemporary world could not but affect the key UN bodies; it was clearly reflected in their composition, and it often undermined their effectiveness. For the secretariats it has been easy to fish in troubled ideological waters; and not all have been able to withstand the temptation.

To take another example, there are reasons to believe that behind the strange procedures adopted by the Expanded Programme in 1954 in the name of country programming lay the dexterous manoeuvres of some who wanted to pit the recipient countries against the specialized agencies, while still continuing direct allocation to the agencies for regional projects. This was considered to be a master stroke that helped establish and maintain peace in the Technical Assistance Board. So indeed it was, but only politically. For this the Programme had to pay a high price.

A senior executive, addressing the Technical Assistance Committee at one of its sessions once stated, inter alia, that the prerogative of the governments of assisted countries to decide what kinds of assistance they wanted was one the administration had tried to foster and to protect. It is casicr to flatter sovereign governments than to serve them wisely and conscientiously; and not a few have in the past opted for the easier course.

Now, contrast the above with the following remark made by the World Bank in its last report: "In providing external finance for projects of high economic priority, and in offering advice on a wide range of development problems in the less developed countries, the Bank Group may help bring about a more effective use of domestic resources and of assistance made available under bilateral programs."[72] Active professional advice to governments to help build their own economies is in no way incompatible with meticulous respect for their sovereignty.

Then there is the principle of equitable geographical distribution of secretariat posts. An international organization must perforce abide by this principle. Yet it also introduces certain risks in the form of opportunities for patronage and of the temptation to recruit "safe" men even at the cost of competence. The secretariats have a rather heavy turnover of personnel, especially at certain professional levels,

---

[72] World Bank and IDA—Annual Report 1966-67, page 6-7.

because of the question of geographical representation and of the rotation between the headquarters and the field. The result is a curious situation where people rotate around problems which tend to acquire an everlasting quality, or where one might more poetically say: Men may come and men may go, but problems live on for ever.

No wonder that Lincoln's well-known dictum—that one can fool all the people some of the time, and some of the people all the time, but not all of the people all of the time—should have a strictly limited validity in the UN environment. Because of the vast spread of the UN system, and its programmes and operations, the size and nature of its "clients," the composition of its governing bodies, over-rapid changes of personnel at certain levels, it is possible for a great many people to be fooled for a surprisingly long time, sometimes not excluding the decision-makers themselves from this category.

The great social reformers of Britain, Sidney and Beatrice Webb,[73] —as the wit put it, they had blue reports in their veins—used to say that a public corporation should work within glass walls. As a custodian of public interests it must be fully accountable to the public; and for the same reason its operations should be fully exposed to the public gaze.

The Webbs' maxim is, of course, valid for a wide range of public undertakings, and it should be equally applicable to the development programmes of the United Nations. It cannot be said that it has always been adhered to in the UN family, For example, the records of TAB sessions were not accessible to the public. Had they been so, they would have revealed how much of lengthy discussions was compressed into the same agenda year after year. The same remark would apply, in varying degrees, to several other documents and records. The reports of the EPTA experts were generally not available to the public. Yet they would have been useful to the professional world; and if regularly published, they would have enabled interested outsiders to judge the performance of EPTA more intelligently.

At the same time there has been no lack of discussions in the governing bodies and in various committees and conferences. The main difficulty here was due to the factors listed earlier—the diffused pattern of UN organizations, programmes and operations, the kaleidoscopic character of the key UN organs, the unsophisticated nature of the majority of the legislative masters, the rotating membership, the shifting personnel. Anomalies could persist in programmes and procedures despite endles discussions and a good deal of publicity. In such con-

---

[73] Later Lord and Lady Passfield.

ditions one might well enjoy something like, to quote Wordsworth in a prosaic context, "a privacy of glorious light."

The predicament is clear; nor is there any easy way out of it. The search for a solution will be possible only when there is a greater realization of an indisputable fact that has been ignored all these years, namely: Political compromises made in the UN forums hurt development in the field.

Given this realization, the next step should be perfectly clear: higher legislative organs of the United Nations—particularly the Economic and Social Council which makes crucial recommendations to the General Assembly—must legislate far more actively than hitherto, based on their own independent judgment and in the overall interest of the programmes and their objectives, and not rely so heavily on views and proposals that emanate from below and are invariably slanted towards the special interests of the various parties involved.

The reform proposals of 1961, the vicissitudes of which have been reviewed in the last two chapters, came to grief mainly because far too much was left to the secretariats of the UN family and far too little initiative was taken at the ECOSOC level. All that the Council did was to bless the mosaic of compromises that was served to it, after it had been designed and embellished in successive stages by the secretariats of the UN and the agencies, by TAB, TAC, and the ACC. Such an approach could not help reform and improve programmes and procedures; it could only perpetuate their anomalies.

Can the Economic and Social Council perform such a legislative function, particularly when decisions will often require high-level professional judgment? Much will depend on the level at which the member-states of the Council are represented at its sessions. As the activities of the UN family grew in the field of development, Mr. Hammarskjöld, especially in the later years of his service, increasingly felt the need of holding at least some sessions of the Council at the level of finance ministers. Obviously, such meetings of busy ministers can only be few and far between, and they can be held only for relatively short durations.

What is particularly important is that the Council, in addition to holding its sessions at a ministerial level as and when circumstances demand, should engage high level experts or consultants, as individuals or as teams, of independent professional standing to study and advise the Council on major problems of development, especially when they transcend the competences of individual agencies or programmes as was, for example, the case with the problems that were entrusted to the

Ad Hoc Committee in 1961. This is the only way decisions can be freed from the shackles of special interests, the only way the policies and achievements of the UN family can be subjected to a higher audit.

Some of the most urgent problems that have long been crying out for effective legislative treatment will be dealt with in the next few chapters. Two suggestions may, however, be made at this point, even though they are likely to shock the status quo-minded.

First, the time has come when the functions and responsibilities of the Resident Representatives, including their status, should be fixed by legislation on the direct initiative of the ECOSOC. These field representatives, as will be shown more clearly in a later chapter, are the pillars of the UN development programmes. On their stature and performance will depend the performance of the UN family, and in many ways its own stature. Yet hitherto it has badly failed on this vital issue, mainly because its members have been unable to disentangle themselves from their own narrow interests. Reform from below has been tried for years, but has been found wanting. It should now come from above.

It would be worth reviving Mr. Hammarskjöld's idea of appointing some Resident Representatives at the under-secretary level, which he tried in Nigeria. It would be meet and proper to designate, say, half-a-dozen countries or groups of countries, that are most important from the angle of the UN programmes, and provide them with representatives with under-secretary status.

And with such legislation could be logically coupled another innovation—rotation of appointments between the field and the headquarters, not only at the junior professional levels as is now more or less the custom, but also at the director and under-secretary levels. This would correspond to the practice habitually followed by the ministries of foreign affairs in national governments, which rotate appointments between headquarters and embassies at high as well as medium and junior levels.

Such rotation will have two solid advantages. The firsthand field experience of senior staff members, if drawn upon in framing basic policies and decisions, will enrich their quality. Besides, the rotation will act at least as a partial antidote to excessive "inbreeding" and "nest-building" at headquarters; it will create new openings in the established "channels of habit," and will in many ways help raise the morale of those engaged in development work.

The second suggestion, quietly pondered so far only by a handful of people smacks of even greater heresy. Simply put, it is this: Some of the highly sensitive posts in the UN system, especially in the topmost echelons of its hierarchy, might be deliberately earmarked for no more than single-term appointments of, say, five years each. Within this period an individual should be able to make his best contributions, so runs the rationale; and normally there should be little to lose and much to gain if thereafter a new man were to step in with a fresh mind and a new set of ideas.

Moreover, proper discharge of responsibilities on these jobs constantly involves the need to take firm stands on a host of contentious issues, which cannot but build up enmities and opposition and thereby steadily erode the effectiveness of the officeholders.

There is a third argument as well, namely, the ever-present temptation to run these high offices the "soft" way, that is, not by serving the cause, but by pleasing people; not by tackling tough issues, but by evading them; not by settling conflicting interests for the common good, but by accomodating them skilfully, not shirking the use of hidden patronage when found convenient. In such cases, ability to serve and the durability in office tend to be inversely correlated; and the so-called experience has to be rated not as an asset, but as a liability.

The underlying idea, despite its heretical look, is not entirely new. For example, U Thant made a powerful plea in 1966 that the post of the UN Secretary-General be confined to a single term. Mr. Clark Clifford, it has been said, believes that three years is about as long as an individual should stay on the top jobs of the Federal Government in Washington because of the pressures involved. Others have expressed the view that the federal regulatory agencies of the U.S. Government should ideally be headed by men with single-term appointments because of the sensitive character of the problems and the decisions involved. And some, today, would like to apply the same principle to the Presidency of the United States!

Probably the turnover in at least some of the top posts in the UN system would have been greater but for one important factor. In an ideology-ridden world the big powers, without exception, apparently preferred that their own nationals had better stay in whatever top positions they happened to occupy, rather than run the risk of seeing these positions filled with men of different nationalities, possibly with allegiance to a rival ideology. It is very doubtful however if, on balance, this attitude has helped matters.

There are abundant reasons why anomalies die hard within the UN system. The suggestions made above will by no means remedy all the ills. They may be no more than half-cures and half-antidotes. Nevertheless, they should be better than none.

PART IV

STRATEGY FOR THE FUTURE

CHAPTER 16

Some Fundamentals

"So few people really understand the imperatives of management."

DAVID E. LILIENTHAL

It is worth restating, even at the risk of sounding pedantic or simplistic, that the purpose of the UN development programmes is to promote development of the economically backward countries to the utmost possible extent. They have no other *raison d'être*.

While all are agreed on this as an incontrovertible starting point, it is surprising how easily its implications are missed, or by-passed, by the policymakers who often end up by supporting policies and actions that are incompatible with the basic objective. The search for an effective UN strategy will be fruitful only when we are able to steer clear of a number of common fallacies and to get firm hold of certain fundamentals. The ingredients of such a strategy—its "don'ts" and its "musts"—could, to start with, best be spelled out as a number of straigtforward propositions.

2

First, economic progress will depend on the capacity to resolve problems in the field, i.e., in each developing country. It is the nature of these problems that should dictate the overall strategy.

It follows that programmes, policies, organizations, and methods— all must be derived from, and directly geared to, the problems to be solved.

It also follows that where, for historical, political or other reasons, a divorce has occurred between the two—the programmes, policies,

153

organizations and methods on the one hand and the actual requirements of the field jobs on the other—it is the former that must be adjusted to the latter. Nothing could be more irrational, and more detrimental to the cause of development, than to perpetuate such a divorce and then to cut and shape jobs arbitrarily to meet the supposed needs of pre-existent programmes and organizations.

Second, what is called technical assistance is at bottom only *development assistance.* Its sole purpose must be to promote economic and social development, and not just to provide technical advice at random. This was quite clear from Resolution 222 (see Chapter 3), which still remains in force notwithstanding all subsequent amendments.

Now, development is much more than normal administration; it is primarily a *business* and, as such, it constantly calls for competent business judgment. It is therefore extremely important to have a clear understanding of the role of an expert—what we should, and should not, expect from him. The old cliché that an expert sees more and more of less and less has lost none of its profundity. In fact, as specialization proceeds apace, it gains even more, and not less, in validity. Vision, to be penetrating, has to be narrowed. Yet this development business calls for two opposing characteristics—the *breadth* of vision as well as its *penetration.*

Mr. John Gardner once remarked that the ablest people in every field must "come out of the trenches of their own specialty and look at the whole battlefield." But the fact is that very few experts are inclined, or able, to take such a panoramic view of things; the vast majority remain entrenched in their trenches.

Here, then, is the dilemma: We cannot do without experts, but expertise alone will not do. Development, one might say, is too serious a business to be left to experts, just as war is too serious a business to be left to generals. In short, we need the non-specialist specialist to integrate meaningfully the expertise of experts, the generalist general who would both respect and command them. In a modern business enterprise this function is performed mainly by the General Manager.

The UN family, organized as it is with a series of autonomous specialized agencies, has shown no appreciation for this critical function. This is a grave weakness in the UN programmes which needs to be urgently rectified.

Third, a high degree of *selectivity* is essential in choosing projects, especially since the resources are limited and only a small number of projects can be undertaken in each country.

The importance of this, too, was clearly recognized in Resolution 222 which laid special stress on the concentration of effort. It was, of course, implied that effort would be concentrated on projects which promised the best possible results in a given situation. This brings us to the hoary question of *fixing priorities*.

The most common error made in the UN programmes is to select and justify projects in absolute terms without regard to their "opportunity costs," i.e., the alternative possibilities that exist and are being ignored. In a developing economy, as observed by Mr. Cleveland in his statement to TAC cited earlier, "almost any project that is undertaken is 'right' in the sense that the need for it is demonstrable. But whatever is undertaken has to be done at the expense of something else that might have been done instead." Rational priorities, he emphasized, is "the fundamental requisite for rapid yet sound development."[74]

All this is no more than an economic truism. Yet how often are we apt to ignore it in practice! What is right from an agency's angle may not be right at all from an overall economic and business angle because the time, effort and money could be much more fruitfully employed on other projects within the same country. In fact, the general thrust of the UN programmes is towards over-concentration on infrastructure at the expense of immediately productive projects, and towards pushing efforts too soon too close to the margin, sacrificing the "potential surpluses" in the process. Their net effect may well be to slow down rather than to speed up economic growth.

Priority-fixing is the soul of all programming operations. And it is also one of the most difficult tasks, more so as it usually requires mature judgment based on practical experience. This inherent difficulty is in no way alleviated by the fact that "priority-fixing" has long been accepted in the UN family as an appealing slogan and has been liberally used to decorate documents and speeches, but without revealing much concern for its practical implications. A conscientious and imaginative search for rational priorities in a developing country must be firmly geared to several other fundamentals as explained below.

Fourth, all assistance must be directed to promote projects that would produce the maximum possible benefit under the conditions prevailing at a given time in a particular country. The decisive criteria for selecting projects must therefore be: *how much benefit, at what cost,* and *within what time.*

---

[74] See Chapter 13, Section 2.

It is not simply good enough to pick out projects at random and show some good results. The effort must be continuously directed to identify and promote those projects which would give the most favourable input-output or cost-benefit relationship, without involving unduly long waiting periods.

The growth rate of the underdeveloped countries will depend, above all, on satisfying this condition. In most cases there are, here and now, countless possibilities for high-yielding, quick-maturing projects. These are the trump cards which should be used to the fullest possible extent. But hitherto this has been far from the case.

Fifth, the most pressing need of the developing countries today is increased *productivity,* which should therefore be the primary objective of all programmes and projects.

Here, again, Resolution 222 showed a good deal of foresight. It did not underestimate the importance of social development, but it had the practical wisdom to recognize the fact that higher productivity alone would provide a nation with the wherewithal to finance social welfare.

It is true that infrastructure, including social services, cannot be isolated from productivity, that it can often make a direct contribution to it. But it is equally true that infrastructure needs are vast; that they cover an extremely wide range, and call for large sums of money; and that all of them are not equally urgent, nor can they make the same impact in terms of productivity. Unless great care is taken in choosing infrastructure projects, there is always a very real danger that they will absorb a disproportionate amount of the available resources, and thereby impede projects for raising production. In a weak low-income economy the delicate balance between the two can be easily upset.

In fact, all developing countries (sometimes also others) show a strong tendency, for historical, political and psychological reasons, to overemphasize infrastructure projects far beyond their capacity at the expense of productivity-oriented projects. One of the most urgent tasks is to counteract and reverse this bias. Without this the prospects of economic growth will be dimmed from the start.

It is here that the UN family has one of its greatest opportunities: to help the governments work out an optimum project mix. But it is also here that it has booked one of its major failures. For the upshot of its indiscriminate programming has been not to rectify, but to reinforce an already existing bias in the programmes of the less-developed countries towards less-productive projects.

Sixth, technical assistance is essential for development; but by itself the contribution it can make to development is severely limited.

Purely knowhow-intensive projects where expert services, with or without some small equipment, can produce worthwhile results in terms of productivity, are extremely rare. A poultry expert working with an incubator or an agricultural expert introducing a better sickle for crop-cutting can effect noticeable improvement, as has actually been the case. But such examples are few. Besides, even in such cases, the projects can make real impact only when they incorporate provisions for country-wide demonstration of the improved methods coupled with adequate supply, maybe also local manufacture, of the improved tool or equipment.

Some corollaries may be added. The inherently limited potential of purely technical assistance projects would be further circumscribed where experts are assigned for undefined periods to do ill-defined jobs. The advisory role of experts, despite the high premium placed on it, has a very limited practical value; where expert advice is treated as an end in itself, it tends to end without giving much return in terms of actual development.

Conferences, seminars, symposia may have their value as a means of exchanging ideas. But, in general, their relation to development is only tangential. They may even be, and sometimes are, a distraction leading away from the primary tasks, and thus turn out to be counter-productive. The UN technical assistance programmes are littered with them. The quality of their performance will visibly improve if they are drastically cut down to, say, ten per cent of their current level and are restricted to what will directly promote development, and if the resultant savings are transferred to other and more productive projects.

In general, technical assistance projects, even at their best, represent only one phase or aspect of development. They are particularly valuable for making people aware of the possibilities and for stimulating their expectations. Their true relationship to development is not unlike that of an overdose of appetizers to a real good meal.

Seventh, by far the best results can be achieved when development projects are prepared not *horizontally* in separate layers, i.e., technical assistance, pre-investment, investment, actual execution, and future operation, but *vertically in depth* and in appropriate dimensions comprising all these phases and giving due heed to integrally related problems.

Such a package approach, covering the whole gamut from "planning to planting," has obvious advantages. It provides built-in safe-

guards against dissipation of efforts and disappointments which frequently result from such causes as lack of follow-through action, neglect
of closely related problems, inadequate opportunities for training up
nationals to meet future operational needs, non-availability of investment capital. It is the surest, the quickest and, in the end, also the most
economical way to promote development. But it is precisely here that
the UN family, with its multiplicity of programmes and its conspicuously piecemeal approach, has been at its weakest. Hitherto its
approach has been ideally suited to achieve the opposite result—to
maximize dissipation of effort and to minimize the ultimate impact.

Eighth, a high growth rate will depend very largely on an effective
utilization of the domestic resources of a developing country. A
primary objective of the UN programmes must therefore be so to select
projects as to make the largest possible contribution towards that end.

The net amount of foreign aid—grants, subsidies, loans and commercial credits, all taken together—is estimated at $6 billion a year,
or thereabouts.[75] The actual contribution of the UNDP to this total is
still less than $200 million. Even if all the other programmes—the
World Food Programme, UNICEF, and the regular programmes of the
United Nations and the specialized agencies—are added to this figure,
the total for the entire UN family would still be only about $350 mil-
lion a year. This is less than six per cent of the total "foreign aid"!

The domestic resources of the underdeveloped countries that are
currently invested in development would, according to the best available estimates, amount to $24 billion, or four times larger than the
total "foreign aid" in the widest sense of the term.[76]

These figures have a twofold significance. In purely financial terms,
the UN family can play only a marginal role. The sums at its disposal,
even when lumped together from all sources, would still be woefully
small; no matter how equitably they are distributed, they can meet
only a tiny fraction of the overall needs.

Yet with the same sums of money the UN family can play a central
role if it decides to use them deliberately to help direct the investment
of the other resources—$24 billion domestic and $6 billion foreign—
into the most productive channels in the developing countries.

---

[75] World Bank's estimate, also quoted by Mr. George Woods. "...the flow of
official aid net of amortization has not increased much above the $6 billion a year
reached in 1961." Mr. Woods' address to the Swedish Bankers Association,
Stockholm on 27 October 1967.

[76] "Four-fifths of the investment being made today is being made out of the
resources of the developing countries themselves." Mr. George Woods in his address
to the Board of Governors of IBRD in Rio de Janeiro, 25 September 1967.

As a purveyor of development finance, the UN family can at best play a peripheral role and show some pedestrian progress. But as a purveyor of creative ideas and advice, of active guidance and wise inducements, it can make a spectacular contribution and can tremendously speed up the rate of progress. This is the unique role which history has thrust on the UN family; it is a role which no other organization can effectively play in today's world, a role which must be played well if the great drama of this age—the development of the two-thirds of the human race—is to attain a truly inspiring quality.

All this is unmistakably clear. Yet how often we are apt to overlook its implications! The UN programmes are all confined to technical assistance and preinvestment activity without the support of development capital;[77] the UN is therefore unable to function as a supplier of capital, at least for the present. Yet in actual practice the preoccupation has been overwhelmingly with their purely financial or their quantitative aspects—the amount of funds available, their distribution among countries and regions, among agencies, the number of projects authorized, of experts assigned. Whatever may be the theory of technical assistance, some policymakers have in practice been frankly inclined to treat the UN programme funds as so much additional money to supplement, though to a very modest extent, the financial resources of the recipient countries.

The UN family must recognize that its small programme can only be a means to an end, not an end in itself; that the only valid end is to induce, through strategic use of its own slender means, the investment of the far larger national resources in the most productive channels. In other words, the actual *resource-value* of the UN programmes is negligible; but a *resourceful use* of the same programmes to secure a high *leverage value* can make them both unique and invaluable.

Ninth, a high leverage value of the UN programmes would be possible only when programming is carried out on an *economy-wide basis*—after a full investigation of the whole range of possibilities or options that exist, careful weighing of all relevant factors, and deliberate concentration on well-screened high-yield projects.

The quality of performance under the UN programmes will depend, to a very large extent, on the ability to satisfy these conditions. For this there are three solid reasons.

---

[77] A Capital Development Fund has been established, but contributions to the UNCDF have so far been nominal. At the last pledging conference held on 18 November 1968, 31 countries made voluntary pledges amounting to $1,356,716; the major industrial countries, including the USA and the USSR, made no contributions. See Chapter 12, Section 3.

First, an underdeveloped economy is like a patient with widespread symptoms of anaemia, and sometimes with preconceived notions about the cure. Random treatment by independently functioning specialists is not the answer. The patient must be treated as a whole based on a comprehensive diagnosis.

Second, the outside help measured in absolute quantity, as indicated above, is bound to be small. The cure and growth must therefore come mainly through self-help.

And third, the modest quantum of outside help can be put to the most effective use only when it serves to carry out the overall diagnosis, to highlight the ailments, to pinpoint their causes, to lay down the right remedies, to create the right motivation, to initiate action, and to set in motion a process of self-help leading to a wiser use of all available domestic and other resources.

Even if the projects aided from the UN programmes are of good quality, the bigger problem of growth-stimulation will not be necessarily solved. For, a government may well transfer a few good projects to the UN programme and at the same time spend its own and very much larger resources on projects of poor quality and low return.

Substantially the same ideas were emphasized several years ago by Mr. Harlan Cleveland in somewhat different words. A country programme, he said, should be the "result of examining the whole situation" into which the outside aid "fits as a marginal factor—often a very small factor indeed." "Aid," he further stressed, "should be regarded primarily as an instrument for fostering the development of desirable institutions, *a lever for influencing the situation as a whole.*"[78]

These two concepts—using aid as a lever and influencing the situation as a whole—are all-important. Here lies the heart of the problem, also the greatest opportunity for the UN family. If it can use this lever deftly and wisely, it can, even with the limited funds at its disposal, achieve remarkable results and securely set a good many underdeveloped countries on the road to real progress. If it fails to do so, then even with far greater resources it will barely make a dent in their economies.

Tenth, such a strategic reorientation of the UN programmes calls for a radical overhaul of the UN family's own approach and organization, both at the headquarters and in the field.

---

[78] The Theory and Practice of Foreign Aid." Maxwell Graduate School of Citizenship and Public Affairs, Syracuse University. Mimeographed, November 1956, Page 52. Italics supplied.

The UN programmes and their activities have grown at random over the years, on the strength of resolutions that sprang from laudable impulses felt by different UN bodies at different times. There never was a predetermined pattern, nor a clear-cut policy, nor even a serious attempt to weld the different parts retrospectively into a more meaningful whole. The result of this haphazard growth could not but be disappointing and frustrating: The UN family, as perhaps the world's largest and most disparate body, has been grappling with problems of the developing economies that call for a rare vision and high managerial skill, in a strikingly superficial, at times even amateurish, fashion that does scant justice to these solemn responsibilities.

The reorientation of the UN programmes on the lines indicated above will require deep rethinking and considerable readjustment, at several points: the headquarters setup of the UNDP, internal organization of the United Nations and of the specialized agencies, field establishments, inter-agency as well as UNDP-field and agency-field relations.

This is the hardest task that faces the UN family today. And it is also the most urgent.

3

The fundamentals set forth above have some corollaries which are well worth noting. They will also help liquidate some long-cherished misconceptions.

The administration of a UN programme, it has been held, is like that of a holding company. The analogy was often cited on behalf of the Technical Assistance board, it being implied that the function of TAB was to "hold together" the participating organizations, i.e., UN and the specialized agencies, which, as its "member-companies," should be allowed to operate as largely independent units. The same line of thinking was at times encountered in the case of the Special Fund. For example, Resident Representatives were sometimes told by headquarters officials that they should keep away from the operations of the Special Fund projects for which the executing agencies, like members of a holding company, had the sole responsibility.

The validity of this analogy can be questioned on two grounds. It is an accident of history that the UN family has been set up in artificially divided segments and scattered over many places (*vide* Chapter 18). Yet though physically separated, functionally they are interlinked. In fact, they are at bottom only parts of an embryonic world government; and as such, they broadly correspond to the individual ministries of a national government. It follows that the UN family, despite all its artificial divisions, is as a whole responsible for the administration of the UN development programmes and cannot therefore afford to behave like a holding company any more than government of a country can do so in handling the problems of national development through its different ministries or departments.

The second objection is even more fundamental. The holding company concept, though inappropriate in the way in which it has been used, may still be evoked, but in an entirely different sense. The business of the UN programmes, or of the UNDP, lies not in the agencies but in the field, and the business is to build up the economies of the developing countries. If the UNDP is to be treated as a holding company, then surely its operating units are not the agencies, but the developing economies of the recipient countries. Pushing the business analogy a step further one may, with very good reason, argue that each of these units or "member-companies" should, in the interest of efficient management, be placed in charge of a single "country director" or "country manager" with unified responsibility and a substantial delegation of functions. The case for such a decentralized set-up at the country level will be examined at some length in Chapter 19.

The ultimate impact of the UNDP, for reasons already explained, will depend on its ability to adopt the aid-as-a-lever approach and to apply it on a whole-country basis. These vital truths have long been recognized by clearheaded people, and there *are* people within the UN family who have not allowed their thinking to be vitiated by inter-agency or inter-programme rivalries or to be smothered by an overdose of platitudes. Yet the UN programmes have so far failed to grasp these twin concepts firmly enough, not to speak of applying them systematically.

The saddest, also the oddest, example of this failure is the country-programming concept *à la* EPTA as discussed earlier (*vide* Chapter 10 in particular), its inability to see the simple distinction between country-*level* programming and the bizarre brand of country-programming *procedures* it has evolved and followed all these years. Seldom has a responsible administration walked so unwarily into such a yawning semantic trap with such woeful consequences. This is a matter of momentous significance. It would therefore be worthwhile to reflect a little more deeply on the right and wrong kind of country-programming with a brief recapitulation of the essential points.

It is one thing to insist that all projects must originate at the country level; that they must emerge out of a thorough investigation and a careful screening of all the possibilities that exist within a country so that, as a result, they may correspond to its top-priority needs; that they must be formulated on the right scale with the right combination of experts, fellowships and equipment so as to ensure the best possible results; and that every single project must be fully backed by the government with all essential counterpart support.

But it is quite another thing to make allocation of funds virtually *in advance;* to do so without a prior look at the substantive aspects of the projects, simply in the hope that the right projects prepared in the right form and on the right scale will, somehow or other, manage to find their way into the programme, and that they will do so despite the pulls and pressures of political forces and of conflicting sectional interests; and to allow, even after the programme has been formally approved, almost unrestricted freedom to switch funds from one project to another as and when found expedient, in a way that often tends to nullify the very concept of a development project.

The case for country-*level* programming, as defined above, is incontestable. Certainly no headquarters-based programming operations carried out on a global basis and far away from the actual realities of the underdeveloped world could ever be an adequate substitute. A country programme must be prepared within the country. This is as good as an axiom.

But the country-programming *procedures,* as now practised, are a totally different matter. They rest on spurious premises, and more or less assume away the complexities involved in formulating a sound programme, such as priority-fixing, the economics of scale, the right mix of the three key ingredients—experts, fellows and equipment; and they often violate the accepted canons of budgeting and finance. As long as such procedures persist, a marriage of the UNDP funds with the real needs of a recipient country will remain an elusive goal. To call this country-programming is a misnomer. It is a travesty of what should be programming based on a thorough country-wide analysis.

That the present procedures tend to fritter away the technical assistance resources has already been seen (*vide* Chapter 7 in particular). This direct loss, though unfortunate, is however not what matters most. Much more serious are the indirect and intangible losses in terms of opportunities sacrificed and results unrealized. But the worst consequences of the EPTA or UNDP/TA parody of country-programming lie somewhere else—in its capacity to disrupt priorities, to misguide investments, to aggravate distortions.

Referring to the Special Fund resources, Mr. Hoffman aptly called them *"seed money*—millions to attract billions." The metaphor has another aspect which must not be overlooked. What the UNDP—its technical assistance as well as its Special Fund component—supplies, serves also as what one might call *lead money*. It directly ties up a country's resources to varying extents. Even more significant, particularly from a quantitative angle, is the fact that it often sets up signposts to guide future investmens. Thus how the UNDP, in its Technical Assistance or Special Fund wing, spends its own money, no matter how small the amounts, can, and almost always does, have a direct bearing on how the scarce domestic resources are going to be invested. The UNDP can, to a considerable extent, be the pace setter for the development of a poor country. Conversely, it can, unless it approaches its tasks with vision and a due sense of responsibility, become a powerful instrument for promoting professional amateurism and retarding economic progress.

The late Mr. Gordon R. Clapp, who was chairman of TVA during 1946-54, once made some pertinent observations on this subject, which are well worth quoting: "... beginning in 1949 during a UN mission tour in the Middle East, as chief of mission, I was exposed to the sales efforts of several of the specialized UN agencies of that time. This intensive but limited experience led me to some gloomy predictions —to myself—as to the effects country by country the built-in rivalries among specialities and the competition for funds, seemingly divorced from any sense of program orientation related to the "clients" needs, would produce. In occasional exposure to the workings of UNTA since that time I have become more and more disheartened by what you refer to as 'fragmentation' and 'dispersal'. This is not just a matter of how funds available for TA are spent. More serious is its effect sooner or later on the wasted talent that flows through this process and the wrong lesson it administers, and the wrong attitudes it engenders in the recipient countries."[79]

In short, aid *is* being used constantly as a lever, but unwisely and maladroitly. The developing economies *are* being influenced year in and year out, but haphazardly, thoughtlessly, and often wrongly. They *are* reaping the results of the UN programmes, but mostly in terms of expectation and excitement without commensurate economic growth. The most urgent task before the wellwishers of the UN programmes today is to rescue them from these outrageous contradictions.

---

[79] Extract from a personal letter dated 12 April 1962 to the writer.

CHAPTER 17

Need For A Unified Programme

"Nothing is so liberally given as advice."

In the UN family's arsenal of clichés the one in most frequent use, and abuse, is "coordination." Perhaps never before in history has a large organization or undertaking cared less to enquire why problems of coordination multiply, far less to control them at birth; has so readily engaged in long and dreary exercises in coordination; and has so heavily relied on them to undo the effects of its own follies.

This unique approach of the UN family is writ large over its past record. For example, first establish two programmes—EPTA and Special Fund—as two spearate entities, strenuously defend their arbitrary separation, and incessantly plead for close coordination between the two.

When this coordination game begins to look too conspicuously illogical and the pressure for a merger mounts, put the two under the same roof but in separate compartments, erect a thick procedural wall between them, defend this artificial design with a wealth of casuistry, and again launch a fresh series of sermons on the need for better coordination.

Or, give technical assistance at random and in bits and pieces year after year, uninhibited by considerations of priorities, duration, scale and costs, and then indiscriminately coordinate good, bad and indifferent projects, in the fond hope that this newly-discovered fetish will, by some primitive magic, produce economic development in the newly-independent countries.

Or, pass resolutions year after year, in the UN General Assembly and in the legislative bodies of the agencies, setting up in a piecemeal fashion new programmes, mostly of a tiny size and to be financed from the regular budgets, then begin to worry about their coordination with

165

the other programmes—especially EPTA and the Special Fund, now accommodated in the UNDP.

And when these august bodies, gnawed by occasional doubts, begin to wonder about the effects of the confused trail of legislation they have been leaving behind, and seek some light and guidance from those concerned with their day-to-day administration, the secretariats get busy to safeguard the status quo, quote appropriate chapter and verse from the governing bodies' own legislative records, outline the intricate network of coordination they have dutifully erected, and, with all the ingenuity of a skilful bureaucracy, reassure their masters, mostly inexperienced delegates of the underdeveloped countries, that all is well with the programmes and their operations except that they need to be invigorated with the infusion of more funds.

Or, when too many programmes, too many agencies, and too many field representatives create a chaotic situation in a recipient country, sound periodically the clarion call for coordination from some olympian heights, which would help quiet any lingering uneasiness of conscience, and then laboriously work out some consensus-based long-winded rigmarole that would systematize the chaos with some marginal adjustments.

And so it goes in the UN family, also within each agency where coordination has been duly accepted as the panacea for all administrative ills.

Then there is the all-important business of interagency coordination. The classic example of this in the development field was, of course, the Technical Assistance Board which, for fifteen years ending in 1965, provided the forum to each agency to protect its interests in the Expanded Programme, and to make sure that they were "coordinated" with those of others without fail.

Finally, there is the apex body—the Administrative Coordination Committee (ACC)—which is supposed to look after top-level interagency coordination. There is "a vast orchestra of interests, decisions and strategies," so said the Secretary-General in his report on the development decade at midpoint,[80] but no conductor and no score, nor any suggestion of central guidance. Yet the whole system did call out for "a greater measure of harmonization" and "coordination becomes absolutely essential if the strategy is to succeed." As the operations of the specialized agencies expanded, the need for "coordination and

<hr>

[80] "The United Nations Development Decade at Mid-Point—An Appraisal by Secretary-General." October, 1965, pages 11-12.

cooperation" was increasingly felt. The task to meet this need devolved on the ACC which comprised the executive heads of all the UN organizations under the chairmanship of the UN Secretary-General. Thus the ACC, in the words of the report, has "come to play a central role" in the UN system in association with the Economic and Social Council.

It is true that in the present UN system the ACC and the ECOSOC are the two key organs for tackling interagency problems. But to imply that because these organs exist, the problems are resolved satisfactorily would be unwarranted. Here, as in other UN bodies, decision depends, above all, on the ability to evolve a consensus on a given issue; and this is arrived at mostly through a process of compromises which can be, and in general are, quite far-reaching. In other words, consensus-based decisions must rest on the lowest common denominator, and this in the UN family can be very low indeed.

That this is particularly true of the chief interagency coordinating body—the ACC—is no secret. The Committee meets twice a year and takes stock of the standpoints of its members on important issues. It exchanges views, but changes little. It harmonizes interests, but mostly by mechanically accommodating them. It coordinates with the due ceremony and care, and leaves things very much as they are. No wonder, then, that the UN programmes have been hoist with their coordination.

2

Oddly enough, even talks about coordination, in the UN literature and discussions, are not always well-coordinated.

The Secretary-General's report quoted above expatiates on the "critical importance" of inter-agency cooperation in this development decade. And to illustrate the point it cites the "relatively simple example" of a rural resettlement programme which is likely to require assistance from FAO, WHO, UNESCO, UN, UNICEF; maybe also IBRD or its affiliate IDA will need to be brought into the picture.

The report then proceeds to extol the Expanded Programme of Technical Assistance (EPTA) as "another vital factor making for coordination." The reasoning used can hardly be called profound: EPTA has brought the agencies together as participants in a development programme and thus it has promoted cooperation among them. What is not asked, and perhaps not even considered relevant, is whether there is the right kind and the right degree of cooperation among the agencies to make a real success of the Programme.

Meanwhile, this is how a project is defined in EPTA's own bible: "A project may involve the services of one or several experts, one or several fellowship awards, or a combination of both. However, it is confined to a single, self-contained subject—e.g., a geological survey, development of a fishing industry, establishment of a TB-control centre, etc."[81]

This can hardly be reconciled with the view quoted above regarding a rural resettlement programme which predicates intimate inter-agency cooperation because of its many-sided character. The fact is that the Expanded Programme has, in practice, shown far more concern for agency jurisdictions than for the character and needs of the field problems. It has cut down projects to fit them neatly into the respective spheres of individual agencies even when an integrated multi-agency approach was essential. That is why so often EPTA projects are, in effect, non-projects.

In the same strain the Secretary-General's report goes on to point out how the Special Fund and the World Food Programme have been instrumental in promoting cooperation within the UN family. Again, the reasoning is much too superficial. Emphasis is laid on how the creation of new programmes has brought the agencies together and stimulated cooperation among them. Yet the question at issue is: how effectively and how efficiently are they functioning, given the multiplicity of autonomy-minded programmes and jurisdiction-conscious agencies. In UN literature this question is glossed over, or obfuscated.

3

For many years it has been customary for the UN programmes, particularly for EPTA, to lay stress on the need to strengthen the coordinating units in the recipient countries. It has been assumed that where a strong coordinating machinery is in existence, it would override sectional interests and establish the right priorities to serve the best interests of the country.

This, however, has always been a question-begging assumption. Many governments—and this is particularly true of the newly independent countries of Africa—are simply not able to set up strong coordinating units. Priority-fixing, as emphasized before, is an exceedingly difficult exercise, the preconditions for which they can seldom satisfy. In both respects they need help and guidance—genuine technical assistance—from the UN family.

---

[81] "The Expanded Programme of Technical Assistance—An Explanatory Booklet." Fourth Revision 1963, page 12.

What do they get now? Mostly ill-disguised sales talk from junior agency representatives anxious to promote immature projects supposed to bring credit to their respective agencies. And how easy it is for them to distort and disrupt priorities! The unsophisticated ministers and officers would in any case be psychologically predisposed to trust to the superior wisdom of the awe-inspiring world organizations. Their native goodness and politeness would normally make it hard for them to reject suggestions and proposals offered in the name of reputable international bodies. And human nature being what it is, their own self-interest would impel them in the same direction since they too would, as a rule, not be disinclined to do more business and build up their own ministries and departments. If strengthening the programme coordinating units of the governments is the objective, one could hardly make a worse beginning.

The emphasis laid on the need for a strong coordinating unit in a recipient country has another aspect which is no less curious. Without such a unit, it is argued, there can never be a sound programme; for, almost inevitably, it will then represent not the high-priority needs of the country as established through objective eyes, but only the resultant outcome of a great many pressures, mainly of a political nature, exercised from different directions. Is it not equally clear that, for fundamentally the same reason, the UN family, too, needs a strong overall authority, not simply to coordinate the powerful special interests impinging upon its programmes from a dozen different sources, but to keep them in check and to bring them in harmony with a rational pattern of priorities for development?

And how can there be effective coordination in the field—whether in the government or in the UNDP office—unless such an authority is, in the first instance, firmly established at headquarters, functioning in close consultation with the agencies as far as technical matters are concerned, but also controlling and overriding their narrow special interests, whenever necessary?

In the background of such facts, talks of coordination sound hollow and unreal. Yet the coordination activities of the UN family have grown into epic proportions, and in the process they have eclipsed what should have been its foremost concern, namely, good management. Today, as one scans the vast establishments of the UN family, one might, following the *tour de phrase* of a famous utterance of a Frenchman, cry out in desperation: "I look among you for managers. But I can find only coordinators."

4

What the UN family must recognize are some simple facts: that the multiplying problems of coordination are not the outcome of any immutable law, but are very much its own creation; that they reflect, and are a measure of, the grave weaknesses—yes, of the mismanagement—it has tolerated so long—fragmented programmes, splintered projects, irrational procedures, neglected priorities; that they not only consume much of its time, energy and money, but also disrupt and nullify most of its efforts; that they can be, and must be, reduced to a fraction of their present dimensions in the interest of effective management of its programmes.

The conclusion emerging from these facts should be no less clear. Given the fragmentation of programmes and responsibilities, and the pressures of special interests, the next big impulse towards effective coordination and improved management must come not from the field, but from headquarters, and not from the administrative but from the legislative end. The most crying need is what has been unmistakably clear for years—to scrap the crazy procedures of the technical assistance component of the UNDP; to merge its two components, fully and unequivocally, into one single programme; to adopt, for the unified programme, the far more sensible procedures of the Special Fund; and to adjust and improve them in the light of the past experience.

The two-component UNDP, as it now stands, is an affront to reason, a monument to the kind of damaging compromises that have been all too common in the UN family. The arguments used in support of this halfway house evinced little reason, nor undue scruple. They were not examined seriously—hardly anybody had the patience or inclination to do so. The decision was political, the result of tenacious lobbying quietly organized by entrenched interests; and it was decently camouflaged to escape critical eyes, of which there were in any case not too many around.

For example, speaking at the July 1965 session of the Economic and Social Council in favour of the proposal to erect a two-compartment UNDP, Lord Caradon remarked that "the case for merging the two into a single Development Programme which would embody the best features of both was overwhelming."[82] He based his support on the need to simplify administration, to strengthen cooperation with

---

[82] Statement to the ECOSOC made on 5 July 1965 by Lord Caradon, Minister of State for Foreign Affairs and the Permanent Representative of the UK to the United Nations.

the participating organizations, to enable the priority needs of the developing countries to be more adequately assessed, and to assure that the resources available, in experience as well as funds, would be used more fruitfully.

Obviously, Lord Caradon, well-known for the generosity of his outlook and the warmth of his support for the UN programmes, did not consider it necessary to probe deeper into the so-called merger proposal. He accepted it at its face value and, in the goodness of his heart, gave it his full blessing in perfectly good faith. And so happily for the anti-merger lobby, "the best features" of the Expanded Programme remained unspecified. Yet the interesting fact is that all the four points cited by Lord Caradon were most pertinent, and all four pointed inexorably in one direction—towards a full merger of the two programmes.

The case for such a merger has always been unanswerable, as should be abundantly clear from what has been said in the earlier chapters, especially on the Expanded Programme. However, in view of the dense fog in which this vital issue is still shrouded, it may be restated in plainer words.

First, the retention of two programmes in the UNDP has in no way simplified the administration; on the contrary, it has continued a vast amount of duplication. As before, each component maintains a separate fund to which voluntary contributions are pledged; makes separate arrangements for currency utilization; follows separate procedures for assessing and collecting local costs for experts, those for the technical assistance component being particularly cumbrous; executes its own standard agreement with each recipient government; does its own book-keeping with separate auditing and accounting, which also involves allocation of common costs, e.g. for the field offices, to the two components. A full merger would eliminate all this duplication and thereby save an enormous amount of administrative work at the headquarters of the UNDP and of the participating organizations as well as in the field offices.

Second, the country-programming of EPTA or UNDP/TA, as we have seen, is not only a negation of what country-programming should really be; it has, in effect, become a major obstacle to it. Despite all the laboured justification of the past, it has been, and still remains, a de facto handout programme, not too far removed from a thinly-veiled system of patronage. This, more than anything else, is the real source of the support it has been enjoying. For, as in all such cases, it is only natural that its numerous beneficiaries would discover a good deal of virtue in the system and would spontaneously rally to its defence.

Clearly, no amount of coordination can cope with or wipe out its unfortunate effects. The code of rules evolved to establish harmony and equity can at best impart to it a misleadingly dignified look. It is time to see the facts as they are, and to end a system which, though sanctified by long practice, has greatly impared the effectiveness of the UN effort. And the best way to end it is to merge the technical assistance component into the Special Fund and, with some minor changes, to apply the procedures of the latter to the entire programme. A mountain of coordination problems will then be swept aside; the two programmes will stand automatically coordinated; and the ground will be cleared, at long last, for the UN family to launch systematically on country-programming, not only in name but also in substance.

Third, the worst feature of the Expanded Programme or UNDP/TA has been, and continues to be, its fragmentation; and as already explained, given the scope, the approach, and the modus operandi of the Programme, it could not be otherwise, (see Chapter 7 in particular). A well-known physicist working as a senior executive in one of the UN organizations expressed[83] the case for concentration of effort in a rather original way that is well worth recalling. Referring to Einstein's formula $E = MC^2$ (where E = Energy, M = Mass, and C = Velocity of light), he argued that it could be well adapted to the field of development if we took E for Effort; M for men, material, money, machinery and management; and C for cooperation. His adaptation of another formula ($P = \dfrac{F}{A}$ where P = Pressure, F = Force, and A = Area) was no less significant. For the field of development, he wanted to read P for impact, F for funds, and A for the area of activities. The ideas, though rather simple, were interesting as the physicist's version of some basic concepts of economics, such as economies of scale, marginal productivity, and opportunity cost. They were revealing also for another reason. They provided fresh evidence of the fact that thoughtful people within the UN family are well aware of the very considerable waste that now results from the dispersal of the technical assistance activities. The amalgamation of the two components and the adoption of the Special Fund procedures for the unified programme, with concentration of effort on carefully selected projects, would unquestionably bring about a great improvement in the UNDP's operations.

---

[83] In informal discussions in 1966.

Fourth, technical assistance, as now administered, is wasteful also in other important respects. It is confined mostly to advice, but there is no assurance that this will be acted upon. It nibbles at problems; there is a general lack of attempt to work out adequate resolutions of given problems over a long enough period. It is defective both in concept and design, and is patently inappropriate where a concerted attack involving different disciplines is needed to tackle inter-related problems of development, as is frequently the case in backward economies.

It escapes evaluation, and its meagre results are easily lost in the perpetual penumbra created by piecemeal programming, while its costly evaluation missions can do no more than provide glimpses only to confirm what has long been known—that a plethora of expertise is inversely matched by the paucity of results.

Here, then, is another distressingly wasteful feature of the technical assistance programme: its grand army of experts is poorly mobilized, and chronically and chaotically under-used. And this happens at a time when there is a growing shortage of experts, with demand outrunning their supply. The Secretary-General's report on the development decade at midpoint stressed this point with the following remark: "Coordinated action is all the more important in that the experts needed in every field of development are becoming more and more scarce."[84] The trend towards a growing scarcity of experts is undeniable, though coordination, the pet panacea of the UN family, is certainly not the answer.

Some bureaucratic pundits have come up with another suggestion to cope with this shortage, increasing difficulties of recruitment, and rising costs in an age of inflation. They have, in all seriousness, argued that the UN family should "lower their sights" regarding the calibre of experts and recruit less expensive ones. There is no doubt that, under the force of circumstances, sights have, in fact, often been lowered. Officials in recipient governments have, from time to time, expressed misgivings about the quality of experts though, out of a sense of decorum, they refrain from airing them in public.

What is needed is certainly not a lowering of the calibre of experts —that would be fatal—but to recruit really competent experts and to make the best possible use of their services on the most worthwhile projects. The simplest, also the most rational, step for the UNDP/TA would be to copy, almost in toto, the methods of the UNDP/SF, (see Chapter 11). With such a model available at its elbow, there never was any justification for the technical assistance programme to persist

---

[84] Ibid., page 33.

in an outmoded course. To do so even after a loudly proclaimed *merger* of the two programmes is not only indefensible, but also disingenuous.

A UN stalwart, cheered by the snail's pace progress made in certain directions, recently remarked: "Things are getting better and better." This makes one wonder when they will be—good! It is hard to be enthused by the prospects of betterment that, even in elementary matters, threatens to stretch into eternity.

Evidently, the above remark was prompted mainly by the impending transition to project programming and project budgeting on a continuous basis. This prodigious procedural overhaul will, as explained in Chapter 9, make some changes in form, but very little in substance; it will reshuffle some anomalies, and will stabilize the worst ones; its net effect will be to apply cosmetics where surgery is overdue.

The wall that separates the two components within the UNDP— let there be no illusion about it—has not been dictated by logic or reason. It is a wall of bureaucratic politics that has become a potent source of confusion in thought and action, in programming and in execution. There is one, and only one, way to end this confusion, namely, by their fusion.

5

Where, then, are the "best features" of EPTA referred to by Lord Caradon, and its "special characteristics" referred to in the merger resolution[85] as something to be treasured and protected? Is there nothing to be said in favour of the UNDP/TA as it now operates? Yes, there is, but surprisingly little, as should be clear from a brief review of the arguments that were used to defend its separate existence.

First, there was the country-programming à la EPTA. This was the biggest vote getter. The label itself enticed a lot of people; its implicit flattery to the sovereignty of the recipient governments pleased them; its money-sharing approach won the support of its beneficiaries. All this could explain, but not justify the resultant compromise. On the contrary, it provides the strongest argument *against* its continuation.

Second, it has been held that the governments of the assisted countries should be the best judges; and that the verdict given by them has been favourable, as is borne out by the fact that "they have asked, and they continue to ask, far more in volume from the Expanded Programme than it has been able to give"; also by the fact that while there have been "complaints about delays" in delivery and performance in

---

[85] General Assembly Resolution A/RES/2029 (XX), clause 1. See Appendix III.

respect of individual projects, there has never been "a serious question-ing" on their part of the value of the programme.[86]

Such reasoning is more likely to delude than to convince. It ignores the fact that money may perform poorly and yet be in unlimited demand. It pretends innocence of the economic concept of waste—doing, say, a fifth-rate job instead of a first-rate one. It assumes, rather sanctimoniously, that the governments are able to judge correctly, also to decide freely uninfluenced by international forces. And it shows how hard it is for some UN bodies to take an objective view of their own work, and how prone they are at times to prevaricate.

Third, there is the stock argument that EPTA and the Special Fund can help and supplement each other, that the two are well "coordi-nated" in practice. The fifteenth anniversary review cites examples to support this thesis.[87] It emphasizes how EPTA can sometimes give assistance specifically designed to explore the possibilities of viable Special Fund projects; and how it can step in to provide supplementary assistance in the follow-up stage. It also points out how more than 100 Special Fund-assisted projects grew out of EPTA-initiated activities.

Such reasoning, it cannot be denied, duly impresses the UN audi-ence which is well-attuned to respond favourably to all superficial co-ordination. Yet its weaknesses are not hard to detect. It assumes that a development project can be safely divided into parts and smoothly passed back and forth from one program to another, and forgets the numerous hitches that inevitably occur in the process. That so many Special Fund projects had their origin in activities first initiated by EPTA cannot necessarily be construed as a tribute to its creativity. Rather, it proves once again how little heed it has been paying to con-siderations of optimum size, duration and cost, and how it has encour-aged slipshod programming.

And finally, many developing countries, it has been argued, need the services of single experts—or of experts in small numbers—which can be provided only from EPTA, but not from the Special Fund.

There is truth in this, though it is mixed with a lot of alloy. Single experts working in isolation can seldom achieve much, all the more so since, under EPTA, they normally function only in an advisory capacity. Experience has repeatedly shown that in the vast majority of cases where single experts are assigned, really worthwhile results can be produced only through a much broader-based approach involving teams

---

[86] "An Anniversary Review of the United Nations Programme of Technical Assistance," E/TAC/153. Rev. I, New York, 1965, page 50.

[87] Ibid., page 49.

of experts with a sizable quantum of equipment and fellowships, generally on the lines of Special Fund projects.

Such an approach will, of course, mean far fewer projects within a given amount of resources. There is, however, no valid alternative to this, no point in financing a congeries of tiny projects, no sense in attempting to do too much with too little and inevitably ending by achieving too little.

The case for single experts has been grossly overstated; and once overstated, it has also been overdone in practice. The resources for the UNDP/TA have gone up significantly in the last few years; they crossed the $70-million mark in 1968,[88] and this should have facilitated the grouping of experts to build larger and more useful projects. But there has been no such suggestion. The continued over-emphasis on the need for single or isolated experts has, as in earlier years, been prompted by a shrewd calculation: the technical assistance component must look different in order to survive as a separate entity; and to do so, it grimly clung to its clumsy cloak.

6

All this gives to the operations of the UNDP/TA a distinctly amateurish touch. Experts are assigned by thousands according to meticulously defined rules to serve on promiscuously chosen jobs. Pursuit of specialties has been the first order of the day. The experts, in their turn, have been enjoying in the underdeveloped countries—no doubt on invitations of their governments—a kind of an open season to shoot at random at whatever problems might excite their fancy.[89] The result has been a crescendo of motion and commotion, and little solid progress.

This anarchy stems from a single root cause—the failure to recognize, or to admit, that the preinvestment work of the UNDP is nothing but technical assistance in a far more effective form; and that, conversely, its technical assistance is intrinsically no different from its preinvestment work, and should in any case be restricted to it. A difference between the two has been loudly proclaimed and strenuously upheld with ingenious bureaucratic props. Nevertheless, it remains a difference without a distinction.

---

[88] The approved programme for 1968 amounted to $71.7 million; for 1969 it showed a farther rise—to $79 million. Also see Appendix 1A.

[89] A fish biologist serving as an expert in a certain country was reportedly more interested in the "sexual life of shrimps" than in the development and use of this resource. Pursuit of expertise only too often tends to become an end in itself.

The first task here is to gear the programmes back to the fundamentals discussed earlier. Both programmes, or both components of the UNDP, have one, and only one, valid objective, i.e., to promote development to the utmost possible extent. Therefore, the only "special characteristics" they are entitled to are those that would clearly subserve this end, and no other.

The Special Fund deals with preinvestment work; therefore, by definition, it must concentrate on projects *only at one remove* from the point of actual investment and production. Should it not be the same with technical assistance as well? Of course, it should, and it must. In numerous statements Mr. Hoffman has stressed the urgency of expanding the preinvestment work of the Special Fund, and to include within its scope new high-priority functions in the fields of education, medical and health services, food production, population growth, and betterment of rural life. And he has been constantly pleading for a target of $350 million to be reached by 1970. When pre-investment work can immediately absorb 200 to 300 per cent more funds than are currently available, there can be no justification to fritter away resources on non-preinvestment activities in the name of technical assistance.

Then there is the question of short-term experts. That there is need for them no one will deny. Its extent must not, however, be exaggerrated. The services of short-term experts can and should be employed more effectively and more purposefully. And the most important jobs that short-term experts can most usefully undertake are to prepare longer-term projects, with the right components and on the right scale, based on a careful appraisal of the problems involved in a given field and the results of studies and investigations already carried out. Once prepared, such projects can be handled under various programmes, depending on their nature; the Special Fund component, IBRD, IDA, various bilateral programmes; some of them may be taken up by the governments and financed from their domestic resources; some may be appropriately tackled by private enterprise.

Short-term experts or consultants, either as individuals or as teams, may also be needed to carry out reconnaissance studies in important fields and to advise governments on the best lines of approach to tackle the problems involved. At times their services may be required for quick evaluation of projects or programmes already drawn up. Such evaluation by competent consultants, prior to the initiation of projects, is particularly important where heavy commitments of funds are involved.

Short-term missions, it should be noted, are now financed from both components of the UNDP—from technical assistance either in country programmes or as contingencies, and from the Special Fund, essentially as contingencies from its so-called revolving fund and mostly for "appraisal" of projects. It follows that the need for short-term experts and consultants is not a valid argument for keeping two separate components in the UNDP.

Until recently Special Fund projects had a minimum cost level of $250,000, while projects costing less than this amount went automatically to EPTA or the UNDP/TA. This line of demarcation is no longer treated as sacrosanct. In fact, the Special Fund is now taking steps to abolish the cost floor in order to accommodate what it calls "mini-projects." The reasons adduced in their favour are: some projects, such as feasibility studies, may actually cost less than the minimum amount; owing to the new procedures of continuous programming in the technical assistance sector, such projects can no longer be accommodated within it; and then there are "mini" economies which will in any case need much smaller projects.

Typical mini-projects are expected to cost $50,000 to $100,000 or even less provided that the figures are not "ridiculously low." The net effect of the change is to underscore once again how artificial is the difference maintained between the two programmes or the two sectors.

Finally, there is the question of supplying OPEX experts or "operational executives." The OPEX programme was created by General Assembly resolution 1256 (XIII) with the United Nations in charge of its administration. Its purpose was to supply experts, on specific government requests, to serve not as advisers, but as executives in government ministries and departments; who, in other words, would tackle technical and administrative problems on a day-to-day basis virtually as employees of the governments concerned and would in the process train up their nationals.

The need for OPEX-type experts has been particularly acute in the newly-independent countries of Africa. And experts employed under the Expanded Programme with the *de jure* status of advisers often function as *de facto* OPEX experts.[90] But the programme suffered from two major handicaps: its size was too small—only 90 to 95 experts were supplied annually; and under its terms the experts were only subsidized from the programme while the recipient governments were required to bear a substantial part of the costs. In general, they had to pay

---

[90] This, for example, was true of more than half of some 40 EPTA experts who were serving in Ghana in 1962.

salaries and allowances according to the scales applicable to their own civil servants; the excess over this needed to attract qualified international experts was payable from the UN programme. The question of cost alone made it difficult for many governments to request OPEX experts. They preferred to ask for EPTA experts, and to use them for OPEX functions.

The UN-OPEX programme was not restricted to the UN fields of activities but covered also those of the agencies, although in such cases experts were supplied only after due consultation with the agencies concerned. Later, UNESCO and WHO established their own OPEX programmes to supplement that of the United Nations. And starting with its programme for 1965-66, the Expanded Programme was authorized to entertain requests for OPEX-type experts. The step was introduced on an experimental basis, but it has continued since then.

Without doubt this was a step in the right direction. International experts actually shouldering executive responsibility and working closely with nationals of the developing countries can render much more effective service than adviser-experts, assuming that really competent people are recruited to perform clearly defined functions within given time limits. The point not to be missed, however, is that the Special Fund component contains most of the elements of OPEX experts, and that the main difference lies in the fact that it combines the OPEX-type duties of several experts in much larger projects to carry out what are usually much more significant jobs.

All this leads up to a simple conclusion: most of what is now attempted under the technical assistance sector can be done easily, and far more fruitfully, under the Special Fund; that the idea of an independent technical assistance programme or component—to supply isolated experts, short-term missions of experts or consultants, or OPEX personnel, or to provide what is in effect pre-preinvestment and post-preinvestment aid—has no justification whatever despite the unflagging effort to establish the contrary.

There never was a case for two separate programmes or components, whether in 1959 or in 1966. What was needed then, and is needed now, is one single programme in order to serve, single-mindedly, the common cause of international development. Those who have been fighting this axiom and straining themselves to make out a case for separating the two are, in effect, doing something else—they are unwittingly making out a case against themselves.

True, a simplified programme, to be fully effective, will need the support of short-term expert missions for project selection, preparation, appraisal or evaluation; and it may also provide isolated experts, of OPEX or EPTA trademark, in those exceptional cases where there is a demonstrable need for them to do specific jobs over definite periods of time. These supplementary needs, important though they are, are only peripheral to the main programme; and taken together, they should not consume, say, more than five per cent or about $10 million a year, which is less than what is now spent, in one form or another, on contingency-type activities.

This, then, is the ounce of reason in the tonnage of special pleading. It was shown through a vast magnifying glass to prove how radically different was the character of EPTA. The stratagem worked; and it secured explicit legislative protection for the programme to continue as a separate entity.

7

Of late much has been made of new procedures adopted for the technical assistance component. But as shown in Chapter 9, they will leave its basic weaknesses more or less intact. The anarchy will continue as before except that—and this is the real meaning of the "fourth generation" of procedural changes—it will henceforward be possible to defend it with more fully centralized authority.

Much has also been said about "continuous programming" which will now become a major feature of the technical assistance sector, as if this represented some revolutionary progress such as, for example, continuous casting in steel production. The new programming technology, it has been suggested on behalf of the UNDP administration, is nothing but contingency programming except that it will be conducted on an uninterrupted basis. This is an apt characterization. Thus, it has taken some twenty years to make the truly novel discovery that the last word of wisdom in programming lies in living from contingency to contingency!

The UNDP administration has lately been making some soothing statements to the effect that bridges are being steadily built between its two components. For one thing, these bridge-building activities have already become a major distraction, the relevance of which to development is not easily recognizable. Besides, since bridges work both ways, they are already producing some unexpected, and unsuspected, results: some of the dubious factors of the technical assistance component have begun to move across these bridges to infect the Special Fund as well. This is clearly reflected in a renewed dedication to the orgy of coordination which is implicitly regarded as synonymous with management.

Perhaps it is symptomatic that this trend coincided with another change. In the earlier years of the Special Fund when Mr. Hoffman was its Managing Director, the UN family, under his leadership, evinced for the first time a refreshing concern for problems of management, and some real progress was made in that direction. After the merger Mr. Hoffman's designation was changed, and he became the Administrator of the UNDP. At the same time the emphasis visibly shifted towards more traditional administration; its tone and temper, too, showed a marked change. It has grown in size in the last few years, but largely at the expense of the initial drive for improved management. This last word is no longer heard in the UN corridors. It has been quietly erased from the UNDP's vocabulary.

The damage done by the merger, or rather the no-merger, resolution which conserved the "special characteristics" of the two programmes, irrespective of their intrinsic merit, maintained two separate funds, and gave blanket protection to their respective "principles, procedures and provisions," has been incalculable. Through this masterpiece of equivocation the legislative masters, whether duped by vested interests or impelled by their predilection to make artful political compromises on economic issues, have created what is an arrant administrative aberration.

Whatever may have been the reason, the masters alone can undo the mischief. To do so, they must demolish their farcical handiwork, take fresh legislative action to establish one indivisible programme, with one clear-cut set of streamlined principles and procedures, and build firmly into it the essentials discussed earlier and in the chapters that follow. And they must do so as the first item on the UN agenda for economic development if the UN family is not to fail demonstrably in its tasks, thereby betraying the trust and the hopes of the underdeveloped countries.

8

What about the regular programmes—of UN, IAEA and the specialized agencies? Should they be merged, too, with the new unified programme to be created by fully merging the two UNDP components as urged above?

Questions regarding the regular programmes have been reviewed in Chapter 14, especially those that cropped up during the merger debate; also how the status quo was defended with all its eccentricities. The arguments used for the purpose were, as we have seen, far from flawless. This becomes even clearer when judged in the light of what has been said above and the fundamentals set forth in the previous chapter.

The regular programmes of all the UN organizations, including UNIDO, would add up to about $40 million a year, as compared with $183 million available to the UNDP for 1968. Of this WHO alone accounts for almost 75 per cent with an annual programme in the neighbourhood of $30 million; the United Nations for another 15 per cent or about $6 million, while the balance is made up of four small programmes respectively of the ILO, UNESCO, IAEA and FAO.[91]

The merger debate went largely astray because the real issues were missed. It is not just a question of size, but of quality; and size matters only to the extent that a bigger programme created by a merger would definitely lead to better programming and greater efficiency in performance. It follows that the matter can be settled only on the basis of three related questions: Are there any concrete advantages to be gained by merging a regular programme into a larger UN programme? What are they? And assuming that they are substantial enough to make the merger worthwhile, what legislative action should be taken to bring it about?

In the merger debate, as it happened, the first two questions were treated superficially, if at all, and attention was concentrated primarily on the third. For example, on behalf of WHO it was time and again stressed that the agency had a constitutional mandate "to assist Governments, on request, in strengthening health services" and "to furnish appropriate technical assistance and, in emergencies, necessary aid upon the request or acceptance of Governments."[92] This mandate was quoted as if it clinched the matter once and for all. Yet a constitution, however important juridically, is a man-made instrument. Besides, an agency constitution is subordinate to the United Nations charter, and all its provisions must therefore be designed to promote, and be kept continuously in harmony with, the charter objectives which alone must prevail in case of a demonstrable conflict.

There was no such conflict in this particular case however, and therefore no case for altering the WHO mandate. For, there was nothing to be gained from the proposed merger and, one might legitimately argue, much to lose from it. This was the right reason against merging WHO's regular programme into the UNDP, and not its constitutional provision.

---

91 Prior to the establishment of UNIDO on 1 January 1967. See Section 8 below.
92 See Chapter 14, Section 5.

In the first place, the agency has the largest regular programme, which is about four times as large as its average annual share in EPTA or UNDP/TA. The size of its programme makes it possible for the agency to develop sound country programmes without spreading the resources too thinly.

Second, WHO has consistently shown a high quality-consciousness in its programming and operations, aided by its decentralized structure, high standards of the medical profession, a keen sense for the right priorities, and systematic adherence to the principle of project programming and project budgeting.[93] In these respects it actually set an example to others.

Third, merging WHO's regular programme into EPTA would have been doubly wrong. First, the tail would have wagged the dog—a $30-million programme would have been merged into the EPTA-WHO programme of $7.5 million. And second, the dog would have been wagged the wrong way—the agency's scrupulous concern for substantive programming would have been swapped for a stereotyped set of financial formulae.

In fact, the only desirable kind of merger has long existed in this case: WHO started its technical assistance programme in January 1947; it did so on a sizable scale; when, a couple of years later, the Expanded Programme came into existence, it adapted the EPTA procedures to its own;[94] and it has continued to do so ever since, despite the strange vicissitudes the latter have been undergoing. It is to the credit of WHO that it has uncompromisingly merged its EPTA activities into its regular programme.

And finally, the WHO fields of activities, despite all their importance, are in general not so directly linked to economic development. This is also clear from its low share in the Special Fund activities. By February 1968, the Fund had approved 873 preinvestment projects; of these, only 22 fell within WHO jurisdiction; and most of these 22 projects, which are mainly for water supply and sewerage, have been authorized rather recently.

The decision not to merge the WHO regular programme was right, though based on wrong reasons. The decision about the UN regular programme, however, was wrong; so also were the reasons given in its

---

93 See also Chapter 19, section 6.

94 "For the most part there is no distinction between the type of technical assistance given by WHO under the two programmes." EPTA Explanatory Booklet, Ibid., para. 75. The only difference between the two is that EPTA is confined to the developing countries, while the regular programme serves all member states.

support. This programme is much too small—$6 million a year or even less—to be used for sensible programming. Most of its fields of activities are identical with those of EPTA or UNDP/TA and the Special Fund; the UN shares in both have always been substantial, and they have been growing in keeping with the growth of the UNDP.

The first argument used against the merger, as we have seen, was that it provided much-needed flexibility not possible under EPTA because of its country targets and two-year programming cycle. But this, as mentioned before, only pointed to the need for changing the EPTA procedures to eliminate its excessive rigidities. In any case, this obstacle will disapear if the two components of the UNDP are merged as proposed above.

That the WHO regular programme, by far the biggest of all, was not being merged with EPTA or the UNDP was regarded as the strongest argument against the idea of merging the regular programmes of UN and other agencies. But the analogy was weak, and argument by precedent had no validity in this case since, for reasons just explained, WHO stood conspicuously in a category by itself.

The UN regular programmes, as approved for 1967 and 1968, amounted to $5.35 million and $5.41 million respectively; the proposed programme for 1969 will be on the same level as this year's.[95] Each programme consists of five main components which, for 1968, were: economic development, GA resolution 200 (III)—$2.57 million; social development, GA resolution 418 (V)—$1.67 million; public administration, GA resolution 723 (VIII)—$874,300; human rights advisory services, GA resolution 926 (X)—$222,000; and narcotic drugs control, GA resolution 1395 (XIV)—$75,000.

The first three of these categories are very much in the UNDP fields; and in each of them there are numerous technical assistance and Special Fund projects. There is no valid reason to continue them separately as diminutive development programmes.

The other two components—human rights and narcotic drugs control—fall, however, in a different category. They are not directly related to economic development and to the UNDP's sphere of activities. The question of their merger with the latter should not therefore arise.

The same principle ought to apply also to the regular programmes of the other agencies—the ILO, UNESCO, IAEA and FAO. A distinction ought to be drawn between the activities that are directly related

---

[95] Exclusive of industrial development which, with effect from 1 January 1967, was transferred to UNIDO.

to economic development and those that are not. The former had
better be merged with the UNDP, just as the latter should not or need
not.

Why worry about these regular programmes at all when they are
so small, it has sometimes been argued. It would be more relevant to
ask why such tiny programmes should at all exist, more so when the
same resources, as part of a bigger unified programme, could be put
to much better use. Besides, they may be too small to do much good,
but not too small to do much harm through random promotion of
projects, thereby blindly influencing domestic priorities.

As for the oft-repeated question of flexibility imparted by these
programmes to the operations of the agencies, what is overlooked is
that there are more rational methods of achieving the same end. As
suggested in the next chapter, once the internal administration of an
agency has been revamped, and all its development activities have
been placed in charge of a competent general manager, the UNDP
would be wise to place a sizable lump sum at his disposal to enable
him to attend to essential contingency type of activities on behalf of
the UNDP, without being hamstrung for lack of funds. This will provide legitimate flexibility and will also make for better management.

9

Since the UNDP was established, another agency has been added to
the UN family with a separate programme. The United Nations Industrial Development Organization (UNIDO), which came into existence on 1 January 1967, is financed from four different sources. The
cost of its administrative and research activities is borne by the regular
budget of the United Nations; a sum of $8.23 million was approved by
the General Assembly for these purposes in 1968.

Voluntary contributions amounting to $7.26 million were pledged
for its so-called Special Industrial Services (SIS).

Like other agencies, UNIDO participates in the UNDP—25 industrial projects, with Governing Council earmarkings of $22.47 mil-
lion, have been assigned to this agency; and $2.54 million has been
allocated to it from the technical assistance component.[96]

And finally, the UN regular programme of technical assistance has
allocated $991,400 for industrial projects in 1968.

The reasons behind this turn of events are well-known. For years
industrial development had received stepmotherly treatment under

---

[96] Position as of mid-1968.

the UN programmes; member-governments belatedly woke up to this fact and demanded greater attention to this field; many of them, especially those representing the developing countries, were persuaded that the best guarantee against a lapse into inaction was to set up a separate agency with an independent source of finance.

Yet what is really needed to stimulate industrial development is not a separate UN regular programme, nor voluntary contributions for SIS, nor perhaps a separate service like this, but high priority for industrial projects within the UNDP, better organized field offices with competent heads able to develop high-grade country programmes with a more pronounced accent on industry, and a determination to see that, as far as feasible, every country is provided with some attractive and economically viable projects in the industrial field. Where conditions for such projects are not immediately propitious, action should nevertheless be taken to create a favourable climate for them in suitable stages and as fast as possible.

The merger debate and its aftermath, the example of UNIDO, as so many other cases underline an old but oft-forgotten truth: it is easy to pass legislation, create programmes and set up new activities and new institutions; but once the die is cast, it is hard to retract or to reform, and much more so in the international field. The ideal time for coordinated action is *before,* and not *after,* the passage of such legislation.

It is up to the legislators, particularly the ECOSOC and the General Assembly, first, to minimize, through fresh legislative action, the ill effects of the multiplicity of programmes that have already been created; and second, to insist on greater circumspection, and to practise much more self-restraint, in handling legislative proposals for new programmes or new activities in future.

10

The philosophy of action-packed coordination that now prevails in the UN milieu urgently needs rethinking on four important counts, if it is not to pave the way to global frustration.

First, problems of development, as they exist in the field, are difficult in themselves. It should not be necessary to aggravate them by projecting senseless procedural complexities which are not pre-ordained by nature, but bear a distinct "made-in-UN" stamp; which do not promote but visibly hinder development; and which can and should be treated as readily dispensable.

Second, technical assistance and preinvestment work should not be confused with development. They are, with rare exceptions, only a *preparation* for it. The hiatus between preinvestment and investment-execution-operation has created problems which have by no means been resolved (see Chapter 18, Section 8). It is quite unnecessary to create or maintain another arbitrary hiatus—between technical assistance and preinvestment. This can be, and must be, dispensed with.

Third, skills do not, by themselves, produce development. There is need for the skill to integrate skills. This is preeminently a function of modern management, a crucial skill in this age of supertechnology and hyperspecialization, a skill that one in vain looks for in the UN world.

The Special Fund partially recognized this need—in insisting that each of its projects must be headed by a qualified project manager. And this is what made its projects much more effective as compared with the skills dumped in underdeveloped countries in the name of technical assistance. By the same token, however, a country needs a programme manager to integrate the skills of the agencies for the benefit of an entire economy and to help channel them in the most promising directions.

And finally, development is not simply a function of skills and money. There are other hurdles to be overcome, of which the political are often the most obdurate. The UN cannot stay away from them; it must face them, and try and negotiate them as best it can. For this it needs a new skill—a new brand of diplomacy. It must therefore plant, as its field representatives, men who are competent to serve the developing countries as "guide, philosopher, and friend," in addition to being good managers.

This, then, is the gear-shifting the UN family immediately needs —from the dreary philosophy of sterile coordination to a lively and imaginative one of better management and friendly diplomacy.

CHAPTER 18

Development As Business

*"We acknowledge little failings only to persuade
ourselves that we have no great ones."*

LA ROCHEFOUCAULD

A unified programme brought about through a real merger, particularly of the two components of the UNDP, will be a big step forward. It will remove what has been the worst negative factor in the UN operations and a needless drag on their effectiveness. But it will not be enough. The UN system, as organized at present, is *not* suitable to administer aid and promote development. It was *not* designed for this purpose; and only at a later stage the UN family stumbled into, or was saddled with, these additional responsibilities. The result is what one might have expected—some palpable structural deficiencies. These have in their turn led to the practice of applying a piecemeal approach to what are mostly interrelated problems of development, and to unbusinesslike handling of what are preeminently business functions.

The structural problem of the UN family has deep historical roots. The architects of the United Nations probably had too vivid a memory of the fate of the League of Nations—how this first experiment in world organization had foundered on the rock of international politics. In an apparent desire to play safe, they decided not to lump together in one monolithic organization, the highly sensitive political functions, such as harmonizing big power rivalries, averting threats of war, and localizing and extinguishing "brush fires," along with the vital but essentially nonpolitical tasks of building a better world. And so they designed a new pattern, a kind of a satellite system, with the United Nations as the parent body placed in the center and a group of spe-

188

cialized agencies revolving on their respective orbits, yet held together, as it were, by gravitational pull from the central body.

Once the design was adopted, the satellites began to multiply, sometimes through spin-off, but mainly through new creation. For one thing, the world that emerged out of the throes of the second world war was more complex and more compact, also more dynamic and more interdependent. And this in turn inexorably pointed to the need for greater initiative on a global basis covering a wide range of functions such as: development of agriculture, promotion of health, spread of education and culture, safety in civil aviation and maintenance of international standards, growth of telecommunications on modern and reasonably uniform lines, weather forecasting with greater dependability, peaceful uses of atomic energy and steps to forestall its abuses, maintenance of a sound international currency system, supply of long-range development capital, promotion of industries in the underdeveloped countries, improvement of the terms of trade to secure better prices for their staple exports. Even this incomplete enumeration of international functions should be enough to explain why the specialized agencies have tended to multiply rapidly. The UN family, in its widest sense, now consists of nineteen organizations and related bodies.[97]

There has been another powerful factor that has worked in the same direction. The United Nations family has thus far evinced little inclination to practice—family planning. On the contrary, the law of bureaucracy—Parkinson's law, if you like—has been the dominating force. Its effects have been manifest in the growing number of the specialized agencies, and even more so in the rapid expansion of the bureaucratic apparatus within each agency.

2

This proliferation, or explosion of international institutions on the world scene, has become a matter of deep concern even to the most ardent supporters of the UN cause. For example, speaking in February 1967, Mr. George Woods urged all those serving in international organizations to take what he termed "an anti-proliferation pledge." These organizations, he warned, were in danger of disappointing the publics that supported them because of their tendency to contribute more to the "already world-wide surplus of oratory than

---

[97] Counting UNICEF and GATT in addition to UN, IAEA, the specialized agencies, IMF and the Bank Group.

to the stock of new ideas and useful activities;" and of the confusing sight of "so many hands outstretched from so many different directions, in gestures either of help or of supplication."[98]

Mr. Woods pleaded that the creation of new entities should be reserved only for functions that demonstrably could not be accommodated within the existing set-up of the UN family; that, meanwhile, attention should be directed to improve the existing efforts, and to work out more effective coordination and a better distribution of labour among themselves.

This is an eminently rational plea. Without doubt the UN family badly needs its own nonproliferation treaty. Nevertheless, proliferation has already been allowed to go so far that a moratorium at this late stage will be of little avail. It is the second part of Mr. Woods' expostulation which is now more relevant. However, mere exhortation for better coordination and better division of labour is unlikely to produce much tangible result. What is needed is a thorough diagnosis of the chronic problems already created by the multi-agency structure of the UN system along with a rigorous search for practicable remedies. It is precisely here that the UN family has been unable to make much headway. The general nature of the problems has long been known. But the specific measures needed to undo, or at least to minimize, their ill effects have not been pinpointed in sufficiently concrete terms.

Whatever may have been the wisdom behind the decision to set up a series of specialized agencies, it has enormously complicated the task of using the UN system for sound international development.

Writing in 1956 Mr. Harlan Cleveland bluntly said:[99] "The UN is very badly organized to administer aid effectively." The Point Four Programme, he recalled, had started with the theory that "each agency of the Government would conduct its own world-wide functional programme—the Public Health Service killing mosquitoes all over the world, the Department of Agriculture promoting seed selection and the use of fertilizer in every agricultural country, and so forth." But soon the administration realized its policy error and discovered that "the important types of coordination had to do with relating health to agriculture to industry to education in a single country's

---

[98] Address by Mr. George D. Woods as President of the World Bank Group at the United Nations Conference on Trade and Development in New Delhi on 9 February, 1968.

[99] "The Theory and Practice of Foreign Aid" by Harlan Cleveland. Maxwell Graduate School of Citizenship and Public Affairs, Syracuse University. Mimeographed, November 1956. Page 71.

development programme, rather than with the day-to-day coordination of the malaria control efforts in Sardinia, Egypt, and Indonesia." The United States quickly modified the system, brought all its experts in one mission headed by one single mission chief serving under unified leadership in Washington. The UN started with the same initial error and stayed with it. "The ultra-sovereign specialized agencies," he said, "are much too jealously conscious of their independence to permit effective direction of the programme by the United Nations secretariat."[100]

Ideally, one might conceive of a single development programme for the world, administered by one single organization with individual departments carrying out the functions now entrusted to the specialized agencies. Under such a system, which would substantially resemble the structure of a national government, the problems of coordination would, by definition, be greatly simplified. Whatever may be the attractions of such an approach, it is bound to remain an academic exercise. It is too late in the day to undertake such a radical redesign; we can no longer start with a clean slate; the specialized agencies are there and we shall have to live with them. It is therefore far more fruitful to direct efforts to make the best of the existing situation. In other words, given the UN system with the specialized agencies, the question is: What steps could and should be taken to enhance their effectiveness?

An attempt to make the best of the present structure of the UN family will be meaningful only when it is based on a full realization of an all-important fact. Economic development of the underdeveloped countries differs fundamentally from the traditional duties of the UN and the specialized agencies, which consisted of such functions as numerous surveys, research and investigation on a wide range of subjects, compilation of statistics on a regional and world-wide basis covering a great many fields, publication of a enormous variety of reports annually or otherwise, dissemination of news of all kinds, and of course the vast amount of work that goes with the legislative bodies and their offshoots in each agency. Development, on the other hand, is business; and as such, it calls for business judgment of a high order at all major decision-making levels—in UN and in the agencies, in the UNDP, and in the field offices. For the same reason it calls for the adoption of the established principles of management with a rational division of functions, and larger and clearer delegation of responsibilities, subject to necessary overall supervision.

---

[100] Ibid., pages 55-56.

3

The problems resulting from the fragmented structure of the UN family have been compounded by another factor, also of historical origin though in a different sense. The United Nations and the larger specialized agencies were set up, as already noted, at a time when there was no development programme in existence. This vital function has been a later accretion; in the last two decades it has grown in volume and importance; yet the internal organization of the UN and the agencies does not adequately reflect the change. By and large, it is still the old setup trying to handle the new responsibilities in old-fashioned ways.

As a result, there is at present an unholy mixture of the two different categories of functions within each organization. Not only that; its various departments tend to operate with a large degree of independence, sometimes almost as subagencies. Indeed, some agencies, especially the larger ones, did develop something like a "sub-TAB" system, under which the available funds, especially those of EPTA, were virtually shared among the different departments according to some tacit formula. This sub-TAB spirit is still haunting most of the organizations. Thus, the UN family, organized as a system of satellites, has come to develop, within each agency, a sort of a subsatellite system, like wheels within wheels.

The result is a more or less complete domination of investment decisions by specialties and subspecialties. Far too much is left to the experts, while the overall manager continues to be conspicuous by his absence. In a modern business undertaking it would be inconceivable to leave the basic policy decisions to individual specialists or groups of them, without a qualified general manager to exercise the final judgment. Yet this is precisely what has been happening in the UN family in dealing with problems of development.

No wonder that priorities within an agency are not determined after a careful review of all the options that may exist at a given time; that on the contrary, they should emerge as resultants of the divergent pulls and pressures that may happen to be at work. A good deal often depends on the individual personality of the departmental heads. For example, livestock, fishery, and poultry are all vitally important subjects in many developing countries. Within FAO, however, these departments may be headed by people who are outstanding as experts in their respective fields, but who are not equally adept in administration and in inter-departmental manoeuvres for securing necessary priorities and funds for their projects. As a result, development in these fields may suffer from neglect despite their large potential to step up food production quickly and at a relatively low cost. Meanwhile, the personality factor may enable another department to pile up a great many projects, say, for land-and-water surveys, even though they are too large, too time-consuming, and too capital-intensive. For similar reasons, forestry development may be overemphasized to the neglect of food crops like wheat, rice and maize. Or, there may be premature stress on basic research and academic studies in a particular country, while the immediate need for developing an effective agricultural extension service may be neglected. Such examples are not the exceptions, but the rule in the UN family.

Besides, it is by no means rare for experts who are competent in their own specialties, to be saddled with administrative and operational responsibilities for which they demonstrably lack the aptitude and skill. The result is a loss of valuable expert man-hours to produce inexpert administration.

This loss was, if anything, aggravated by a decision taken a few years ago by several organizations such as UN, UNESCO and FAO. Until then, the practice for them was to maintain a sizable administrative unit to effect coordination of EPTA, Special Fund and the regular programme activities. This arrangement was never liked by the so-called "substantive" departments which supplied the expertise or what, in their view, was the real substance of the projects, on the ground that a non-technical administrative unit showed little understanding for the technical aspects of the problems and was therefore not qualified to do the coordinating job. At bottom, this was only another facet of the old conflict between experts and laymen. As it happened, the experts practically carried the day; the administrative units were truncated both in size and in functions, and were left with only such residual duties as channelling routine communications, drawing up schedules for visitors including field representatives, preparing periodic reports. The substantive responsibilities, both for programming and for operations, were transferred to the experts in the departments.

This was a retrograde step. For one thing, procedures had become a new specialty in the UN family, thanks to the multiplicity of programmes and the maze of rules and regulations that had grown around them. It is pathetic to see how experts struggle to get acquainted with them, often to end up with what is neither good administration nor good expert advice. Given the pluralism of programmes and the complications of procedures, even the non-technical coordinating units had been performing a useful function if only because of their specialized knowledge of the intricacies involved.

194

The decision was a retrograde step for a second and more important reason. It ignored the fact that development cannot be achieved by expertise alone, that the specialties have to be integrated meaningfully and informed with business judgment (*vide* Chapter 16, second fundamental). There was need for reform, but its character was misjudged. The real need was not to weaken and retrench the coordinating bodies, but to strengthen and expand them, and at the same time to place them under business-oriented general manager-type of administrators, possessing enough practical experience to evaluate a wide variety of expert opinions and advice, and to use them constructively as elements in formulating policies.

The divorce between the nontechnical—that is, administrative-cum-financial—and the technical functions has been, and still remains, a major weakness within the UN system. And the recent decentralization of the decision-making responsibility by giving wider powers to the technical departments has certainly not helped matters. A similar dichotomy has been a characteristic feature of the administration of the two programmes combined in the UNDP. Its technical assistance component (that is, former-EPTA) has all along maintained a non-technical headquarters setup since its declared policy was to leave all technical functions to the UN and the specialized agencies. Its Special Fund component, on the other hand, employs a sizable number of experts and consultants, but solely to render technical advice to non-technical executives who are the custodians of financial and administrative powers.

It is not surprising that such a system should lead to a duplication of technical service with frequent conflicts of expert opinions. The executives rely heavily on the views of their own experts which they themselves are unable to evaluate, and which are often pitted against those of the agencies. The same process may be more or less repeated within the agencies, depending on the extent to which the two functions are separated. Few experts are temperamentally disinclined to take part in these battles in expertise, especially when they can do so comfortably from the sidelines while forging the shield of technical advice that their nontechnical masters so clearly expect them to supply.

All this greatly slows down the decision-making process. There have been examples where the same projects have been "reviewed" or "appraised" by several missions. The delays are, of course, duly attributed to the complex nature of the problems. That they are far more the result of an illogical administrative setup is seldom realized, as also the fact that delays do not, by themselves, contribute to the soundness of the ultimate decisions.

No development programme can run efficiently with such built-in contradictions. From the structural angle, by far the most important reform needed is to end the artificial division between technical and nontechnical functions, and to unite them into one single managerial function—in the UN and in each agency, in the UNDP, and in the field offices.

4

The first and most obvious task in UN and the agencies is to separate all development activities financed from the UNDP, WFP, regular programmes and related sources, from all other nondevelopmental functions and to place them directly in charge of a fully qualified top-ranking general manager. As this designation implies, he should have the overall responsibility for all development-oriented activities. More specifically, it will be his task to counteract the centrifugal tendencies of the individual departments; to coordinate and, more than that, to integrate their activities; to take important policy decisions; and to supply that critical but hitherto missing element called business judgment. The advantages of such unified management will be enormous, especially if, as is hoped, the general manager and his staff are able to function broadly on the lines indicated below.

The development wing of an agency (or of UN) should of course draw heavily on the technical personnel of the non-development wing. And it could most appropriately do so on a reimbursable basis. This will ensure fuller utilization of the technical personnel; it will eliminate the waste of their valuable time on nontechnical jobs; it will keep down operational costs; and it will help resolve old controversies about the appropriate level of agency costs on UNDP projects.

Once the general managers have been installed in the UNDP, in UN and the agencies, it would be possible to work towards a new partnership within the UN family for efficient management of the development programmes. The UNDP should deal with the UN/agency general managers; respect, and heavily rely on, their technical-cum-business judgments, frame major policies and decisions in frequent consultation with them. It should then no longer find it necessary to maintain a large technical personnel on its own payroll to use them either against or as a crosscheck on the UN/agency experts. This duplication is not only costly and superfluous; at present it is also a constant source of friction and mutual frustration.

Nor should it be necessary for the UNDP administration to insist that UN and the agencies must approach it for every single financial authorization, large and small, including marginal cost adjustments on authorized projects and all kinds of contingencies. Such meticulous financial control, which an attempt is now being made to tighten further,[101] can only lead to overcentralization, creating needless work and causing undue delays without improving the quality of management. Worse still, such control is not compatible with the concept of partnership and mutual trust on which alone the UN family can expect to build a real *esprit de corps* and a unity of purpose.

Once the new system is introduced, the obvious next step for the UNDP would be to delegate substantial financial powers to the UN/ agency general managers. More specifically, they should be given the authority to make, within pre-determined limits, adjustments in the cost estimates of going projects subject to periodic reporting to the UNDP. A sizable sum of money could be appropriately placed at the disposal of each general manager to enable him to meet certain specified types of contingencies, such as minor adjustments in the estimates of authorized projects, and expenses for preliminary missions to help prepare new projects, subject to the submission of, say, a half-yearly report on the expenditures actually incurred. The sum might be of the order of $500,000 for UN and each large agency, and half that amount or less for each of the other agencies.

The general manager system, as outlined above, provides the best hope for building durable interagency bridges. Development, it cannot be emphasized too often, is "an integrated multidisciplinary activity," and "progress depends upon the simultaneous prosecution of a number of different but interrelated activities."[102]

Yet integration of disciplines is a most difficult task in the UN family because of the autonomous character of the specialized agencies. The guiding motto for them still continues to be: Agency first, UN next. Even when agency representatives get together in a committee or conference for joint deliberation, every move and every single proposal or resolution is jealously scanned primarily from the angle of how much an agency will stand to gain or lose from it. Sectional viewpoints tend to prevail over the imperatives of development. There are numerous examples where interdependent activities have been deliberately split into arbitrary parts and parcelled out to different agencies.

---

101 This will be the result of the procedural changes that are now being introduced for UNDP/TA. on 1 January 1969. See Chapter 9 on "Plus Ça Change. . . ."

102 The quotation is from the Second Report (page 9) of the Advisory Committee on the Application of Science and Technology to Development. United Nations (E/4026), May 1965.

Even when several agencies work on the same project, the cooperation is usually more apparent than real. The joint approach may simply be the outcome of the fact that several agencies have successfuly staked their claims on a project and have therefore joined it as suppliers of their own specialties. On a water development project, for example, the main responsibility may rest with UN, but FAO will be involved for irrigation and drainage, WHO for prevention of water pollution, WMO for hydrology. In home economics, the organizations contesting for an active part are UN, FAO, UNESCO, maybe also WHO and UNICEF from the angle of nutrition, while on a community development project the claimants would be all these five plus the ILO. On such multiagency projects the specialties are mostly juxtaposed, not integrated; and there is seldom any suggestion of a single unified management in the business sense of the term.

Sometimes even this limited interagency cooperation may be too much to expect. The case of an important river valley project may be cited as an example. Apart from flood control, power generation and navigation, the project aimed at drainage and reclamation of large tracts of fertile agricultural land. A senior FAO executive, speaking in the name of his agency, remarked *inter alia*:[103] His department was fully organized to handle such jobs in their entirety, and they would be very happy to take over this Special Fund project, but only if FAO were designated as its Executing Agent. If, on the other hand, the primary responsibility were given to the United Nations, they would not be interested. To clinch his point he then added that FAO had enough river valley projects on hand or in view, for which it was, or would be, the Executing Agent. He therefore saw no reason why the agency should come in to "play second fiddle" to somebody else.

The executive made the statement without a blush. This was not surprising. To grind the axe of an agency, or of one of its departments, is accepted as the normal order of things within the UN family. In fact, this is what the administration mostly expects from its executives and rewards them for the success they achieve. What is considered abnormal is to question these facts of the UN life.

As it happened, the project was reduced in scope to cover only river regulation; the United Nations was designated as the Executing Agent; the agricultural part of the project, despite its extraordinarily high potential for future production, was indefinitely shelved though, ostensibly, only for further evaluation.

---

[103] In personal discussion with the writer in 1965.

There is no ready-made answer to the deep-seated interagency rivalry or to the all-pervading professional parochialism. Nevertheless, there can be no doubt that one major reason why these symptoms are present in such acute form is the absence of an overall authority to hold them in check, to treat development, first and foremost, as business, and therefore to apply to it, as far as possible, the fundamentals of management despite the strong pressures from special interests. The installation of general managers in each of the UN bodies will create countervailing forces and should set in motion a trend in the right direction. The common language of management which they may be expected to speak should go a long way to create a common concern for what is, after all, a common cause. This, is any case, remains our best hope.

5

The structural change proposed here—the separation of all UNDP and other development activities in UN and each agency and placing them in charge of an experienced general manager in each case—will be a big step towards better management of the UN programmes. Clearly, the full benefit of this change can be realized only when the UNDP itself is reorganized on the lines of a modern business. The most urgent need here has already been indicated; to end the separation of "administrative" and "technical" functions and to introduce the general manager system.

There can be no question that the UNDP administration functions with high efficiency in several areas. It excels in rule-making and rule enforcement; its document factory runs to full capacity—for example, it could rightly pride itself on having turned out on time some 3000 pages of documents before one single session of the Governing Council; it shows rare skill in maintaining political balance in personnel matters; it has great experience in managing committees and conferences, and in piloting them in the desired direction. But it is decidedly weak in business judgment at the critical levels. And its "think factory" runs mainly on truisms and clichés.

At the 1968 January session of the Governing Council, the Italian delegate, Mario Franzi, himself a former president of the 37-member council, wondered aloud if "governing" should not be eliminated from the council's title unless it got more effective power. In reply to the points raised by Mr. Franzi and others, the Administrator Mr. Hoffman stated that, although the programme responded only to requests from governments, its field representatives were active as "consulting architects" in the preparation of these requests.

Another suggestion made was that the council should be advised not only of projects recommended for approval, but also of those not recommended. To this Mr. Hoffman replied: "The council would have to meet 365 days a year. Right now we have some 400 requests under consideration."

These replies sufficed—at least for the present. The council bowed before the great idealist reverentially, but apparently still unconvinced. How long will the *argumentum ad vercundum* carry the day? And how long should it?

Mr. Hoffman was unquestionably on sure ground so far as the principle was concerned. The Governing Council, which is a political body with heterogeneous composition and wide differences in ideology, outlook, competence, even in comprehension of the essentials of good management, can function only as an overall policy-making body. Management has to be insulated from political pressures.

But Mr. Hoffman would have been on far surer ground had the headquarters and the field offices been demonstrably so organized as to ensure that high-grade business judgment was, in fact, applied to the projects at all phases. That there is wide room for improvement in this respect has long been an open secret. The misgivings that stemmed from this knowledge were echoed in the Governing Council. And it is most unlikely that they will be allayed until the essential reforms are carried through to inspire greater confidence in the management.

As for the "consultant architects" (i.e., the Resident Representatives) in the field, their functions will be scrutinized in the next chapter to show the utter inadequacy of the existing arrangement, why they have to serve as impotent consultants mainly as architects of routine compliance with little or no elbowroom to take creative initiative. It will also be argued why they must, as a matter of overriding urgency, be elevated to the status of fullfledged general managers at the country level and endowed with unified responsibility, adequate powers, and a high diplomatic status.

What cannot be stressed too strongly is that the UN family will be able to pursue development as business only when: first, the UN programmes, or in any case the two components of the UNDP, are fully merged—in the financial, procedural and managerial sense—to create a single unified programme (see Chapter 17); and, second, the three-dimensional structural reform is carried through and general managers are installed at the three decisive points of the sprawling

international conglomerate—that is, in the UN as well as in each
agency for managing all its development activities, at the UNDP headquarters, and in each recipient country as argued in this and the next
chapter. These two reforms must come first. Only then will it be possible to take other necessary measures to raise the quality of UN
performance to a markedly higher level.

6

The most significant benefits that will follow once the UN programmes and the administrative structures of the UN family have been
rationalized along the suggested lines, can be briefly indicated.

The Special Fund procedures, as we have already seen (*vide* Chapter
11), marked a vast improvement as compared with those of EPTA.
The preparation of each project in depth and on a sizable scale; clear
definition of its objectives with attention to related problems; provision
of essential expert services, equipment and supplies, award of fellowships to selected nationals for advanced training in foreign countries
in order to qualify themselves for specific jobs to be performed later
on the project; insistence on adequate counterpart support by the
receiving government not only as matching contribution but also in
terms of national personnel; authorization of each project for its full
duration; a plan of operation agreed to by all concerned in advance;
a joint UNDP-government approach to execute a specific job, and not
simply to provide technical advice from outside—all these are unquestionably sound in principle and conform to the best business
methods.

Even the Special Fund operation, however, are far from perfect and
need to be improved in several important directions. The supply of
projects is at present left too much to chance; the method of screening
the requested projects at headquarters can no doubt be improved; there
is a marked overemphasis on infrastructure projects at the expense of
those oriented towards productivity; the preparation and execution of
the plan of operation often consume too much time; the implementation of authorized projects could be more efficient and expeditious.
All these factors directly affect the performance of the programme and
are therefore well worth some further elucidation.

The fundamental most commonly violated by the UN programmes
—and here the Special Fund is certainly no exception—is the need
to apply the *whole-country* approach with a thorough investigation of
all the possibilities that exist, leading to the selection of the *topmost
few* that are immediately realizable, and that would give the best

results within a short time and at a low cost. Or, to put it in more modern terminology, what is needed is the application of the multi-discipline, problem-oriented, or "systems approach" to an entire economy. This, incidentally, is what some private business organizations are already doing in isolated instances. For example, the Litton International Corporation, a subsidiary of the Litton Industries, which has been advising the Greek Government on economic development, made the recommendation, in February 1967, that the proposal for constructing five large and costly dams in the island of Crete be abandoned and replaced by a system of ground water storage. Such a system would be far less spectacular than the proposed dams, but the payoff, Litton argued, would be high.

The UN family, whatever may be its professions, has in practice deplorably failed in adopting the "systems approach." The UNDP/TA (former-EPTA) has been talking about country-programming, while moving away from it in reality. The UNDP/SF, under the leadership of Mr. Hoffman, had a clearer vision of the goal; but encumbered with the shackles of the UN system, it could take only a few faltering steps in that direction. The fact is that the UN family—this will be even clearer from the next chapter—is simply not set up to perform this essential task in the recipient countries. It is not disciplined enough to think in terms of a multi-discipline, problem-oriented approach embracing a whole economy. Instead, it has been applying what is, in effect, a series of single-discipline, agency-oriented random approach to the problems of a developing country.

It is futile to expect that the unhappy effects of this specialty-mongering could be remedied by the *ad hoc* wisdom supplied by short-term planning missions which it is now becoming the practice for the UNDP to depute to individual countries. These missions look like teams, but they lack the team spirit; they are dominated by the special-interest approach; in general, they are deficient in practical experience in dealing with problems of economic development. All this is usually reflected in their end-products which are mostly summations of specialty-inspired proposals, make poor sense from a business angle, and constitute a precarious basis for committing large funds.

It is essential to get away from the illusion that the tasks of programme-planning can be fulfilled through such cursory treatment. Obviously, the first and foremost need here is for the UNDP, and for the UN family, so to reorganize the field offices that they can take care of the brunt of this programming function along with all other related activities. And there is one, and only one, way of achieving this, namely, to install competent general managers at the country level and to give them adequate support, from the UN and the agencies, with technical personnel, as and when necessary, to work with and under them. The functions and responsibilities of the country-level general managers—that is, those of the Resident Representatives—will be further discussed in the next chapter.

In addition, the UNDP will be well advised to hire from time to time the services of competent bodies from outside, especially reputed public corporations, to apply the "systems approach" to entire economies. Such a service, like all other forms of assistance, can of course be offered by the UNDP only when specifically requested by the governments. However, the governments may be informed that this service would be available to them if they feel interested, and may even be encouraged to give it serious consideration.

The "system analysis" would be a most desirable kind of preinvestment activity for the Special Fund.[104] It would help lay down the broad framework of a country programme with all its essentials and with a rational order of priorities, which should greatly facilitate the preparation of projects for the Special Fund and other programmes. Nor would the employment of private corporations for carrying out the analyses in question involve any new principle. It has now become a common practice on a variety of Special Fund projects to farm out the main jobs on a contract basis to outside bodies, particularly to private corporations.

In recent years there has been a rapid growth of corporations that are competent to apply the "systems approach" to each developing economy in its entirety. And more of them are likely to spring up, especially if a programme like the UNDP, maybe also the World Bank, decides to make use of their services.

Employment of competent private firms will have some clear advantages. A high-grade firm will be able to mobilize, on short notice, a group of experts welded as a team to apply a truly multi-disciplinary approach, unlike the UN family which, to do the job with its own staff (that is, on a "force account" basis), must every time assemble experts on an *ad hoc* basis, who, coming from very different sources and representing special interests, seldom mesh to form a real team. Besides, a private firm, if well chosen, will bring with it wide experience in integrated development of natural resources along with seasoned

---

104 The World Bank has shown greater awareness of this need; hence the stress on periodic review of national economies by its ad hoc missions. The national development plans—5-year or otherwise—can seldom meet this need if only because they are usually all-embracing and not realistic enough.

business judgment, without which an exercise like this will have little practical value. The quality of the analysis coupled with the reputation of the firm should make it easier to attract investment capital from outside. It can also provide valuable on-the-job training to qualified nationals of the recipient country in what is a difficult but extremely important field of activity. An obligation to provide such training may well be written into the contract.

What about the cost? The services of such firms may, and probably will, cost more than what the UN family now spends on its "force account" planning jobs. But this is where it should learn *not* to economize. Development pursued as business rather than as a bureaucratized affair implies, among other things, that the UNDP administration should have the wisdom to pay, in a vital matter like this, the full premium warranted by the superior quality of work based on experience and mature judgment.

<h2 style="text-align:center">7</h2>

The Special Fund projects requested by the governments would greatly improve in quality if they were to emerge out of an in-depth investigation and careful weighing by competent people of the wide range of alternatives that exist in each country. Meanwhile, the process followed at UNDP headquarters for appraising and screening the projects actually requested leaves much to be desired.

The general practice is to subject each request to an independent technical review and evaluation either by the UNDP's own personnel or by a short-term consultants' mission in the field. This would, *prima facie,* look like a praiseworthy concern on the part of the administration to be doubly sure about the merit of a project. The facts are however less reassuring. The headquarters' independent appraisal is by no means superior to the two other technical scrutiny to which a Special Fund project is subjected as a general rule—first, in the field at the time of formulating the request, and later in the hands of the agency concerned.

What should be a partnership approach among the three parties —the UNDP, the agencies, and the field representatives—in the interest of producing the best possible projects, tends to grow into a tug-of-war among experts. The multiple technical reviews substantially add to the costs, without necessarily adding to the quality of the final decisions. As part of its independent evaluation process, the headquarters raises questions that may be surprisingly superficial and off the mark. Its authority to make financial allocations is not matched by its capacity to supply worthwhile business judgment. What it supplies instead from headquarters-based sources are fresh doses of expertise which duplicates that of the agencies, and an overdose of "bureaucratese" that delays decisions.

The fact that the number of projects formally submitted to the Special Fund far exceeds the available resources—in recent years the requests have been two to three times as large—creates a dilemma for the headquarters: It is unable to accept them all for lack of funds, and it is unwilling to take the responsibility of turning down requests for fear of displeasing the governments. The problem is usually resolved by adopting two devices. The requesting governments are frequently asked to indicate their *own* order of priorities for the projects submitted to the UNDP for assistance so that these could be considered in that order as and when warranted by the financial status of the programme. And the process of evaluation of projects is suitably lengthened so as to keep them long enough in the pipeline.

Such a solution may be ideal from the angle of political and bureaucratic convenience, but is nonetheless inappropriate. It is incompatible with business methods, and it can hardly help build up confidence in the administration. There is little doubt that it is this lack of confidence that lies at the root of the growing demand of the Governing Council members for a larger say about the projects submitted to it for approval, starting from the earlier phases of screening, scrutiny and selection. It would be wise for the administration to recognize this fact rather than to continue to treat the demand as unreasonable.

The most serious weakness of the Special Fund projects, as pointed out previously,[105] arises from the fact that they are confined only to the preinvestment phase. This means that, in general, one must shop around for investment capital after the projects have been completed, but without any guarantee of success. Thus, Special Fund projects, carried through with so much effort and having aroused so much expectation, may well remain paper projects and never lead to the end-objective of investment and actual development. This danger is far from imaginary. In fact, while political compromises led to the establishment of a Special Fund deliberately restricted only to pre-investment work, thoughtful people, both inside and outside the UN family, were not unaware of the risks involved. Some whispered, even at that early stage, their misgivings about the future of this newborn half-programme.

---

105 See especially Chapter 12.

Time has not allayed, but only confirmed the initial misgivings. By the end of February, 1968 the Governing Council had authorized 873 projects (excluding 20 projects which were subsequently cancelled) and had made allocations totalling $862 million. By the same date 178 projects were completed; of these only 37 were able to attract "follow-up" investments, amounting to some $1,900 million.[106]

Not all the completed projects, it may be rightly argued, called for follow-up investment since they consisted not only of resource surveys (108), but also of technical education and training (43), applied research (25), and economic development planning (2). Information is not available on the precise number of projects that did call for follow-up financing, nor on the appropriate level of such finance. What cannot be questioned, however, is that the proportion of completed projects that needed but failed to attract long-term capital remains disconcertingly high.

The follow-up investments of $1,900 million on 37 completed projects look quite impressive, as compared with the Governing Council allocations totalling $185 million and government counterpart expenditures of some $225 million. Allowance should, however, be made for the fact that they include a few rather large projects and that on a number of them investments, mainly from domestic sources, were either under way or had been assured.[107] This fact, of course, made the Special Fund support even more, and not less, desirable so as to improve the quality of the projects and their cost-benefit relationship. The relevant point, however, is that not all the follow-up investments in the 37 projects were new; nor did they necessarily result from the Special Fund's preinvestment activity.

Since a much larger number of projects are now approaching completion, the gap between preinvestment work and follow-up investment threatens to widen correspondingly, giving rise to serious concern. To counteract this trend, the UNDP took some "practical steps" which were reported to the Governing Council in January 1968. Among these were:[108]

---

[106] See Appendix 1B, Table 3; also Governing Council document DP/L. 67/Add. 3 dated 12 April 1968.

[107] Four projects accounted for $1,742 million as follow-up investments, or over 90 per cent of the total: Electric power study, Argentina—$333m; hydro power study, Brazil—$371m; Niger dams survey, Nigeria—$238m; Skopje urban plan, Yugoslavia—$800m (mainly domestic resources).

[108] Some details were reported in the "Preinvestment News" of the UNDP, February 1968 issue. Also see Governing Council document DP/L. 61 dated 5 December 1967.

—The establishment of a Development Finance Service within the UNDP. Its business will be to establish and maintain contacts with the international financial community and "to stimulate interest" in the investment possibilities that were being uncovered in the developing countries.

—Increased use of the services of financial advisors during the implementation of "more promising" preinvestment projects "to assist governments" in locating and, as far as possible, in exploiting the sources of funds.

—Building up cooperative arrangements between the UNDP and international and regional banks and other main sources of financing. The World Bank now entrusts to the UNDP preinvestment studies costing over $200,000 each. The African and the Asian Development Banks are also looking to the UNDP in the preinvestment phase. And the UNDP hopes that the Banks in turn will provide finance for an increased number of completed Special Fund projects.

—Bringing the investment opportunities to the attention of public and private investors, such as the main bilateral aid programmes and broadly based international investment companies like ADELA which consists of over 40 financial and industrial groups interested in financing development projects in Latin America.

All these are admittedly steps in the right direction; and they reflect a welcome recognition of the urgency to solve the problem of follow-up investment. Nevertheless, the nagging question remains: Are they going to be enough? The answer, if given with a due sense of responsibility, must be in the negative. A completed preinvestment project not carried through the actual investment phase imposes a needless burden on a poor developing country, since it ties up much of its slender resources —financial, material, and human—without giving any tangible return. The plain fact is that the present method—carrying out preinvestment work *first* and *then* looking around for investment capital—is simply not good enough. It involves too much of a gamble in the future. In no worthwhile business undertaking would one assume, or tolerate, such high risks. Clearly, the task is to reduce the risks to a minimum and, wherever possible, to eliminate them altogether. This can be done—provided the UNDP decides to satisfy two basic conditions:

First, every preinvestment project must be chosen with the same meticulous care and after the same hardheaded economic evaluation that would, for example, be insisted upon as a matter of course by an organization like the World Bank before it decides to commit investment funds to a particular project. Such self-discipline is absolutely essential. Without it preinvestment activity would cease to be a responsible affair.

And second, a preinvestment project should, as a general rule, be undertaken only when there is adequate advance assurance that, on its completion, the required investment capital would be forthcoming from internal or external sources, or from a combination of both.

These conditions are now honoured mostly in the breach. The present practice *ostensibly* rests on three arguments: the preinvestment projects are opening up *new* investment opportunities; feasibility studies are essential to establish whether or not actual capital investment would be justified; and only such studies, when completed, could reveal the order of the capital as well as of the expertise, equipment and training that would be needed for individual projects. The arguments no doubt sound plausible. That is why so many minds have been trapped by them. Yet they do not bear scrutiny.

A country-wide systems approach discussed earlier will reveal that in every developing economy—large or small, relatively developed or primitive—there are, here and now, plenty of opportunities for productive investment of all the capital that could be mobilized in the foreseeable future from domestic and international sources. To detect them, all that is needed is a systematic approach and keen, trained eyes. The developing countries have by no means reached the saturation point where all known and easily detectable high-payoff investment possibilities have been exhausted, giving rise to a desperate need for *new* investment opportunities that could be uncovered only through a series of longrange preinvestment studies. That point, in almost all cases, is a long way off.

Even where feasibility studies are a prerequisite, it should not be forgotten that most of the investment capital must in the end come from domestic sources, which at present account for 80 per cent of the annual capital formation in the developing countries taken together. In the great majority of cases the governments could, therefore, give advance undertakings to the effect that they would find the necessary capital for investment should this be warranted by the findings of the feasibility studies. Even where external capital is envisaged—from the World Bank or the IDA, from the regional banks, bilateral programmes, or other sources—an advance understanding, even if on somewhat flexible terms regarding the supply of investment funds could be entered into, and ought to be insisted upon, as a precondition for launching an expensive, time-consuming preinvestment study.

The *real* reasons for the lax practice now followed in promoting preinvestment projects lie, however, somewhere else: the large number of projects stimulated by special interests; the absence of able managers with overall authority to keep them in check and to judge projects by applying strictly objective criteria; political considerations that frequently tend to sway decisions rather than their economic implications. And to all these must be added something even more fundamental: A preinvestment programme, from its very nature, can escape certain elementary discipline, and can, if it so chooses, launch its projects without concern for their ultimate fate. It can do so because, unlike the IBRD, IDA and similar organizations, it need not cater for investment capital, and has therefore no reason to worry that the capital is invested only in productive, self-liquidating projects in order not to jeopardize its repayment prospects.

It is the absence of this compulsion that helps to explain why the number of infrastructure projects dealing with research, surveys, training, etc. at several removes from the point of actual production and requiring little or no investment capital, has been increasing rapidly, despite the great urgency of multiplying projects that would stimulate production more directly and more immediately. And it also explains why the UN family could be gripped by a kind of *quantomania,* or a deep concern for a quantitative expansion of the programmes, without evincing an equivalent zeal for their *qualitative* improvement.

8

Certain other shortcomings in the Special Fund administration apparently flow from the same root cause. The preparation and execution of the plan of operation is a sluggish process; as a result, the time lag between the Governing Council approval of a project and its formal initiation is frequently much too long. Nor could these delays be, in good conscience, attributed to any relentless pursuit of high quality in producing what is admittedly a key document. On the contrary, the consensus among knowledgeable people is that they are the result of a lengthening red tape coupled with what is often little more than repeated clerical overhaul of drafts. It should certainly be possible to standardize much of this document and to handle it with far greater dispatch.

Finally, the implementation of Special Fund projects contains considerable room for improvement. The most important single step needed here is delegation of responsibilities from the agencies to the field representatives. At present the main function of the Resident Representative, once the plan of operation for a project is executed, is to keep a general watch over its progress;[109] all responsibilities are concentrated in the hands of the executing agency; and the agency, to all intents and purposes, treats the Project Manager as its field representative for the project in question. Thus, in a country with, say, half a dozen Special Fund projects, there are as many Project Managers; each of them is operated from the agency headquarters under a remote control system which extends not only to technical matters but also to administrative details; and since the head of the department concerned is already overloaded with other work, the Project Manager is, in practice, placed in charge of some junior officer at headquarters with whom he engages in massive correspondence.

Clearly, the delegation of responsibilities in this case should be not from the head of an agency department to one of his junior officers *at headquarters,* but from him to a senior officer serving as general manager *in the field* and accepted by the agency as its own representative. It is also clear that this should be done by all the agencies for all Special Fund projects that are under way in a particular country.[110]

This is what should be done according to the accepted canons of public administration and the established principles of business management. That this will greatly improve the efficiency of the field operations and will result in large savings in terms of both money and time goes without saying. But what are self-evident truths seem to escape the UN family with surprising ease. In the next chapter will be discussed the man-made obstacles which its own ingenuity has hitherto created to frustrate this overdue reform.

In a programme that specializes only in preinvestment work, here then are the fatal pitfalls of the prefix *pre:* projects can originate more from specialty-cum-political pressures than from systematic coun-

---

[109] This is the case even where projects are developed by a Resident Representative through his personal efforts. In short, the business of a Resident Representative is to procure business for an agency. Once this is done, he must keep his hands off.

[110] An Executive Agency representative, while on a field trip to Belgrade, described his concept of a Resident Representative's functions in the following endearing words: "As a Resident Representative, you should keep aloof from the project. You are like a spare tire and should step in only when the project is in trouble." "And what should this spare tire do," I asked, "when there is a whole series of flat tires?" Ironically, this is what was happening on this important project and it could be kept going only with a great deal of personal effort from the Resident Representative.

try-wide studies; there is no urge to develop the best possible activities within a country, no concern to maximize the leverage effects of the programme, no heartache if "completed" projects remain incomplete for lack of investment; screening of projects tends to become a closely-guarded prerogative of a few; political expediency or bureaucratic fiat may, without undue qualms, be substituted for business judgment; there is little incentive to efficiency, and a great deal of it to—muscle-flexing. All this is possible because the programme is not obligated to respect the fundamentals of development and to show results. It can prosper in the twilight zone of preinvestment, fascinate the world with a colourful display of activity, and escape accountability.

All this underscores once again the great fallacy of separating technical assistance from preinvestment activity, and preinvestment activity from investment and development. This multiple divorce cannot but breed irresponsibility and create a fictious sense of progress, not only in those who are directly in charge of the programmes, but in a great many other people who are prone to accept unquestioningly the UN family's complacent self-evaluation.

The folly of dividing an indivisible development process into arbitrary stages is all the more damaging in its effects because it comes on top of what is a disunited UN family with deep organizational cleavages. The satellite pattern of the UN system, it may be assumed, has come to stay and, consequently, it has to be accepted as an unalterable fact. Nor would it be practicable to reduce the number of UN agencies. What can be reduced, however, is the number of UN programmes, and the extent of their autonomous behaviour. This points emphatically to the need for the two major reforms mentioned earlier —to end the multiplicity of the programmes and to merge, at least to start with, the two components of the UNDP fully and completely into one; and to install general managers in UN and in each agency, in every recipient country, and at UNDP headquarters. These reforms are practicable and indispensable. No "feasibility study" should be needed to arrive at this conclusion. Nor should it be hard for the UN family to realize that, without these two crucial reforms, it can never do anything like justice to the responsibilities it has so zealously assumed for world development.

9

The confusion that now reigns within a participating organization is due primarily to a failure to separate its relatively new dynamic business activities from its traditional administrative functions. At present it is trying to ride two animals—a horse and a mule—without realizing that they are different in build and gait, and therefore call for quite different handling; that, in any case, they cannot be kept comfortably in harness since they do not lend themselves to coordination; that, in fact, the more strenuous is the effort to coordinate them, the more awkward will be the result. The only rational solution is to separate the two and to concede to each the specific treatment it needs.

The business functions—that is, activities mostly financed from the UNDP, possibly also from other programmes—must be headed by a general manager for reasons explained earlier. He would be the pivot in each agency, not simply to coordinate its sub-specialties, but to control them and weld them as and when necessary so as to make the utmost possible business sense for particular projects. Similarly, a responsible general manager will not blindly assert the rights of his agency, nor will he rest content with purely mechanical coordination with other agencies. He will readily agree, whenever the need arises, to *coalesce* the specialties of his own agency with those of others in order to secure the best possible overall results in terms of development.

A general manager will no doubt need his own whole-time staff. It has to be high grade and business-oriented, but it need not be large, especially if, as suggested earlier, an arrangement is made for him to draw professional experts from the non-development wing of the agency on reimbursable cost basis.

Though stationed within an agency, a general manager will, because of the nature of his functions, have a somewhat different orientation. On the legislative side, he will have a stronger link with the UNDP Governing Council, perhaps also with the ECOSOC and the Second Committee of the General Assembly, than with the legislative body of his own agency. On the operational side, he must clearly maintain very close day-to-day contacts with the UNDP administration, with all the field representatives (see next chapter), and with his counterparts in the other agencies, especially where multiagency activities are involved.

Obviously, a general manager, as conceived here, will be effective only when he functions as the right-hand man of the Secretary-General or Director-General of his organization, but with a large delegation of responsibilities and with undivided authority over the activities concentrated in the development wing. In short, this wing would be the business department, or *de facto* a sub-agency, of the organization to conduct all its development activities in close collaboration with other UN bodies. It follows that this business department, or the sub-agency, and not the organization as a whole, would, ipso facto, be the "executing agency" for carrying through Special Fund projects.

There is no exact precedent for the kind of relationship envisaged here between the executive head of a participating organization and the general manager of its business department. However, it does bear some resemblance to the relationship that now exists between the UN Secretary-General and the Executive Director of UNICEF, or between the UN Secretary-General or FAO Director-General on the one hand and the Executive Director of the World Food Programme on the other.

The case for a large delegation of powers to the general manager should be fairly obvious. For one thing, the Secretary-General or the Director-General is over-loaded with work. He must perforce devote a great deal of his time to the legislative bodies, to the delegations, to committees and conferences, to public relations, to world travels and, last but not least, to fund-raising. He simply does not have the time to deal with problems of development, except in a very general way. Besides, his strengths almost always lie in administrative *cum* diplomatic work, and very rarely in the business field which calls for a different background of experience. And finally, business administration requires freedom of initiative and flexibility in operations, which can be best secured only when it is insulated from other kinds of activities.

There are two factors which, though somewhat concealed, are of paramount importance in this context. Both have hitherto tended to escape the notice of the UN family, and even of the member governments of the developed countries who ought to know better.

First, the UN programmes are confined to technical assistance and pre-investment work, unconnected with any capital development fund; nonetheless, functionally, they *are* business programmes since their sole purpose is to promote development. The decisions they involve are akin to those of business; and what cannot be stressed too often, they directly influence government decisions for allocation of the available resources for development. That they are divorced from a capital development fund does in no way alter their inherent quality and turn them into non-business activities. The sole effect of this divorce is to make this pitfall more treacherous, to deprive the programmes of high grade business judgment, to make their selection and preparation less stringent, also less conscientious.

Second, the development and nondevelopment activities are now lumped together, in UN and in each agency, under the oldfashioned departmental administration. Yet the first category clearly needs a different treatment. For example, in recruiting experts and consultants, also in selecting firms and awarding contracts, rigid conformity to rules often affects quality. There should be wider room for seasoned judgment and discretionary powers to be exercised by competent managers in the best interest of projects and programmes.

The proper line of functional demarcation—in UN and in each agency—must run not between technical and nontechnical activities as at present, but between those that have business characteristics and those that have not. The first division is illogical—it cannot but hurt development. The second is indispensable—without this no development business can succeed.

10

Can the UN family attract general managers with the requisite background of experience? And can it afford them? These are suspiciously familiar questions that are mostly raised not to facilitate the search for truth but to foreclose it. In the world of business, it is an axiom that success depends on two things: the ability to hire good men, and to take their advice. How can it be different with what is perhaps the world's most complicated business today—the development of the underdeveloped world?

The question of cost would have been more convincing if it were uniformly applied to *all* levels. And what are the facts? In recent years the secretariats of the UNDP, UN and the agencies have undergone rapid expansion; the number of their employees has gone up steeply; and in keeping with the standard behaviour of modern establishments, the expansion has taken place mostly in the lower ranks, that is, at and near the bases of the organizational pyramids. The administrative budgets have soared; the investments in experience, creative imagination and managerial ability have tended to remain relatively low; but there has been no sign of stinting on expenditures for routine administration, for the mounting volume of clerical work, and for the growing international army of coordinators.

And to this, according to the judgment of knowledgeable people, should be added an even more dubious type of investment. A veteran administrator with long experience in the field of development once made the following significant comment: "The patronage problem is serious enough in a national government. For a specialized agency it has to be multiplied by about five because of the sovereignty issue."[111]

---

[111] During a personal discussion in 1967.

The Director-General of one of the UN organizations explained, in the course of an informal personal talk,[112] the dilemma he had been faced with. On joining the organization he had found it considerably overstaffed; he therefore initiated a policy of retrenchment in the interest of economy. But pretty soon he encountered opposition coming mostly from the delegations, until he was forced to the conclusion that the delegations liked to *talk* about economy, but in fact did not *want* it. And so he reluctantly had to suspend the effort.

No one with inside knowledge of the UN family would deny that feather-bedding is a fairly common phenomenon, though its extent varies from one organization to another. This frequently leads to a scramble for the available work, which in turn builds up a twofold pressure: first, to inflate the existing work sufficiently—usually through committee discussions, memoranda-writing, ad hoc studies, field inspection, periodic reports, correspondence—in short, through a judicious lengthening of the whole decision-making process; and second, to secure more new work, above all, by promoting new projects. That too many experts can spoil development is something the UN family has yet to recognize and worry about.

The principle of "geographical distribution" of jobs is no doubt a complicating factor in an international organization. Nor can it be denied that it opens the door rather wide to patronage. On the other hand, an international organization, because of its very character, must maintain a certain geographical spread in job distribution. If this has become more of a handicap than it really need be, it is mainly because of the way the principle has been put to practice. A determined effort, at the top levels, to seek out the right men within the framework of geographical representation would yield far better results. Such an effort is, however, none too common. Instead, the temptation to seek out politically convenient men to build up the influence of a programme or organization, or of some individuals, has often proved much too strong to resist in practice.

The facts just cited show the real nature of the problem. The UN family does not lack the *financial* ability to attract high grade men to serve as general managers; indeed, a shift to the managerial system proposed here will lead to substantial savings, apart from greatly improving the entire programme operations. What the UN really lacks is the *will* to treat development primarily as a non-political, non-bureaucratic business, freed from half-concealed patronage, and firmly

---

[112] In late 1966.

geared to the essentials of management. If success in business depends on the ability to hire good men and then to take their advice, the converse is no less true: Good men can be hired only when they know that they will be listened to and their advice will be accepted. Creative minds instinctively shun duels with power-loving bureaucrats and self-serving politicians. But they can be tempted with challenging tasks and real opportunities to create and to serve even if accompanied by surprisingly small sums of money. It is this fund of idealism that the UN family has yet to tap.

The development programmes of the United Nations have, in recent years, grown into the biggest international show business, so said some cynics. It would be hard to deny that there is truth in the remark. The gap between the show and the substance is without doubt much too wide today. It can be bridged only when the UN family is able to accept and apply fully the axioms of development discussed earlier and to abandon its establishmentarian approach in favour of a managerial one.

11

The changes proposed above, it is needless to say, will in no way diminish the role of the agencies. If they are indispensable for speedier and more orderly progress in the developing countries, they are no less needed in the interest of the agencies themselves.

The agencies have assumed a major role for development. Yet they are cultivating these avidly acquired responsibilities in a perfunctory fashion, and are thus sowing the seeds of future frustration, for the world and for themselves. How much more could they achieve even with the resources they now have if they were freed from the procedural shackles of the technical assistance programme (or UNDP/TA), and if they could free themselves from a senseless interagency rivalry, inject greater quality-consciousness into all their activities, use their outstanding technical personnel to the best possible advantage on well-chosen development projects, instead of leaving them to plough lonely —and largely sterile—furrows of narrow specialties on their own, and instil all along the line a higher degree of service-mindedness! A great many people, technical and nontechnical, in the specialized agencies and elsewhere, are aware of these needs and would welcome such a wholesome change.

Even from the purely selfish angle of the volume of business transacted by them, the agencies should have nothing to fear. It is true that if the reforms suggested above are put through, the size of their activities as between the countries will have to be modified, sometimes considerably. But on a global basis, after offsetting the pluses and minuses, there should be no significant difference. After all, the agencies were created in response to the urgent needs of mankind. Those needs are not only there but have been growing continually; and, pari passu, the financial resources of the various programmes have also gone up, though rather haltingly in the last few years.

The case of the Special Fund well illustrates the point. Unlike EPTA, the Fund never parcelled out money to the agencies and the countries; instead, it has always authorized individual preinvestment projects and has allocated funds on a case-by-case basis for their execution. What has been the result? The agencies have been loaded with projects, far more than most of them can easily cope with.

For a good many years there have been talks about multilaterization of development activities, for channelling more funds through the UN family. Little progress has been made so far in that direction. It is safe to assume, however, that progress here will depend largely on the ability of the international organizations to demonstrate their own effectiveness. Quality of performance and service—this is the trump card of the agencies. Given the quality, they will not have to run after business; business will run after them. And it will do so in a far more orderly fashion, making possible more orderly and also more solid development.

In this context it is worth recalling a phrase used by Mr. Arthur M. Okun, former Chairman of the Council of Economic Advisers, about the wage-price spiral and labour-management tussle in the USA. Speaking in April 1968, he stressed that the respective shares of the business community and the working class in the increased productivity had remained surprisingly steady in recent years; that the only effect of their fight for a higher share was to push up wages and prices in a spiral. It was like viewing a parade, he said, with all the spectators "standing on tiptoe"; nobody gained or lost, and everybody suffered discomfort.

The interagency rivalry for a larger share of the UN programmes has produced similar results: little net gain or loss for an agency, and a lot of discomfort for them all. Meanwhile, the saddest feature of it is that the developing countries have been kept on the tiptoe of expectation which is likely to remain largely unfulfilled. The rivalry is not helping the agencies, and it is clearly hurting the latter.

CHAPTER 19

Role of Resident Representatives

Where there is no will, there is a way.

MODERN PROVERB

It is time to face the fact that the vast apparatus of the UN system has been yielding woefully small development, that for this the apparatus itself is overwhelmingly at fault.

The UN family, structured as it is as a system of satellites, each with an independent orbit, could be adapted to serve as an effective vehicle of development only if what may be called the *triangle of general managership* is riveted into it. The case for general managers at the UNDP, at UN and each agency headquarters has been dealt with in the last chapter in an attempt to uncover its practical implications. There remains the case of the field representative, that is, of the country-level general manager, which will be examined in this chapter.

Under the scheme of things envisaged here, the field representative accredited to each aid-receiving government would be the keystone of all UN programmes at the field level; he would be the logical counterpart of the general managers at the UNDP, UN and agency headquarters; and in that capacity he would function both as their spokesman and as their adviser. Since the sole purpose of development is to build up the backward economies of the underdeveloped countries, and since the problems of development—economic, political, social and technical—are all in the field, the questions surrounding the role of the field representative easily overshadow all others. And how they are tackled in actual practice will, more than anything else, determine what success the UN family can hope to achieve with its development programmes.

217

The issues have many facets. They can be best understood only when seen against the relevant background facts, all the more since they have been clouded both by misconceptions and by vociferous special pleading. It would be particularly useful to consider: why, in such a vital matter, so little headway has been made so far; how the question of agency country representatives and mission chiefs has frequently complicated matters and inhibited objective thinking; what kind of technical support the field representative should receive from the agencies; what should be his functions and responsibilities—why, as general manager, he must have overall charge of all activities under the UN programmes, and why at the same time he must, as "development diplomat," frequently engage in negotiation and persuasion at high levels in the government; and finally, what facilities, what powers and what status would be appropriate to enable him to discharge these high responsibilities adequately.

The bigger agencies, it should be noted, maintain regional offices headed by regional representatives; this is true of WHO, the ILO, FAO and UNESCO. In addition, they frequently have their own country representatives, the smaller countries being usually grouped together for this purpose. Many of them are given the status of mission chiefs under arrangements made directly between the agencies and the governments concerned. In general, the regional and country representatives deal directly with the respective ministries of the governments in matters relating to programme formulation and execution.

The United Nations field setup is somewhat different. It has its regional economic commissions which, however, have little direct concern with the development programmes of the UN. It maintains Information Centres at the country level, but the primary duty of the UNIC directors is to disseminate information about the activities of the United Nations, especially at its headquarters in New York. So far as the UNDP and its regular programmes are concerned, the UN relies almost exclusively on the Resident Representatives. In a few countries they are also called upon to serve as heads of the Information Centres. In the great majority of cases, however, the UNIC directors run their separate offices, function rather independently of the Resident Representatives, and are often endowed with the status of mission chiefs.

The smaller agencies cannot, as a rule, afford to mantain country representatives; they, therefore, rely on periodic visits of their senior officers to the field to hold discussions with the ministries or departments of the governments, and on correspondence with them, which may or may not be channelled through the Resident Representatives.

Thus, the picture varies a good deal, depending on the importance of a country and the size of its programme. The main point to be noted is that at a given time, in a recipient country with a sizable programme, there are usually several agency representatives who, in that capacity, deal with questions relating to their own agencies and are virtually independent of the Resident Representatives.

Could there be a single country representative for the UN family as a whole? This is not a new question. The need has been long recognized; it has been keenly felt, hotly debated, also warmly recommended in numerous conferences and documents. Yet the labour of all these years has produced only the proverbial mouse. It has ended in a noisy tinkering with an obsolete status quo.

From time to time there have been talks of investing the Resident Representative with the role of the field coordinator of all programmes, both multilateral and bilateral. For example, two resolutions to that effect—851 (XXXII) and 856 (XXXII) respectively—were adopted by the Economic and Social Council at its mid-1961 session. Resolutions, like these, well-intentioned as they are, contain an overdose of wishful thinking. As things now stand, they are wholly unrealistic because they fail to make allowance for the severe limitations under which a Resident Representative must work.

The fact is that while a Resident Representative is given wide functions, the *de jure* powers he enjoys are close to nil. As a result, he has to depend, almost exclusively, on persuasion. He may be a man of great ingenuity, a genius in persuasion, but even then he inevitably ends up by making many compromises, far more than can be good for the UN programmes.

Nor should one overlook the fact that he has numerous masters to serve in the UNDP (formerly TAB/SF), UN, and the specialized agencies. He knows that two to three times a year these masters will sit in judgment over his performance. And he also knows only too well that the participating organizations will judge the quality of his performance by applying one crucial criterion: how well he has defended their own special interests and whether or not he has done his best to maintain their volume of business.

For the same reason a Resident Representative must continuously propitiate the agency representatives, mostly junior professionals who descend on the scene from time to time, even though he himself may be far superior to them both in experience and in ability to develop good projects and to guide the programmes in the right direction.

In coordinating the EPTA (now UNDP/TA) country programme, as mentioned before,[113] he is faced with a thankless task: how to find ways and means to reduce the inflated number of projects stimulated by the agencies and by government departments and to compress them within the financial target set for the country. In doing so, he must move warily. He must make sure that each agency is given a reasonable share. It is important to keep the agencies on the right side even if, in the process, priorities get pushed to the wrong side or to the wrong place.

Or, take the case of evaluation reports on technical assistance activities. A Resident Representative is called upon to submit such reports once a year, and he is urged to be objective and frank. But how will frankness and objectivity be evaluated if the facts served happen to be unpalatable? He knows from experience, at least that of others, that such instructions have to be taken with more than a grain of salt. In any case, the reports will be read and commented upon by all the agencies. And so he must be cautious and tactful, and play sufficiently safe. He must emphasize the positive results and soft-pedal the negative ones.

The Resident Representative is supposed to coordinate the activities of the agencies. The logic of circumstances works inexorably the other way. Willy-nilly, he himself gets "coordinated" with them.

2

Following ECOSOC resolutions, the Administrative Coordination Committee (ACC) considered, in October 1961, the problem of coordinating the EPTA activities at the field level and laid down the following guidelines:

1. EPTA programming discussions between officials of participating organizations and governments concerned should be held "with advance knowledge of Resident Representatives," and "with their participation, as appropriate."

2. No request for a change in the approved programme for a given country should be forwarded by a participating organization to TAB headquarters without prior consultation with the Resident Representative, and through him, with the coordinating unit of the government concerned.

---

[113] See Chapter 5, especially Section 5.

3. Chiefs of mission or country representatives should be briefed by their headquarters on the new coordinating role of the Resident Representative, and be told "to work closely with him," keeping him fully informed of any major proposals or developments concerning EPTA programming.

4. Resident Representatives should be directed by the Executive Chairman of TAB to keep each agency fully informed of matters of interest to that agency, in particular, of all discussions which they may have with the government.

5. Resident Representatives and chiefs of mission should "act in closest cooperation with each other, and mission chiefs should serve as technical advisers" to the Resident Representative, government authorities being informed of this arrangement.

6. The Executive Chairman of TAB and the Resident Representative concerned should be informed promptly of the appointment of chiefs of mission who should be instructed to call on the Resident Representative at the outset. Appropriate use should also be made of his help in establishing government contacts.

7. Resident Representatives should be fully informed, beginning with the "request stage," of all comparable programmes of technical assistance carried out by a participating organization, and their cooperation sought in ensuring coordination between these programmes and EPTA.

8. Resident Representatives and all chiefs of missions should hold periodic meetings under the chairmanship of the Resident Representatives, to increase mutual understanding and coordination at the country level.

9. Participating organizations should keep Resident Representatives fully informed as regional projects in which their countries might participate are being developed and carried out.

10. Resident Representatives should be given advance notice of all visits of headquarters officials of the participating organizations concerned with technical assistance, and kept fully informed of the purposes and results of discussions at the country level.

These are the famous "ten principles" which have been cited from time to time as concrete evidence of TAB's, and later UNDP's, con-

cern for coordination of field activities. They are remarkable not for
the degree of coordination they set out to achieve, but for highlighting
the extent to which coordination had so long been lacking in the
field. They represented a belated effort to find a partial remedy for a
near-chaotic situation. And they aimed at what may perhaps be termed
flexible coordination based on a balancing of agency interests.

Even this mini-consensus looked rickety from the start. For one
thing, the ten principles were not officially communicated to the governments; they remained a kind of a gentlemen's agreement among the
participating organizations; and it was left more or less to the individual
Resident Representative to find ways and means to ensure that the
agreement was something more than an expression of a pious hope.
A good deal therefore depended on his personality, his ingenuity, and
on his luck. It was, of course, essential for him to tread cautiously
in invoking the agreement. He could hardly forget that his own
survival postulated the agencies' support. The upshot was clear. Under
the gentlemen's agreement the burden of acting like a gentleman fell
overwhelmingly on him.

After six years the UN, it appears, is engaged in assessing the effects
of the ten principles, and the extent to which they have been adhered
to in practice. Such a review must, of necessity, be based on the information received from the field offices. Again, in furnishing this information in response to the headquarters questionnaire, the Resident
Representative will need all his habitual tact. For he knows that his
report has to be factual and also—innocuous. It is hard to see how
such an exercise could lead to any new revelations or to any profound
conclusions. It will, as usual, be prolific of paperwork, and barren of
result.

The weakness of the ten principles is that they are still ten, and
not one. As every good bureaucrat knows, where there is *no* will, there
is a way. The ten principles are a good device, even if somewhat outworn, to sidetrack the main issue.

3

It has long been customary for the UN family to recruit experts
on the basis of job descriptions drawn up well in advance. Not that
they are always prepared with the requisite care; their quality varies a
great deal from agency to agency, and sometimes within the same
agency. Nevertheless, the practice is undoubtedly sound. The better
the job descriptions and the more precisely they spell out the duties
and responsibilities involved, along with the qualifications and ex-

periences needed for the post in question, the greater are the prospects of landing the right type of experts. Even with the best job descriptions there will always be some poor recruitments; but without them recruitment will be too much of a hit-or-miss affair.

What about the job description for a Resident Representative? It is no exaggeration to say that it does not exist, nor has any effort been made to produce one. There has been ceaseless talk about the great importance of his role, but there has never been a clear concept of what this role should be, not to speak of an incisive analysis of how best he should function and what specific services he should render.

Take, for example, the following description emanating from a high administrative level: "A Resident Representative can be successful only if he has the confidence of the Government, the Participating Organizations and their personnel. A position of confidence can only be earned by the exercise of personal qualities of high character: objectivity, intelligence, tact, skill at negotiation and communication, firmness balanced by flexibility, and complete personal devotion to the objectives of the Programme, as well as to the broad principles of the United Nations. A successful Resident Representative must develop a deep interest in his country of assignment. He must possess a determination to know, understand and respect its people. Ability to deal with human problems in a friendly, understanding and sensible way is also essential, for the effectiveness of technical assistance depends very much on the well-being of experts and their families living far from home."

This is a masterly statement, despite some of its schoolmasterly overtones; excellent as far as it goes, but unfortunately it does not go far enough and deep enough. It lists a lot of high qualities which a Resident Representative will need for his job, most of which are more or less axiomatic; but it fails to define the job itself and what constitutes his *raison d'être*—the specific part he is supposed to play in the context of the total development effort of the country to which he is assigned. And so the statement, with all its sparkling phrases, can dazzle but not inspire, certainly not enlighten. As a job description, it remains eloquently obscure.

This was perhaps, the reason which impelled Mr. Paul Hoffman, then Managing Director of the Special Fund, to add the following words: "The Resident Representative/Director of Special Fund Programmes has the further function of mobilizing and integrating total United Nations technical and preinvestment assistance in such a manner as will utilize to the maximum the United Nations family's potential for contributing to the best interests of the Government and the country he serves."

This comes tantalizingly close to what is the heart of a Resident Representative's functions. It also evokes some further questions: How, exactly, should he "mobilize and integrate" total UN assistance; what concrete steps should he take to ensure maximum utilization of the UN family's potential to subserve the "best interests" of the country to which he is assigned; what role can he play in identifying and clarifying the best interests; and what, finally, should be the relationship between the UN assistance, which is bound to be extremely small, and the far larger domestic resources of the government.

Perhaps what could pass for a near-ideal job description for a Resident Representative was given, several years later, by Mr. Hoffman in a serio-comic vein at the global meeting of the Resident Representatives held at Turin, Italy in June 1966. "We need men and women with unique qualities to head our UNDP offices," said Mr. Hoffman. "Sometimes I wonder how long our supply of supermen and superwomen will last." If he were to begin a search for such people by placing an advertisement it would read something like this:

WANTED FOR A CHALLENGING OPPORTUNITY:

A well-educated, widely experienced man or woman to serve as a Resident Representative. Must have a broad experience in economic growth problems; qualities of leadership; capability to analyse problems quickly, accurately and deeply; maturity of judgment; infinite patience; tolerance; a sense of humour; a genuine love of his fellowmen without prejudice as to colour, creed or national origin; experience in negotiating; facility in oral and written English, with preference to candidates who speak one or more of the other official UN languages or other important languages; prepared to travel extensively within his country of assignment; ready to reside for periods of four-to-five years, usually under conditions of climatic discomfort, sometimes hardship, and occasionally danger; be prepared to assume representational functions and entertain extensively both for the home team and for visitors. Salary at UN rates, allowances minimal, psychic rewards tremendously satisfying.

Having found the men and women to fill these posts, Mr. Hoffman added, the UNDP headquarters would try to give them "the tools for the work—not only the tools of authority but necessary supporting staff and facilities"; and it would "continue to press for satisfactory arrangements with the cooperating and executing agencies."

The advertisement[114] for "supermen" was superb. It was the nearest thing to a job description that the administration has ever produced for a Resident Representative. His functions and the qualities needed to fulfil them were set forth with a clarity that had hitherto been sorely missed. There was of course still need for some further distillation, particularly to single out the most important elements from this comprehensive list and to establish an order of priority among them.

In any case, the "advertisement" was intended only to provoke some fresh thinking—and to amuse. It was not used—nor indeed anything remotely similar to it—in making the recruitments. The Resident Representatives, now about 70 in all, have been drawn at random from widely different fields with the most heterogeneous background of experience. The result is that at present they make no pattern at all, or perhaps only a crazy quilt pattern.

4

It should be noted that, since 1960, some tangible progress has been made in strengthening the general position of the Resident Representatives, also in evolving somewhat better order in the EPTA or UNDP/TA operations. The progress has been due not so much to the ten principles mentioned before as to two other factors: the strong stand taken by Mr. Hoffman as Managing Director of the Special Fund and later as Administrator of the UNDP, and the rapid growth of the Special Fund activities which, within a few years, surpassed the volume of TAB operations.

Mr. Hoffman's views on this issue were emphatically clear from the day he took charge of the Special Fund, and he never ceased to reiterate them whenever the occasion arose. For example, in April 1962 he restated them as follows: "... the one change of paramount importance" for the more successful operation of the United Nations programmes "requires at the country level a single Director," who is recognized both by the governments receiving assistance and by the

---

114 As Mr. Hoffman read out the text of his unusual ad., deliberately giving lighthearted touches to what was not intended to be lightly set aside, a colleague sitting next to me whispered into my ear: "All this is to be taken only as a humour. In life you get only what you pay for!" The UN family, he clearly implied, was already getting the best it could expect for the salaries it was willing to offer.

United Nations agencies providing assistance, as having "general responsibility for the planning, administration and operation of all United Nations technical assistance and preinvestment activities in the country." Internal coordination and proper planning of social and economic development are among the greatest needs of the governments. They are entitled to be asisted by "an effectively co-ordinated external aid" and it is the "duty of the United Nations family" to provide this service "at least with respect to its programmes."

Ideally, the government should, Mr. Hoffman stressed, set up an effective coordinating or planning machinery, while the United Nations in its turn should have "one focal point for the programming, planning and coordination of its activities in the country concerned." This was and it still remains the goal, but it has so far remained beyond the reach of the UN family.

To facilitate the field coordination between the Special Fund and the Expanded Programme, the General Assembly Resolution 1240 (XIII), as noted in Chapter 11, had laid down that "the Managing Director shall enter into an agreement with the Executive Chairman of the Technical Assistance Board concerning the role of the resident representatives in the work of the Fund." Thus, Mr. Hoffman's obligation under this Resolution was to make use of the existing network of the Resident Representatives, but he was left entirely free to decide what should be their responsibilities. Accordingly, an agreement was reached with the Executive Chairman of TAB, and the Resident Representatives were designated "Directors of Special Fund Programmes" in the countries to which they were assigned. As Managing Director's representatives at the country level they were given undivided responsibility for all Special Fund activities, which greatly strengthened their position.

The Resident Representatives, in general, seized the new opportunities with alacrity. They gladly carried the additional load which was quite heavy in many cases and was growing rapidly. And they waited wistfully for the day when the Expanded Programme, too, would be rationalized and streamlined on the same pattern.

They are still waiting. For, the technical assistance programme stubbornly stuck to the "ten principles." And true to its old tradition, it continued to work for a different kind of "rationalization"—to find enough plausible arguments to uphold the existing status of the Resident Representative with multiple fractures in his responsibiilty.

5

Should the agencies have country representatives and mission chiefs? And what should be the relationship between them and the Resident Representative? Though these questions have long vexed the TAB and the UNDP administration, no adequate solution is yet in sight.

The Expanded Programme evolved its own philosophy about agency representation, which bore the stamp of the usual TAB approach.[115] Its main points are worth noting, since they clearly show the tortured reasoning and its negative impact. Where the programme of an agency, FAO for example, in a particular country is small and consists of a few experts and several fellowships, it would at best need a senior agricultural adviser; he could very well be chosen from among the experts in the country, to serve as a coordinator of the FAO team and as general adviser to the ministry concerned. But when the country programme, comprising both technical assistance and Special Fund projects, grows to a considerable size and embraces a number of distinct fields e.g. soils, fisheries, forests and nutrition, the case for "a senior agricultural adviser and mission chief" becomes very much stronger. Sometimes "an agency country representative" may also be needed to develop or fully articulate a programme in a particular country.

The growth of programmes pointed to the need for high-level technical advice. The governments should therefore be encouraged to approach the agencies concerned to seek appointment of senior advisers or country representatives.

As for their relationship with the Resident Representatives, there were the ten principles which, by now, had become the sheet anchor of TAB policy. It was time and again implied that these principles, backed as they were by the ACC, embodied all conceivable wisdom on the subject and should therefore settle it once and for all.

Attention was drawn to the "constitutional autonomy" of the participating organizations, which would of course "continue to be respected." Therefore, "the formal channels of communication and other arrangements established by the organizations" would remain as before; and they should, as necessary, "be brought to the attention of the Governments by the Resident Representatives concerned." Shorn of circumlocution, this meant that the agencies should continue to deal directly with individual ministries in a government (e.g. WHO

---

[115] What follows is a summary of the conclusions reached by TAB in September 1964, after considering the matter at the request of its governing body, i.e., TAC.

with the health ministry, FAO with the agriculture ministry). In most cases it was supposed to be their constitutional right to do so.[116]

What, then, should be the responsibilities of the Resident Representatives? His office would continue to provide "administrative and housekeeping services to agencies who wish to rely on him for such assistance." The general representational responsibility for the UN family of organizations should reside, "so far as EPTA and Special Fund and the World Food Programmes are concerned," in the Resident Representative. He would, however, be "available" to assist with the representation of other programmes of assistance carried out by the organizations "at their request."

This process of rationalization culminated in all-too-familiar conclusions. At least in countries where the programmes have attained "a substantial level," the roles of Resident Representatives and country representatives "are mutually complementary"; they do not "conflict or overlap nor are they interchangeable"; in such countries it is no longer feasible to ask the Resident Representatives "to assume the duties of an agency mission chief, except on a temporary basis"; ergo, agencies should be "encouraged to appoint mission chiefs as and where appropriate."

This was the considered thesis submitted by TAB to TAC in December 1964. How glaring is the contrast between this and the "Hoffman advertisement" quoted above! The misconceptions, and the motivations, underlying this thesis are still very much at work. They explain why real progress on this critical front has been unconscionably slow.

The logic used in support of the above thesis is vulnerable on several counts, even though it may appear plausible at first sight. For one thing, the United Nations does not appoint country representatives or mission chiefs, though in most countries it has relatively large programmes. Instead, it relies heavily on the Resident Representatives for all its activities[117] and uses them as its channel of communication with the governments. The UN is often the best served of all the organizations; it asks for, and in return it gets, the best from the field representatives.

The Government of Yugoslavia has, from the start of the UN programme, insisted that there should be one and only one representa-

---

[116] See Chapter 14, Section 5.

[117] The only exception, as mentioned earlier, is the information service for which the UN maintains a network of field representatives, and sometimes this function, too, is entrusted to the Resident Representative.

tive[118] of the UN family and has consistently refused to entertain suggestions for separate agency representatives. The result has undoubtedly been salutary. It has facilitated coordination of the field operations. Besides, the absence of special-interest pressures, in marked contrast to the normal practice in other countries, has been a most helpful factor in developing projects based on a country-wide study of the possibilities. This, in the final analysis, has made it possible to serve also the agencies more, and not less, effectively, as they themselves have readily acknowledged. In this respect Yugoslavia has set an excellent example, which, in its essentials, deserves to be emulated by other countries irrespective of the size of their programmes.

Mission chiefs and country representatives are appointed on the ostensible ground that technical heads are needed to handle technical problems. Yet quite often the same technical experts get bogged down, sometimes with surprising willingness, in nontechnical matters of a purely administrative character, such as office accommodation, secretarial facilities, housing for experts, local transportation, internal travel, leave authorization, currency questions, and what not. The result is a triple waste. Technical experts are diverted from the fields for which they are best qualified, in order to do jobs for which they are ill-equipped and which they often handle maladroitly, sometimes with awkward results; while this piecemeal handling of logistics and similar matters pushes up the administrative costs of the agencies and of the programmes.

When an agency, for example FAO, has a sizable programme in a country, it may very well need a whole-time technical adviser. But why should the adviser be an agency country representative, perhaps with the status of a mission chief? This is not explained and is simply taken for granted. The obvious, indeed the only logical, arrangement would be to attach him to the Resident Representative and to make it clear that he will function under the general supervision of the latter. In other words, the setup can and should be the same as in embassies with only one chief of mission but with attachés—agricultural, educational, medical and others, whose number and rank will depend on the size of the programmes and the actual requirements in individual countries.

The Resident Representative with such advisers or attachés, assuming that really competent men are chosen for these positions, will

---

[118] In Yugoslavia, he is called simply "Representative" without the qualifying word "Resident", on the ground that there are no non-resident representatives of the UN family.

make an effective team incomparably superior to the present chaotic setup in the field. It will make for significant savings in costs, more efficient administration, better programming, quicker implementation of projects. Above all, it will enable the Resident Representative to intervene at the right moment and at the right level, to secure necessary support whether for better execution of current projects or for promotion of new projects of exceptional promise. There is not the slightest doubt that such teamwork would immediately raise the performance of all concerned—of the UNDP, of UN and the agencies, their technical advisers in the field, the Resident Representatives and their staff—to a significantly higher level.

The existing system which was given a strong blessing on weak and superficial grounds, errs most grievously on yet another count. It ignores the need to adopt the "whole-country analysis,"[119] or the so-called "system approach," without which the search for high-priority projects will be futile, also the need for mature investment judgment along with high-level persuasion frequently needed for selecting and promoting them.

Meanwhile Mr. Hoffman, in hot pursuit of his "advertisement," has been striving to bring about better order in the field offices. Late in 1966 FAO, faced with budgetary difficulties, urged the UNDP to finance its country representatives. The opportunity was seized by Mr. Hoffman, and an elaborate agreement was worked out. In essence it meant that henceforward, in return for the UNDP's financial support, the FAO country representative would be located in the Resident Representative's office, use the same administrative services and facilities, function as his agricultural adviser for the UNDP activities but would retain a semi-independent status for the agency's non-UNDP activities within the country.

A similar agreement was due to be negotiated with the ILO, also for the same financial reasons.

All this represents motion in the right direction, though for the wrong reasons. Part of the cracks has now been cemented, belatedly and somewhat clumsily. The rest remains thinly papered over, as before.[120]

---

[119] See Chapter 16, especially the "Fourth Fundamental" and Chapter 18, Section 7, also see Section 7 below.

[120] The Director-General of FAO had remarked that "the Resident Representative should in effect be the head of a cabinet of Agency representatives." Commenting on this, Mr. Hoffman left no doubt that he would like the head of the so-called cabinet to be "modelled more on the USA practice than on that of a parliamentary government." Address at the Global Meeting of Resident Representatives held in Turin, Italy on 27 June 1966.

6

Much has been made of the "constitutional autonomy" of the specialized agencies and, consequently, of their right of direct negotiation and communication with the ministries concerned in a recipient country. The implication is that for the agencies to go through the Resident Representative's office, not to speak of having their technical experts function under his general supervision, would be an infringement of their autonomy.

This superficial view has been a part of the TAB syndrome. It has been assiduously propagated for many years; as a result, it has been so deeply embedded in the UN family's thinking that it cannot be easily dislodged. To refute it, however, should not be difficult.

The United Nations is certainly no less an autonomous body than the specialized agencies. Yet as mentioned before, it has systematically used Resident Representatives as its spokesmen in the field. It has never felt that its rights have in any way been infringed or abbreviated. There is no reason why it should be otherwise with the specialized agencies, especially if they *voluntarily* decide to use the Resident Representatives in the same way.

That they can do so is shown by the new agreement negotiated between FAO and the UNDP. Indeed, it is possible to go a step further and to argue that the agencies must do so in the overall interest of the UN programmes, the UN family, and, above all, the underdeveloped countries. One might even hold that this is implicit in their constitutional *duties,* and that their constitutional *rights* must be tempered accordingly.

In any case, the UNDP and the programmes established by General Assembly resolutions have the clear mandate that they must all be operated efficiently and effectively in the sole interest of the recipient countries. It follows that any agency desiring to participate in these programmes must be ready to give up whatever practices or attitudes are not compatible with this overriding mandate. This is the price an agency must be prepared to pay if it wants to be enlisted as a participating member. Even juridically it cannot both assert its constitutional autonomy and claim the right to participate in the Programme on its own terms. The UNDP, in its turn, would be fully entitled to lay down what essential preconditions the participating organizations must satisfy to make its operations fully effective. In fact, not to do so would be tantamount to a serious omission on its part.

To a considerable extent the Special Fund did so from the outset. And what was the result? The agencies fell in line with the Special Fund policy more or less without demur.

Of all the specialized agencies WHO is supposed to be the most autonomous in spirit. This is probably true, and there are also good reasons for this. The WHO operations have been genuinely decentralized through its regional offices established in accordance with the provisions of its charter. Other agencies—FAO and the ILO, for example—and the United Nations have regional establishments, but actual decentralization in terms of responsibility for decision-making has not been remotely comparable with that of WHO. As a result, its programming and operations have always been close to the grassroots.

Besides, WHO built up its technical assistance activities, along with a network of field offices, even before the Expanded Programme came into existence. It could do so on a significant scale because of its substantial regular budget including the special fund for malaria eradication.[121]

It is also true that much of WHO's activities has no direct relation to economic development in a business sense and can therefore be separated from the latter without too much difficulty.

And finally, the quality of WHO programming and operations has always been high because of a combination of factors: the high standards traditionally maintained in the medical profession; the automatic safeguards in matters literally involving life and death; the willingness of the member-governments to contribute generously to its exchequer; and, as just mentioned, its genuinely decentralized operations with careful programming and concentration of effort and money on matters worthy of high priority, such as control and eradication of malaria, smallpox, tuberculosis and other communicative diseases, environmental sanitation, water supply and sewerage, medical training, and infrastructure for health administration.

Like all large administrations, WHO too has its weak spots. But by and large, it is a well-run agency. The quality of its performance cannot but compel admiration.

No wonder that WHO should have been loth to surrender its autonomy. The TAB/SF, now the UNDP, field offices have been weak in command, mostly ineffective in programming and other responsibilities. Admittedly, WHO had little to gain, and much to lose, by agreeing to be an integral part of such a field setup. It chose to

---

121 See also Chapter 14, Section 5 and Chapter 17, Section 8.

remain aloof as far as possible. And in defence of its isolationist attitude it adduced its constitutional autonomy as the principal argument.

Yet the interesting fact is that whenever a Resident Representative had any worthwhile services to render—whether some new projects or ideas, or help in high-level negotiation, or in procuring some essential facilities—WHO has readily seized them. Time and again, this has been borne out by actual field experience.

It is safe to conclude that if the field offices are set up along the right lines, and if, in the true spirit of the "Hoffman advertisement," they are headed by competent men equipped with the requisite authority, responsibility and status, the agencies—including WHO—will increasingly realize the intrinsic value of what the Resident Representative can do for them; and, despite current reservations, they will then veer round and increasingly accept his leadership.

The need for reforms has long been clear, also their nature. They have been delayed so long mainly because the will to reform has been lacking. Given the reforms, it should not be difficult to overcome any lingering resistance from the agencies and to win their full support. Instead, their resistance has been, and is still being, used as an argument, or as an excuse, for not carrying out the sorely-needed reforms.

7

The really significant value of UN aid—a fact that cannot be emphasized too often—lies not in doling out funds to the recipient countries to supplement their resources, but in using them deliberately to set up the right guidelines for development, to bring about a purposeful and productive orientation of domestic investments, to help structural transformation where needed. The fact that UN aid is confined to technical assistance and preinvestment work without investment capital is all the more reason why it must be handled in this way, as a "lever for influencing the situation as a whole."[122] Otherwise its worldwide operation will continue to yield poor results in terms of actual development.

Now, wielding aid as a lever is not everybody's job, far less of a specialist of the run-of-the-mill type. It is the job of an entirely different kind of specialist, who may not be a specialist himself but who has respect for specialists and knows how to make the best use of their

---

[122] See Chapter 16, Section 2.

knowledge and experience; who understands, above all, the economics of development and has an eye for the hidden potential—unused natural resources, unemployed man-hours, wasting physical assets, underused plants, untapped savings; and who combines with these traits something else—diplomatic ability of a high order. For, he must deal with the high-level policy-makers, and, through suggestions and proposals for using the available aid, he must frequently try and persuade them to his way of thinking. Such a specialist would represent a new breed, a hybrid, whom Mr. Eugene Black labelled as a "development diplomat," and for whom he carved out a crucial role in his strategy for economic development. A development diplomat, says Mr. Black, should be "a man with a vocation"; and as "an artisan of economic development," he should use "the tools of economics and other disciplines as best he can to place in perspective, to shed light on and to illuminate the choices before the decision-makers in the underdeveloped world."[123]

Illuminating the choices—this is the most potent tool of persuasion one could use in promoting sound projects and in preparing sound country programmes. What is particularly reassuring is that so often it works, even in what might at first appear disheartening circumstances. Once the choices are effectively illuminated before the actual decision-makers—politicians, civil servants, perhaps also businessmen, the chances of securing the right decisions are multiplied a great many times. This was repeatedly confirmed by the writer's personal experience in such different countries as India, Ghana, West New Guinea/West Irian and Yugoslavia, as it has been confirmed by the experience of other people in other countries.

A UN Resident Representative should, it is submitted, function primarily as a development diplomat in Mr. Black's sense. He should not therefore be shackled by any other principles—ten or less. This is all the more important since the governments of the developing countries desperately need precisely the kind of informed and sympathetic guidance that development diplomats alone could provide, while, in the political climate prevailing in today's world, the United Nations is no doubt in the best position to recruit and assign such diplomats.

The search for a new strategy will remain a fruitless endeavour until this obvious truth is firmly grasped and unequivocally put into practice by the UN family.

---

[123] *The Diplomacy of Economic Development.* Harvard University Press, 1961. Page 24.

8

The Resident Representative must be the kingpin of all field activities, functioning as the country director and manager of the UNDP, also as a development diplomat vis-à-vis the government. Given these functions, the questions of his responsibility, authority and status, as also of the setup of his office should be easy to resolve.

Debates on these issues have been long and wearisome because of the inability, and the unwillingness, to define the appropriate role of a Resident Representative. They have been handled mostly on a case-by-case basis; far too much has been left vague or left to chance; as a result, the status a Resident Representative enjoys and the facilities he is provided with have varied enormously from country to country;[124] worst of all, his responsibility and authority have all along remained nebulous, and they still suffer from well-documented obscurity as revealed by the ten principles. No Resident Representative can effectively operate from such a shaky base and do justice to the functions outlined above.

An argument that has been used with tedious frequency to justify continued indecision or uncertainty in these matters is that a Resident Representative is not a conventional diplomat; that his position and setup are therefore not comparable with those of an ambassador. The first part of the argument is unquestionably valid; but the second part reflects not a logical deduction, but only a familiar attitude.

A conventional ambassador primarily serves the country he represents, and often sets his gaze on narrow political and commercial objectives. A Resident Representative's sole business, on the other hand, is to serve the country to which he is assigned, to help promote its economic and social development. He has no political objective, although he must have the ability to navigate through political shoals in serving the country he is accredited to. He is a diplomat, though admittedly of a new vintage.

What must be equally borne in mind is the fact that the Resident Representative must be a diplomat and must function as such. This is where the affinity between the two begins. The objectives in the two cases are poles apart; but the tools needed to achieve them are strikingly similar.

---

[124] This was stressed by the UNDP again in February 1968. An Interagency Working Party, appointed in 1967, submitted a report on the subject. The ACC considered it but took no action because it was found incomplete.

A little reflection will show why it must be so. In both cases the esential tool of work is persuasion through discussion, which, to be fruitful, has to be carried out at top levels. A Resident Representative therefore needs the same rank and status as an ambassador. Only then it will be possible for him to deal with important matters at high enough levels, e.g. of ministers, as and when this becomes necessary. To deny him the status of a chief of mission with ambassadorial rank can only handicap him in his work and needlessly diminish his usefulness.

It is also clear that a Resident Representative, like a regular ambassador, will need the services of technical advisers. In fact, given the nature of his functions, the need for such advisers will be even greater in his case. The important point, however, is that the advisers should serve *under* his general supervision, like the technical attachés assigned to an ambassador. Here again, the embassy set-up provides a near-perfect model which the UN family would be wise to emulate.

Several countries have, on their own initiative, conferred the full chief of mission status on the Resident Representatives. This, for example, was the case in Ghana and Yugoslavia. Experience showed what an essential tool it was for adequately serving the governments, the UNDP and the UN family.

There is no reason why the UN administration should not take up the matter with the recipient governments and negotiate a standard agreement with them, ensuring that all Resident Representatives will be given appropriate diplomatic rank and status, that they alone, within the UN system, will be regarded as the chiefs of mission, and that their technical advisers representing the specialized agencies will be accorded due rights and privileges substantially similar to those now extended to the technical attachés in embassies. There is every reason to assume that the recipient governments will readily agree to such an arrangement, provided that the UNDP takes the initiative. But will it do so?

A Committee appointed by the US Department of State in 1963 to advise on the administration of the UN programmes made the following significant recommendations: At the country level, the role of the Resident Representatives of the UN system of organizations should be further strengthened by:

"(a) a new and clear definition of functions which will leave no doubt about the central role of the Resident Representatives in coordinating the technical cooperation activities of the UN system in their countries of assignment, in acting as the spokes-

men of the UN system, and in dealing with representatives of
nations carrying on bilateral programs. In this connection *consideration should be given to the appointment of Resident Representatives by the Secretary-General.*

"(b) the provision of adequate staff resources and administrative support."[125]

These recommendations were made five years ago. The problems
are old; the solutions, too, have been known; they have been discussed
and rediscussed, but the core of the problem has still been left untouched. The past record shows a chronic unwillingness to deal with
anything but what are frankly peripheral issues.

The Committee's suggestion that the Resident Representatives
might be appointed by the UN Secretary-General, on behalf of the
entire UN system, and no doubt in appropriate consultation with the
agencies, was a most reasonable one. But reason has not played a prom-
inent part within the UN family in dealing with these matters.
Some greeted the proposal with a derisive smile. Others averred that
this would make matters even worse, but did not care to amplify.
Yet there is no valid alternative to it. If the UN family means serious
business with its development programmes, it must sooner or later
accept it. And the sooner it does so, the better would it be for all
concerned, especially for the underdeveloped world.

9

Are the Resident Representatives qualified to fulfil the role that
has been carved out for them in the foregoing analysis? Misgivings have
been expressed on this score, and not without reason. As mentioned
before, they have been recruited from widely disparate fields of life
to do ill-defined jobs. Even when their qualifications were impressive,
there was no guarantee that they would meet the specific requirements
for promoting economic development.

Several years ago, after Mr. Hoffman returned from his first round
of visits to the field offices as Managing Director of the Special Fund,
whispers went around in the UN secretariat that he had been far
from satisfied with the calibre of the Resident Representatives; that
50 per cent of them were, in his view, not good enough for the jobs.
At that time one of his major concerns was that the Resident Representatives should function as full-fledged country directors, be in

---

[125] "A Report of the Advisory Committee on International Organizations."
Department of State, June 1963. Italics supplied.

charge of all UN operations and speak on behalf of the whole UN family. Evidently, about half of them did not measure up to his expectation for shouldering such responsibilities.

Gradually the whispers subsided, and within a year or so, no trace of his initial reactions could be seen or heard anywhere. What happened exactly is known only to Mr. Hoffman himself; others can only guess.

Perhaps guessing is, after all, not too difficult in this case. For one thing, it was an open secret that his proposal to change the designation of the Resident Representatives into Directors to reflect their leadership and control over the country programmes, encountered much stronger opposition than Mr. Hoffman had bargained for. Ostensibly the opposition came from FAO, but in effect, and in subtler and less identifiable form, from the veteran no-changers at the top administrative echelons. Mr. Hoffman was stymied; sorely disappointed, he decided, at least for the present, to settle for half the objective, and as the executive head of the newly-established programme, he had no difficulty in achieving this. The result was a double-barrelled designation for the heads of the field offices: "Resident Representative of the Technical Assistance Board and the Director of the Special Fund Programme" in a given country.

This cumbersome title lasted for about six years, until the "merger" of the two programmes in January 1966 when its second part was dropped. Since then the heads of the field offices have been designated simply as Resident Representatives of the UNDP.

Did Mr. Hoffman shy away from his initial objective owing to the resistance he encountered from oldtimers? There are good reasons to believe that he did. After his first few moves he must have realized how difficult it was to change ingrained attitudes, not to speak of dislodging entrenched personnel from an international organization, unlike what one would normally experience in a business corporation.

In any case, the fact is that Mr. Hoffman sought to achieve the same objectives as far as possible by other means and turned primarily in two directions. He disparaged the policy of running the field offices on a shoestring basis, insisted on giving them more generous facilities —staff, transportation and a more liberal budget, made sure that the necessary allocations were made from the Special Fund, and urged that the Resident Representatives should spend less time at their desks, travel extensively within the countries they were assigned to, study the local conditions and establish personal contacts with the right people. This policy has undoubtedly strengthened the position of the field representatives and enhanced their usefulness.

The other major step taken by Mr. Hoffman was to appoint a few high-level consultants who were located at New York headquarters, but who were required to go out periodically to the field on inspection-cum-consultation tours to help the field representatives to tackle any major outstanding issues, and to report to him personally. They provided ad hoc props to the Resident Representatives, which, within limits, had their utility but which, from their very nature, could be no more than a poor second best.

But where are the "supermen" sought by Mr. Hoffman to serve as field representatives and to discharge the high responsibilities he had earmarked for them? Are they available in sufficient number? And can the UN family attract them with the means at its disposal?

These questions have been heard over and over again. No knowledgeable person will, however, have any doubt about the answer. Men of the requisite calibre *are* available; they *can* be attracted by the UN family at little or no extra overall cost, *provided* it really means business and is willing to give them the requisite authority, responsibility, and status. But will this proviso be satisfied? Here lies the real snag. The administration has so far revealed no burning desire to attract high-calibre people for these pivotal posts.

Indeed, some senior administrators seem to shudder at the very thought of attracting such people. The virtue they value most is not ability, but pliability; they look for people who would be safe and congenial, not dynamic and original; who would rather take orders from headquarters than lead a field team and serve as active advisers to governments. Apparently, even in the last few years, appointments of Resident Representatives have been largely inspired by such calculations; and the available posts have been filled mainly with men who are eminently qualified for the old TAB-type of routine-ridden operations, but not cut out to function as country directors *cum* managers *cum* development diplomats.

To repeat, men *are* available, men of superior ability and high purpose. It is the business of the UN family to seek out such men, to attract and harness them to its programmes.[126] To the misfortune of the developing countries, it has hitherto shown a strange aversion to do so and has instead sought out alibis to justify a shortsighted policy.

---

[126] Even small countries will need the same high quality of services; the differences will be only quantitative. The number of field representatives assigned to groups of countries could certainly be increased, which would reduce their total number. Here again, the pattern of the diplomatic service is relevant, although smaller countries too will sometimes need local offices headed by deputies or assistants of the regional representatives.

10

Despite all that has been said above, it must be admitted that, even today, most of the Resident Representatives are far superior to most of the officials in the UN family to whom they have to turn most of the time for most of the decisions in their day-to-day work; that they could, here and now, shoulder much greater responsibilities than they are actually vouchsafed. All in all, they constitute what is one of the ablest and perhaps the most under-utilized institution in the entire UN system.

The standard explanation for this situation is that it reflects the fragmented structure of the UN family. This is true; but as we have seen, the situation could be largely remedied, given a clear perception of the potential role of the Resident Representative, and given the willingness at the policy-making level to carry out the essential reforms.

The misconception about the functions of the Resident Representatives and the services they could render does indeed run deep. Take, for example, the role assigned to him by the United Nations in its "Proposals for Action" in connection with the first Development Decade. "He will not normally be a planning expert or economic adviser," says the report, "and even where he may be so qualified his many other duties would not normally permit him to act in that capacity."[127]

Nevertheless, his role "in intensified United Nations action," continues the report, "will be highly important." He should "call to the attention of a government" the importance of establishing development plans if it has not already done so. When "joint planning teams" are envisaged, he should ensure that "all important sectors are adequately covered." He is not responsible for technical matters, but he "reminds the government of the need for sound projects," and he also "draws its attention to ways of utilizing the experience gained from completed or continuing projects." He must be "familiar with the plans and priorities of the government," and he should "be able to suggest critical areas for attention which have been overlooked."

In sum, the primary concern of a Resident Representative is not economic development, but his "other duties," presumably routine administration. He should be an adviser to the government as well, but not an effective one. His role in the development business, despite professions to the contrary, is not central, but peripheral.

___
127 "The United Nations Development Decade—Proposals for Action," United Nations, New York, 1962. Page 22.

Such a concept makes a travesty of what should be his real functions. It overlooks the fact that sound projects do not grow automatically, that they have to be identified and actively sponsored. It shows a blind faith in expertise, and ignores the fact that the specialties, unless carefully chosen and intelligently welded together, may very well not promote, but hinder development. It shows no understanding of the crying need for a unified UN leadership, for seasoned investment judgment, for highlevel negotiation and persuasion.

And the irony of it all is that this superficial concept of the Resident Representative's functions figured in the United Nation's own proposals for action in the first Development Decade! This is not unlike staging Hamlet without the Prince of Denmark. Perhaps it is even worse; for, the experts and emissaries assigned by numerous international bodies of high prestige and authority to an underdeveloped country to play more or less independent roles, mostly according to the promptings of their respective headquarters, can only create a scene of confused excitement in which orderly development may well be the first casualty.

There is yet another factor which is even more important because it is the real source of the misconception about the role of the Resident Representative, something which is keenly felt by insiders, vaguely sensed by outsiders, and which a sense of decorum within an organization would normally forbid one to talk about. It is the extreme reluctance of the headquarters—of the UN, the agencies, and of the UNDP —to delegate or to decentralize; the ingrained love for authority which often inspires top-level executives; which, in extreme cases, may come perilously close to a lust for power. In this age of high mobility and massive organization, the forces of centralization are everywhere constantly at work. The bureaucratic pyramid-building is fast becoming a universal pastime. The UN system, despite the evangelical mantle it prominently dons, is by no means immune from this ubiquitous trend.

The result is what one might expect. As the UN programme grows in size, the organization men expand their own staff at headquarters and increasingly use the personnel, mostly junior officers, to control the field operations. Thus, paradoxically enough, the very expansion of the programme tends to build *up* the headquarters and in practice to build *down* the field representatives. Since the merger, the UNDP has taken some galloping steps in this ominous direction.

This tendency is, of course, not confined to the UN programmes and is also noticeable elsewhere. A former ambassador of the United States, who had served in two African countries, remarked some time ago that an application even for a small amount of money for some desirable activity needed more than thirty clearances in Washington. The programme would be better off, he suggested, with some delegation of responsibility to the ambassadors in the field, reducing the clearances in such cases to one or two.

Whatever may the explanation for the present position of the Resident Representatives, the United Nations must build them up, and not down; it must build them up in reality, and not just on paper. On their stature, more than on anything else, will depend the fate of the UN development programme and, in the final analysis, the stature of the United Nations itself.

From time to time Secretary-General of the United Nations sends out high-level political emissaries to deal with some immediate political crisis. It is fascinating to speculate what would happen if he were to send out handpicked development diplomats as his peacetime emissaries and assign them, to start with, say, to a dozen most important countries in the underdeveloped world, with the sole task of inspiring and promoting their economic development. The United Nations, it may be confidently assumed, will then begin to pulsate with a new life, and the developing world with a new hope.

CHAPTER 20

Some Thoughts on Priorities[128]

"Cieco per troppo vedere, freddo per troppo sentire."

An internationalist, in the words of an Italian historian as quoted above, is often "blind for seeing too much, cold for feeling too much." The description, in spite of its harsh implications, contains an undeniable core of truth. And it does hold good for a great many development planners serving in the international field. They look at the underdeveloped countries, find them backward, poor, bristling with problems, needing almost everything, and they are confused by what they see. They are, as a result, constantly at a loss to know where to begin, how to go about this business of development, and where, above all, to invest the limited resources that are available for development.

Their vision is further warped by something else—the specialties galore. How could it be otherwise when a dozen powerful specialized agencies are zealously advertising their skills and persistently offering them to their prospective clients? Talks of priorities have been on the increase, and they continue to embellish official reports and high-level utterances, but only like the foam on the crest of a wave at rising tide.

For example, the Secretary General's 'Proposals for Action" for the development decade of the 1960's was prefaced with the remark that they represented the areas in which action by the United Nations system was expected to produce "the maximum leverage effect on development as a whole," and "the maximum linkage effect in promoting

128 Chapters 20-21 include much of the text of a paper on "Nation-Building: Economic Development," which was presented, on 20 April 1968, at the first University of Rhode Island Conference on the Problems and Prospects of the Developing Nation-State (reproduced as Occasional Papers in Political Science No. 11). Permission to use this material is acknowledged with thanks.

243

advances in other sectors."[129] The statement had the virtue of being up-to-date as regards the latest refinements in some key economic concepts and terminology. On the substantive side, however, the action programme contained little to excite one's imagination. It looked very much like a medley of mostly agency-inspired proposals that revealed no well-considered sense of priorities.

The extent of the concern shown by the UN family for priorities in actual practice can be better judged from the following comment which occurred in a more recent UNDP document:[130] "The Programme has come to the end, more or less, of a first phase based largely on satisfying individual requests for assistance as they came in..." The wording is somewhat oblique, but the meaning is nonetheless clear. It is an admission of the fact that hitherto fixing priorities has not been a burning issue in the UNDP. As usual, the plea advanced is that the UN family has been learning from experience, ignoring what was said long ago by Benjamin Franklin: "Experience keeps a dear school, yet Fools will learn in no other."[131]

Priority-fixing, it need hardly be emphasized, is the soul of development planning. If things go wrong here, development will inevitably suffer, and no amount of coordination or administrative efficiency will improve the outcome. This has been readily accepted by all concerned; in fact, the question of priorities has long been accorded a priority status and, by constant repetition, has been turned into a trite cliché. Its impact has, however, been barely noticeable on the actual contents of the programmes which have been left at the mercy of all kinds of internal and external pressures.

The problem has been enormulsly complicated because powerful forces have been allowed to work virtually unchecked to promote dispersal within the specialty-ridden UN family. The quest for priorities must begin with an attempt to bring, and to keep, these forces under firm control. This is the first obvious task, which means that the procedural and managerial reforms discussed in the previous chapters must be unequivocally adopted and put into practice.

The second task is to identify, say, half-a-dozen most important and most promising areas of development in each country, as measured in terms of production and productivity, and to direct towards them the main thrust of the UN programmes. Once the framework of a

---

[129] "The United Nations Development Decade—Proposals for Action" (E/3613), United Nations, New York, 1962, page ix.

[130] "Future Needs of Pre-investment Activity," etc., DP/L. 57, submitted to the UNDP Governing Council in January 1968.

[131] In "Poor Richard" (1743).

country programme has been nailed down in this way, it should be quite easy to assess what supplementary effort would be needed to reinforce or to facilitate the execution of the central programme and to project it into the picture. A really effective programme to stimulate economic growth can be developed only on this basis, and on no other.

What, then, are these high-priority areas which should constitute the heart of a country programme? And what is the rationale behind them?

These are large questions; and it would be pretentious to suggest that anything like full justice could be done to them within the limited scope of this book. Within each priority field a good many problems are involved, and these often vary rather widely from region to region, and from country to country. An action programme cannot be based on generalizations; it will have to give due attention to interrelated problems in the light of the specific conditions prevailing in a country.

Nevertheless, generalized thoughts have their own value; in fact, there is no escape from them since detailed planning must be firmly anchored on the right fundamentals. Otherwise it may easily go astray, and the planning exercise may dissolve itself into a mass of details more or less artifically assembled, as has often been the case in the UN family. The main purpose of the reflections offered in this chapter is to help counteract this risk and to clarify the fundamentals or the broad priorities.

The reflections fall logically into two main divisions: on population control (Sections 2-3), since this has become a major condition for raising living standards in the low-income countries; and on other investment priorities for economic and social development. Though these are discussed in Sections 4-10 below in a certain sequence, no particular order of importance among them is implied. All the items together constitute what should generally be the group of topmost priorities in a country. And as a rule, progress will depend on the ability to tackle them more or less simultaneously.

2

The question of priorities can be best judged only in the context of this explosive age with its multiple revolutions—political, economic, social, scientific and technological, all of which have been simultaneously at work, affecting all parts of the world in varying intensity (see Chapter 1). Discoveries and breakthroughs have come thick and fast. By all tokens, this bewildering trend will continue in the years ahead and will probably be further accelerated.

Inevitably, this is also an age of lags, gaps, and imbalances. The results of many technological advances are penetrating into the remote corners of the earth, but mostly in a haphazard, arbitrary fashion, bringing about far-reaching changes in many spheres of life, upsetting old balances with no immediate prospects of creating new ones in their place. The imbalances are no less marked in the psycho-sociological field. Under the impact of science and technology the world is changing fast, and with it the external life, but the human mind is often unable to keep pace with the changes and to work out their full implications, far less to adjust the old pattern of values and behaviour to the new environment.

This is particularly true of the phenomenon which has come to be called, though not too elegantly, the "population explosion." At bottom this is only one facet of this revolutionary age, an effect of the multiple lags and imbalances which the dizzy tempo of scientific and technological discoveries has brought in its wake.

In the Western countries where the wheels of industrial revolution began to move a couple of centuries ago, the process of development, it is worth recalling, was spread over a long period; and throughout this period economic growth kept well ahead of population growth. For a good many decades social problems, including public health and environmental sanitation, were more or less ignored. They began to receive increasing attention only at a rather late stage of development.

In the underdeveloped countries the course of history has been different, and in a good many cases even reversed. By and large, their economies stagnated, barring the growth of some export-oriented plantation and extractive industries. And the enlightenment of the colonial rulers expressed itself, above all, in measures to combat famines and epidemics as was, for example, the case in India under British rule.

Meanwhile, progress in another vital sector of the social infrastructure, i.e. in eduction, remained painfully slow. The concern for mass protection through measures for famine relief and control of epidemics was not matched by a policy of mass enlightenment through education, not to speak of mass welfare through overall economic development. The stage for population explosion was set long ago through these basic imbalances.

This sequence—public health first, economic development next—which was noticeable in the past has continued and become more pronounced in recent times. The amazing progress made in medical science produced the means—DDT, sulpha compounds, vaccines, antibiotics and other "wonder drugs"—to launch mass attacks on what had long been regarded as mass killers, such as malaria, cholera, small-pox, tuberculosis. With these wonderful tools so readily available to fight diseases, a government, functioning no matter under what system, had to give high priority to the promotion of public health. Pressures of public opinion would in any case push the government towards such a policy; just as the people themselves, guided by the strongest of all human instincts—the instinct of self-preservation—would refuse to compromise, on economic or financial grounds, in dealing with fatal diseases. The profit-motivated pharmaceutical industries in the West have been vigorously active to boost their output and to expand their international markets. Meanwhile, the World Health Organization (WHO) has patiently and systematically pursued its malaria and other eradication programmes. together with numerous projects for improvement of public health and environmental sanitation.

The result of this biomedical revolution, as is well known, has been a steep decline in death rates in recent years, particularly in infant and child mortality, accompanied by a rapid rise in life expectancy. For example, in India the death rate per 1000 was 27 in 1951, in 1966 it was 16, and by 1969 it is expected to fall to eight. Since the early 1940's the average life expectation has gone up from 27 to 50 years; it has practically doubled within the brief span of 25 years. Meanwhile, birth rates still hover around the traditional level of 40 per 1000. Essentially this is what has been happening, with some marginal varia-tions, in the entire underdeveloped world.

A rise in life expectancy, however sudden, is something devoutly to be wished. Yet it has become a cause for grave concern, for the simple reason that the fruits of the modern medical science have been applied one-sidedly—to curb deaths, but not births.

This, in turn, has been due to two major lags. First, there has been a psychological lag. "To anyone who thinks in biological as well as in economic, political and sociological terms," says Aldous Huxley, "it is self-evident that a society which practises death control must at the same time practice birth control—that the corollary to hygiene and preventive medicine is contraception."[132]

This is a self-evident truth, but initially it received only tardy recognition. Yet as the world population surged ahead—at the rate of 60 to 70 million a year—a revolution set in with a quick "revaluation of old values." The changes in the last few years have been truly dra-

---

[132] Quoted in "Does Overpopulation Mean Poverty?" By Joseph Marion Jones, Center for International Economic Growth, Washington, D. C., 1962.

matic. For example, in 1959 President Eisenhower had declared that his Government would have nothing to do with the problem of birth control. "This is not our business," he said. But since then there has been a complete turnabout. Allocations to provide assistance for family planning, at home and abroad, begun as a trickle in 1967, are expanding fast. Despite some stubborn pockets of resistance, the psychological lag, it may be assumed, will soon be overcome.

The ideological battle has been largely won. True, the Catholic Church still remains a stronghold of conservatism. But even here the stirrings of conscience have been increasingly audible, accompanied by frequent questioning of old dogmas. Conservative forces within the church are now fighting what clearly looks like a losing battle.[133]

Secondly, there has been a technological lag. The available means of birth control left a great deal to be desired; they were either crude and primitive, or too expensive, and not reliable enough. It is only in the last few years that this gap has been finally bridged with new chemicals and new devices. The mortality-curbing media have now been almost matched—in sophistication, effectiveness, and cost—by those for curbing fertility; and one may confidently count on further refinement and improvement. At last the technical means are available to stage a counterrevolution in the demographic field.

3

What about the attitude of the people in the developing countries? It has too long been assumed that the people are too conservative and tradition-bound, too indifferent to their own interests; that they would not respond positively to the idea of family planning.

Experience shows that such generalized assumptions are mostly ill-founded. In many countries the people, even in rural areas, are exposed to new ideas; movies, transistor radios, spread of education, rising urban population are bringing about a significant change. They may still want a family of four, even five, children, preferably with a son; but they would still be willing to limit births because they know that far fewer babies would now die than before. Even when the desired size of the family is the same, a childbearing mother knows that with sharply lowered infant mortality, her risk-bearing factor has changed.

---

133 The ferment continues despite Pope Paul's encyclical "Humanae Vitae" ("Of Human Life") since issued. Indeed, to justify the stand against this ruling one might cite Pope Paul's Easter Message of 1967 quoted at the beginning of this book.

The motivation for family planning is already present in many cases, as has been repeatedly confirmed by experience in such countries as South Korea, Taiwan, Hong Kong, Singapore, India, Pakistan, Egypt, Turkey, Chile, Mexico and Venezuela. And in a great many more cases the motivation can be created. Indeed, it would seem that in many developing countries the people are well ahead of their governments in this respect.[134]

Nevertheless, formidable tasks remain. We may build our hopes on "knowledge, chemicals, and women's instinct." But knowledge has to be disseminated; chemicals and devices have to be produced, or procured, and made available to individuals with proper instructions and guidance; then only can women's instinct come into full play.

Even if the worst predictions do not come true, one thing is certain: the world population curve will rise more steeply and go much higher before it begins to flatten out. The next three decades seem destined to go down in history as the period when the human species multiplied at the fastest rate.

Even on a conservative estimate, some three billion more people will be added to the world total between now and the end of the century. And the major part of this increase will occur in the developing countries where population is now growing at an average rate of about three per cent. During this period their share will rise from two-thirds, or over two billion, to at least three-quarters, or 4.5 billion.

This means that even if *maximum efforts are made* from now on to hold down the population, by 2000 A.D. the developing countries will have more than double their present numbers to be fed, clothed, housed, educated, protected medically, and employed gainfully.

The tasks are stupendous even with the present size of their population; its accelerated growth will greatly add to their magnitude and complexity. Mankind is faced with what President Johnson called "the multiplying problems of the multiplying population." "Let us face the fact," he added, "that less than five dollars invested in population control is worth a hundred dollars in economic growth."[135] Anything that the world can do to moderate this grim multiplier will be an aid to development; it will make the future tasks correspondingly less grim.

---

[134] For a reassuring account of the trends see, for example, Mr. Frank W. Notestein's article, "The Population Crisis: Reasons for Hope," in *Foreign Affairs,* October 1967.

[135] At San Francisco in June 1965.

What should be the role of WHO in this context? With its far-flung organization, its high professional standards, its international status, and the prestige and confidence it enjoys in the developing countries, the agency could play a role that is truly unique in stimulating, formulating and guiding national policies for population control. It is one of the major ironies of this age that the World Health Organization which, for the last twenty years, has done a superb job in combatting death, disease and disability, consistently refused even to consider the very idea of giving any assistance in the field of birth control.[136] The tacit assumption behind this negative policy was that its function was to save lives, not to control births. Thus, by its very efficiency and its determined one-sidedness, WHO became a major factor in aggravating the population explosion.

In summer 1966 the agency veered round to accept for the first time the idea, in principle, that family planning should form a part of its activities. A resolution passed by its governing body authorized it to give technical advice, "on request, from member governments," in the field of family planning "as part of an organized health service." The decision was modest, almost timid. No request, it seems, has so far been received from the governments for any significant assistance in family planning. Nor, apparently, is the agency in the least upset over this lack of initiative.

The 1966 resolution has so far produced little tangible result. Its real importance was ideological in the sense that it represented the first breach in the solid facade WHO had maintained so long. Yet it was hailed with jubilation as if it marked the beginning of a new era in world population policy. No wonder that a well-known demographer should have been provoked to the remark: "With the beating of drums and the blaring of trumpets, WHO is bringing up the rear."

Some time ago the United Nations began to give assistance in the demographic field, mainly for research, studies and training. This is far from enough and can be no substitute for large-scale WHO initiative directed to limit or regulate population growth. The question therefore arises: how long should this world body be allowed to shirk what is preeminently its responsibility for tackling a world problem of such great urgency? And there is a cognate question too: Is it, after all, not primarily a duty of the influential members of the United Nations

---

[136] This has been due, as is well known, to the opposition of the Catholic and the "Marxist" countries. But the explanation in no way mitigates the effects of this one-sided policy.

and the specialized agencies to take the initiative, pass appropriate legislation, force WHO out of its present passivity, and compel it to assume a far more active role on a global scale on the population front?

Meanwhile, the task before developing countries is clear. Population must be controlled. The western world could spread out its demographic transition over a century or more. But they must telescope the whole process into a couple of decades. This has become the *first* imperative of our times. They must therefore give or, as far as possible, be persuaded to give, a correspondingly high priority to it in their own development programmes.

4

The *second* imperative is no less clear: the development of agriculture and production of food must be speeded up and vigorously pursued. This was the crux of the forthright recommendations made in May, 1967 by the President's Science Advisory Committee on the World Food Problem:[137]

> "1. The scale, severity, and duration of the world food problem are so great that a massive, long-range, innovative effort unprecedented in human history will be required to master it.

> "2. The solution of the problem that will exist after about 1985 demands that programs of population control be initiated now. For the immediate future, the food supply is critical.
> . . . .

> "3. Food supply is directly related to agricultural development and, in turn, agricultural development and overall economic development are critically interdependent in the hungry countries."

Here, again, it is essential to see things in the right perspective. The food crisis that now threatens to engulf two-thirds of the world has, like the population explosion, been in the making for a long time; and, like the latter, it is the outcome of a number of historical and technological gaps. These gaps, far more than any mistaken priorities, explain why food production has lagged behind in the developing countries and is now frighteningly outpaced by population growth.

Until recently agriculture was, by and large, a neglected subject in the underdeveloped world. In the newly-independent countries of Asia

---
137 "The World Food Problem. A Report of the President's Science Advisory Committee." The White House, Washington, D. C., May 1967. Vol. 1, Page 11.

and Africa the neglect pre-dated independence by several generations. And after independence it continued mainly because, until very recently, the incentives as well as the means for modernization were lacking. Seasonal overproduction, periodic slump in agricultural prices, sharp fluctuations of commodity prices on the world market have long acted as deterrents to agricultural development. The domestic markets for food grains were usually limited until the recent upsurge in population boosted demand and suddenly created the threat of an acute shortage.

There was yet another spectacular lag which is often overlooked. Agricultural research in the developing countries had long been confined to tree or plantation crops—coffee, cocoa, tea, jute, rubber, palm oil, coconut, sugarcane—and did not extend to food crops. Great strides had been made in the temperate zones in evolving improved and heavy-yielding varieties of foodgrains, but they were generally not suitable for the soil and climatic conditions of the tropics and subtropics. This is an important point to remember. Industrial technology can be readily transferred across the oceans not only from east to west, but also from north to south—a steel mill, a textile or chemical factory, even a nuclear reactor, for example, can be set up in almost any country; the limitations are economic, not physical. But it is not so with agricultural technology, such as improved seeds, new varieties, pesticides, weed-killer, which cannot be transferred across major climatic barriers. They must be evolved through years of painstaking research and experiment to suit entirely different physical conditions. In short, tropical ecology called for a different food production technology, and this was almost completely lacking.

It is only in the last few years that this critical research gap has been largely closed, as a result of the initiatives taken by the Rockefeller and the Ford Foundation. Some vastly improved varieties of wheat and maize evolved in Mexico, and of rice developed in the Philippines can, with minor local adaptations, be grown in most tropical countries. The new varieties are spreading rapidly in India, Pakistan and other developing countries, raising yields to levels which would have been unthinkable only a few years ago. The result is what Mr. William Gaud recently called the Green Revolution.[138]

This green revolution also gives the green light, and shows the direction in which the developing countries in general must move.

---

[138] "The Green Revolution: Accomplishments and Apprehension." Address before the Society for International Development on 8 March 1968 in Washington, D. C., by Mr. William S. Gaud, Director, U.S. A.I.D.

Incidentally, this is what happened in Japan where improved seeds and fertilizers played a vital role in the early stages of her economic development. Even today, Japan's agriculture provides the best model for the heavily populated countries of South and South East Asia. She has demonstrated how even on tiny 1-to-2-acre farms one can build a prosperous agriculture with high-grade seeds, heavy doses of fertilizers, pesticides for plant protection, skilful conservation of water and soil, and a whole range of small tools and implements—for ploughing, seeding, weeding, spraying, harvesting, thrashing, perhaps also for processing—all tailor-made to suit the small farms and to give the optimum combination of man and equipment.

Many areas in the developing countries, which now grow only one crop, often a precarious one, could be brought under double-or triple-cropping, provided, of course, adequate supply of water can be assured. Besides, most of them have excellent opportunities for mixed farming, comprising not only foodgrains, but also fruits and vegetables, poultry, animal husbandry, and sometimes also pond fishery, which will help diversify agriculture and very substantially raise the value of its output.

Intensive agriculture on such lines will give a tremendous impetus to production, employment, and income. Apart from the farming population directly employed in agricultural operations, it will be able to support indirectly large sections of the population in various ancillary industries and services, including marketing, transportation and distribution.

5

How effective has been the role played by FAO for stepping up food production? In the last decade the agency, and more specifically its Director-General in person, did pioneering work to focus world attention on the race between food production and population growth, a looming food crisis of staggering dimension, and the urgent need for concerted global effort in time to forestall it, which led, in July 1960, to the launching of a worldwide Freedom from Hunger Campaign.

In addition, FAO did something else no less farsighted. It championed the cause of population control through family planning as a matter of overriding urgency and the highest priority, and it worked incessantly to arouse public opinion in its favour at a time when WHO, the most logical agency to be preocupied with this grave problem, seemed irrevocably set on a negative course.

In recent years the importance of FAO, a key agency dealing with a key problem, has grown rapidly. Its offices—at headquarters and in the regions—have expanded; its staff has multiplied; its budget has soared; its activities have widened in scope and volume; its participation in the UNDP has been very substantial—for example, of the 873 Special Fund projects approved by February 1968, FAO accounted for no less than 344 or 40 per cent. Yet its impact in terms of actual production has been barely noticeable.

The agency, it seems, is not altogether unaware of this. For example, in a report reviewing the trends in food and agriculture in the second postwar decade it was stated that, though immense progress had been made in agriculture during this period, it has "proved more difficult than expected" to apply the technological advances to the developing countries "largely because of institutional defects."[139] The same report, in its Foreword, also emphasized that the greatest single obstacle to increased farm production, "probably even greater than ignorance of modern methods of agriculture," was the lack of any real incentives to cultivators in many countries to increase their production for the market.

Both points are undoubtedly true. Both are also exaggerated, and in any case they almost amount to a doctor blaming his patient for illness. The relevant question is not how difficult the conditions are in the developing countries to increase agricultural production, but *given these conditions,* how much more FAO could and should achieve.

The real reasons why FAO's success in practical terms has so far been severely limited, have been indicated in the preceding chapter. It has been, and continues to be, strong in expertise, but weak in management; it has overcentralized responsibilities and allowed too little freedom and initiative at the grassroots level; it has over-emphasized its advisory role and maintained a passive stance; it has exaggerated its helplessness and blamed government attitudes, and has done too little to change them.

And perhaps worst of all, it has failed to realize the importance of what should have been its foremost concern from the day the agency was established—to help develop competent agricultural extension services in as many countries as possible and to bring the benefits of modern science and technology to the door of the farmers coupled with actual field demonstration and the requisite practical guidance. This, as all agriculturists know, is the most potent instrument FAO

---

[139] "The State of Food and Agriculture 1965. Review of the Second Postwar Decade" (C/65/4), FAO, Rome, 1965. Page 5.

could and should have used to raise output, to change the farmers' outlook, and to prepare the ground for basic reforms, including land reform, and for building and strengthening other essential services and institutions. This is the instrument FAO has yet to develop.

According to the report cited above, the total food supplies for the developing countries would have to be increased fourfold in the next 35 years to give their vastly increased numbers "an adequate, though by no means a lavish diet." To make the leaders alive to the issues at stake, FAO launched on the preparation of what it called an "Indicative World Plan," which would broadly chart the "goals and objectives" for the governments and would also outline the "means and measures" by which these goals might be realized. All this is indicative of FAO's general approach. The agency has shown a strong predilection for grandiose schemes, instead of sorting out and coming to grips with the practical tasks. It has worked hard to mobilize world public opinion, but not hard enough to meet the actual needs of underdeveloped farming. It has dealt with the agricultural problems of the developing countries massively in its reports and studies, but has not sufficiently cared to explore the practical ways and means to resolve them.

No wonder that this great international agency should have played such a small part in ushering in the revolution in tropical agriculture. Only now it is waking up to the new vistas of possibilities that have opened up, and is beginning to realize that agricultural progress in the developing countries need not be perpetually stymied by their institutional defects; that the seeds of revolution can be planted in the fields and nourished with fertilizers; that the new forces of dynamism thus introduced in rural environment would be a powerful factor in changing the farmer's attitude; and, working backwards from the field, they would, sooner or later, help burst the institutional rigidities and even compel the authorities to forge new policies and to make necessary institutional and other adjustments. With this realization belatedly dawning on the agency, it has begun to react to the new revolution essentially like WHO to family planning. "With the beating of drums and the blaring of trumpets," it is now engaged "in bringing up the rear."

The miracle seeds of rice and wheat, which have begun to double and treble output per acre, are packed with revolution. This is now being demonstrated beyond any shadow of doubt in the countries of Asia—in the Philippines, Taiwan, India, Pakistan, Ceylon, Iran, Turkey, and others. They are fast becoming "engines" of far-reaching change in the social and economic field. "They may be to the agricultural revolution in Asia what the steam engine was to the industrial revolution in Europe," says Mr. Lester R. Brown.[140]

The U.S. Secretary of Agriculture, Mr. Orville L. Freeman, is even more categorical. For example, referring to IR-8, the rice seed developed in the Philippines, he said: "This seed is to agriculture what the steam engine was to industry."[141] These statements can no longer be dismissed as idle rhetoric. Already there are enough telling facts to bear them out, also to warrant the prediction that the revolution will spread rapidly in Asia and will soon—perhaps within the next few years—spill over to the continents of Africa and Latin America.

To capitalize on this agricultural breakthrough, a host of other problems, however, will have to be faced and solved including continued genetic research, supply of improved seeds and of fertilizers and pesticides, water development and better water-use, equipment for farm mechanization and for grain handling and processing, transportation and storage facilities, also farm credit, marketing, price incentives. These are the tasks to which FAO could most profitably address itself systematically, today and in the coming years.

And to do so effectively, it must turn its attention to develop that vitally important institution without which no agriculture can be modernized: a modern extension service with men competent to provide demonstration and guidance for improved farm management. This has acquired greater urgency than ever before because, to take full advantage of the new opportunities, the farmer will need a wide range of essential services. In addition, he will have to be initiated into far more up-to-date techniques of soil-and-water conservation and management, which must go hand in hand with the high-yielding seeds, heavy doses of fertilizers and pesticides, and multiple cropping.

To underscore this urgency and to dramatize the opportunities now unfolding, it would be worth creating a global pool of, say, up to 100 handpicked experts with long experience in agricultural extension work—drawn largely from the USA in view of its unparalleled achievements in this field, and partly from West Europe, Japan, and perhaps also Israel,[142] and to make their services available to the gov-

---

140 "The Agricultural Revolution in Asia," Foreign Affairs, July 1968. The article gives a vivid account of the latest developments with a prognosis.

141 New York Times, 7 July 1968.

142 The governments of these countries could make experts available on secondment and, in any case, actively help in their recruitment. Newly retired members of the Agricultural Extension Service of the U.S.D.A. should often deserve serious consideration.

vernments as part of the UNDP's top-priority activities, to help them build up their own agricultural extension services in suitable stages.

In some countries, such as India and Pakistan, young men trained in agriculture are available in sizable numbers who, with some supplementary practical training, could be drafted into the service. In many countries the training of nationals will, however, take a longer time. Initially, therefore, such countries may very well need larger teams of extension service experts from outside. In a good many instances Peace Corps volunteers would be ideally suited to serve on such teams.

For almost a decade FAO has worked hard to mobilize public opinion to face the facts of the demographic revolution and the threat of a world food crisis. Will it now mobilize its own forces to speed and guide the blossoming agricultural revolution, to mount a big effort to step up food production, and to lead the underdeveloped countries from the brink of near-famine conditions towards the promise of abundance which has been miraculously brought within their reach? No other task could be more challenging, and none more rewarding—for FAO, for the UNDP, and for the entire UN family.

6

The threat of a famine in foodcrops which only a couple of years ago seemed inexorably to be overtaking mankind, may yet be averted if the use of the miracle seeds spreads fast enough and if the green revolution attains quick momentum. A large part of the world is, however, already caught in a protein famine. The per capita intake of protein has long been abnormally low in most developing countries, with widespread symptoms of malnutrition resulting primarily from this deficiency. In recent years this has been aggravated by the upsurge in population with damaging effects which have been particularly marked on children. A rapid rise in the production of all kinds of edible protein—plant and animal, conventional and industrial—deserves a very high priority.[143]

Luckily, the means to combat the protein famine are already there. Production of protein food from animal sources can be rapidly stepped up. Poultry, in particular, has a large potential almost everywhere, and it can also show the quickest results within the shortest

---

[143] The Advisory Committee on the Application of Science and Technology emphasized the urgency in its Second Report, E/4026, United Nations, New York, 1965. See paras. 47-67 in particular. This is the best document the UN family has produced on the question of priorities, and it deserves much greater attention than it has received so far in the formulation of country programmes.

time. Similarly, pond culture of fish has tremendous possibilities in many tropical countries, and can be rapidly expanded at a low cost. The world's fisheries resources—both inland and marine—are yet to be surveyed and tapped. At present "only a minute fraction" of these resources provided by nature has been used for human food; and the fraction supplies only one-tenth of the animal protein and about one-hundredth of the world's total food supplies.[144]

A separate Department of Fisheries was created in FAO in 1965 when a permanent Committee on Fisheries was also established. Fisheries are now receiving greater attention, but the efforts need to be intensified with a more definite policy to bring about a rapid increase in actual output.

Supply of protein food from conventional sources—animal, poultry, fish, also various pulses and other plant products—can be dramatically increased within a decade or so. The world need not in this case wait for new breakthroughs. By and large, the required knowledge and technology are already there and can, with minor adaptations, be put to use on a massive scale. What is needed is a well-conceived action programme on a much larger scale, backed by larger resources and greater determination.

Meanwhile some scientific breakthroughs of great promise made in recent years for producing protein-rich foods by industrial processing techniques still await commercial exploitation. Of these the most important are protein concentrates derived from the byproducts of oil-seed crushing and fisheries industries. The technological problems for producing safe and inexpensive highprotein concentrates have been resolved. But the human problem—that of consumer acceptance—still remains, more so since food habits are among the hardest to change. Nevertheless, it should not be beyond the wit of man to overcome resistance to what is intended to meet one of the primary needs of man to promote his own well-being. The obstacle is an argument not for helpless inaction, but for more spadework and greater ingenuity.

Food losses in the developing countries continue to be heavy. This, again, is due largely to technological gaps. Spectacular progress has been made in the developed countries in evolving techniques for food storage and preservation, but they cannot be transferred to the tropical countries where conditions are radically different—high temperatures, poor communications, lack of industrial facilities, low level of hygiene, and general poverty of the masses. There is need for more tailor-made technology to meet the specific requirements of the developing coun-

---

[144] Ibid., para. 50.

tries. The emphasis will have to be largely on methods of low-cost, small-scale storage and preservation that would minimize losses. It should be possible to work out the appropriate solutions by adapting the available knowledge and techniques.

Measures to prevent food losses deserve high priority for a double reason—to augment considerably the net supply of food in general, and to conserve protein food in particular since animal and fisheries products deteriorate quickly in tropical temperatures. The nature of the problems and their urgency have been known for many years, though they are hardly reflected in the FAO programmes. Only very recently some Special Fund projects have been authorized to help improve the storage and preservation, mainly of foodgrains, in some countries. The steps taken are still much too modest. They need to be multiplied many times, and they must go beyond preinvestment to actual development.

7

Development of industries should easily rank as the next, or *third*, high-priority field.

Here again, the historical lags and gaps have been quite conspicuous. One may, for example, recall the thesis that was at one time fashionable and occurred in many textbooks on economics, viz. that tropical countries were inherently suitable for agriculture, but not for industries. From this there followed the corollary that concentration of efforts in these countries on the production of primary commodities while depending on manufactured goods imported from abroad, represented an international division of labour which was more or less preordained by nature and which, consequently, best served the interests of all parties.

Theories, however, changed; and for some time it almost looked as though the above thesis would have to be reversed. Trends in many tropical countries seemed to indicate, until very recently, that they could develop industries far more easily than agriculture.

The old thesis has now been set aside as an interesting piece of rationalization that belonged to the heyday of colonialism. Nevertheless, the bias it reflected against industries became a powerful psychological factor that helped create a counter-bias in favour of industries, once the colonies attained independence and became the masters of their destiny. And this new bias could only have been helped by the example, and the ideology, of Soviet Russia with its emphasis on central planning and its focus on rapid industrial development.

By a curious coincidence, the inaction in the field of industries, which was the hallmark of the colonial era, came to characterize also the United Nations programmes of development. Over the years the specialized agencies multiplied, the programmes proliferated to cover an ever-widening range of activities, but the industrial sector was either ignored or held at best in a precarious embrace. The omission, in the eyes of some people, suspiciously looked like a hangover from an anti-industrial past.

The delegates of Soviet Russia at times also of the other socialist countries, drew pointed attention year after year at the sessions of the various UN bodies—TAC, the ECOSOC, the Second Committee, the Governing Council of the Special Fund and later of the UNDP—to the need for laying greater emphasis on industrial development under the UN programmes. Nor is there any doubt that their tenacious pleading was a major influence in producing the concensus that ultimately led to the creation of a new agency, with effect from 1 January 1967— the United Nations Industrial Development Organization or UNIDO— to fill this yawning void.

The long and sterile debate on agriculture versus industry has already done enough damage and should be shelved once and for all. The debate, for one thing, could not halt action; it only helped produce wrong action in many instances, especially since there was no competent body to provide impartial guidance. The governments of many developing countries proceeded to set up industries according to their own light, or lack of it, often under relentless pressure, or under temptation of enticing offers from outside, and ended up by retarding rather than stimulating their economic growth.

The world—in this case mostly its developed part—has taken a long time to discover what was always obvious, namely, that traditional agriculture cannot be modernized without the support of a thriving non-farm sector. The President's Science Advisory Committee was emphatic on this point, as is clear from their recommendations quoted above. Farmers cannot be expected to raise production unless there is a large enough market for it. And only an expanding non-farm sector can create the market for the expanding output from agriculture. Besides, in many developing countries, especially in the heavily populated countries of Asia, a flourishing non-farm sector is essential also to reduce the pressure of population on land which at present acts as a powerful drag on agricultural productivity.

There is a third reason as well. Modern agriculture is directly dependent on a host of non-farm, but farm-supporting industries, such as fertilizers, pesticides, farm equipment, seed production, livestock feeds, electricity supply, storage facilities, refrigeration, transportation and marketing, and a whole range of processing industries.

Talks about high priority for agriculture will be futile as long as these three elementary facts are ignored. The question cannot be: agriculture or industry. It must be both, and in any well-conceived programme of economic development, agro-industries must be given special emphasis side by side with agriculture.

The industrial sector in many developing countries, such as India and Pakistan, contains cottage industries and handicrafts which deserve far greater attention than they have received. There is an all too common tendency to sacrifice them for the sake of modern large-scale factories. This blind imitation is hurting many developing economies today. For, it involves heavy capital outlay with expenditure of scarce foreign exchange; it often fails to produce commensurate benefits in terms of productivity; and instead of creating new jobs for the people, it may, through premature adoption of labour-saving machinery, actually aggravate unemployment.

This misguided trend stems from a failure to perceive an important fact—that modern science and technology have altered the old picture of the economies of scale; that today not only the big, but also the small can benefit from them. That is why even tiny farms, with heavy chemical and other inputs, can comfortably survive as productive units, provided the essential inputs are available at a low enough cost. That is also the reason why, with better tools, better techniques and better organization, it is possible to build up the productivity of handicrafts and small industries to a level that would make them viable even in a competitive environment.

There are no doubt cases where the economies of scale will call for large units, as in the case of a power station, a fertilizer factory, a seed production industry, a machine tool or equipment manufacturing concern. Nevertheless, industrial planning in the developing countries will, as a rule, make a great deal more sense both for creating employment and for generating economic growth if, at least initially, it centres round mainly these two sectors—agri-business, and handicrafts and small industries, barring, of course, such exceptional cases as Kuwait and Libya which are dependent on one single natural resource, that is, oil.

Food-processing industries, such as canning, preservation, and refrigeration, constitute an important group of agri-business. In most cases they deserve priority treatment even in the early stages of industrialization, although greater refinements can be introduced only in stages as supply of electricity, refrigeration plants, transportation and other facilities become more fully available. It is important that, in developing such industries, prevention of waste and conservation of nutritional values are both given due emphasis right from the start.

To meet the protein famine referred to earlier, promotion of industries for producing fish and oil-seed protein concentrates should receive urgent consideration in certain developing countries, such as India and Pakistan, where it should be possible to create large enough markets for their profitable operation.

Another general high-priority field is the development of building and building materials industries. For the vast majority of people in the underdeveloped countries the housing conditions are deplorable. And with the fast-growing population, both urban and rural slums are expanding at a frightening rate. Since housing, as an essential of life, ranks only next to food and clothing, it should receive a correspondingly high priority treatment in all programmes intended to raise living standards and to promote mass welfare.

Yet housing in the deevloping countries has hitherto suffered not only from inadequate initiative, but also from a wrong approach. There has been altogether too much imitation of the West in this matter. That the physical conditions in the tropics and sub-tropics, and therefore the housing requirements, are radically different has received little recognition. The genius of the colonial masters was applied to expensive western-style residential houses for the benefit of the few, in addition to government buildings also standardized according to the western pattern. And that tradition has continued more or less unchanged. The result is a tragic waste. The cities in the developing countries are not only expanding fast and planlessly, they are in most cases cluttered with buildings that are expensive, ill-designed, and mostly ill-suited to the climatic conditions. Meanwhile, even the most pressing needs of the masses, both in rural and urban areas, continue to go largely by default.

The Advisory Committee referred to above drew pointed attention to these facts. The evidence presented to the Committee indicated that "from one third to one half of all resources available for investment in the developing countries is currently being used for housing construction and for essential urban services and facilities."[145] Moreover, practically all the roofing materials used in towns have to be imported at present. But neither these materials nor the roofing designs are suitable

---

[145] Ibid., para. 97.

for the hot climate because of "insufficient protection from heat radia-tion."[146] Thus, the present practice, at a high cost in terms of capital and foreign exchange only provides high discomfort.

The need for low-cost housing suited to the tropics is obvious. It calls for more intensive reesarch and investigation in the locally avail-able building materials, more careful studies of designs, improvement of construction methods, and the upgrading of local trades personnel. The Advisory Committee rightly urged that all this, along with mass production and distribution of roofing, is "eminently a subject demand-ing a concerted attack on a worldwide scale." The problems are certainly soluble on the basis of the scientific knowledge and techniques already available, but they will need a greater input of effort and imagination.

Apart from these general areas, there should be numerous other possibilities in many countries to develop consumer goods industries —textiles, leather goods, furniture, household utensils, to mention some of the most obvious; also mining and processing of minerals, though to a more limited extent. Such cases would require much more specific on-the-spot study and appraisals. Where the domestic market is limited—and this is particularly true of countries in Africa, Central America, and the Middle East—many industries would be viable only when they are conceived and developed on a regional basis to cater to groups of countries.

8

The creation of UNIDO has been greeted as the beginning of a new era for the developing countries. It does reflect a new awareness in the UN family about the urgency to promote more actively the growth of their industries. What are the prospects that this newborn agency will actually deliver the goods? Unfortunately, the signs are none too reassuring.

The purpose of UNIDO, as laid down in General Assembly Resolu-tion 2152 (XXI) of 17 November 1966, is to promote industrial devel-opment and assist in accelerating industrialization of the developing countries, "with particular emphasis on the manufacturing sector."

At its first session, held in April-May 1967, the 45-member Industrial Development Board, which is the principal organ of UNIDO, decided that the agency would carry out its functions essentially on the basis of "meeting the urgent needs" of the developing countries. And to

---

[146] Ibid., para. 102.

fulfil this purpose, it would undertake two basic types of activities, namely, "*operational* activities and action-oriented *studies and research* programmes." The Board then laid down the activities to be covered by the first category which would be financed from voluntary contributions made by governments. Accordingly, UNIDO is authorized to:

— Encourage, promote and recommend national, regional and international action to achieve more rapid industrialization of developing countries;

— Contribute to the most effective application in the developing countries of modern industrial methods of production, programming and planning, taking into account the experience of countries with different social and economic systems;

— Build and strengthen institutions and administration in the developing countries in the field of industrial technology, production, programming and planning;

— Disseminate information on technological innovations originating in various countries and assist the developing countries in the practical application of such information;

— Assist, at the request of developing countries, in the formulation of industrial development programmes and in the preparation of specific industrial projects;

— Aid in the regional planning of industrialization of developing countries within their regional and sub-regional economic groupings;

— Offer advice and guidance on problems relating to the exploitation and efficient use of natural resources, industrial raw materials, by-products and new products of developing countries;

— Assist the developing countries "in the training of technical and other appropriate categories of personnel needed for their accelerated industrial development, in cooperation with the specialized agencies concerned";

— Propose "measures for the improvement of the international system of industrial property, with a view to accelerating the transfer of technical know-how to developing countries";

— Assist, at the request of developing countries, in obtaining external financing for specific industrial projects.

These are the guidelines the Board laid down for UNIDO's work. It set out to meet "the urgent needs" of the developing countries, and then discovered that almost everything pertaining to industries was urgent. This resolution suffers from the same besetting sin as EPTA, the over-Expanded Programme, namely, an attempt to compress too many things into too little money. Blanket legislation of this type, so characteristic of the UN programmes, can only lead to a blurring of all sense of priorities, and to a guaranteed dispersal of money and effort. Once again, the stage is set for an unbusinesslike approach to a vitally important business sector.

What the developing countries need most is not a multiplicity of services, nor ambitious international conferences, nor seminars and symposia, however well-meaning and well-organized, but manufacturing industries that are productive, viable and profitable, that create wealth, employment and income. The task before UNIDO is to choose such industries wisely and to see that they are carried through all the phases, from preliminary study through blueprint and construction to actual opertion. The General Assembly resolution is quite specific on this point. It wants industrialization to be accelerated "with particular emphasis on the manufacturing sector." These words contain in a nutshell the fundamental guideline that UNIDO should stringently follow.

The primary objective of UNIDO should be to establish successful industrial projects, and to do so as far as possible in every single developing country. Only then will the newborn agency fulfil the primary function for which it has been created, and only then will the UN programmes begin to make belated amends for the long neglect this crucially important sector has suffered from all these years.

9

The *fourth* high-priority field, it is suggested, should be comprehensive public works programmes, especially in rural areas, to create jobs for the surplus man-power, to increase productivity, and to promote social welfare. These programmes could lay special stress on such items as small irrigation projects, various types of soil-and-water conservation measures, reforestation of waste-lands, flood protection levees, construction of irrigation and drainage canals, wells and tanks, village feeder roads, transmission lines for rural electrification, storage silos, godowns and workshops, buildings for schools and hospitals, and rural housing. Many of these items could be promoted as self-help projects with appropriate support from governments on a matching basis.

To carry out such programmes it would be unrealistic to rely exclusively on the so-called community development approach. Conditions vary enormously within the developing countries; and in most cases they are far from propitious for its success. There is ample room, and clear need, for other types of organization, such as the Civilian Conservation Corps of the New Deal era, labour camps, youth brigades, boy scouts, a domestic Peace Corps. Nor is there any reason why the army should not be mobilized, wherever feasible, to carry out public works projects including construction of major roads and highways.

While it is primarily for the recipient governments to formulate and execute such programmes, the UNDP can certainly help by providing ideas, guidance, incentives and, where appropriate, by introducing Special Fund-type of projects. Some of these activities are already supported by the World Food Programme in a few countries.

10

Fifth, that education must be treated as a top-priority need no one will question. Outlays for education and research are nowadays regarded as the best national investment and, in the long run, the biggest booster of the gross national product. This is no less true of the developing countries where, without education, economic progress would be inconceivable. For them, freedom from ignorance remains a precondition for freedom from want.

It is, however, not enough to recognize the *need* for education. There must be greater realization of the *kind* of education that is needed, and of the *tempo* at which it must spread.

In evolving their systems of education, almost all developing countries are faced with two major handicaps due to historical reasons: for too long, education has been the privilege of too few people; and almost everywhere it has been geared to the humanities, especially language and literature, to the neglect of natural sciences.

The most urgent first task of education in these countries is also the most obvious, namely, mass literacy. Expenditure for education should be treated as an investment and not be relegated to the category of "social services" as distinct from "development services" and "security services," urged Professor John Kenneth Galbraith in 1961, then U.S. Ambassador to India.[147] He recalled Jefferson's dictum: "If you

---

[147] Convocation address at the Rajasthan University in December 1961.

want a country to be ignorant and free, you expect what never was, and never will be." And then he made the most pertinent point which no development programme, national or international, can afford to ignore: "Nowhere in the world is there an illiterate peasantry that is progressive and nowhere is there a literate peasantry that is not."

A UNESCO study made in 1962 underlined the magnitude of the task: 700 million persons, or 44 per cent of the world's population aged 15 years or over, were illiterate; 52 per cent of the school-age population in 1959 went without primary education; between 1950 and 1960 the incidence of illiteracy rose sharply in certain heavily populated countries, notably in Asia.

That was the world situation around 1960. Since then, despite increased attempts to spread education, there has been, according to UNESCO surveys, further deterioriation from year to year because of the rapid growth of population.[148]

Many developing countries have more or less instinctively given high priority to primary education. This is particularly true of a number of African countries—Ghana, for example, took the bold step, in 1961, of introducing free compulsory primary education. The investments, however, are not yielding the return they should in terms of development. In many instances they have even proved counterproductive.

That education may very well hinder economic growth, at least in the short run, is well illustrated by what, according to Mr. Nathanial McKitterick, is happening in Senegal. The system of primary education in rural areas, he remarks, is both primitive and expensive, costing 20 per cent of the central budget, and it produces "graduates highly motivated to escape the basic problem of Senegalese economic life: the problem of greater agricultural production." The reason, in the words of one Senegalese cabinet minister quoted by him, is that "l'école est l'animation française."[149]

This, however, holds good for a great many countries other than Senegal and for schools with "animation" other than French. Education of the 19th century vintage cannot meet the late 20th century

---

[148] According to recent estimates of UNESCO specialists, in 1970 there will be between 760 and 770 million adult illiterates with the vast majority in the developing countries, the current primary education enrolment often being below 50 per cent.

[149] "A Mass Attack on Low Productivity in Peasant Agriculture." International Development Review, September 1967. The account given in this article is instructive also as an example of how development projects should be planned and executed without artificial distinction between technical assistance, pre-investment work, etc.

needs. Literacy will make better peasants only if the literates stay on their farms, an assumption that was implicit in Ambassador Galbraith's remark quoted above. And this applies equally to craftsmen, mechanics and workers in general, whose skills will improve with literacy provided they continue to pursue their skills. People, in short, must be educated and trained *for* the tasks of development, and not *away from* them.

The UN family has been busy discovering these rudimentary truths. And like WHO in population control, FAO in food production, UN/UNIDO in industrialization, in the last few years UNESCO in education has been "bringing up the rear" with customary elan and fanfare.

For example, two Special Fund projects were approved, in January 1966, for Algeria and Iran respectively, as an experiment in relating adult literacy to skill-upgrading. They carried the characteristic title "work-oriented adult literacy pilot projects." Thus does the great agency for education hope to pilot, at the pace of the mid-Victorian era, toward freedom from ignorance an impatient underdeveloped world that has been plunged into an explosive age.

The agency has been paying more attention, especially in the last few years, to primary and secondary education, also to science teaching, school curricula, textbook production, and teacher training. The right guidelines for action are painfully emerging after years of enthusiastic amateurism.

To some people, though admittedly a very few, within the UN family and its immediate entourage, UNESCO's tasks in providing education for development have long been perfectly clear, almost from the day the Expanded Programme of Technical Assistance was established: first, to launch and conduct a worldwide campaign for adult literacy and to mobilize support for it, moral and material, on the broadest possible front; and second, to concentrate at the same time utmost possible effort on an expansion of primary and secondary education with teacher training, introduction of improved techniques for teaching, and modernization of curricula with much greater emphasis on science teaching and practical training. There was no need, in their view, to grope around for the priorities, and no justification to squander the modest financial resources on a mass of tiny projects, most of which vanished into thin air without leaving any tangible results behind.

It is intriguing, even though futile, to speculate what tremendous services UNESCO could have rendered to the developing world if it had enough vision, enough tenacity and practical commonsense to press ahead with these historic tasks. It missed its mission; and the underdeveloped world was deprived of an essential service at a critical time.

The priorities have not changed. They are still the same. Only, because of the past neglect, they have enormously grown in urgency. There is an old Chinese proverb which says: "If you plan for one year, plant rice; for ten years, plant trees; for a century, educate the people." Such long-range planning for education, starting presumably with the three R's and taking generations of children laboriously through school, will no longer do. The vastly different tempo of this age calls for a far more daring dimension in thinking and action.

The case of India well illustrates the point. About 75 per cent of her population are still illiterate; and the flood of newcomers—currently more than a million per month—is constantly swelling their ranks, despite all the strenuous efforts made to extend school education. And yet the people must be enlightened rapidly about a host of vital problems, such as the urgency and methods of birth control, better agronomic practices with new seeds and more fertilizers, the folly of carrying the surplus cattle population, improved nutrition through better and cheaper food. The stakes are high, and the time is short. India must try and compress a century's progress into a single decade.

There is only one way out. In order to plant rice and trees, and to educate the people at the same time and with the fastest possible speed, India must plant—television. Amazing progress has been made in recent years in mass communication media which can tremendously facilitate the dissemination of knowledge and quicken the process of mass education, or enlightenment. The construction of a network of television services embracing the whole country deserves top priority in India's development strategy today, with free or subsidized TV sets and screens for community use in rural areas and in the poorer sections of the urban centres.[150]

Immediate introduction of television will not be practicable in all developing countries. What is important is that the modern mass media of communication should be pressed into service to the utmost possible extent to accelerate the process of mass enlightenment. In a revolutionary age the process of education must also be revolutionized.

---

[150] From recent press reports it appears that the Government of India has decided on a plan to make television available to the whole country by lofting a broadcasting satellite into a central position over the subcontinent. This is a most timely and commendable decision which should be pushed through with maximum speed under the most competent technical guidance.

11

Sixth, that public health must indefinitely continue as a top-priority area, goes without saying. Long classified as a "social service," it must also be treated as an inescapable development service. Better health can help raise productivity in the developing countries almost immediately, often quite significantly. In that sense public health expenditures must be regarded as a productive investment.

The creditable record established by WHO in the last two decades, it may be assumed, will continue in the future and will be further improved upon. The ready support the agency receives from its member-governments, its sizable regular budget, its practical approach to problems, and the experience and momentum it has gained from the past would warrant such optimism. Meanwhile, it is absolutely essential to broaden its programme as well as its participation in the UNDP/SF in several directions.

The first requirement should be abundantly clear from what has been said earlier. The world cannot, and must not, be indefinitely deprived of the services of the World Health Organization in dealing with what has exploded into mankind's second biggest problem of survival, second only to the threat of a nuclear war. Its professional services must be mobilized, on a far bigger scale and as a matter of utmost urgency, to promote family planning and population control.

This, as things now stand, will almost certainly require greater initiative at the highest policy-making levels of the UN family—the ECOSOC and the General Assembly. Meanwhile, the UNDP, too, can do a great deal more in this field even within the fragile framework of the existing WHO legislation. It can, through its field representatives, persuade the governments, where conditions are favourable, to ask for WHO assistance in family planning as part of their organized medical service, and then to make more liberal allocations to the agency.

As for public health, the supply of pure water in adequate quantities should be a matter of the highest priority. More than two-thirds of the world's population, it has been estimated, at present lack such supplies. The result is the high incidence of water-borne diseases; according to the WHO Director-General, no less than 500 million people are estimated to suffer from them. Besides, WHO studies have revealed that among the diseases recorded in the developing countries, gastroenteritis and related conditions account for the highest mortality; that their high incidence is particularly marked among children of one to four years; and that the rate of mortality from this cause is actually on the increase, no doubt a result of population growth.[151]

Water supply has been recognized as a Special Fund field of activity. And by February 1968, 11 projects for water supply and/or sewerage were authorized: three for Calcutta, dealing with different aspects of the problem; two for Accra-Tema (Ghana) in two phases; the rest were for Istanbul (Turkey), Taipei (China), Ibadan (Nigeria), Manila (Philippines), Kampala-Jinja (Uganda), and Malta.

There is undoubtedly a case for many more projects of this type. And what is no less important, projects for supplying pure drinking water—through tubewells and other means—should also be rapidly developed for the country-side as part of a programme for promoting rural welfare and for countering the exodus to the urban areas (see next section).

Will WHO be able to cope with a greatly expanded programme of water supply? It will certainly have to subcontract the jobs to competent commercial firms, as is already the practice, instead of trying to tackle them on a "force account" basis. Besides, unlike the normal activities of WHO, water supply projects will involve much of the characteristics of an engineering-cum-construction business and will therefore require management of a different kind.

A no less vital field is nutrition, particularly to help combat protein malnutrition and vitamin deficiency, both of which, as mentioned earlier, are appallingly widespread in the developing countries. The gravity of the problems has been recognized; and WHO, FAO and UNICEF are already active in this field, working jointly on some projects. Greater investment of funds and efforts here will be fully justified.

The Advisory Committee on A.S.T.D. recommended that the control of the tsetse fly and of African trypanosomiasis (sleeping sickness) should be given high priority and cited three reasons in support of this view: large tracts of fertile agricultural land are now lying idle because of the widespread prevalence of this disease; if the tsetse fly is brought under control, these wasting assets could be put to productive use; this would encourage cattle-raising for which the land is particularly well suited and, in addition, it would help eliminate human trypanosomiasis; like the elimination of other vectors (e.g., the mosquito), the problem should be amenable to scientific study and solution, provided adequate resources were allocated to it.

[151] World Health Organization, *WHO Chronicle,* Volume 19, No. 11 (November 1964) pages 425-428.

The Committee urged that "high priority be given not only to such scientific studies but equally to the subsequent measures needed to apply the results on the necessary scale."[152] This is an eminently constructive recommendation, of which the ultimate reward should be considerable. It would liberate a large part of African population from a crippling disease; and it would stimulate cattlebreeding and meat production, and thereby substantially increase the supply of animal protein.

As the first step in giving effect to this recommendation, a Special Fund project was authorized, in January 1967, with an allocation of $1,211,600 for "operational research on human and animal trypanosomiasis eradication" in the Nyanza and Western Provinces of Kenya. The subject ought to be vigorously pursued until the goal is fully achieved. This means that once the research phase is successfully completed and the actual eradication phase begins, it will be necessary to launch several projects and to allocate correspondingly larger funds.

For the last few years, WHO has been taking active interest in water and air pollution control. Some projects for control of river pollution have already been authorized. This is a welcome trend, and it deserves continued attention on the principle that a dollar in time will save nine. Pollution control measures in the early stages of development will no doubt tend to push up the immediate costs of projects and the need for investment capital. But the extra cost will be small, and it will forestall the ultimate need for vast expenditures as social overheads.

There are a number of other fields which deserve high priority for substantially the same reasons as those cited above:

> —*malaria* eradication, in which WHO has established a unique record,[153] although it needs additional support to speed up the work in Africa where progress has been slow because of delayed start and other reasons.

> —*Bilharziasis,* which is widespread in Asia, Africa and Latin America and is a serious obstacle to development. Control of this water-borne parasitic disease, as WHO has frequently urged, needs to be intimately integrated with the numerous water-and-land-use projects initiated by FAO under Special Fund auspices.

---

152 Second Report of the Advisory Committee, Ibid., paras. 20 and 63-67.

153 Some 1,560 million people, or over 50 per cent of the world's population, lived in what were originally malarious areas, according to WHO estimates. Today 75 per cent of them live in areas that are already freed or are being freed of malaria.

—*Onchocerciasis,* or river blindness, is another communicable disease prevalent in several areas of Latin America and, in a more virulent form, in Africa. It causes blindness among substantial sections of the population, and also prevents the use of land and water for economic development.

—*Smallpox,* one of the oldest communicable diseases. Medical and technological advances have now made it feasible to stamp out the disease completely. A global programme for smallpox eradication has its humanitarian appeal and would also make a lot of economic sense.

—*Zoonoses,* which is the generic name for diseases transmitted between animals and man. The Advisory Committee, referred to earlier, specifically urged that the work on African trypanosomiasis should not impede efforts to bring other kinds of zoonoses under control.[154] A Special Fund project was authorized, in January 1966, for strengthening the Pan American Zoonoses Centre in Ramos Mejia and Azule, Argentina.

All the five fields listed above, judged by the combined criteria of social welfare and economic development, unquestionably deserve liberal support. It may be legitimately argued, however, that the support should come primarily from WHO's own funds since it has a substantial regular budget. What is important is that the activities in these fields should continue, and, as far as possible, be enlarged with financial backing, if necessary, from both sources.

Today what WHO needs to realize is that all its excellent work to improve health and to lengthen life in the developing countries is threatened from an entirely different front—from an undreamt-of upsurge in population; that it must get busy on this new front as well, with the same professional skill and devotion it has hitherto displayed; that it must do so without further delay if these countries are to derive lasting benefit from its valuable services.

12

Seventh, there is the disquieting concomittant of the explosive population growth in the developing countries—urbanization, premature, uncontrolled, over-rapid, an explosion within explosion with tragic consequences, tragic in terms of the misery and suffering it entails and of the crushing economic burden it imposes.

---

[154] Ibid., para. 68.

Cities are growing, the world over, at about 4.5 per cent a year. Some of the largest cities in the developing countries are expanding at twice that rate. About 5,000 newcomers per week move into Rio de Janeiro, according to the UN figures. The capital cities of tropical Africa have doubled in about a decade.[155] The total urban population of the developing countries was estimated at 300 million in 1960; according to current projections, it will, by 1980, more than double to 700 million.

But the cities are unable to accommodate—economically, socially, even physically—the migrants that are pouring in. Urban unemployment has been mounting; its incidence is particularly heavy among young people—50 per cent of the urban unemployed in Indonesia and 80 per cent in Ceylon are under 25 years of age. Public utilities in the cities—power supply, water supply, and sewage disposal, transport and communication—are being strained far beyond their capacity, sometimes perhaps beyond repair. All major cities in the underdeveloped world have their "densely crowded shanty towns in which 20 to 30 per cent of their inhabitants may be living—without water, without sewers, without roads,"[156] and, one might add, with uncertain jobs, meagre food, little light and fresh air, and no hope.

Thus, the masses of people disgorged by rural slums are crowding into the cities only to make the urban slums worse than before, to pile up problems for the cities and misery for themselves. "The city reduces the new migrants to the rawest struggle for survival," says the UN report noted above.[157] Or, as the late Ambassador Stevenson put it, "This rootless, hopeless, workless urban poverty is the greatest single cause of misery in the world."[158]

Of late a good deal has been said in the UN family about the importance of regional planning to reduce this blind mass migration. Will it help? It will, but only as much as fresh light and air would help a heart patient. For a real cure one must treat the root causes, not the symptoms. The urban pull-factors and the rural push-factors are well known. The exodus to the cities can be reduced only when these two sets of causes are resolutely tackled.

The pull of the cities is easily explained. First of all, there is the high level of wages, for which the pattern is usually set by manufacturing and building industries, government offices, foreign commercial

155 "Development Decade at Mid-Point," Ibid., page 8.
156 Ibid., page 7.
157 Ibid., page 8.
158 In his last address, delivered to ECOSOC on July 1965.

and diplomatic establishments. Such wages are, as a rule, completely out of line with the rest of a developing economy; yet they have been helped and sustained by a number of factors. Cities have been running away with the lion's share of public investments; that political leaders mostly live in cities has no doubt helped to tilt the scale in their favour; and in any case large expenditures are needed to expand the city utilities and services to cope with the flood of new-comers. Private investments, too, have followed the same trend, often stimulated by soaring real estate values in the cities.

In many developing countries trade unions are already well-organized, and are able to push up wages faster than productivity. Inflationary forces—of money-push, demand-push, and wage-push variety— have been at work in all these countries, further widening the wage differential in favour of urban areas. High wages for factory workers and domestic help have accelerated the adoption of labour-saving machinery and gadgets, which are mostly imported from abroad at a high cost of foreign exchange and whose net effect is to reduce job opportunities.

The urban employment market can absorb only a fraction of the migrants. But the lure of high-wage jobs is there and continues to act as a powerful magnet. Even casual jobs at urban wages may be found much more attractive than the low-income, and often no-income, life in villages.

Cities offer amenities like electricity and piped drinking water which are no less coveted by the rural poor. Even though they are often beyond the reach of the shanty-town-dwellers, these are the first items of civilized life they long for.

The young are attracted to the cities largely because of the better facilities for education and the windows they open on a brighter future.

And finally, cities offer excitement and distraction with their cinemas and radios, political and other movements, their hurry and bustle, even their milling crowds, all of which have appeal to the young and the old, especially to the young. Life for new migrants is often miserable in cities. It is, nevertheless, an escape for them from the more monotonous and more fully assured misery of rural life. Every developing country, in short, is today faced with its own variant of the old question: "How you gonna keep 'em down on the farm after they've seen Paree?"

Meanwhile the push-factors, long at work in rural areas, have become more relentless with the passage of time. Starved of capital investments, with agriculture withering in neglect, with little or no expansion in employment, the stagnant rural economies have experienced an unprecedented growth just where they can least afford it—in population. With soaring unemployment, the trickle of exodus to the cities has turned into a flood.

If the world is divided today between rich and poor nations, an underdeveloped country is divided between rich cities and poor villages. And while the bulk of the domestic resources, including scarce foreign exchange, flows to the cities to push up what are essentially nonproductive expenditures, the rural areas are denied the most promising high-yield investments, especially in agriculture and agri-business. This palpable imbalance has widened the gap between urban and rural incomes, weakened the infant economies of the developing countries, and held back their rate of growth.

These, in brief, are the causes of the urban population explosion and its effects. No research is needed for the diagnosis, nor any elaborate regional planning for evolving action programmes. The UN family would do well not to waste precious time in exploring the obvious.

The priorities discussed earlier in this chapter will go a long way toward arresting the present disastrous trends and will help establish a healthier urban-rural balance. Today the best hopes lie in the budding agricultural revolution which, with multiple cropping, can fast multiply the demand for farm labour, as well as the job opportunities in a host of agriculture-related activities.

Of the other policy measures needed to counteract the rural push-factors, a few may be specifically mentioned, even though they have been implied in the above analysis. Location of new industries is a matter of great importance. Heavy industries, such as iron and steel, do not offer too many economically sound alternatives; their location is largely dictated by the sources of the primary raw materials. With light industries, on the other hand, the initial choice is much wider, and it can be further widened by judicious fiscal and other incentives.

Location of new industries in carefully chosen rural setting would give an impetus to agriculture as it would create new markets close to farmlands; it would help relieve the growing congestion in capital cities, bring about a more equitable distribution of urban amenities, and lead towards a more optimum distribution of population within a country.

This, however, would call for correspondingly greater emphasis on the development of transportation and communication. For, it is primarily the absence of these facilities that has been driving industries to a few cities, mostly the capitals of the developing countries.

Rural electrification has not been receiving the attention it deserves, even in densely populated areas where it would be an economic proposition. Subsidized power rates for rural areas should pay off handsomely in the end. Yet the rates in many instances are kept too high, much higher than the rates allowed to the cities.[159] This deprives the rural areas of what could be a powerful lever for their development, apart from neutralizing an important push-factor.

Supply of pure drinking water is another amenity which can no longer be neglected. In many areas investments in dual-purpose tubewells—for irrigation and drinking water—would be richly rewarded, and would lessen the rigours of rural life. The agricultural revolution now in the making demands that top-priority be given to power and water supply in rural areas. The rising income now in prospect should make both economically more feasible today.

Provision of medical facilities, a primary need in every society, has acquired a new urgency. For, it is only as part of an organized medical service that family planning can be made effective in rural areas.

Finally, there is need for more and better and quicker education, geared deliberately to the practical needs of development.

The importance of rapid development of communication facilities on a country-wide, often on a regional, basis has already been emphasized. The pace of development will, among other things, directly depend on the ability to disseminate the right knowledge to the masses of people, and this would be possible only if the underdeveloped countries are equipped with modern mass communication media. Given their overwhelming importance, these media deserve to be added, as the *eighth* item, to our list of foremost priorities. It is a good sign that the UNDP/SF is authorizing projects to develop telecommunication systems on a continental scale. One hopes, however, that the work will not end with the preinvestment phase, that when the blueprints are ready, the necessary investment capital will be found to implement the projects and to make the systems a reality.

13

A country programme built around the priorities considered in this chapter cannot go wrong. And if properly prepared and systematically carried through, it cannot but give a powerful impetus to economic growth. It must, however, consist of projects prepared *in full depth*. This means that there must not be any artificial phasing under differ-

---

[159] This, for example, is true of Calcutta and the surrounding region.

ent programmes with multiple hiatus, that every single project should be conceived covering all phases—from technical assistance—to pre-investment—to investment—to execution—to operation and/or production.

Supplementary support will no doubt be needed from time to time from various agencies to carry through such a country programme. Such support should, however, be sought and authorized only when there is a *demonstrable necessity* for it. What must be avoided is to plant a multiplicity of skills in the developing countries on the facile assumption that, because the countries are underdeveloped, every skill will in due course render some good somewhere, that nothing can therefore really be wasted.

The problem of fixing priorities has been grossly exaggerated in the UN family. There is no need to hunt for them. They are glaringly visible even to the naked eye, provided, of course, it is open enough and is turned in the right direction.

This volcanic age has been erupting problems, aided by the rapid march of science and technology, and aggravated by their mal-application and non-application. Many of them are crying out for solution. And those that cry out the loudest also proclaim, and dictate, what must be the highest priorities.

Why, then, does the UN family make so much fuss about priorities, and miss them so easily? The answer was given earlier—it is "blind because it sees too much." It is also stricken with a peculiar kind of double vision—it has its eyes simultaneously fixed on the problems in the field and on the specialties in its armoury, and all the while its heart is set at least as much on marketing these specialties as on solving the actual problems.

Now, specialty-marketing is not compatible with priority-fixing. In the vast majority of cases, it is bound to get in the way of the latter. Essentially, this is what has been happening in the UN family all these years. And this is what has made a clear-eyed view of development priorities so unconscionably difficult.

It also explains what has been, and still remains, a fatal policy gap. Each agency has enlarged its arsenal of specialties, expanded its army of experts, and placed them in the field to fight the war on poverty in the underdeveloped world. But there has been no overall strategic planning; nor, indeed, any clear recognition of its need.

In the absence of such recognition there could be no realization of another inescapable truth, namely, that the war on poverty cannot be fought and won solely on the technical-cum-economic front; that it must be fought—at least as much, perhaps even more—on the political-diplomatic level in order to persuade the governments to recognize, to accept and to act upon a clearcut set of priorities in their own interest, and thereby to make it possible for the UN programmes to serve them effectively and really to help them help themselves. To ignore this vital front and to go on fielding specialties and technicians is both futile and foolhardy.

The truth is that, despite appearances, the UN family has, in effect, been moving from agencies to specialties, to projects, to priorities. This has been the most potent single cause for turning the war on poverty into a war of attrition. The course has to be reversed. The UN family must make an about-turn and move, both in appearance and in reality, in the opposite direction—from field priorities to projects, to specialties, to agencies. This is the revolution needed today—to put development on the right track, and to end a worldwide beating about the bush.

CHAPTER 21

A Dull Decade of Development

"We were passengers on a train that disappeared into the mist, its destination unknown to us, the surrounding scenery hidden from our view. As a result, we could not even determine at what speed we were moving."
Netherlands Minister Mr. B. J. Udink on the UN Development Decade.[160]

The developing countries desperately need to escalate their economic growth—to win the fateful race between population and food, and to raise their living standards to more tolerable levels. They need a resolute two-pronged attack on both fronts—to bring down the fertility rates with all available means, and to speed up their economic progress.

With the latest advances in birth control media, the prospects of accelerated progress on the demographic front have considerably bright ened. The more recent breakthroughs with the "miracle seeds" augur equally well for the future agricultural development. The developing countries are now poised on the threshold of an era of rapid economic growth. Psychologically, too, they are better prepared than ever before. Many of them display a new mood of optimism and self-confidence. Their capacity to absorb additional resources in high pay-off projects has greatly increased, especially in the context of the new agricultural revolution. Yet, ironically, just at this critical juncture in their history when they badly need a much larger quantum of development finance, its prospects have definitely worsened. The net volume of external finance, instead of expanding, threatens to decline.

---

[160] Statement made in the Second Committee of the General Assembly on 20 October 1967.

2

It is now certain that the modest targets set by the General Assembly in resolution 1710 (XVI) on the United Nations Development Decade[161] will not be realized. According to this "programme for international cooperation," the minimum annual rate of economic growth was supposed to go up from about 3.5 per cent to five per cent in ten years, that is, by 1970; and this would have given a *net* increase of about two per cent in per capita income, after making allowance for population growth. The actual increase will, on an average, not be significantly higher than what it was at the start of the decade, although a few countries, such as Greece, Iran, Israel, South Korea, Malaysia, Mexico, Pakistan, Taiwan, Thailand, Tunisia and Yugoslavia, have recorded quite impressive progress, mostly owing to some specially favourable factors, such as the volume of bilateral aid, geographical location, and oil.

It had been further assumed that the total flow of external finance —grants, subsidies, loans, commercial credits, contributions to international programmes, all put together—should reach one per cent of the national incomes of the developed nations. This level has never been reached. The developed nations, it has been estimated, have added to their combined gross national products some $50 billion a year on an average since 1961. The net flow of official aid—that is, after making allowance for amortization—has shown practically no change since then and has remained more or less stable around $6 billion a year.[162]

Only two countries fulfilled the goal of one per cent in 1967— France with 1.24 per cent and the Netherlands with 1.01 per cent; the average for the 16 nations[163] was 0.75 per cent. The USA provided about half of the new funds to the "third world" or the developing countries, and this amounted to 0.7 of its gross national product. A special feature of 1967 was a sharp rise in West Germany's capital flow to the poorer countries; this accounted for an eight per cent rise in the overall volume as compared with the previous year. The total net flow was $11.4 billion; of this, almost $7 billion came from government loans and grants, and the rest from private sources.

According to UNCTAD estimates, the average capital outflow (net of amortization and capital repatriation) from development market-

---

[161] For the text of the resolution, see Appendix IV.

[162] See, for example, the World Bank's Annual Report for 1966-67, page 5.

[163] Members of OECD; see Report of its Development Assistance Committee (DAC), July 1968.

economy countries amounted only to 0.68 per cent of their combined gross national products in 1965-66 compared with 0.87 per cent in 1961. If all these countries had reached the one per cent target in 1966, there would have been additional outflows of about $5 billion to the developing countries and the multilateral agencies. As for the socialist countries, the assistance provided by them has, on an average, remained below one per cent of their gross output during the 1960's.[164]

Much of the assistance provided was "tied"—that is, it had to be spent in the country providing the loan or grant; and while the volume of aid has flattened out, the proportion of tied aid has been increasing. According to the DAC, 50 per cent of the official aid in 1967 was directly tied. The actual proportion spent in the donor countries was, of course, much higher. For example, 88 per cent of all foreign aid funds disbursed by the US Agency for International Development (AID) in fiscal 1967 was spent in the United States on US goods, products and services (against 82 per cent in fiscal 1966). The net impact on the US balance of payments was an outflow of $82 million (against $213 million in fiscal 1966).[165]

The US foreign aid, which had totalled $3.3 billion in fiscal 1967, dropped to $2.3 billion in fiscal 1968, the lowest figure on record so far. For the next year it is likely to show another sharp fall.[166]

While the volume of aid is tending downwards, the burden of debt-service payments has been rising steeply. Here are some eloquent facts:[167] 95 developing countries made service payments totalling $3.96 billion in 1966—$2.8 billion as amortization and $1.2 billion as interest; between 1962 and 1966 these payments grew at an average annual rate of ten per cent, much faster than their exports; their total outstanding external debt—public and publicly guaranteed—grew even more rapidly, at about 16 per cent a year, and by mid-1966 reached $41 billion.

Between 1962 and 1966 the debt-service payments more than doubled in East Asia, increased by about 90 per cent in South Asia (mainly India and Pakistan), rose almost 75 per cent in Africa, and continues to be heavy in Latin America. They now offset 40 per cent of the official flows of capital to the developing countries. And if this trend con-

---

164 UNCTAD II, document TD/7/Supp. I.

165 The Foreign Assistance Program, Annual Report to the Congress—Fiscal Year 1967. Pages 17-19.

166 The Administration's Foreign Aid Bill for fiscal 1969, amounting to $2.95 billion, has been subjected to several cuts in Congress.

167 World Bank and IDA, Annual Report 1966-67, pages 30-31.

tinues, the net transfer of capital from some donor countries would soon reach the zero point.

Meanwhile, the International Development Association (IDA), the "soft-loan" affiliate of the World Bank, has been marking time for a second replenishment of its empty coffers. The cumulative total of IDA's usable resources since its start stood, as of 30 June 1967, at $1,781 million and consisted of: the original subscription of its 18 "Part I members," their contributions towards the first replenishment, and ad hoc allocation of $200 million made from IBRD's net earnings in three instalments during 1965-67, and IDA's net income of $14 million.[168] The resources have already been committed. In anticipation of the needs, steps were taken in July 1966 for a second replenishment. Official approval is still awaited.

The proposal made by the USA and now pending before the 18 nations, would raise their annual contributions from $250 million a year under the past agreement to $1 billion in three stages—$600 million in the first year, $800 million in the second, and $1 billion in the third. For the three years starting in November 1968, the total would thus be $2.4 billion.

As the major donor, the USA has agreed to provide 40 per cent of the total as its share, subject however to two conditions intended to ease its current balance of payments difficulties: first, a percentage of the contributions would be earmarked for making purchases in the USA; and second, nations with payments deficits, including the USA, would be allowed to delay their contributions until the final years of actual loan disbursements. Other donor countries are none too happy over these stipulations since the first would militate against the principle of free and internationally competitive bidding, while the second would virtually place on them the burden of making the initial payments. The two conditions are being debated; agreement on the new proposal is not yet in sight. In the meantime, IDA has put off all fresh commitments, and the developing countries concerned are waiting in suspense, with projects ready to be launched but no finance.[168a]

In foreign aid, as in the general cause of world development, the United States has been the undisputed leader—the originator, inspirer and pace setter. As goes the USA, so go the other rich nations—this has been an axiom. Its faltering attitude is quickly followed by a

---

[168] Ibid., pages 19-20.

[168a]. The Congressional bill raising the U.S. contribution to the IDA was finally signed on 27 May 1969 by President Nixon.

hardening mood in other countries. "Foreign aid has a great future—
behind it," so remarked a US Congressman. As things now stand, it
would be hard to disagree.

3

In international trade the results have been no less disheartening.
It was hoped that, during the current decade, the share of the developing countries in the world trade would show a modest increase—from
26 to 28 per cent. Since 1961, the world trade has expanded at an
average rate of eight per cent per year;[169] the value of the exports from
the developing countries increased from $27 to $42 billion in the six
years ended 1966, but as a proportion of the global trade their share
came down to 23 per cent. Even a one per cent increase in their share
today would add close to $2 billion per year to their precious foreign
exchange earnings. It has been suggested, no doubt somewhat cynically,
that had they been able simply to maintain their share in the expanding world trade at the 1960 level of 26 per cent, the problem of their
external finance would have been largely solved, and the developed
and the underdeveloped could perhaps have jointly celebrated the end
of the foreign aid era.

It may be briefly noted that the trade between the socialist and the
developing countries has shown a more rapid rate of growth—since
1955 it has doubled every five years. During 1960-65, the exports of
the developing countries to the socialist countries grew at an annual
rate of 15 per cent, and their imports from the latter at 18 per cent a
year. During the same period, their share in the import trade of the
developed countries fell from 25 to 20 per cent, while their percentage
share in the overall volume of imports into the socialist group of countries rose from 7.4 to 10.[170]

The second United Nations Conference on Trade and Development
(UNCTAD II), which had met in New Delhi in February 1968, ended
its eight weeks' deliberations with no tangible results and in an atmosphere of despondency for the developing nations. No headway was
made on any of the major issues considered vital to their future, such
as additional international aid on easier terms; a larger share for
their primary commodities, which account for 80 per cent of their export trade, in the expanding markets of the developed countries;

---

169 During 1956-60, the average was 6.4 per cent. The growth slowed down to
five per cent in 1967.

170 UNCTAD II, Documents TD/5 and TD/18.

freer access to these markets for their manufactures and semi-manufactures which at present amount to a bare five per cent of their exports; adoption of a system of general nondiscriminatory preferences applicable to all developing countries; and stabilization of commodity prices. The developing countries had placed high hopes on UNCTAD II. It turned out to be a case of much cry and little wool.[171]

The benefits of the Kennedy Round of tariff cutting have been virtually confined to the high-income countries; they will spill over, at best marginally, to the underdeveloped world. The GATT communique of May 1967, announcing the results of the marathon negotiations, had suggested that the next order of business should be to liberalize the policies of the high-income countries with regard to their trade with the low-income countries. This remains an unfinished item on the agenda of GATT and UNCTAD.[172]

Not long ago there was some lively debate over the question "aid or trade." By now, it has crystallized into two more or less unanimous conclusions: first, the developing countries need both, need them on a far more liberal scale, and will continue to do so for a long time to come; and second, by far the most important form of aid is trade.

This second conclusion has been greatly reinforced by several factors. The support for aid, as seen above, has been fading; the supply of external finance is unlikely to expand, and may even begin to decline—in real terms, after making allowance for price increases, it has already been doing so; the debt-service charges are building up to intolerable levels. It is only through an expansion of their export trade that the developing countries can earn the foreign exchange they sorely need to service past debts and to finance future development. This remains their only hope today.

Besides, many of them, as a result of the efforts made in the past two decades, have reached the stage where they have the capacity to produce and to export more—both primary commodities and processed or semiprocessed goods. To utilize this capacity, to build it up further, and to reap the economies of scale, they must have easier access to the export markets.

---

[171] The renewal of the International Coffee Agreement after September 1968 was for some time in doubt. The question of instant coffee almost created a tempest in a "coffee-cup"! Luckily, a new accord has been reached, assuring $500 million of foreign exchange a year to the coffee-growing countries of Latin America, Africa and Asia. The new Agreement, which replaced that of 1962, entered definitively into force on 30 December 1968.

[172] For a succinct statement of the case with practical recommendations, reference may be made to: "Trade Policy Toward Low-Income Countries," Committee for Economic Development (CED), June 1967.

These markets lie mostly in the developed industrial countries where the world's purchasing power is overwhelmingly concentrated. To recall some simple figures, 27 rich nations with per capita incomes of $750 and above, and with only one-quarter of the world's population, today own three-quarters of the world's wealth.

Economics and commonsense have always dictated the need for a liberal trade policy which would raise the export earnings of the low-income countries and speed their development, and would also create expanding markets, especially for capital goods from the developed nations.

A sense of historical equity, too, would point in the same direction. The dominant economic ideology in the days of colonialism was free trade with international division of labour. It was pushed to the point where even the validity of the infant industry argument was ignored; the victory of the Manchester School was complete; the voice of Friedrich List hardly reached the remote colonies; and their markets were thrown open, sometimes mercilessly, to manufactures from abroad. In the teeth of this competition, and denied even temporary protection in the transitional stage, they were unable to develop even simple processing industries; their established handicrafts often fell easy victims to an arbitrary system of free trade.

In the decolonized world the old dogmas are no longer in vogue. And one seldom talks about the benefits of an international division of labour. The infant economies of the developing countries are largely denied its advantage. Their products, only too often, are unable to surmount the artificial tariff and nontariff barriers that surround the markets of the developed economies.

The blind march of modern technology has meanwhile introduced massive distortions in the world economy. The old thesis of an international exchange of goods according to comparative advantages largely based on natural factors, no longer holds good. The flood of synthetics and substitutes, developed with huge capital investments, has drastically cut into the markets for the primary produce of the poorer nations. Technology, as now applied, has worked remorselessly against them.

4

The advocates of more liberal aid and trade, and there are many highminded people in this category—Eugene Black, Paul Hoffman, George Woods, Barbara Ward, Arnold Toynbee, to mention only a few names at random—have been eloquently arguing the case of the developing countries. They have tirelessly pointed out how the dictates of justice, altruism, and self-interest—all converge on the need for a more liberal policy. The outpourings of these anguished souls seem to be of markedly less avail today. They are easily submerged in the rising tide of a new callousness.

What the rich nations could spare at very little sacrifice to themselves, they have repeatedly stressed, could spell the difference between stagnation and progress for the poorer nations. Supply of external finance, public and private combined, to the tune of one per cent of the combined incomes of the industrial countries as was envisaged at the start of the decade, would be equivalent to as much as 20 per cent of the resources that the poor nations are now able to invest in their development. What would be only "marginal" to the rich nations, stressed Mr. Woods, would be "greatly magnified" in the finances of the poor.[173] Or, suppose the developing countries were able to raise their share of the world trade just by one percentage point. This, as seen before, would have added close to two billion dollars to what they actually earned as foreign exchange in 1967.

Mr. Hoffman has emphasized on countless occasions that development assistance is not charity or a "giveaway." It is good business for all. "An expanding world economy," he has insisted, "is as critically needed by industrially advanced nations as by underdeveloped ones."[174]

Similar views have been expressed by many people on a great many occasions. While the aid programme is "a generous expression of the American humanitarian tradition, it is also firmly rooted in American self-interest."[175]

The advocates of a liberal aid-and-trade policy have also reminded the world about the mounting bill for armaments. "There is a fantastic disproportion," says Barbara Ward, "between what the industrialized powers are prepared to think 'essential' in terms of arms and what they cry 'bankruptcy' over in terms of aid." Annual spending on arms by all the developed nations she estimated at $120,000 million, and aid from all sources at $9,000 million.[176]

Armaments, on a rough estimate, absorb about ten per cent of the combined national incomes of the industrialized nations, and development assistance in all forms—official and private taken together—three-

---

[173] Address to the Board of Governors by Mr. George D. Woods, President, World Bank, at Rio de Janeiro on 25 September 1967.

[174] "World Without Want," page 119.

[175] *New York Times* in a leader on 10 July 1968.

[176] "Two Views on Aid to Developing Countries," by Barbara Ward and P. T. Bauer. Occasional Paper 9, The Institute of Economic Affairs, London, 1966, page 27.

quarters of one per cent, probably even less. The advocates of larger
foreign aid, and a great many other thoughtful people, speculate
wistfully what would happen to the world if a tiny portion of the
colossal sum could, by some miracle, be deflected away from the stock-
piling of weapons towards the tasks of world development.

There is no indication that this miracle is likely to happen, at least
in the foreseeable future. "The rich in any country," said Arnold
Toynbee reflecting sorrowfully, "have always been more willing to
spend on arms than on a welfare state. They begrudge less being taxed
for war purposes than for social purposes." Then he added with his
native objectivity: "This has been true in Britain, too. It is something
in human psychology. I don't know why."[177]

5

There are enough reasons today for widespread pessimism about
the future outlook for aid and trade. Efforts to liberalize them must
be continued by men of vision, representing both rich and poor nations. Meanwhile, the most rational course of action would be to shun
wishful thinking, to take cognizance of the facts as they are, to work
out, and to stick to, the best conceivable strategy to achieve the maximum possible growth in the less-developed countries with the resources,
domestic and foreign, that can be confidently counted upon.

Indeed, there are good reasons to feel much greater concern about
what happens within the developing countries themselves—about their
own policies and the mobilization of their own effort—than about the
future of foreign aid. The arithmetic alone—that is, the ratio of
domestic to external finance—is sufficiently telling. The developing
countries, taken together, now save and invest about 15 per cent of
their national incomes to finance development; this generates 80 per
cent of the capital invested by them every year; and only the balance
of 20 per cent comes from outside. The rate of their economic growth
will depend far more on how productively, and profitably, they can
utilize the much larger domestic capital than on what happens to the
remainder, despite its value particularly in terms of foreign exchange.

Even more relevant, however, is the definition of resources, which
has to be broadened. Hitherto they have been conceived far too much
in purely financial terms—savings in terms of domestic currency plus
the net inflow of official aid and private investment, and far too little
in real terms, that is, the natural resources of the developing countries
—their lands, waters, forests, minerals, and their manpower.

---

177 "Toynbee on America," *Life*, 8 December 1967, page 111.

The real assets of the developing countries lie here, in the rich physical resources which constitute the foundation of their future wealth and welfare. The rate of their economic progress will depend on the imagination and the practical wisdom with which they are able to put them to actual work. What they need today is a far more resource-oriented strategy in the place of the present overwhelmingly finance-dominated approach.

The most important priorities to be embodied in a country programme have been indicated in a previous chapter. Their focus has been on higher production and productivity through better utilization of natural resources, leading to higher employment and income. But where will a country find the wherewithal to finance such a comprehensive programme, especially at the time of a capital famine—with stagnant foreign trade, dwindling external finance, inelastic domestic savings, a crippling load of debt-service payments, with little or no access to foreign capital markets, with interest rates at the highest level since 1920?

The present pattern of allocation of the available financial resources, domestic and foreign, is far from ideal. There is substantial room for improvement. In most cases the resources need to be reallocated in close conformity with the priorities already indicated. Such reallocation will generate greater momentum for growth within a developing economy.

Besides, a good case can be made out for applying deficit finance, in measured doses, though financial orthodoxy is apt to run it down as inflationary and as the royal road to currency devaluation.

Not long ago the orthodox school used to reject the thought of deficit finance also in the developed countries, even when the economy was operating in low gear, with substantial plant capacity lying idle, and a high proportion of workers out of employment. Yet it has gradually come round to accept much of Mr. Keynes' recipe for a full-employment economy, based on flexible fiscal and monetary policies. Today, the New Economics has become a familiar affair, and it makes liberal use of the Keynesian tools for managing an economy in order to keep it as close to full employment as possible.

The underdeveloped countries, too, need their own brand of New Economics to create jobs for their growing numbers of men and women who are now unemployed or underemployed, and to put to work the natural resources that are now unused or underused. The vast reservoir of idle manpower ought to be treated not simply as an embarrassment, but also as a valuable resource.

A policy of manpower mobilization for productive purposes will have a threefold advantage. By providing employment to the people, it will reduce their misery and will directly contribute to their welfare, which, after all, is the ultimate aim of all development. It will speed up the rate of capital formation and of economic growth—the idle manpower represents a kind of savings and can therefore provide an escape from the dilemma facing a developing country because of the low level of its conventional savings and the slow rate of its capital formation. And finally, it will reduce the net burden of population on the economy.

The developing countries, as mentioned before (Chapter 20, Section 3), are now required to carry a heavy burden of *child* dependency since 40 to 45 per cent of their population fall in the age categories below 15. What they should not be required to do is to carry a heavy additional burden of *adult* dependency with mounting millions of able-bodied but unemployed and under-employed men and women.

Will not a policy of deficit finance and manpower mobilization be inflationary? It need not, and should not, be so. Indeed, properly conceived and carefully applied, such a policy will be *anti-inflationary*. A large proportion of the growing population in the developing countries now live, in some form or other, off their meagre economies, contributing little or nothing in return. As a result, these countries are already in the grip of a *population-push inflation*. The only effective means of combatting this inflation would be to mobilize the unemployed and underemployed people and to put them to productive work.

Deficit finance, like all finance, can admittedly be abused. Nor is there any doubt that, along with the misallocation of other financial resources, deficit finance, too, has frequently suffered the same fate. Clearly, the task is to avoid its abuse and to channel it in the right direction rather than to treat it as financial anathema.

It follows that projects must be selected with great care. Fortunately, the underdeveloped world contains vast opportunities for low-cost, high-yield, quick-maturing projects; and modern science and technology have further widened their scope. The growth rate in a poor country would depend primarily on its ability to select, promote and execute such projects. Deficit finance, when exclusively used for this purpose, could only benefit a developing economy. And it would have the same economic legitimacy as credit expansion directed to finance productive, self-liquidating projects in the developed countries.

The idea of manpower mobilization is sometimes objected to on the ground that it would be an encroachment on individual freedom, that it would involve regimentation. Yet what value has freedom to individuals who have no jobs and no income, who live in misery and despair, who are left free only to suffer from hunger and starvation? It would be far more merciful to compel men and women to work, even if this involved an element of regimentation, than to leave them to such hopeless, dismal fate. Here is something for which the developing countries could cheerfully take a leaf from the history of Soviet Russia and other socialist countries. And if they do so, it will give a powerful stimulus to their economic growth.[178]

What about the administrative capacity of the governments in the developing countries? Will they be able to carry out such programmes? Here, again, commonsense dictates a twofold approach: make the best of whatever capacity now exists, and build further on the present foundation. That the administrative systems in the developing countries will have to be strengthened as a matter of urgency goes without saying. Meanwhile, it is vitally important to avoid a "misallocation" of the limited capacity now available.

A wise state will therefore try to work out a rational division of labour between the government and private enterprises or citizens. It will concentrate on those indispensable functions which only the government can discharge—health and family planning, education slanted towards development, a wide range of services for agriculture including a countrywide organization for extension work, modernization of handicrafts and small industries, transport and communications, large irrigation and power projects, manpower mobilization, public works programmes—in addition to the traditional functions of a government, such as national security, maintenance of law and order, foreign policy, collection of revenue, currency management. Even this incomplete listing shows what an overwhelming burden a modern government must carry, if its essential nation-building responsibilities are not to go by default. In view of this, it would be nothing short of a tragic folly for a government to burden itself with additional functions, such as farming operations, processing and manufacturing industries, trade and commerce, which can be discharged by private enterprise, where individual initiative is essential for efficient operations, where the interplay of market forces, supplemented by wise state

---

[178] For the types of programmes for which the manpower could be mobilized, see Chapter 20, Section 9.

regulation, will yield better results than management by a centralized bureaucratic apparatus.

This is the costly lesson that Soviet Russia and other socialist countries have learnt from their long experience; and as a result, they are now struggling to bring about the painful transition towards a more decentralized system with greater emphasis on market forces and even on a special brand of profit considerations. This historic lesson should not be lost on the underdeveloped countries. They should be on their guard not to complicate the gigantic tasks of development by repeating a well-established error of judgment.

6

This brings us to what must be treated as a major task in the development process—the creation of a favourable climate for private enterprise. For a number of reasons it has so far been neglected in the developing countries. The one-sided behaviour of private enterprises, owned and managed by foreign capital in the colonial days, left behind an unhappy legacy. Misconceptions about socialism, often powerfully fed from outside, have played, and are still playing, an important part in influencing policy decisions. The inherent limitations of state enterprises have been easily lost sight of in an atmosphere of conflicting ideologies.

These limitations have, as a rule, been ignored also by the aid-giving agencies. For one thing, aid programmes, both bilateral and multilateral, have to work perforce on a government-to-government basis. This has strengthened the already existing bias of a developing country in favour of public-sector business, and has further circumscribed the elbowroom for private enterprise.

In fact, the aid-givers, from the "West" as well as from the "East," have themselves often shown a similar bias, due in no small measure, to a failure to grasp fully the great importance of private enterprise to a developing economy. And only too often, they have rationalized it with the stock argument that there is no alternative to state enterprises since private entrepreneurs are non-existent. This is a hasty generalization. In many developing countries, there is even now much entrepreneurial talent that is running to waste, and a good deal more is lying dormant. It will sprout and blossom in a more favourable climate.

The climate must be changed. It must be freed from the ideological penumbra to reveal some stark realities: First, all countries today are socialistic so far as the broad social objectives are concerned; all states are welfare states—they must all cater to the welfare of the masses of people; what varies is not the goal, but the means for its realization. Second, all economies today are mixed—with a public and a private sector; what varies is no longer the principle, but the respective spheres demarcated for each. And as mentioned above, even those who had, at one time, relied almost exclusively on state enterprises, or *étatism*, are veering round towards a decentralized mixed pattern. And third, economic and social development shows itself at its best when a progressive government concentrates on its basic responsibilities, allows a vigorous private enterprise system to function side by side, and regulates it wisely in the interest of the general public.

It cannot be different in a developing country. Progress is bound to suffer where a government with too little capacity attempts to do too much and rushes into fields where private individuals could do the jobs at least equally well with a little state supervision. It is now common knowledge that, in a centralized state, bureaucracy expands, initiative withers, and economic growth flags.

There are other compelling reasons that lead to the same conclusion. Much of the capital of the developing countries—of Latin America, the Middle East, of India, Pakistan, and others—seeks refuge abroad, usually in the financial centres of the capital-rich countries. This is a drain on national resources which a developing country simply cannot afford. Most of this refugee capital, along with the savings that are habitually hoarded at home, could be put to productive work if official policy were directed to create a more favourable milieu for private business.

In such an environment it should also be easier to attract foreign capital on a larger scale. If available on reasonable terms and conditions, it would alleviate the capital shortage in the developing countries and give a powerful impetus to their economic growth. In addition, it would bring with it the technology and the management techniques they unquestionably need to modernize their economies.

What, then, are the reasonable terms and conditions? The developing countries must recognize that the rich countries, strange as it may seem, are suffering not from a surfeit, but from a shortage, of capital because of their sky-rocketing demand for investment—to finance booming economies, technological advances with rapid obsolescence and replacement of equipment, ever-expanding armaments of ever-increasing sophistication, space exploration and, more recently, urban reconstruction and allied public undertakings. Whatever capital the prosperous economies are able to spare has tended to be invested mostly in other developed countries for mutual benefit. It follows that to attract foreign investment capital, the developing countries will have to compete with the other demands, and to do so, they will have to offer adequate inducements.

Clearly, they must provide: guarantees against nationalization or confiscation; exemption from foreign exchange and other regulations to permit transfer of profits and capital according to mutually agreed schedules; protection against punitive taxation, maybe coupled with fiscal incentives; and opportunity to earn enough profits, which, obviously, will have to be higher than what the same capital would earn at home or in other foreign countries.

The developing countries are now showing increasing awareness of the need for foreign private investments, also of the conditions on which these could be attracted. Many of them have already taken steps to provide the essential guarantees or assurances. At this point, therefore, the reverse question becomes more pertinent: What guarantees should the developing countries themselves be entitled to? And what should be the obligations of foreign private enterprises in these countries?

These questions have seldom been discussed with sufficient objectivity, practical insight, and frankness. The virtues of private enterprise and foreign capital have been extolled in the abstract, and the developing countries have been blamed for their failure to see them. Yet things are not quite so simple. There are some real snags which no objective analysis can circumvent.

In the western countries there has been much glorification of the profit motive, just as the developing countries have looked askance at it. Both attitudes suffer from exaggeration. Profit motive is no doubt the main force that propels private business. But history in the West has abundantly shown that it needs to be bridled, that otherwise it can be extortionate, sometimes ruthlessly so. The West has largely resolved this dilemma with two effective tools: competition within a national economy and a whole series of regulatory bodies to protect public interest. In the USA, for example, where giant corporations dominate the scene, there is still a lot of competition among these giants, despite the tendency of some social scientists to underrate its importance; and there are a number of federal regulatory agencies which, despite their occasional lapses, have rendered invaluable service to the public as watchdogs of their interests.

These are vital safeguards, but they operate only within the boundaries of the developed countries. Unfortunately, they do not accompany foreign enterprises when they move across the oceans to the underde-veloped world. A large private corporation setting up a business in a developing country is almost always immune from competition because a backward economy has none to offer, and so it becomes almost a born monopoly. And it naturally enjoys immunity from the kind of regula-tion to which it would be subjected automatically at home. The weak government of a developing nation is unable to regulate a large foreign business concern. Attempts to do so may easily create a foreign-policy impasse.

Here lies the crux of the matter, which largely explains the present ambivalent attitude of many developing countries towards foreign capital. They realize how foreign capital could help their develop-ment, but they also know how helpless they are likely to be in dealing with it. They want it; at the same time they are afraid of it. And they are none too sure that they would really derive adequate benefit from its presence in terms of fair prices, a fair share in the profits, participation in management, transfer of modern technology, and training of their own nationals. Such attitudes should not, after all, be too difficult to understand when countries of West Europe and even Canada publicly express nervousness from time to time about the influence of US capital on their economies.

Clearly, it is not enough to extol foreign capital and private enter-prise based on profit motive. Who profits from profits, and in what proportion—this is the crucial issue. To overcome the lingering suspi-cion or nervousness of the developing countries, they will need to be assured of an equitable share in the profits and other benefits resulting from investments of foreign capital. Otherwise, they will have little incentive to invite it on a large scale.

7

Given such a background, it is not surprising that the flow of private capital to the developing countries should have been small. Net of amortization, it has fluctuated around $3.4 billion a year.[179] Much of it goes to a few countries for petroleum and some metal ex-porting industries. Another sizable part consists of suppliers' credits with fast amortization schedules, which account for about half of the current burden of debt-service. The total inflow of private capital to

---

[179] For the "18 IDA Part I members," the figures given by the World Bank were: $4 billion in 1965 and $3.4 billion in 1966. Ibid., p. 24. The total for 1967 was perhaps slightly over $4 billion, mainly owing to an increase in capital export from West Germany.

all developing countries, net of amortization and recorded capital outflows, has been around $2 billion a year. And only a fraction of it
consists of long-term finance capital to promote industrial growth
outside petroleum and some metal industries.

The International Finance Corporation (IFC), the equity-capital
affiliate of the World Bank, has broken new ground by supplying risk
capital to promote private enterprises in the developing countries,
particularly in the fields of manufacture, processing and mining. The
cumulative total of the gross commitments made by IFC in 11 years
stood at $221.4 million on 30 June 1967. Of late, the volume of its
operations and the size of individual commitments have both tended
to increase. The total reached a new peak with $49.1 million in 1966-
67.[180]

It may be noted in passing that the Agency for International Development (AID) of the USA has, for the last few years, been engaged
in attracting American and local private resources for development.
For this it has relied mainly on three sets of measures.[181] Its Investment Insurance Program insures American investments in the developing countries against certain risks. By June 1967, the number of countries participating in the Program had risen to 78.

More recently, it has introduced the so-called Extended Risk Guar-
anty Program to enable US institutional investors to make long-term
loans for important projects in the developing countries. Under this
Programme AID protects up to 75 per cent of American private investment against virtually all risks. Nine such guarantees were authorized
in fiscal 1967; they covered $42 million of US investments in projects
costing $158 million.

Secondly, AID has encouraged American private investment in the
developing countries, particularly to promote agricultural industries.
About $70 million were made available in fiscal 1967 to industrial
development banks in the developing countries for investment in private ventures. In addition, AID obligated $84 million in direct dollar
loans to private borrowers, American and foreign.

And finally, AID shares with US firms the cost of surveying specific
investment opportunities in the developing countries. It pays half of
the survey cost if the industry does not materialize. Under the Investment Survey Participation Agreements, 280 surveys were authorized
since fiscal 1963. Of these, 134 were completed by fiscal 1967; 36 firms

---

180 International Finance Corporation, Annual Report 1966-67.
181 For more details, see Annual Report to the Congress for Fiscal Year 1967
on the Foreign Assistance Program, pages 13-16.

made positive decisions and invested a total of $81 million; 98 completed surveys ended without investments.

The examples of IFC and AID show how, with businesslike methods, it is possible to widen the scope for private enterprise in the developing countries and to create new opportunities for investment of foreign private capital on mutually advantageous terms. This is an encouraging trend. Nevertheless, the rate of progress is still much too slow, and the net volume of such finance remains far too small.

8

Can the process be accelerated, and the flow of private capital be significantly enlarged in the coming years? This is a question of great moment to which the United Nations should address itself more energetically.

The General Assembly resolution on the United Nations Development Decade was quite specific on this point. It called upon the member-states to adopt measures which would "stimulate the flow of private investment capital for the economic development of the developing countries, on terms that are satisfactory both to the capital-exporting and the capital-importing countries."[182] This basic principle has been reaffirmed by the General Assembly and the Economic and Social Council in a number of other resolutions, and more specifically in a recommendation of UNCTAD I on the promotion of private foreign investment.[183]

The United Nations has, for a good many years, published valuable studies on international flows of private capital, and on questions relating to their promotion through measures for protection and incentives. More recently, it has published a report, crystallizing the conclusions reached in its earlier studies, to facilitate further discussion and to help formulate concrete recommendations to serve as the basis for future action.[184] It has suggested "a dialogue" between governments and investors, in an effort to find "bases of reconciliation" between the "sometimes divergent interests of investors and governments."

---

[182] Resolution 1710 (XVI), Clause 2(d). See Appendix IV.

[183] E.g., General Assembly Resolutions 2087 and 2091 (XX) of 20 December 1965; ECOSOC resolutions 1271, 1273 and 1270 (XLIII) of 4 August 1967, and 1286 (XLIII) of 14 November 1967. For UNCTAD recommendation, see Annex A. IV. 12 of the Final Act.

[184] "Foreign Investments in Developing Countries," E/4446, United Nations, New York, 1968.

These are all commendable suggestions which will find ready support from large sections of the world public. But very few today will
consider them enough. The time has been ripe to go beyond the
dialogue stage and to come to more resolute grips with the practical
problems. The creation of UNIDO has added to the urgency. It has
kindled fresh hopes that industries, long neglected in the developing
countries, will receive greater attention in the future. A great deal
will, however, depend on the ability to mobilize private capital from
abroad on a much bigger scale for investment in the developing countries, either directly or through the intermediary of the newly-established institutions—international, regional and national—to handle
development finance.

A most valuable service which the UN family could render at this
stage would be to work out a standard agreement, within a reasonably
flexible framework, spelling out the rights and obligations of both
parties, i.e., the capital-exporting and the capital-importing countries,
along with the essential guarantees and assurances they are respectively
entitled to. The UN family is ideally suited to bring enough judicious
and experienced minds, from both the developed and the developing
nations, to bear on the thorny issues, to work out equitable solutions
which it could then recommend for serious consideration to the member countries with the stamp of its own approval.

The World Bank, it may be noted, recently applied a somewhat
similar approach in an attempt to help improve the use of suppliers'
credits. It has recommended, among other things, that the governments
in both debtor and creditor countries should restrict the use of such
credits only to economically sound projects, that their terms should
take into account the life and productivity of the projects, and that
they should not impose an unduly heavy burden on the overall debt-
servicing capacity of the borrowing country.

Attempts to involve competent consulting firms for carrying out
economy-wide investigations, or systems analysis, as suggested in an
earlier chapter (Chapter 18, Section 6) will improve the prospects of
attracting private investment capital from abroad. Employment of
industrial consulting firms to carry out both broader surveys in order
to identify promising industrial projects in a country and to assess
specific investment proposals for particular industries could help open
up new avenues for private capital, both domestic and foreign.

And finally, the Resident Representatives could play a most valuable role in this context if, from their vantage point, they are allowed
to function (as suggested in Chapter 19) as general managers and

development diplomats at the country level on behalf of the entire UN family.

The next decisive push to economic growth in the developing countries, it is no exaggeration to say, could come most logically from a widening of private enterprise, coupled with its natural concomitant—an increasing flow of private capital from abroad. Foreign capital will augment the resources for development, especially in terms of valuable foreign exchange. This, by itself, should be a major argument in its favour at a time of declining official aid.

More important, however, is the fact that unless there is enough room for private enterprise with enough freedom from stifling bureaucratic control, many potential industries may never see the light of day, or even if they do, they will never be run with enough efficiency to be sufficiently competitive.

And finally, a flourishing private enterprise system, with growing cooperation between domestic and foreign capital, could spearhead faster progress on another vital front—foreign trade. Because of better management, a cost-conscious approach, greater initiative, keener alertness, and improved contacts with the outside world, it would be the surest means to secure for the products of the developing countries wider access to the export markets.

In this neglected sector the UN family has a critical role to play. It can persuade, with all legitimate means at its disposal, the governments of both developed and developing nations to overcome their present inhibitions and to adopt a more enlightened and forward-looking policy that would redound to the advantage of both. To do so, it will have to go beyond studies and discourses, however well-meaning they may be, and will have to launch on a concerted programme of responsible action. One thing is certain. Greater UN initiative in this all-important field will in the end bring some of the richest rewards to all concerned.

CHAPTER 22

Essentials of a New Strategy

"Un jour tout sera bien, voilà notre esperance:
Tout est bien aujourd'hui, voilà l'illusion."

VOLTAIRE

A dull decade of development is drawing to its dreary close. Performance has lagged behind even the low targets that had been set for this ten-year span. Worse still is the change in mood that has meanwhile intervened. The decade began with a glow of hope for the future. It is ending in an atmosphere of deepening gloom.

The United Nations is now engaged in working out a strategy for the second decade of development, that is, the 1970's; and tentative proposals to that effect have been on the anvil since the fall of 1967. What are the chances that it will draw the right lessons from past experience and will use them, intelligently and realistically, for the future? The indications, at this moment, are none too reassuring.

The Committee working on the future strategy has not distinguished itself by an originality of approach or incisive thinking on the subject; nor has it evinced any outstanding capacity to diagnose the ills that have afflicted the current decade and have frustrated its noble intentions. It seems comfortably set on the beaten track, concentrating on what are no more than the symptoms of a deeper malaise.

The Committee[185] agrees that the progress in the current decade has been "unsatisfactory" and that this makes it imperative for the UN bodies "to redouble their efforts." It therefore proposes that the United Nations "might adopt a charter" for the coming decade; and

---

[185] Committee for Development Planning. See Report on its Second Session, Annex II, E/4362, New York, 1967.

that this charter should declare the "common interest" of all nations to secure more rapid advance in the developing countries, stress the need for "concerted action," and set up certain targets, such as for income per capita at a level representing a "significant increase" in the rate of their growth, also for minimum per capita food consumption, for standards of health and education, and for employment.

The charter, furthermore, should specify the means to be employed, by the developed and the developing countries, to attain these targets, with particular reference to such difficulties as plan implementation, the mounting foreign debt service, foreign exchange shortage, rapid growth of population. It should include measures to overcome the foreign exchange gap, such as more aid, better access to the markets of the developed countries, greater efforts by the developing countries to expand exports or to replace imports, especially by stepping up agricultural output.

And finally, there should be "pledges" in the charter, in both "qualitative and quantitative terms"; by the developed countries regarding "the scale and character of their aid and trade policies"; by the developing countries regarding institutional improvements, mobilization of domestic resources, social reforms when they are a precondition for economic development, and family planning in countries burdened with excessive population growth.

All this bids fair to produce no more than a slightly different mixture of the noble platitudes which paved the road for the first development decade. It assumes that what is needed is more of the same, only backed by increased fervour, and that a fresh charter adopted by the UN will be enough to generate it in a hardheaded world. It seeks to focus attention, somewhat more sharply this time, on the goals to be achieved and the means to be employed. And the means, as conceived by it, will in effect be confined to a listing, perhaps in greater detail, of the obligations of the two parties—the developed and the developing nations.

Such a concept of means remains largely meaningless since, as in the past, it suffers from one grievous omission: there is no mention of the United Nations system itself, although it must be regarded as by far the most important means in this context. For, it is the malfunctioning of the UN system that has been primarily responsible for the poor results in the first development decade. The search for a more effective strategy must therefore begin here, with the attempt to tackle this basic weakness, to overhaul the UN machinery and procedures in order to improve its performance.

Declaration of high ideals and proclamation of appealing goals will, by themselves, have little practical value. They will set the stage only for a repeat performance—enthusiasm at the start, frustrated hopes in the end, and voluminous analysis in between, covering the causes of the shortfalls, the sins of omission and commission of others, that is, of the aid-givers and aid-receivers, but never of the aid-administering intermediary, the UN family.

There should be no excuse for reenacting this dreary drama, and no justification for bypassing the incontrovertible fact that, once again, progress will depend on the quality of leadership and management to be provided by the UN family, far more than on any other factors. No strategy for future development can ever succeed unless it embraces the role of the UN family as well, shows clear understanding of what that role should be, and spells it out in advance in sufficiently concrete terms.

2

The UN family, it has often been argued, is ideally suited to administer aid and sponsor development of the low-income countries. Some have been at pains to stress its superiority as compared with bilateral aid agencies, especially of the USA.

This thesis has been consistently upheld by Mr. Hoffman. Of what he calls the "unique advantages" of channelling aid through the UN system he mentions four in particular.[186] First, the United Nations and the specialized agencies have "accumulated the richest experience" covering practically all fields of development activity.

Second, the UN assistance is a cooperative enterprise in which both rich and poor nations participate in a spirit of partnership. This stimulates self-help in the recipient countries and reduces the cost to the donors.

Third, the UN assistance, unlike a bilateral programme, is immune from the risk of political charges such as grinding a particular national or ideological axe, and there is no suggestion of "hateful strings." This enables UN officials to talk tough and act tough with recipient governments in the interest of the programme without rousing their ill-feeling. The latter have often indicated their preference to receive aid through th United Nations since it is given "without political, commercial, or military motives."

And finally, the UN draws its experts and technicians from all over the world. This enables it to pick and choose the right experts to

---

[186] *World Without Want.* Pages 122-24.

match more precisely the specific needs of a recipient country in the early stages of development. Expertise supplied from the highly developed countries may be, and has often proved to be, oversophisticated, and therefore unsuitable, for the developing economies. "With all the good will in the world," says Mr. Hoffman, "advanced countries are not always the best qualified to help."

And he leaves no one in doubt as to what should, in his view, be the most desirable course: in giving aid the correct policy is to select the channel which will give "the most effective results at the lowest possible cost." The USA should therefore use the UN much more frequently than it has done in the past. Its limited resources for development should not be wasted "in a futile attempt to buy friends, obtain commercial advantage, or get national credit."

The arguments are familiar. They have been pressed by a good many other people on different occasions. For example, Mr. Harlan Cleveland, as Assistant Secretary of State, developed them at considerable length in 1961 while speaking in support of the appropriations for the Foreign Assistance Act of 1961, and made a strong plea for channelling American aid increasingly through the international agencies.[187] In the US Congress, powerful voices have been heard from time to time in favour of this view.

As for the UN family, it has never had any serious doubt about its own superiority as a medium for administering aid. The points made by Mr. Hoffman have long been more or less taken for granted. They are looked upon by many as self-evident truths.

Yet to regard these points as the whole truth would be an exaggeration. And even more so would be to assume that they have all been realized in practice. For too long there has been too strong a tendency to treat what are largely *potential* advantages of the UN family as if they were all *actual*, and to ignore the difference between things as they could be and things as they really are.

The UN assistance has been free from "hateful strings," but it has also failed to provide much-needed directions. The UN officials can talk tough, but they seldom exercise this right, except when turning down requests on financial grounds. The Expanded Programme, or the UNDP/TA, abdicated its responsibility in the name of country-programming and has glorified this laissez faire policy. The UN record in helping recipient governments to fix their priorities has been as

---

[187] Hearings, Subcommittee of the Committee on Appropriations, House of Representatives, August 26, 1961. At the same time Mr. Cleveland initiated an attempt to improve the UN machinery. See Chapter 12.

good as blank. In fact, the UN has not been, and is still not, able to speak to the governments in one single voice; as a result, it has sounded not "tough," but confused.

Nor is it correct to suggest that the UN assistance is free from politics. The fact is that the UN family has its own politics, though of a different brand—the politics of delegations, of the specialized agencies, and of large bureaucratic establishments, all of which has unquestionably affected its overall performance.

Even the freedom to draw on experts from all over the world has proved to be a mixed blessing. It has no doubt helped avoid some pitfalls, such as supplying oversophisticated experts from the most advanced industrial nations. But it has also worked the other way—the developing countries have at times been unable to draw experts from these sources even when the latter would have best served their interests. For example, in agricultural extension work, in planning multipurpose river valley projects and also in the field of management, the US experience, though more relevant to the needs of some developing countries, could not be made available to them. The question of higher cost of US experts was no doubt a factor. But more so was the fact that, in the UN, professional judgment must be tempered, quite often rather heavily, by considerations of the geographical distribution of experts, sometimes also of currency utilization.

How to mesh experts recruited from a number of countries into efficient teams is a serious problem, especially on larger projects. A group of experts belonging to different nationalities and working on problems of development is an ennobling sight. But it has also its drawbacks.

A romantic view of the UN family, however natural, cannot be very helpful. It is the hard facts—the results achieved and the record established—which will ultimately swing public opinion one way or the other.

3

The woes of the US bilateral programme have been repeatedly diagnosed by outstanding experts, from inside and outside. They spring primarily from three main causes: overexposure to domestic, especially Congressional, politics; hand-to-mouth appropriations in dealing with what are long-range tasks of development; and the pursuit of heterogenous goals through one single economic, political, commercial, and military programme. There is general agreement, both inside and outside the USA, that, in administering its foreign aid programme, the USA did not put its best foot forward, that the fortuitous mix of economics and politics has helped neither, that it has in fact tended to frustrate both in a good many instances.

Students of America's history sometimes speculate how different things would have been had she been able to combine three of its outstanding elements in administering foreign aid: the liberal, humanitarian tradition which no doubt was the mainspring of the foreign aid programme; the autonomous corporation as the institutional device to administer it on the lines, for example, of the TVA with freedom of action, and with a clear mandate to pursue development abroad as a business and to steer clear of politics at both ends; and the genius of management which could be applied only within the framework of the corporate device. The history of foreign aid, it may be argued, would have been differently written in that case with more benefit packed into each aid dollar; development abroad would have proceeded at a faster pace; and the programme would have established for itself a more shining record of achievements.

Meanwhile, the record has suffered for another transparent reason: a disposition, more pronounced in the last few years, to overpublicize the shortcomings of the US foreign aid programme and to deny it the credit due for its past achievements, a disposition that is inspired by the ingrained opposition of some sections of the public to the programme itself. By contrast, the UN aid is more fortunately placed. It has no opposition lobby to contend with, nor is it faced with political detractors determined to run down its record. And its shortcomings, grave as they sometimes are, are comfortably invisible from outside.

There are many examples in economic history to show that "comparative advantages" enjoyed by a country because of natural factors do not, by themselves, suffice in building up its competitive capacity in international trade, that such advantages can be squandered away through mismanagement. The UN case has been essentially similar. It has emphasized the advantages it enjoys in handling aid, but has at best been indifferent to the quality of its management.

4

The UN family was expected to function as a catalytic agent in the developing countries; instead, it has managed to catalyze itself. This has been, and continues to be, the worst predicament of the UN family, a fact that is manifest in the plethora of programmes, agencies, and field representatives, directors who are unable to direct adequately, and leaders who cannot, or will not, lead.

As the UN Secretary-General stated in his report on the development decade, "In international society no one is ultimately responsible for success. There is no government to take final praise or blame."[188] This statement is as accurate as it is significant. In the UN family there is no focus of responsibility, without which sound management is inconceivable. Superimposed on this are intense interagency rivalry and inter-programme competition. No wonder that the UN family, instead of providing the needed leadership to the developing countries, should find itself stymied so often at so many critical points by its own incohesiveness.

The reasons for this state of affairs, and for its continuation over the years, have been analyzed at considerable length, especially in the last five chapters, also the practical measures needed to rescue the UN system from its inner contradictions, to revitalize it and to turn it into a more potent instrument of economic progress. Only a few brief remarks, mainly by way of summing up the major recommendations, need be made here.

The worst offender in the UN system has been the Expanded Programme, later metamorphosed into UNDP/TA. Its bad procedures have produced bad programmes and poor leadership. They have been more conducive to bureaucratic growth than to economic growth. The entangling cobwebs of procedures spun by the Expanded Programme in self-justification and self-defense have been a massive diversion away from the tasks of development; so, too, has been the long and obdurate debate to defend an arbitrary distinction between technical assistance and preinvestment work.

All this represents one of the worst examples of "misallocation" of resources—of effort and energy—and misdirection of policy and action in the field of development. The *first* task, which cannot be repeated too often and too strongly, is to scrap the technical assistance procedures, merge the two components of the UNDP, create one single programme, and apply to the whole of it the Special Fund procedures with the suggested modifications (Chapter 17-18).

As a corollary to this step, the regular programmes of the United Nations and the agencies, in so far as they directly relate to economic development, should be merged into the UNDP. The WHO regular programme, which has different characteristics, and which is large enough to function effectively by itself, may be allowed to continue its separate existence, the more so since the agency has been system-

188 "The United Nations Development Decade at Mid-Point—An Appraisal by the Secretary-General," Ibid., page 11.

atically integrating all activities financed from the UNDP into its regular programmes to secure the best overall results (Chapter 17).

The *second* set of recommendations relate to the most pressing reforms needed within each headquarters setup. Clearly, disciplines need to be disciplined; skills have to be meshed in a managerial sense; development has to be pursued as a business. The old-style treasury-cum-bureaucratic coordination is patently out of place here. Economic development in the modern world needs modern business managers.

Such managers, with clear-cut overall responsibility and with supporting managerial assistance, have to be installed at the headquarters —of the UNDP, of UN and the specialized agencies. And in each agency, all development activities need to be separated from all non-developmental functions and placed directly in charge of the general manager and his staff.

An accident of history has led to the present fragmented structure of the UN system—with a whole series of nearly-independent agencies with separate constitutions, legislative bodies and secretariats, and scattered over a large segment of the globe. Yet functionally they are interrelated; and no sensible development is possible unless policy and action are constantly based on, and are guided by, a full realization of their mutually complementary character.

Here, then, is the biggest challenge posed by the UN system: how to create a unity of purpose out of the plurality of organizations; how to evolve unified leadership in the face of the centrifugal forces upheld by law and practice, yet contradicted by logic; how to rescue development from falling a victim to the special interests of the specialized agencies. The problem is unique and difficult, but it is not insoluble. However, given the disjointed structure of the UN system, it can be resolved only if general managers are installed at the key points, as proposed, and if they work as a team in a real ésprit de corps (Chapter 18).

This internal redesign at the headquarters of the UNDP, UN and the agencies has a corollary for the field offices, which constitutes the *third* major recommendation. Should it be necessary to establish that, like all large business organizations, the UN family too—despite its fragmented structure, and more so because of it—must have a single unified representation in a recipient country through competent men, able to speak from experience and with authority, enjoying a high enough status to speak at a high level in the government in order to serve it effectively with advice and suggestions? Should all this not be an axiom both in business and in public administration? The UN family has for years been fighting this axiom and has lavishly invested its diplomatic and bureaucratic genius in the vain attempt to make out a case against it. This, far more than any other factor, has made the UN system so impotent; and this, more than anything else, limits its ability to administer aid on a truly significant scale and to pioneer development in the world's economic backyards.

The present setup and operations at the country level constitute what is little more than a well-planned chaos. No amount of tinkering here will help. The remedy has to be radical; and it should not be further delayed (Chapter 19).

Once these procedural, managerial, and infrastructural changes have been carried out within the UN system, it would be possible for it to deal more nationally with the question of priorities, and to reconstruct country programmes with the central emphasis on what must be treated as the most urgent problems and also as the most promising opportunities (Chapter 20).

The UN family will then be in a position to assist the governments much more actively in the utilization and mobilization of their own "resources" in the broadest sense of the word (Chapter 21).

And only when development is treated primarily as a business, and experienced managerial minds are brought to bear on it for key decisions, would it be possible to create, or widen, the room for private enterprise. This will not merely improve the prospects of attracting investment capital and modern know-how from abroad, but will, given a favourable climate of incentives and regulation, grow into a powerful engine of economic progress (Chapter 21).

These, in a nutshell, are the essential reforms the UN family badly needs today. And only when these reforms are carried out in toto, without shirking some surgery when needed, will it be possible for the UN system to acquire the properties of a true catalyst and to achieve truly outstanding results in serving the developing countries.

5

But how will the reforms be carried out? The self-catalyzed UN family has time and again demonstrated its helplessness in this regard. It has been incapacitated to an extent that it is unable to carry out objective self-analysis as a preliminary to self-reform and self-improvement.

It should, clearly, be the function of the legislative bodies to undertake periodic probes into the UN operations, to form independent judgment on critical issues, and to lay down appropriate policy guidelines. But the legislative arm of the UN family has been stricken with a paralysis of its own for two fundamental reasons.

First, there are too many legislative bodies—the UN General Assembly which, in theory, is the supreme legislative organ, and the governing bodies of the specialized agencies. Their composition is too heterogeneous—the vast majority of their members are unable to exercise their legislative prerogatives, quite often even to comprehend the implications of the basic issues. They depend helplessly on the secretariats not only for facts and information, but also for views, opinions, and recommendations. These are usually given uncritical blessings, provided that they are not open to any serious political objections. It is the politics of economics that seems to matter most. The secretariats know the game well enough, and are usually quite adept in taking care of the pitfalls well in advance.

And second, the member-governments have developed a tradition of speaking in different voices in different legislative bodies. They have thus been instrumental in accentuating rather than moderating the particular interests of the agencies and in further feeding their separatist tendencies.

Years ago Mr. Harlan Cleveland made a pointed reference to this discouraging trend. After stressing that the "sovereignty" of the specialized agencies violated the principles of a unified country programme, he proceeded to argue that the problem seemed insoluble because "we are doing nothing to solve it." And then he added: "The Americans who represent the United States in the international councils of FAO, WHO, UNESCO, and the others are not proposing the submersion of their respective jurisdictions in a single technical assistance agency, though many of them would privately concede the value of such a move."[189]

A distinct echo of the same thought, though in a fainter form, can be heard in the following remark made more recently by the UN Secretary-General: "Although the agencies were constituted by more or less the same governments, each tended to reflect the specialized interests of particular ministries in the governments."[190]

Here, then, is the interlocking dilemma of the UN family. Progress in the developing countries calls for strong UN leadership, which the UN system, as a multifractured body, has been unable to provide. These congenital handicaps could be remedied through appropriate

[189] "The Theory and Practice of Foreign Aid," 1956. Ibid., p. 71-72.
[190] "The United Nations Development Decade at Midpoint." Ibid., page 12.

legislative measures, which the competent legislative bodies have so far shown little disposition to undertake or even to consider.

This is an untenable situation that has to be ended. It can be ended only when the legislatures decide to legislate with imagination and courage, on the basis of independent judgment, in the overall interest of the entire UN system. This means that, above all, the ECOSOC and the General Assembly must take a far more active initiative for overhauling the UN machinery. And within these two bodies, the leading members, especially the USA, will obviously have to take the lead for pushing through the urgently needed reforms.

Not that the leading members of the UN system have been unaware of its crippling limitations. There is truth in Mr. Herbert Feis's remark that "its members (except the Soviet Union and France) have been lenient to these imperfections lest by harsh criticism they weaken the main structure of the United Nations. They have kept their mouths shut and their purse strings tight."[191] Such a policy, even if understandable, has certainly not been helpful. The leading members can avoid negative criticism, yet open their mouths, speak out frankly, press for and carry through the badly needed reforms to strengthen the UN machinery, and then loosen their purse strings. This is what they can do and they must do, if they are not to shirk a responsibility that so conspicuously rests on them.

6

In a recent address Mr. George D. Woods, after expressing his conviction that "the record of the developing nations is far better than the popular image suggests," urged the governments of the developed nations to carry out a "grand assize" by a dozen or more leading world experts in development, who would review 20 years' history of development assistance, assess the results achieved, identify the errors made, and lay down policy guidelines for the future.[192]

A similar grand assize of the UN system, by renowned experts with independent status, would be eminently desirable today. The broad

---

191 *Foreign Aid and Foreign Policy.* By Herbert Feis, Dell Publishing Co., Inc., New York, 1966. Page 223.

192 "Development—Need for New Directions." Address to the Swedish Bankers Association, Stockholm on 27 October 1967. Mr. Woods repeated his proposal in February 1968 at the United Nations Conference on Trade and Development in New Delhi.

The World Bank has meanwhile announced (on 23 October 1968) the formation of an 8-member Development Group headed by Mr. Lester B. Pearson, former Prime Minister of Canada; the Group should report before the end of 1969.

contours of the verdict that will emerge from such an independent review by a judicious body of world experts should not be difficult to foresee:

The problems facing the developing countries are staggering in magnitude and complexity, due not to any fault of their own, but to the arbitrary march of history and of modern technology. The achievements they already have to their credit in the face of unparalleled difficulties are remarkable. Their overall record merits not cynical criticism, but sympathy, even admiration.

True, there have been some glaring examples of misallocation of resources, even of wasteful glamorous projects. But in relation to the total picture their proportion has been small, if not inconsequential. The really serious misallocation of resources—and there has no doubt been a good deal of it—often stemmed from extraneous causes, from pressures to sell to the developing countries: ideologies, at times also military hardware, along with aid from some bilateral programmes; machinery and equipment from profit-motivated commercial concerns whose primary interest was to transact business without paying much heed to the real needs of their customers; a whole range of skills from the UN organizations, mostly without proper regard for the priority needs of the governments they set out to serve.

In the final judgment, this last point will no doubt be regarded as the saddest feature of all. For, in the contemporary world it is only the UN that could have provided the leadership, helped protect the interests of the governments, and direct their meagre resources into the most productive channels. This was its mandate from history. This is where it has woefully defaulted, and instead of conteracting the ills, has often accentuated them.

"The mustard seeds that should drive away the spirits are themselves possessed," says an Indian proverb. The means of reform are themselves vitiated. This sums up the position of the United Nations in economic development. The faltering development decade reflects a faulty UN system. The dilemma is clear. The UN family must resolutely set its house in order and rise to its historic responsibilities. A reorganized and revitalized UN body can arrest the current drift toward despair and usher in a new era of hope and progress.

It can, by providing the long-awaited leadership in the developing countries, help direct their resources toward more productive goals, provide visible evidence of greater production of tangible wealth, and create the sensation of forward motion at a faster pace.

It can, through this and other well-conceived actions, reassure an aidweary West that its aid dollar is being well-spent and is well serving the cause; that its weariness comes at an inopportune moment; that the developing countries are beginning to reap the results from the past effort, while many of them are now on the verge of taking a decisive leap into a brighter future.

And finally, it can, through imaginative policies and demonstration of improved results, convince an increasingly inward-looking West that the little it spares from its swelling affluence spells the difference between progress and stagnation in the struggling poor nations; that even the little it decides to spare is not a sacrifice, but a high-yield investment, not just in a moral or spiritual sense, but in cold business terms since it will underwrite a steady expansion of its own future trade.

The world has travelled a long way from the 19th century economic doctrines, and has come to recognize it as an axiom that prosperity in a national economy depends not on the wealth of the few, but on the welfare of all. This precious discovery should hold good also for the world economy. Higher living standards in Asia, Africa and Latin America—in the world's long-neglected resource-rich areas—will help raise world economy to higher levels of prosperity. The New Economics needs a new dimension, a new frontier transcending national boundaries, to come to firmer grips with the problems of international development. The time is apparently not ripe for this vision to become a reality. It may very well take another decade or two, or even more. How long it will actually take will depend, first and foremost, on how well the UN family acquits itself of its own responsibilities, and how creatively it fulfils its own functions in the developing nations. It can, by its performance, hasten the ultimate victory of the new New Economics that will some day lead beyond the national frontiers—to build bridges between the rich North and the poor South, and to create a more compact world community.

Appendix I

APPENDIX IA: STATISTICS RELATING TO EXPANDED PROGRAMME*

Table 1. Yearly Expenditures (million $)

Year	Project Costs	A.O.S. Costs[1]	Total Programme Costs
1950-51	4.52	1.92	6.44
1952	18.80	4.17	22.97
1953	17.82	4.99	22.81
1954	15.11	4.35	19.47
1955	21.31	4.57	25.88
1956	25.32	5.15	30.48
1957	25.79	5.72	31.52
1958	27.71	6.10	33.82
1959	26.54	6.30	32.84
1960	27.91	6.50	34.41
1961	31.28	6.82	38.11
1962	44.64	6.94	51.58
1963	39.50	8.43	47.93
1964	51.78	8.71	60.49
1965	42.50	6.30	48.80
1966	59.00	6.80	65.80
1967	50.60	8.10	58.70
1968	64.60	8.09	72.69

*Source: Official documents of TAB and UNDP.
1. Administrative and Operational Services costs.

313

TABLE 2. SHARES OF PARTICIPATING ORGANIZATIONS IN PROGRAMME FUNDS (MILLION $)*

Year	UN	ILO	FAO	UNESCO	ICAO	WHO	ITU	WMO	IAEA	UPU	IMCO	TAB
1950-1	1.20	0.34	2.01	1.08	0.30	1.33	(included in UN figures)					0.18
1952	5.43	1.88	6.36	3.53	0.94	4.35	—	—	—	—	—	0.48
1953	5.28	2.26	6.05	2.73	1.11	4.18	—	—	—	—	—	1.30
1954	4.65	1.99	4.73	2.31	0.75	3.76	—	—	—	—	—	1.28
1955	5.75	2.64	7.65	3.08	0.99	4.40	—	—	—	—	—	1.36
1956	7.12	3.06	8.02	3.79	1.18	5.18	0.26	—	—	—	—	1.56
1957	6.66	3.21	8.62	4.15	1.29	5.20	0.30	0.30	—	—	—	1.78
1958	7.02	3.42	8.35	5.45	1.29	5.60	0.36	0.38	—	—	—	1.96
1959	6.95	3.36	8.10	4.84	1.39	5.17	0.34	0.48	0.28	—	—	1.94
1960	7.31	3.25	8.41	4.87	1.47	5.54	0.38	0.50	0.59	—	—	2.10
1961	7.10	3.56	9.24	6.11	1.61	6.28	0.54	0.51	0.45	—	—	2.70
1962	9.60	4.79	11.46	9.38	1.85	7.98	1.06	0.90	1.16	—	—	340
1963	9.11	4.22	11.55	6.69	1.84	7.82	0.90	1.00	0.76	0.12	—	3.92
1964	11.40	5.82	12.57	10.65	2.46	9.19	1.22	1.53	1.31	0.23	—	4.12
1965	10.30	5.10	11.70	8.30	2.00	7.90	1.20	1.20	0.70	0.40	0.00	4.60
1966	13.30	7.00	15.30	11.60	2.70	10.20	1.80	1.90	1.30	0.60	0.00	4.80
1967	12.70	6.50	15.50	8.90	2.40	8.30	1.50	1.50	0.80	0.50	0.20	5.30
1968	12.80	7.27	16.36	13.40	3.07	9.79	2.39	1.95	1.77	0.54	0.20	6.19

*Includes "project" and "A.O.S." costs. TAB allocation is for A.O.S. costs only, to cover the costs of Headquarters and of TAB Field Offices.; the small allocation to IMCO, which joined the Programme in 1965, was also for A.O.S. costs only. The share of UNIDO, the last organization to join the Programme, amounted to $3.09 million in 1968.

TABLE 3: REGIONAL SHARE OF DIRECT PROJECT COSTS (AMOUNTS IN MILLION $)*

Year	Africa		Asia and Far East		Europe		Latin America		Middle East		Inter-Regional	
	Amount	%	Amount	%	Amount	%	Amount	%	Amount	%	Amount	%
1950-51	0.44	10.1	1.44	31.8	0.16	3.7	1.18	26.2	0.94	20.5	0.35	7.7
1952	1.35	7.2	5.94	31.6	1.94	10.3	4.91	26.1	4.38	23.3	0.29	1.5
1953	1.59	8.4	5.72	32.1	1.56	8.7	4.79	26.9	3.54	19.9	0.72	4.0
1954	1.28	8.5	4.65	30.8	1.50	9.9	3.92	25.9	3.25	21.5	0.51	3.4
1955	1.80	8.5	6.65	31.1	1.71	8.0	5.62	26.4	4.67	21.9	0.86	4.1
1956	2.24	8.9	8.24	32.5	1.73	6.8	7.30	28.8	4.96	19.6	0.86	3.4
1957	2.92	11.3	8.42	32.6	1.86	7.2	7.22	28.0	4.95	19.2	0.44	1.7
1958	3.39	12.2	9.65	34.8	1.74	6.3	7.54	27.2	4.99	18.0	0.40	1.5
1959	3.75	14.1	9.19	34.6	1.69	6.4	6.91	26.0	4.63	17.5	0.37	1.4
1960	4.99	17.9	11.04	39.6	1.66	6.0	7.22	26.0	2.51	9.0	0.42	1.5
1961	6.93	22.2	11.77	37.7	1.47	4.7	7.57	24.2	2.42	7.8	1.05	3.4
1962	13.81	31.0	14.22	31.9	2.54	5.7	9.09	20.4	3.29	7.4	1.60	3.6
1963	14.58	36.9	10.72	27.1	1.77	4.5	7.87	19.9	2.52	6.4	2.04	5.2
1964	17.58	33.9	14.23	27.5	2.66	5.1	10.45	20.2	3.04	5.9	3.81	7.4
1965	14.85	35.0	10.62	25.0	1.67	3.9	9.14	21.5	2.45	5.8	3.75	8.8
1966	20.80	35.3	14.40	24.4	2.70	4.6	11.90	20.2	3.80	6.5	5.30	9.0
1967	18.60	36.8	11.30	22.4	2.20	4.3	10.80	21.3	3.50	6.9	4.20	8.3
1968	21.70	40.9	11.60	21.8	2.20	4.1	10.80	20.4	3.10	5.8	3.70	7.0

*Does not include A.O.S. costs. Prior to 1960, the Middle East includes Iran, Afghanistan and the UAR. From 1960, the first two countries are included in Asia, while the UAR is listed under Africa.

TABLE 4. PERCENTAGE OF FUNDS ALLOCATED FOR EXPERTS, FELLOWSHIP AWARDS AND EQUIPMENT.

(costs in million $)

Year	Total Project Costs	% for Experts	% for Fellowships	% for Equipment
1950-51	4.52	73	20	7
1952	18.80	59	27	14
1953	17.82	76	14	10
1954	15.11	74	17	9
1955	21.31	67	22	11
1956	25.32	69	18	13
1957	25.79	74	16	10
1958	27.71	75	13	12
1959	26.54	78	15	7
1960	27.91	78	17	5
1961	31.28	75	13	12
1962	44.64	70	21	9
1963	39.50	80	14	6
1964	51.78	70	23	7
1965	42.48	81	15	4
1966	58.94	73	21	6
1967	50.62	84	13	3
1968	64.60	77	19	4

TABLE 5A. VOLUNTARY PLEDGES AND LOCAL COST CONTRIBUTIONS

(in million $)

Year	Countries Pledging	Amounts Pledged	Local Cost Contributions
1950-51	54	20.04	——
1952	65	18.80	——
1953	69	22.32	——
1954	73	24.99	0.62
1955	70	27.62	1.10
1956	77	28.83	1.70
1957	84	30.81	1.91
1958	85	31.05	2.21
1959	82	29.42	2.14
1960	84	33.99	2.05
1961	91	41.79	2.16
1962	92	45.37	2.61
1963	105	50.05	2.60
1964	109	51.29	2.99
1965	112	53.87	3.19
1966	111	56.69	4.04
1967	118	60.36	4.13
1968	119	64.57	4.66
1969	119	70.14	4.25

TABLE 5B: MAJOR CONTRIBUTORS DURING 1965-69

(in million $)

	1965	1966	1967	1968	1969
United States	22.67	23.10	24.65	27.08	29.00
United Kingdom	4.75	4.75	4.75	4.75	5.18
Germany, Fed. Rep.	2.65	2.65	3.00	3.00	3.60
Denmark	2.61	3.19	4.05	4.07	4.67
Sweden	2.50	3.00	3.00	3.00	3.00
Canada.	2.15	3.07	3.47	4.43	5.50
USSR	2.00	2.00	2.00	2.00	1.85
France	1.85	1.85	1.85	1.87	1.87
Netherlands	1.79	1.79	1.81	1.88	1.40
Norway	1.12	1.19	1.26	1.26	1.00
Italy	0.90	0.90	0.90	0.90	1.00
Switzerland	0.87	0.93	0.93	0.93	1.20

TABLE 6: EXPERTS SERVING IN THE FIELD DURING 1950-68

Year	UN	ILO	FAO	UNESCO	ICAO	WHO	ITU	WMO	IAEA	UPU	IMCO	Total
1950-1	165	65	271	109	32	155	(included in	UNTA totals)	—	—	—	797
1952	449	159	532	223	70	334			—	—	—	1,767
1953	383	222	522	225	96	377	18	9	—	—	—	1,852
1954	343	180	479	188	84	355	14	9	—	—	—	1,652
1955	415	241	665	232	94	419	23	19	—	—	—	2,108
1956	467	290	826	294	104	479	20	25	—	—	—	2,505
1957	516	296	785	339	111	498	29	29	—	—	—	2,603
1958	524	321	675	336	132	497	24	30	—	—	—	2,539
1959	527	291	604	317	138	476	27	39	4	—	—	2,416
1960	522	251	553	302	116	430	27	35	22	—	—	2,258
1961	588	272	587	327	115	440	33	33	48	—	—	2,443
1962	600	331	707	447	110	512	50	61	76	—	—	2,894
1963	695	323	772	432	111	521	51	62	64	6	—	3,037
1964	822	376	756	631	144	562	61	101	83	10	—	3,546
1965	1,035	333	686	550	125	559	66	65	59	16	—	3,494
1966	1,036	377	816	661	113	616	101	99	108	21	—	3,948
1967	887	344	798	545	114	500	88	99	103	20	6	3,504
1968	782*	363	766	676	111	518	85	95	105	33	7	3,685

Note: Experts who have been in the field for more than a year, are counted for each year they have served. Therefore, although the grand total for the years through 1967 is over 32,000 "expert assignments", the number of different experts serving during this period is closer to 13,500. They were recruited from 99 different countries and territories, and were sent to 136 different countries and territories.

* The drop was due mainly to the transfer of experts in the industrial field to UNIDO which had 144 experts in 1968.

TABLE 7. FELLOWSHIPS AWARDED: 1950-1968

Year	UN	ILO	FAO	UNESCO	ICAO	WHO	ITU	WMO	IAEA	UPU	IMCO	Total
1950-1	451	92	55	130	33	84	(included in	UNTA totals)	—	—	—	845
1952	792	486	223	214	43	369			—	—	—	2,127
1953	235	413	161	75	58	238	5	10	—	—	—	1,195
1954	153	506	238	291	45	278	6	7	—	—	—	1,524
1955	457	573	274	417	106	545	30	29	—	—	—	2,431
1956	632	297	266	244	134	474	31	50	—	—	—	2,128
1957	430	468	313	204	86	487	53	20	—	—	—	2,061
1958	554	288	216	222	45	376	37	21	—	—	—	1,759
1959	667	480	222	208	71	326	29	20	84	—	—	2,107
1960	556	395	266	229	48	373	18	47	85	—	—	2017
1961	506	368	227	172	79	507	60	40	70	—	—	2,029
1962	997	658	468	504	149	745	63	113	134	—	—	3,831
1963	788	365	227	245	107	570	65	83	74	21	—	2,545
1964	1,492	739	453	670	227	861	96	190	175	36	—	4,939
1965	906	336	287	485	122	459	77	112	65	32	—	2,881
1966	1,062	573	549	892	327	860	141	193	161	48	—	4,806
1967	1,446	356	651	374	145	389	69	58	102	83	5	3,678
1968	1,456	630	970	958	411	631	229	222	124	77	13	6,137
TOTAL	13,580	8,023	6,066	6,534	2,236	8,572	1,009	1,215	1,074	297	18	49,040

Note: UNTA Fellowship totals for the 1950-1 Programme also include Regular Programme awards.

Nationals of 168 countries and territories have been granted fellowships by the Programme from 1950-1967. These fellows have been sent for training in 128 different host countries.

The total for 1968 and the grand total include 416 fellowships awarded by UNIDO in 1968.

APPENDIX 1B: STATISTICS RELATING TO SPECIAL FUND

Table 1. Number and Cost of Approved Projects - by Year and Agency

| | | Number of Projects Approved[1,2] | Costs of projects (Million US $ equivalent) | | |
			Total	Governing Council Earmarkings[3,4]	Government Counterpart Contribution[3]
By Governing Council Session					
1959:	May	13	37.1	9.4	21.7
	December	29	48.6	24.7	23.8
1960:	May	29	57.6	22.4	35.0
	December	39	79.2	34.8	44.4
1961:	May	41	74.5	33.0	41.5
1962:	January	44	103.4	40.2	63.4
	May	40	79.4	35.8	43.6
1963:	January	40	95.2	43.0	52.3
	June	39	70.1	30.1	39.9
1964:	January	44	152.3	49.5	102.7
	June	48	84.6	39.5	45.0
1965:	January	64	171.4	69.3	102.0
	June	45	92.3	41.1	51.2
1966:	January	81	254.8	104.4	150.4
	June	55	161.3	63.1	98.2
1967:	January	69	185.2	78.1	107.0
	June	54	129.6	48.9	80.7
1968:	January	95	228.3	91.1	137.1
	June	56	127.2	50.1	77.0
1969:	January	104	226.8	99.8	127.1
By participating and executing agency					
UN		182	367.2	187.2	180.0
ILO		133	303.8	114.7	189.1
FAO		401	864.9	380.4	484.5
UNESCO		133	533.1	156.5	376.6
WHO		27	60.4	25.0	35.4
IBRD		52	79.0	47.2	31.8
ICAO		13	43.1	16.2	26.9
ITU		26	71.3	24.5	46.8
WMO		19	45.7	18.5	27.2
IAEA		5	8.6	3.9	4.7
UNIDO		31	60.4	27.6	32.8
IDB[5]		1	1.4	0.9	0.5
ADB[5]		1	0.4	0.3	0.1
UPU[5]		1	1.8	0.7	1.1

1. Includes completed projects.
2. Excludes cancelled projects.
3. The Government's cash payments towards local operating costs are included under "Governing Council earmarkings" and not under "Government counterpart contribution".
4. Includes residual earmarkings of $2.4 million for cancelled projects.
5. Most recent executing agencies: Inter-American Development Bank, Asian Development Bank, and Universal Postal Union.

TABLE 2. NUMBER AND COST OF APPROVED PROJECTS - BY ACTIVITY, ECONOMIC SECTOR AND REGION

	Number of Projects Approved[1,2]	Costs of projects (Million US $ equivalent)		
		Total	Governing Council Earmarkings[3,4]	Government Counterpart Contribution[3]
BY FIELD OF ACTIVITY				
Resource Surveys	377	666.9	338.4	328.5
Technical Education and Training	330	1007.4	342.9	664.6
Applied Research	197	480.4	187.9	292.6
Economic Development Planning	21	71.3	39.6	31.7
BY ECONOMIC SECTOR				
Agriculture	358	786.6	341.5	445.1
Industry	236	508.3	216.8	291.4
Public Utilities	128	257.7	115.3	142.4
Housing, Building and Physical Planning	16	40.1	15.1	25.0
Multi-Sector	55	129.9	73.6	56.3
Health	8	27.8	7.3	20.5
Education and Science	83	377.5	101.5	276.0
Social Welfare	3	4.1	1.9	2.2
Public Administration and Other Services	38	94.1	35.7	58.3
BY REGION				
Africa	338	743.3	336.9	406.2
The Americas	223	559.4	219.7	339.7
Asia and the Far East	233	573.6	232.0	341.6
Europe	63	207.8	63.7	144.1
Middle East	67	138.4	52.4	86.0
Inter-Regional	1	3.8	3.8	

1. Includes completed projects. The table shows the position as of June 1968 with a total of 925 projects.
2. Excludes cancelled projects.
3. The Government's cash payments towards local operating costs are included under "Government Counterpart Contribution" and not under "Governing Council Earmarkings".
4. Includes residual earmarkings of $2.4 million for cancelled projects.

TABLE 3. DATA ON COMPLETED SPECIAL FUND PROJECTS

A. Number of Projects

(I) By year

1960	1
1961	2
1962	4
1963	11
1964	24
1965	27
1966	47
1967	62
Total	178

(II) By Executing Agency

UN	35
ILO	26
FAO	69
UNESCO	9
WHO	4
IBRD	18
ICAO	4
ITU	3
WMO	7
IAEA	1
UNIDO	2
Total	178

(III) By Region

Africa	43
The Americas	54
Asia and the Far East	51
Europe	14
Middle East	16
Total	178

(IV) By Field of Activity

Resource surveys	108
Technical education and training	43
Applied research	25
Economic development and planning	2
Total	178

(V) By Economic Sector

Agriculture	64
Industry	50
Public Utilities	32
Housing, building and physical planning	2
Multi-sector	14
Health	1
Education and Science	7
Public administration and other services	8
Total	178

TABLE 3. DATA ON COMPLETED SPECIAL FUND PROJECTS (Cont'd.)

B. Cost of Completed Projects

Number of completed projects (as above)	178
Total cost	284.39 (million US $)
Governing Council earmarkings	128.56 " " "
Government counterpart contributions	155.83 " " "

C. Follow-up Investment

(a) No. of completed projects on which follow-up capital investments have been made	37
(b) Total amount of follow-up investments	1,900 (million US $)
(c) These included:	
Electric power supply in Argentina	332.65 " " "
Hydro power study in Brazil	371.00 " " "
Niger dams study in Nigeria	238.00 " " "
Skopje Urban Plan in Yugoslavia	800.00 " " "
Total of four projects	1,741.65 " " "
Total of (c) as percentage of (b)	90.2%

Appendix II

1240 (XIII). Establishment of the Special Fund

The General Assembly,

In conformity with the determination of the United Nations, as expressed in its Charter, to promote social progress and better standards of life in larger freedom and, for these ends, to employ international machinery for the promotion of the economic and social advancement of all peoples,

Conscious of the particular needs of the less developed countries for international aid in achieving accelerated development of their economic and social infrastructure,

Recalling its resolution 1219 (XII) of 14 December 1957,

Further recalling previous resolutions on the establishment of an international fund for economic development within the framework of the United Nations,

Noting the recommendations contained in Economic and Social Council resolution 692 (XXVI) of 31 July 1958,

Part A

1. *Commends* the Preparatory Committee on its work;

2. *Establishes* a Special Fund in accordance with the provisions set forth in part B below;

Part B

I. GUIDING PRINCIPALS AND CRITERIA

1. Pursuant to the provisions of General Assembly resolution 1219 (XII) and pending a review by the Assembly of the scope and future activities of the Special Fund, as envisaged in section III of that resolution, the Special Fund shall:

(*a*) Be a separate fund;

(*b*) Provide systematic and sustained assistance in fields essential to the integrated technical, economic and social development of the less developed countries;

(c) In view of the resources prospectively available at this time, which are not likely to exceed $100 million annually, direct its operations towards enlarging the scope of the United Nations programmes of technical assistance so as to include special projects in certain basic fields as outlined hereunder.

The Special Fund is thus envisaged as a constructive advance in United Nations assistance to the less developed countries which should be of immediate significance in accelerating their economic development by, *inter alia,* facilitating new capital investments of all types by creating conditions which would make such investments either feasible or more effective.

2. In establishing programmes, the Managing Director and the Governing Council of the Special Fund shall be guided by the following principles and criteria:

(a) The Special Fund shall concentrate, as far as practicable, on relatively large projects and avoid allocation of its resources over a great number of small projects;

(b) Due consideration shall be given to the urgency of the needs of the requesting countries;

(c) Projects shall be undertaken which will lead to early results and have the widest possible impact in advancing the economic, social or technical development of the country or countries concerned, in prticular by facilitating new capital investment;

(d) Due consideration shall be given to a wide geographical distribution in allocations over a period of years;

(e) Due consideration shall be given to technical, organizational and financial problems likely to be encountered in executing a proposed project;

(f) Due consideration shall be given to the arrangements made for the integration of projects into national development programmes and for effective co-ordination of the project with other multilateral and bilateral programmes;

(g) In accordance with the principles of the Charter of the United Nations, the assistance furnished by the Special Fund shall not be a means of foreign economic and political interference in the internal affairs of the country or countries concerned and shall not be accompanied by any conditions of a political nature;

(*h*) Projects shall be devised in such a way as to facilitate transfer, as soon as practicable, of the responsibilities of the Special Fund to assisted countries or to organizations designated by them.

3. Projects may be for one country or a group of countries or a region.

4. Projects may be approved for the period of time needed for their execution, even if more than one year.

II. BASIC FIELDS OF ASSISTANCE AND TYPES OF PROJECT

5. The Special Fund shall assist projects in the fields of resources, including the assessment and development of manpower, industry, including handicrafts and cottage industries, agriculture, transport and communications, building and housing, health, education, statistics and public administration.

6. In view of the resources prospectively available at the time of the initial period of the Special Fund's operations, projects to be assisted by the Fund might be in one or a combination of the following forms: surveys; research and training; demonstration, including pilot projects. These may be implemented by the provision of staff, experts, equipment, supplies and services, as well as the establishment of institutes, demonstration centres, plants or works, and other appropriate means, including fellowships, in so far as they are integral parts of a specific project financed by the Fund, in such proportions as are judged necessary by the Managing Director for each project, taking into account the type of assistance requested by Governments.

III. PARTICIPATION IN THE SPECIAL FUND

7. Participation in the Special Fund shall be open to any States Members of the United Nations or members of the specialized agencies or of the International Atomic Energy Agency.

IV. ORGANIZATION AND MANAGEMENT

8. There are established as organs of the Special Fund: a Governing Council, a Managing Director and his staff, and a consultative board. The Special Fund shall be an organ of the United Nations administered under the authority of the Economic and Social Council and of the General Asembly, which will exercise in respect of the Fund their powers under the Charter.

9. The Economic and Social Council shall be responsible for the formulation of the general rules and principles which will govern the administration and operations of the Special Fund; the review of

the operations of the Fund on the basis of the annual reports to be submitted by the Governing Council; and the consideration of the Expanded Programme of Technical Assistance and of the Special Fund in relation to each other.

10. The Economic and Social Council shall transmit the report of the Governing Council, together with its own comments, to the General Assembly. The Assembly will review the progress and operations of the Special Fund as a separate subject of its agenda and make any appropriate recommendations.

Governing Council

11. The immediate inter-governmental control of the policies and operations of the Special Fund shall be exercised by a Governing Council which will consist of representatives of eighteen States.

12. The Governing Council shall provide general policy guidance on the administration and operations of the Special Fund. It shall have final authority for the approval of the projects and programmes recommended by the Managing Director. It shall review the administration and the execution of the Fund's approved projects, and shall submit reports and recommendations to the Economic and Social Council, including such recommendations as the Governing Council may deem appropriate in the light of the relevant provisions of General Assembly resolution 1219 (XII).

13. The States members of the Governing Council shall be elected by the Economic and Social Council from among Members of the United Nations or members of the specialized agencies or of the International Atomic Energy Agency.

14. There shall be equal representation on the Governing Council of economically more developed countries, on the one hand, having due regard to their contributions to the Special Fund, and of less developed countries, on the other hand, taking into account the need for equitable geographical distribution among the latter members.

15. States members of the Governing Council shall be elected for a term of three years, provided, however, that of the member elected at the first election, the terms of six members shall expire at the end of one year and the terms of six other members at the end of two years. Retiring members shall be eligible for re-election.

16. Decisions of the Governing Council on important questions shall be made by a two-thirds majority of the members present and voting. These questions shall include questions of policy, the approval of projects and the allocation of funds. Decisions of the Governing Council on other questions shall be made by a majority of the members present and voting.

17. The Governing Council shall adopt its own rules of procedure, including the method of selecting its officers.

18. The Governing Council shall normally meet twice a year and on such occasions as may be necessary, in conformity with its rules of procedure.

19. The Managing Director of the Special Fund shall participate without vote in the deliberations of the Governing Council.

20. The Governing Council shall make appropriate arrangements in its rules of procedure for the representation of the specialized agencies, the International Atomic Energy Agency and the Executive Chairman of the Technical Assistance Board. To this end, it shall take due account of the practice followed by the Economic and Social Council.

Managing Director

21. The Special Fund shall be administered by a Managing Director under the policy guidance of the Governing Council. The Managing Director shall have the over-all responsibility for the operations of the Fund, with sole authority to recommend to the Governing Council projects submitted by Governments.

22. After having consulted the Governing Council, the Secretary-General will appoint the Managing Director, subject to confirmation by the General Assembly.

23. The Managing Director shall be appointed for a term of four years, or for a shorter period. He shall be eligible for reappointment.

24. Appropriate arrangements shall be made for the participation of the Managing Director in the Technical Assistance Board.

25. The Managing Director shall establish and maintain close and continuing working relationships with the specialized agencies concerned with those fields of activity in which the Special Fund

will operate, and with the International Atomic Energy Agency. He may also establish appropriate contacts with other organizations which may be concerned with the activities of the Fund.

Consultative Board

26. A Consultative Board shall be established to advise the Managing Director. The function of the Board shall be to assist the Managing Director with advice in the examination and appraisal of project requests and proposed programmes of the Special Fund. The Board shall be composed of the Secretary-General of the United Nations, the Executive Chairman of the Techical Assistance Board and the President of the International Bank for Reconstruction and Development or their designated representatives.

27. The Managing Director shall make, as appropriate, arrangements for representatives of the specialized agencies and of the International Atomic Energy Agency to be invited to the deliberations of the Consultative Board when projects falling mainly within their fields of activity are considered.

Staff

28. The Managing Director shall be assisted by a small group of officials to be selected by him or in consultation with him, on the basis of their special competence.

29. For other services, the Managing Director shall rely as far as possible on the existing facilities of the United Nations, the specialized agencies, the International Atomic Energy Agency, and the Technical Assistance Board. These facilities should be made available to the Special Fund without charge except when clearly identifiable additional expenses are involved. The Managing Director may also, as required, engage expert consultants.

30. To facilitate the field co-ordination between the Special Fund and the Expanded Programme of Technical Assistance in the countries seeking assistance, the Managing Director shall enter into an agreement with the Executive Chairman of the Technical Assistance Board concerning the role of the resident representatives in the work of the Fund.

V. Procedures

Sources and formulation of requests

31. Projects shall be undertaken only at the request of a Government or group of Governments eligible to participate in the Special Fund.

32. Governments shall present their requests for assistance in a form indicated by the Managing Director. Requests shall include all possible information on the intended use and benefits expected to be derived from the Special Fund's assistance, evidence of a technical nature regarding the projects for which assistance is requested, data bearing upon the economic appraisal of such projects, and statements concerning the part of costs which the Government itself would be ready to assume. The Special Fund, the Expanded Programme of Technical Assistance, the United Nations, the specialized agencies and the International Atomic Energy Agency should be ready to assist and advise Governments, at their request, in the preparation of their applications for assistance.

33. The Special Fund shall utilize only the official channel designated by each Government for the submission of requests.

Evaluation and approval of requests

34. The Managing Director shall be responsible for the evaluation of project requests. In this evaluation, he will normally be expected to rely upon the assistance of existing services within the Expanded Programme of Technical Assistance, the United Nations, the specialized agencies and the International Atomic Energy Agency. He shall also be authorized to contract the services of other agencies, private firms or individual experts for this purpose, in case the services of the United Nations, the specialized agencies or the International Atomic Energy Agency are wholly or partly unavailable or inadequate.

35. On the basis of the evaluation of project requests, the Managing Director shall periodically develop programmes for submission to the Governing Council. In developing his recommendations to the Governing Council, he shall consult the Consultative Board.

36. The Managing Director shall, at the request of the Government or Governments which have submitted such projects, submit to the Governing Council for its consideration a report on project requests which he has been unable to include in his programme.

37. The Governing Council shall examine the programmes and projects submitted by the Managing Director. Each project shall be accompanied by:

(a) An evaluation of the benefits expected to be derived by the requesting country or countries;

(b) A summary of its technical evaluation;

(c) A proposed budget showing the financial implications of the project in their entirety, including a statement on the costs which would be borne by the recipient Governments;

(d) A draft agreement with the requesting Government or Governments;

(e) When appropriate, a draft agreement with the agent or agents responsible for the execution of the project.

38. The Governing Council shall take final decision on the projects and programmes recommended by the Managing Director and authorize him to conclude the appropriate agreements.

Execution of Projects

39. Projects shall be executed, whenever possible, by the United Nations, by the specialized agencies concerned, or by the International Atomic Energy Agency, it being understood that the Managing Director shall also be authorized to contract for the services of other agencies, private firms or individual experts in the cases mentioned in paragraph 34 above.

40. Arrangements for the execution of projects shall be subject to the approval of the requesting Government or Governments, and shall be specified in an agreement with these Governments. Such arrangements shall contain provisions regarding the cost, including any local costs, which the requesting Government will assume and those facilities and services which it will provide.

41. Where requests for assistance fall within the sphere of two or more organizations, arrangements shall be made for joint execution by the organizations concerned and for proper co-ordination.

42. The Managing Director shall make appropriate arrangements to follow the execution of projects.

43. The Managing Director shall report to the Governing Council on the status of projects and the financial position of the projects and programmes.

44. The Managing Director and the Governing Council shall take appropriate measures to ensure an objective evaluation of the results of projects and programmes.

VI. FINANCES

45. The financial resources of the Special Fund shall be derived from voluntary contributions by Governments of States Members of the United Nations or members of the specialized agencies or of the International Atomic Energy Agency. The Fund is also authorized to receive donations from non-governmental sources. It is recommended that contributions by Governments should be paid as early in each year as possible. Furthermore, while contributions will normally be on an annual basis, it is recommended, in view of the expected longer term of many of the Fund's projects, that contributions be pledged or indicated, whenever possible, for a number of years.

46. The Secretary-General is requested to convene annually a pledging conference at which Governments would announce their contributions to the Expanded Programme of Technical Assistance and to the Special Fund respectively. If a Government pledges an initial lump sum, it should, within a reasonably short period, indicate the division of its contribution between the two programmes.

47. Contributions shall be made by Governments in currency readily usable by the Special Fund consistent with the need for efficiency and economy of the Fund's operations, or shall be transferable to the greatest possible extent into currency readily usable by the Fund. To this end, Governments are urged to make available as large a percentage as they may find possible of their contributions in such currency or currencies as the Managing Director may indicate are required for the execution of the Fund's programme. The Managing Director should, consistent with the criteria set forth respecting the nature and utilization of contributions, endeavour to make the fullest possible use of available currencies.

48. The Managing Director shall, at the end of the first year of the operations of the Special Fund and subsequently as he deems necessary, report to the Governing Council for its consideration on

the extent to which restrictions which may have been maintained on contributions have affected the flexibility, efficiency and economy of the Fund's operations. The Governing Council shall also consider what action may be necessary with respect to currency found not readily usable in order to facilitate the Fund's operations. Any action in this respect shall be subject to review by the Economic and Social Council and the General Assembly.

49. Contributions shall be made without limitation as to use by a specific agency or in a specific recipient country or for a specific project.

50. To the end that the multilateral character of the Special Fund shall be strictly respected, no contributing country should receive special treatment with respect to its contribution nor should negotiations for the use of currencies take place between contributing and receiving countries.

51. Since programmes shall be developed on a project basis, there should be no a priori allocation of funds on a country basis or among basic fields of assistance.

52. Recipient Governments shall be expected to finance part of the costs of projects, at least that part payable in local currency. This general rule may, however, be waived in the case of countries deemed financially unable to make even a local currency payment.

53. The Special Fund shall be governed by financial regulations consistent with the financial regulations and policies of the United Nations. The financial regulations for the Fund shall be drafted by the Secretary-General of the United Nations, in consultation with the Managing Director, for approval by the Governing Council, after review by the Advisory Committee for Administrative and Budgetary Questions. In the preparation of these regulations, account shall be taken of the special requirements of the Fund's operations; in particular, appropriate provision shall be made to permit the approval of projects of more than one year's duration and for an exchange of currencies between the Fund and the Special Account for the Expanded Programme of Technical Assistance. Provision should also exist under which the Managing Director is authorized in consultation with the Governing Council to establish appropriate financial rules and procedures.

54. The administrative budget prepared by the Managing Director with the assistance of the Secretary-General of the United Nations shall be submitted for approval to the Governing Council with the comments, if any, of the Advisory Committee on Administrative and Budgetary Questions. It shall be submitted to the General Assembly at the same time as the annual report of the Governing Council with the comments of the Advisory Committee on Administrative and Budgetary Questions.

55. The Special Fund shall be authorized to build up gradually a reserve fund by earmarking a specific percentage of the total contributions of each year up to an amount to be determined by the Governing Council on the recommendation of the Managing Director.

56. The Governing Council shall be authorized to consider allocating part of the resources of the Special Fund for assistance on a refundable basis at the request of Governments for projects within the terms of reference of the Fund.

Part C

Reaffirms the conditions set forth in section III of General Assembly resolution 1219 (XII) under which the Assembly shall review the scope and future activities of the Special Fund and take such action as it may deem appropriate.

776th plenary meeting,
14 October 1958.

*

*   *

At its 782nd plenary meeting on 5 December 1958, the General Assembly confirmed the nomination by the Secretary-General of Mr. Paul G. Hoffman as Managing Director of the Special Fund in accordance with the resolution above.

---

1 See A/4024.

Appendix III

Resolution Adopted by the General Assembly

[on the report of the Second Committee (A/6111)]

2029 (XX). *Consolidation of the Special Fund and the Expanded Programme of Technical Assistance in a United Nations Development Programme*

The General Assembly,

Having considered the recommendation of the Economic and Social Council, in its resolution 1020 (XXXVII) of 11 August 1964, to combine the Special Fund and the Expanded Programme of Technical Asistance in a United Nations Development Programme,

Being convinced that such a consolidation would go a long way in streamlining the activities carried on separately and jointly by the Expanded Programme of Technical Assistance and the Special Fund, would simplify organizational arrangements and procedures, would facilitate over-all planning and needed co-ordination of the several types of technical co-operation programmes carried on within the United Nations system of organizations and would increase their effectiveness,

Recognizing that requests for assistance on the part of the developing countries are steadily increasing in volume and in scope,

Believing that a reorganization is necessary to provide a more solid basis for the future growth and evolution of the assistance programmes of the United Nations system of organizations financed from voluntary contributions,

Being convinced that the United Nations assistance programmes are designed to support and supplement the national efforts of developing countries in solving the most important problems of their economic development, including industrial development,
65-30323

Recalling and reaffirming section III of its resolution 1219 (XII) of 14 December 1957 and part C of its resolution 1240 (XIII) of 14

335

October 1958 concerning the decision and the conditions under which the General Assembly shall review the scope and future activities of the Special Fund and take such action as it may deem appropriate,

Reaffirming that the proposed consolidation would be without prejudice to consideration of the study which the General Assembly, in its resolution 1936 (XVIII) of 11 December 1963, requested the Secretary-General to prepare on the practical steps to transform the Special Fund into a capital development fund in such a way as to include both pre-investment and investment activities, and without prejudice to the recommendation of the United Nations Conference on Trade and Development on the gradual transformation of the Special Fund, so as to include not only pre-investment but also investment proper,[1] or to the recommendation of the Economic and Social Council and of the General Assembly thereon,

Taking note of the message of the Secretary-General in which he stated, *inter alia,* that, far from limiting the possibilities of a United Nations capital investment programme, the proposals should enhance those possibilities,[2]

Recognizing that the effective working of a United Nations Development Programme depends upon the full and active participation and the technical contribution of all the organizations concerned,

1. *Decides* to combine the Expanded Programme of Technical Assistance and the Special Fund in a programme to be known as the United Nations Development Programme, it being understood that the special characteristics and operations of the two programmes, as well as two separate funds, will be maintained and that, as hitherto, contributions may be pledged to the two programmes separately;

2. *Reaffirms* the principles, procedures and provisions governing the Expanded Programme of Technical Assistance and the Special Fund not inconsistent with the present resolution and declares that they shall continue to apply to relevant activities within the United Nations Development Programme;

3. *Urges* the Governing Council referred to in paragraph 4 below to consider conditions for an effective implementation of the provi-

----

[1] See *Proceedings of the United Nations Conference on Trade and Development* vol. I, *Final Act and Report* (United Nations publication, Sales No.: 64.II.B.11), annex A.IV.8.

[2] See *Official Records of the Economic and Social Council, Thirty-seventh Session, Annexes,* agenda item 19, document E/3933, annex VI.

sions of section III of General Assembly resolution 1219 (XII) and part C of its resolution 1240 (XIII) ;

4. *Resolves* that a single inter-governmental committee of thirty-seven members, to be known as the Governing Council of the United Nations Development Programme, shall be established to perform the functions previously exercised by the Governing Council of the Special Fund and the Technical Assistance Committee, including the consideration and approval of projects and programmes and the allocation of funds; in addition, it shall provide general policy guidance and direction for the United Nations Development Programme as a whole, as well as for the United Nations regular programmes of technical assistance, it shall meet twice a year and shall submit reports and recommendations thereon to the Economic and Social Council for consideration by the Council at its summer session; decisions of the Governing Council shall be made by a majority of the members present and voting;

5. *Requests* the Economic and Social Council to elect the members of the Governing Council from among States Members of the United Nations or members of the specialized agencies or of the International Atomic Energy Agency, providing for equitable and balanced representation of the economically more developed countries, on the one hand, having due regard to their contribution to the United Nations Development Programme, and of the developing countries, on the other hand, taking into account the need for suitable regional representation among the latter members and in accordance with the provisions of the annex to the present resolution, the first election to take place at the first meeting of the Economic and Social Council after the adoption of this resolution;

6. *Decides* to establish, in place of the Technical Assistance Board and the Consultative Board of the Special Fund, an advisory committee, to be known as the Inter-Agency Consultative Board of the United Nations Development Programme, to meet under the chairmanship of the Administrator or Co-Administrator referred to in paragraph 7 below and to include the Secretary-General and the executive heads of the specialized agencies and of the International Atomic Energy Agency or their representatives; the Executive Directors of the United Nations Children's Fund and the World Food Programme should be invited to participate as appropriate; in order that the participating organizations may be provided with the opportunity to take part fully in the process of decision- and policy-making in a consultative capacity, the Inter-Agency Consultative

Board shall be consulted on all significant aspects of the United Nations Development Programme and in particular it shall:

(a) Advise the management on the programmes and projects submitted by Governments, through the Resident Representative, prior to their submission to the Governing Council for approval, taking into account the programmes of technical assistance being carried out under the regular programmes of the organizations represented on the Consultative Board, with a view to ensuring more effective co-ordination; the views of the Consultative Board, when it so requests, shall be conveyed by the Administrator to the Governing Council, together with any comments he may wish to make, when recommending for approval general policies for the Programme as a whole or for programmes and projects requested by Governments;

(b) Be consulted in the selection of agencies for the execution of specific projects, as appropriate;

(c) Be consulted on the appointment of the Resident Representatives and review annual reports submitted by them;

The Inter-Agency Consultative Board shall meet as often and for such periods as may be necessary for the performance of the foregoing functions;

7. *Decides* that, as a transitional measure, the present Managing Director of the Special Fund shall become the Administrator of the United Nations Development Programme and the present Executive Chairman of the Technical Assistance Board shall become the Co-Administrator of the Programme, each to serve until 31 December 1966 or, pending a further review of arrangements at the management level, until such later date as may be determined by the Secretary-General after consultation with the Governing Council;

8. *Decides* that the present resolution shall come into effect on 1 January 1966 and that such action as may be required in terms of this resolution shall be taken prior to that date.

1383rd plenary meeting,
22 November 1965.

Annex

1. Nineteen seats on the Governing Council of the United Nations Development Programme shall be filled by developing countries, and seventeen seats by economically more developed countries, subject to the following conditions:

(a) The nineteen seats allocated to developing countries of Africa, Asia, Latin America and to Yugoslavia shall be filled in the following manner: seven seats for African countries, six seats for Asian countries and six seats for Latin American countries, is being understood that agreement has been reached among the developing countries to accommodate Yugoslavia;

(b) Of the seventeen seats allocated to the economically more developed countries, fourteen shall be filled by Western European and other countries and three by Eastern European countries;

(c) Elections to these thirty-six seats shall be for a term of three years provided, however, that of the members elected at the first election the terms of twelve members shall expire at the end of the year and the terms of twelve other members at the end of two years.

2. The thirty-seventh seat shall rotate among the groups of countries mentioned in paragraph one above in accordance with the following nine-year cycle:

First and second years: Western European and other countries;
Third, fourth and fifth years: Eastern European countries;
Sixth year: African countries;
Seventh year: Asian countries;
Eighth year: Latin American countries;
Ninth year: Western European and other countries.

3. Retiring members shall be eligible for re-election.

Appendix IV

Resolution adopted by the General Assembly
1710 (XVI). UNITED NATIONS DEVELOPMENT DECADE
A PROGRAMME FOR INTERNATIONAL ECONOMIC CO-OPERATION (I) [a]

The General Assembly,

Bearing in mind the solemn undertaking embodied in the Charter of the United Nations to promote social progress and better standards of life in larger freedom and to employ international machinery for the advancement of the economic and social development of all peoples,

Considering that the economic and social development of the economically less developed countries is not only of primary importance to those countries but is also basic to the attainment of international peace and security and to a faster and mutually beneficial increase in world prosperity,

Recognizing that during the decade of the nineteen-fifties considerable efforts to advance economic progress in the less developed countries were made by both the newly developing and the more developed countries,

Noting, however, that in spite of the efforts made in recent years the gap in *per caput* incomes between the economically developed and the less developed countries has increased and the rate of economic and social progress in the developing countries is still far from adequate,

Recalling its resolutions 1421 (XIV) of 5 December 1959, 1514 (XV) of 14 December 1960, 1515 (XV), 1516 (XV), 1519 (XV) and 1526 (XV) of 15 December 1960,

Convinced of the need for concerted action to demonstrate the determination of Member States to give added impetus to international economic co-operation in the current decade, through the United Nations system and on a bilateral or multilateral basis,

---

a See also resolution 1715 (XVI) of 19 December 1961.

1. *Designates* the current decade as the "United Nations Development Decade", in which Member States and their peoples will intensify their efforts to mobilize and to sustain support for the measures required on the part of both developed and developing countries to accelerate progress towards self-sustaining growth of the economy of the individual nations and their social advancement so as to attain in each under-developed country a substantial increase in the rate of growth, with each country setting its own target, taking as the objective a minimum annual rate of growth of aggregate national income of five per cent at the end of the Decade;

2. *Calls upon* States Members of the United Nations or members of the specialized agencies:

(*a*) To pursue policies designed to enable the less developed countries and those dependent on the export of a small range of primary commodities to sell more of their products at stable and remunerative prices in expanding markets, and thus to finance increasingly their own economic development from their earnings of foreign exchange and domestic savings;

(*b*) To pursue policies designed to ensure to the devoloping countries an equitable share of earnings from the extraction and marketing of their natural resources by foreign capital, in accordance with the generally accepted reasonable earnings on invested capital;

(*c*) To pursue policies that will lead to an increase in the flow of development resources, public and private, to developing countries on mutually acceptable terms;

(*d*) To adopt measures which will stimulate the flow of private investment capital for the economic development of the developing countries, on terms that are satisfactory both to the capital-exporting countries and the capital-importing countries;

3. *Requests* the Secretary-General to communicate to the Governments of Member States any documentation useful for the study and application of the present resolution and to invite them to make proposals, if possible, concerning the contents of a United Nations programme for the Decade and the application of such measures in their respective plans;

4. *Requests* the Secretary-General, taking account of the views of Governments and in consultation, as appropriate, with the heads of international agencies with responsibilities in the financial, economic and social fields, the Managing Director of the Special Fund, the Executive Chairman of the Technical Assistance Board, and the

regional economic commissions, to develop proposals for the intensification of action in the fields of economic and social development by the United Nations system of organizations, with particular reference, *inter alia,* to the following approaches and measures designed to further the objective of paragraph one above:

(*a*) The achievement and acceleration of sound self-sustaining economic development in the less developed countries through industrialization, diversification and the development of a highly productive agricultural sector;

(b) Measures for assisting the developing countries, at their request, to establish well-conceived and integrated country plans—including, where appropriate, land reform—which will serve to mobilize internal resources and to utilize resources offered by foreign sources on both a bilateral and a multilateral basis for progress towards self-sustained growth;

(*c*) Measures to improve the use of international institutions and instrumentalities for furthering economic and social development;

(*d*) Measures to accelerate the elimination of illiteracy, hunger and disease, which seriously affect the productivity of the people of the less developed countries;

(*e*) The need to adopt new measures, and to improve existing measures, for further promoting education in general and vocational and technical training in the developing countries with the co-operation, where appropriate, of the specialized agencies and States which can provide assistance in these fields, and for training competent national personnel in the fields of public administration, education, engineering, health and agronomy;

(*f*) The intensification of research and demonstration as well as other efforts to exploit scientific and technological potentialities of high promise for accelerating economic and social development;

(*g*) Ways and means of finding and furthering effective solutions in the field of trade in manufactures as well as in primary commodities, bearing in mind, in particular, the need to increase the foreign exchange earnings of the under-developed countries;

(*h*) The need to review facilities for the collection, collation, analysis and dissemination of statistical and other information required for charting economic and social development and for providing constant measurement of progress towards the objectives of the Decade;

(*i*) The utilization of resources released by disarmament for the purpose of economic and social development, in particular of the under-developed countries;

(*j*) The ways in which the United Nations can stimulate and support realization of the objectives of the Decade through the combined efforts of national and international institutions, both public and private;

5. *Further requests* the Secretary-General to consult Member States, at their request, on the application of such measures in their respective development plans;

6. *Invites* the Economic and Social Council to accelerate its examination of, and decision on, principles of international economic co-operation directed towards the improvement of world economic relations and the stimulation of international co-operation;

7. *Requests* the Secretary-General to present his proposals for such a programme to the Economic and Social Council at its thirty-fourth session for its consideration and appropriate action;

8. *Invites* the Economic and Social Council to transmit the Secretary-General's recommendations, together with its views and its report on actions undertaken thereon, to States Members of the United Nations or member of the specialized agencies and to the General Assembly at its seventeenth session.

1084th plenary meeting,
19 December 1961.

Selected Bibliography

The book is based mainly on the writer's personal experience at the United Nations headquarters and in the field, supplemented by a study of numerous reports and documents, largely unpublished. No attempt is therefore made here to offer anything like a comprehensive bibliography. A short list of publications is given below to serve as a guide to those who may wish to pursue the subject further. Most of them have been referred to in the text.

"The Expanded Programme of Technical Assistance for Economic Development of Underdeveloped Countries." An Explanatory Booklet published by the Technical Assistance Board. United Nations (TAB/I/Rev. 4), 1963.

"15 Years and 150,000 Skills." An Anniversary Review of the United Nations Expanded Programme of Technical Assistance prepared by the Technical Assistance Board. United Nations (E/TAC/153/Rev. I), New York, 1965.

"Guide for United Nations Technical Assistance Experts." Bureau of Technical Assistance Operations, Department of Economic and Social Affairs. United Nations, 1964.

Annual Reports of the Technical Assistance Board and of UNDP/TA.

Anual Reports of the UN Specialized Agencies, especially of FAO, Rome; UNESCO, Paris; and WHO, Geneva.

Annual Reports of the International Bank for Reconstruction and Development/International Development Association (World/Bank/IDA), Washington, D.C.

Annual Reports of the International Finance Corporation, Washington, D.C.

Annual Report to the Congress on the Foreign Assistance Programme, Fiscal Year 1967; Washington, D.C.

"The United Nations Development Decade—Proposals for Action." United Nations (E/3613), 1962.

"The United Nations Development Decade at Mid-Point—An Appraisal by the Secretary-General." United Nations, October 1965.

Advisory Committee on the Application of Science and Technology to Development. Second Report. United Nations (E/4026), 1965.

"International Action to Avert the Impending Protein Crisis." United Nations (E/4343/Rev. I), 1968.

Report of the World Food Congress, 2 Vols.; FAO, Rome, 1963.

The World Food Crisis, FAO, Rome, 1966.

The State of Food and Agriculture 1965 - Review of the Second Post-war Decade. Also later Annual Reviews on the same subject.

"The World Food Problem." A Report of the President's Science Advisory Committee in two volumes. The White House, May 1967.

"Towards a New Trade Policy for Development." Report by the Secretary-General of the United Nations Conference on Trade and Development (UNCTAD). E/CONF. 46/3, United Nations, New York, 1964.

"Trade Policy toward Low-Income Countries." Committee for Economic Development (CED), New York, June 1967.

"Foreign Investment in Developing Countries." United Nations (E/4446), New York, 1968.

Eugene Black: "Economics of Development Diplomacy." Harvard University Press, Cambridge, Massachusetts, 1961.

Harlan Cleveland: "The Theory and Practice of Foreign Aid." A Paper prepared for the Special Studies Project of the Rockefeller Fund. Maxwell Graduate School of Citizenship and Public Affairs. Mimeographed, November 1, 1956.

Paul G. Hoffman: "World Without Want." Harper & Row, Publishers, New York, 1962.

Julian Huxley (Editor): "The Humanist Frame." Allen & Unwin, London, 1960; and Harper & Brothers, New York 1961.

Barbara Ward: "The Rich Nations and the Poor Nations." Hamish Hamilton, London, 1962.

Barbara Ward and P. T. Bauer: "Two Views on Aid to Developing Countries." Occasional Paper 9. The Institute of Economic Affairs, London, 1966.

A Report of the Advisory Committee on International Organizations. United States Department of State. June 1963.

Pope Paul VI: "On the Development of Peoples." Encyclical Letter of His Holiness, 26 March, 1967.

Index*

A

Abbreviations used in this book, *see* List of Abbreviations, vi, vii
Ad Hoc Committee, created, 120-121; enlarged, 126; debates and decisions, Chapter 13, sec. 3-4, Chapter 14, sec. 2-6
Administrative Committee on Coordination (ACC), 139
    interagency coordination, 166-167
    EPTA activities at field level, 220-221
    Resident Representatives' status, 235 f.
Advisory Committee on the Application of Science and Technology to Development (ACASTD), 197 f., 257 f., 258, 259, 262-263, 271
Agencies, UN, *see* specialized agencies
Agency allocation system, EPTA, 39, 41
Agency for International Development (US-AID), 282, 296-297, 304-305
Agriculture, as a priority, 251-257
Aid, bilateral versus multilateral, 302-305
Aid or Trade, 284-287
Anomalies, why die hard, Chapter 15
Armaments, mounting expenditures, 287-288

B

Bauer, P. T., 287 f.
Bilharziasis, 272
Black, Eugene, 236, 286
Brazilian Catalogue of services, EPTA, 30 f.
Brown, Lester R., 256

C

Caradon, Lord, 171
Castle, Barbara, 13-14

Category I and II, EPTA, 44-45, 61
Civilian Conservation Corps (CCC), 269
Clapp, Gordon R., 164
Cleveland, Harlan, 32, 118-119, 142, 155, 160, 190-191, 309
    statement before TAC, 118-119
Clifford, Clark, 149
Committee for Economic Development, 175 f.
Communication, as priority field, 277
Coordination
    in ACC, 166-167
    of EPTA activities, in TAB, 35-36
    at field level, 220-221
    multiplying problems of, 165-170
    versus management, 165-167, 186-187
Coordinating Units of recipient governments, 168-169
Contingencies, Contingency Fund (EPTA), 32, 42-43, 62-64, 77
    suggestions, 185, 196
Continuing commitments, EPTA, 44
Continuous programming, UNDP/TA, 39, 74, 180
Country programming, 39, 161-164, 171-173, 277-279
    procedures, Chapter 5
    right and wrong, Chapter 10
    "systems analysis," 200-203
    Yugoslavia, as example, 83-94
Country targets, EPTA, 43-45, 73-76
Cowper, William, 38
Currencies, utilization problem, 30-31

D

Danish restricted contribution, EPTA, 30 f.
Decolonization, 1, 3-5
Deficit finance, 289-290
Demographic revolution, 1
Development

---

*To keep the index reasonably short, names of agencies, UN organs, governing bodies, and of important persons such as UN Secretary-General U Thant, UNDP Administrator Paul G. Hoffman, have been shown mainly by subject-matter. For a complete list of abbreviations used, see the List on pages vi, vii.

Revolving fund, UNDP, 77
Rochefoucauld, *see* La Rochefoucauld
Rockefeller Foundation, 252
Ruskin, John, 52

S

Secretary General, UN, on
   interagency coordination, 105-106, 306, 309
   Merger, EPTA-Special Fund, 129-132
   EPTA and regular programmes, 134-136
   need for reform, x-xi
   priorities, 243
   Resident Representative's role, 240-241
   Special Fund, 110
   Secretary-General's term, 149
Skopje earthquake, 85
   reconstruction, 86-88
Smallpox, 273
Special Fund, esp. Chapters 11 and 12
   Founding Resolution, Appendix II
   discussion, Chapter 11
   growth of programme, 97, 110, Appendix IB
   problem of follow-up investments, Chapter 12 and 204-208, Appendix IB
   procedures, comparison with EPTA, Chapter 11, 200
    weaknesses and remedies needed, 106, 107, 109-115, 198, 213
   SUNFED or UNCDF, precursor of, 98-99, 108-110, 113-114
   specialized agencies, used in a functional sense, *see* List of Abbreviations
   agency allocation system, EPTA, 39, 40
   country representatives, mission chiefs, 227-230
   interagency coordination, 166-168
    cooperation, 196-198, 307, 309
   proliferation of, 188-190
   relations with Resident Representatives, 220-221, 227-230
    WHO view, 140-141, 230-232
Stevenson, Adlai E., iii, iv
SUNFED, 98-99, 108
Systems analysis, country, programming, 200-203

T

Tagore, Sir Rabindranath, iv, xiii, 142
Technical Assistance Board (TAB), 35,

49-50, 54-55
Technical Assistance Committee (TAC), 35, 49-50, 54-55
Technical Assistance Conference or Pledging Conference, 30, 40
"Ten principles," for field coordination, 220-221
Thant, U, *see* Secretary-General, UN
Thoreau, Henry D., xiii
Tolstoy, Count Leo, xiii
Toynbee, Arnold, 288
Trypanosomiasis, 271
Tupper, M., 81
Two-year programming, EPTA, 39, 50, 68-71, 72-73

U

Udnik, Minister, B. J., 280
Unified programme, need for, Chapter 17
   full merger of EPTA and SF, 170-182
   merger of regular programmes, 182-186
United Nations (UN)
   above criticism, 5-6
   fields of activity, 26
   industries transferred to UNIDO, 26 f.
   regular programmes, merger question, 134-139, 184-185
   Resident Representatives as UN field representatives, 228
United Nations Capital Development Fund (UNCDF), 98-99, 108-110, 113-114
United Nations Children's Fund (UNICEF), 36, 111, 187 f., 212
United Nations Conference on Trade and Development (UNCTAD), 284-285
United Nations Development Decade, 4, 281, Appendix IV
   discussed, Chapter 21
   strategy for 1970's, esp. Chapter 22
United Nations Development Programme (UNDP),
   creation, 4, Chapter 14, esp. sec. 2-3, and 6
   need for a full merger, Chapter 17
   and for procedural improvements, Chapter 18, esp. sec. 4-9
United Nations Information Centre (UNIC), 117, 228
United Nations Industrial Development Organization (UNIDO), 27 f., 185-186, 263-265
UN paradoxes, 9-10

V

Vietnam, xiv
Voltaire, 300

W

Ward, Barbara, 286, 287
Webb, Sidney and Beatrice, 147
Woods, George D., 14, 189, 190, 287, 310
World Bank, 36, 59, 145, 177, 202 f., 298, 310 f.
World Food Programme (WFP), 111, 195, 212
World Health Organization (WHO)
  costing of projects, 45
  decentralization, 232
  family planning, 250-251, 270

health as a priority field, 270-273 -
project programming, 41, 68
regular programmes, merger question, 137-139, 182-184
relations with Resident Representatives, 138-139, 231-233
Special Fund projects, SF-WHO priorities, 270-273
Working Capital and Reserve Fund (WCRF), EPTA, 32, 42-43

Y

Young, Edward, 108
Yugoslavia, programming in, 16, 83-93, 228-229, 281